The Ẓāhirī *Madhhab* (3rd/9th–10th/16th Century)

Studies in Islamic Law and Society

Founding Editor

Bernard Weiss

Edited by

Ruud Peters and A. Kevin Reinhart

VOLUME 38

The titles published in this series are listed at *brill.com/sils*

The Ẓāhirī *Madhhab* (3rd/9th–10th/16th Century)

A Textualist Theory of Islamic Law

By

Amr Osman

BRILL

LEIDEN | BOSTON

Library of Congress Cataloging-in-Publication Data

Osman, Amr, 1978- author.
The Zahiri Madhhab (3rd/9th-10th/16th century) : a textualist theory of Islamic law / by Amr Osman.
pages cm. — (Studies in Islamic law and society)
Revised version of the author's doctoral thesis—Princeton University, 2010.
Includes bibliographical references and index.
ISBN 978-90-04-27619-2 (hardback : alk. paper) — ISBN 978-90-04-27965-0 (e-book) 1. Islamic law.
2. Zahirites—History. 3. Islamic sects. I. Title.

KBP250.O86 2014
297.1'401815—dc23

2014020979

This publication has been typeset in the multilingual 'Brill' typeface. With over 5,100 characters covering Latin, IPA, Greek, and Cyrillic, this typeface is especially suitable for use in the humanities.
For more information, please see brill.com/brill-typeface.

ISSN 1384-1130
ISBN 978 90 04 27619 2 (hardback)
ISBN 978 90 04 27965 0 (e-book)

This book is printed on acid-free paper.

Contents

Acknowledgements

I was more than fortunate to work with four great scholars in the course of completing this study, which is based on my doctoral dissertation that I completed at Princeton University in 2010. I cannot find words that would do justice to Michael Cook's professionalism, dedication, and conscientiousness, and I cannot thank him enough for all his support during and even after the time I spent at Princeton. I have learned a lot from Hossein Modarressi's knowledge of Islamic thought and from Muhammad Qasim Zaman's scholarship and experience. I still seek their advice and they remain generous with their support. My debt to Muhammad Shahab Ahmed has been accumulating since he taught me at the American University in Cairo in 1999–2000, and I have since realized that my attempts to repay it are simply futile.

In the course of writing my dissertation, I benefited from comments on some parts of it by Kecia Ali, Aaron Zysow, David Powers, Susan Spectorsky, Noah Feldman, Muhammad Fadel, and Tony Lang. Similarly, Lena Salaymeh, George Hatke, Dan Stoltz, Jack Tannous, and Sarah Kistler read and commented on parts of it. Luke Yarbrough, however, read the entire dissertation with the care and dedication that he would give to his own writing.

Having said this, I have to emphasize that any weakness or mistakes in his dissertation are my sole responsibility.

I also thank the editorial staff at Brill's *Studies in Islamic Law and Society Series*—particularly Kevin Reinhart, Ruud Peters, Nicolette van der Hoek, Nienke Brienen-Moolenaar, and Ingrid Heijckers-Velt—for their enthusiasm for this study and their patience with me when Egypt's gloomy events in 2013 made it impossible for me to submit the manuscript at the agreed time. Also, I had the opportunity to fully concentrate on revising this manuscript when I was awarded a generous "Zukunftsphilologie" post-doctoral fellowship at the Forum Transregionale Studien in Berlin (2013–2014). My thanks are due to Islam Dayeh, Angelika Neuwirth, and Georges Khalil.

Last but not least, my wife, Marwa Fekry, supported me during my years at Princeton when she was working on her own dissertation and blessed me with two truly precious children, Fayruz and Yusuf. To Marwa I dedicate this book.

Introduction

It is reported that when the Prophet Muḥammad decided to fight the Jewish tribe of the Banū Qurayẓah, he said to his Companions: "Do not pray the afternoon prayer except in the abode of the Banū Qurayẓah."[1] The Companions understood this command variously. Some of them took it to mean that they should pray the afternoon prayer only when they reached the Banū Qurayẓah, even if this meant praying it after its prescribed time. Others inferred that what the Prophet actually meant was that they should not waste any time in setting off to the battlefield. According to this understanding, the Companions were being requested to hurry, but they were nonetheless supposed to pray the afternoon prayer at its due time. The Prophet, it is reported, was silent on the matter. He did not reprimand either group, nor did he endorse one understanding over the other. Surprisingly, or perhaps unsurprisingly, the report does not mention the time at which the Prophet himself prayed.[2]

This report is in fact a classical example to which medieval Muslim scholars have regularly referred to demonstrate two points. The first is that differing conclusions could ensue from sound *ijtihād*, the effort made by jurists to discover God's law in a given case. Since the Prophet did not tell either group that they were wrong, it must have been the case that neither was. Secondly, this report illustrates the difference between "literalists," viz. those who adhere to the "letter" of written or verbal commands, and those who pay more attention to the objectives (*maqāṣid*) which commands, and laws in general, seek to realize. Arguably, the latter understanding fared much better in Islamic legal history than the former; however, the former has not been categorically dismissed, for a report like the one mentioned above lends credence to this mode of thinking. Just as some Companions were more interested in the objectives of the Prophet's command, others were more interested in obeying its letter. Both groups were sincere, even if they proceeded along differing lines.

For a Ẓāhirī scholar like Ibn Ḥazm al-Andalusī (d. 456/1064), however, this report does not support either of the two views that other scholars sought to prove. In his view, all other scholars erred when they thought that the difference between the two groups was due to the way in which they construed the Prophet's command. They also erred when they thought that the Prophet's reported silence meant that both groups were right. How is that so? Ibn Ḥazm

1 *Lā yuṣalliyanna aḥad al-ʿaṣr illā fī banī Qurayẓah.*

2 For a discussion of this well-known report, see, for instance, Ibn Qayyim al-Jawziyyah (d. 751/1350), *Aʿlām al-Muwaqqiʿīn ʿan Rabb al-ʿĀlamīn*, vol. 1, p. 203.

 | DOI 10.1163/9789004279650_002

argues that what the Prophet's Companions were dealing with here was a case of *taʿāruḍ al-adillah*, when conflicting evidence exists as to a specific issue.[3] The Companions knew that there was a general, unqualified command that prayers must be said at their prescribed times. That day, the Prophet gave them a command that could not be reconciled with the general command. A group of them decided to adhere to the original general command, preferring to pray the afternoon prayers at their prescribed time. The other group, however, followed the Prophet's new command and prayed after sunset when they had reached the Banū Qurayẓah. Both, Ibn Ḥazm stresses, were following religious commands. Furthermore, the fact that the Prophet did not reprimand either group only indicates that whereas one of them was right and the other wrong, both were sincerely seeking to obey the Prophet and did not intend to disobey him, for which reason he did not need to reprimand either of them. Those Companions who understood his command rightly, therefore, were rewarded twice, once for practicing *ijtihād* and again for reaching the right conclusion; those who got it wrong were rewarded only once for practicing *ijtihād*.

Ibn Ḥazm points out that had he been among the Prophet's Companions that day, he would have prayed in the abode of the Banū Qurayẓah, for the Prophet's command on that specific day indicates that it was a special case. In other words, had the Prophet wanted his Companions to pray at the prescribed time of the afternoon prayers, he would not have needed to say anything to them and they would have prayed at the appointed time as they normally did. The fact that he said something must indicate that he intended to say something exceptional for that particular day. When making this argument, Ibn Ḥazm had three objectives. He was obviously seeking to resist understanding this disagreement between the Companions in terms of their hermeneutics, a view that would legitimize multiple readings of a single text. He was also seeking to demonstrate his view that religious commands, in the absence of valid evidence to the contrary, must be taken to indicate absolute obligation. Thirdly, he was dismissing the validity of using this report to demonstrate that legal diversity was tolerated by no less a religious authority than the Prophet Muḥammad himself. The beliefs that only one legal view on any issue is correct, that only one reading of any text is valid, and that commands are to be taken to indicate absolute obligation are all pillars of Ẓāhirism, as will be discussed later.[4]

3 For Ibn Ḥazm's discussion of this report, see his *Iḥkām fī Uṣūl al-Aḥkām*, vol. 3, pp. 190–193.

4 On the question of why the Prophet did not order those who prayed *ʿaṣr* in the afternoon to repeat it upon reaching the Banū Qurayẓah in the evening, Ibn Ḥazm argues that we simply do not know when news about this disagreement reached him. It is possible, he surmises,

This controversy over the Banū Qurayẓah report also illustrates medieval Muslim scholars' understanding of Ẓāhirism, the legal theory of the Ẓāhirī *madhhab*. For them, it only meant the blind following of the letter of the law without attempting to grasp what it seeks to accomplish. In this respect, it indicates not only superficiality and narrow-mindedness, but also a true mental deficiency in failing to determine and appreciate what is intended by the law. Yet these scholars may concede the sincerity of the advocates of this approach and perhaps admire their keenness to rid jurisprudence of subjectivity and the personal preferences that usually result from appealing to the "spirit" rather than the "letter" of the law. It was particularly this belief in and admiration of their sincerity that generated my interest in the Ẓāhirī *madhhab*.[5] Yet it was the many unanswered questions about its history and doctrines that prompted me to seek to fill some of what I regarded as important gaps in our knowledge and understanding of this particular *madhhab* and perhaps of Islamic legal history and theory in general.

Arguably, the Ẓāhirī *madhhab* was the most important of the "defunct" medieval *madhhab*s, for despite the fact that it ended up disappearing from the legal scene, the ongoing interest that it has attracted in medieval and modern Muslim scholarship testifies to its importance and distinctiveness. This interest is understandable given that the Ẓāhirī *madhhab* produced far more literature than any other defunct *madhhab*. Ibn Ḥazm—the only Ẓāhirī scholar whose legal works have survived (to our knowledge)—was among the most prolific thinkers in the history of Islam. But it was not only that. Ibn Ḥazm was arguably among the most ingenious of medieval Muslim scholars, and it may have been precisely because of this—and perhaps because of a hidden admiration similar to the one mentioned above—that other medieval scholars felt that the Ẓāhirī challenge was too serious to be disregarded.

Probably for similar reasons, some modern scholars (Muslim and non-Muslim) have showed great interest in the Ẓāhirī *madhhab*. As early as the end of the 19th century CE, Ignaz Goldziher examined the place of Ẓāhirism among the legal trends of the 3rd/9th century and vis-à-vis other legal schools that

---

that the Prophet knew about it the following day, when it was too late to do anything about it (Ibn Ḥazm, *Iḥkām*, vol. 3, p. 292). This kind of appeal to the historical setting and to our inability at times to know all of its minutiae is a recurrent theme in Ibn Ḥazm's legal reasoning and relevant to our later discussion of his presumed literalism.

5 I use *madhhab* rather than "school of law" for reasons that will be discussed later in chapter one.

developed later.[6] Goldziher's study, it must be acknowledged, was an excellent achievement given the limited sources that were available to him at that time. Yet while Goldziher showed an obvious interest in the *history* of the Ẓāhirīs, most later Western scholars maintained only his interest in Ibn Ḥazm and did not build on his effort to place him within the larger framework of the historical development of the Ẓāhirī *madhhab*.[7] The result was that Ibn Ḥazm became the focus of almost all studies on the Ẓāhirīs. This fixation on Ibn Ḥazm, however, is justifiable only if sustained effort is made to study Ẓāhirism without complete reliance on his works. Indeed, this fixation on him seems to have perpetuated the belief that we can hardly know much about other Ẓāhirī scholars, including Dāwūd ibn ʿAlī ibn Khalaf al-Iṣbahānī (d. 270/884)—widely known as Dāwūd al-Ẓāhirī—the scholar credited with single-handedly establishing the Ẓāhirī *madhhab*.[8] Thus, apart from Ibn Ḥazm, the larger history of the Ẓāhirī *madhhab* remains largely unexplored, and hasty conclusions about it are not lacking.[9]

---

6 Goldziher's *Die Ẓâhiriten, ihr Lehrsystem und ihre Geschichte; Beitrag zur Geschichte der muhammedanischen Theologie* was published in 1884.

7 For example, Abdel Majid Turki's article "al-Ẓāhiriyya" in *EI*[2] is less than five pages long, and he makes it clear that he drew mainly on Muḥammad Abū Zahrah's work on Ibn Ḥazm (Muḥammad Abū Zahrah, *Ibn Ḥazm: Ḥayātuhu wa-ʿAṣruhu, Ārāʾuhu wa-Fiqhuhu*). Abū Zahrah himself, who wrote monographs on the founders of the four surviving Sunnī schools of law, did not write a book on Dāwūd and wrote instead on Ibn Ḥazm. In his study on the origin and development of Sunnī schools of law, Christopher Melchert, who was by no means studying the school for its own sake, discusses the history of the school over more than six centuries in less than ten pages (Christopher Melchert, *The Formation of the Sunnī Schools of Law: 9th–10th Centuries C.E.*).

8 The fact that all of Dāwūd's works seem to have been lost is of course an obstacle, but studying the views that the available sources attribute to Dāwūd may prove fruitful. Mention should be made here of Muḥammad ʿĀrif Abū ʿĪd's monograph (based on his doctoral dissertation) on Dāwūd (*al-Imām Dāwūd al-Ẓāhirī wa-Atharuhu fī al-Fiqh al-Islāmī*, the only such work to my knowledge). Unfortunately, although Abū ʿĪd made an impressive effort in collecting information about Dāwūd's life and legal views, his rather uncritical examination of these materials has not added much to our knowledge of the subject.

9 For example, in her "The Beginnings of the Ẓāhirī *Madhhab* in al-Andalus" (in Peri Bearman *et al.* (eds.), *The Islamic School of Law: Evolution, Devolution, and Progress*), Camilla Adang refutes Christopher Melchert's claim that the Ẓāhirī *madhhab* did not have representatives in Andalus before Ibn Ḥazm, who, according to Melchert, founded the school on the sole basis of books that were available to him. Adang has written extensively on the Ẓāhirī *madhhab* and has recently co-edited a volume—entitled *Ibn Ḥazm of Cordoba: The life and Works of a Controversial Thinker*—on various aspects of Ibn Ḥazm's thought.

This fixation on Ibn Ḥazm is at odds with the fact that he belonged to a *madhhab* that he did not himself establish. In fact, it contradicts the very notion that he belonged to a *madhhab* at all, no matter how we define it. Accordingly, two questions present themselves at the beginning of this study. If we assume for the sake of argument that Ibn Ḥazm had not existed, how much could we actually know about the Ẓāhirī *madhhab*? In other words, is Ibn Ḥazm the best-documented representative of the *madhhab*, or is he our *only* source of any meaningful knowledge about it? What do we know about the life and doctrines of Dāwūd al-Ẓāhirī himself? Accordingly, starting with Dāwūd (CHAPTER ONE), PART ONE of this study explores the scope of the spread of the Ẓāhirī *madhhab* in various centers and corners of the medieval Muslim world and discusses the information available on the political and intellectual careers of scholars reported to have belonged to it, including Ibn Ḥazm and his place in and influence on the Ẓāhirī *madhhab* (CHAPTER TWO).

Furthermore, a fundamental question about the history of the Ẓāhirī *madhhab* is arguably that of its failure. What was it about the *madhhab* that made it perish while some other schools that were perhaps less successful than it was at certain historical moments (such as the Ḥanbalī school) survived? In recent years, Islamicist legal historians have sought to account for the success of the four existing Sunnī schools of law and the failure of others by either focusing on their popularity among jurists or state patronage as the main cause of their success. Others have emphasized their ability to make adequate concessions to come to terms with other schools and adapt to social realities as the main factor that determined which schools survived and which perished. These concessions included, for instance, abandoning either excessive rationalism or excessive traditionalism. Scholars of every *madhhab* had to find a formula by which they could combine elements of both. The ability of schools to develop curricula or courses of study for their students is also among the factors advanced to account for the success of some schools and the failure of others.[10] Although these views are taken into consideration when studying the Ẓāhirī *madhhab*, it is our findings here that would ultimately determine the conclusions made apropos its failure. In fact, given the broad spatial and temporal scope of the Ẓāhirī *madhhab*, it is not unlikely that it may have failed for different reasons in different regions, a possibility that is entertained here.

In addition to these questions about the history of the *madhhab*, there are questions related to its doctrines, which are taken up in PART TWO. What

---

10 For these views, see, for instance, George Makdisi, "The Significance of the Sunnī Schools of Law in Islamic Religious History"; Christopher Melchert, *Formation*, pp. 187ff.; and Wael Hallaq, *The Origins and Evolution of Islamic Law*, pp. 167–172.

exactly is Ẓāhirism, and what was Ẓāhirī about Dāwūd al-Ẓāhirī? Most medieval and modern scholars writing on this subject have implicitly or explicitly regarded Dāwūd as one of the *Ahl al-Ḥadīth* scholars of his age. Judging on the basis of Dāwūd's reported rejection of some of the notions of the *Ahl al-Raʾy* (such as *qiyās* (analogy), *istiḥsān* (equity), *maṣlaḥah* (interest), etc.), they conclude that Dāwūd cannot have had any relation to them or to their juridical thinking. However, this conclusion can only be sustained when we have collected and investigated enough biographical and doctrinal evidence about Dāwūd's life and jurisprudence. This investigation is carried out in CHAPTER ONE, whereas CHAPTER THREE and CHAPTER FOUR seek to explore the characteristic features of the *Ahl al-Raʾy* and the *Ahl al-Ḥadīth* to determine the group in which Dāwūd fits better and to which side he may have been closer in terms of legal doctrine.

But what was it that distinguished Dāwūd's jurisprudence if he was already affiliated with one of these two groups of scholars? Ẓāhirism is commonly regarded by modern, and possibly some medieval Muslim scholars, as a "literalist" approach to reading religious and legal texts. In other words, what distinguished Dāwūd and subsequent Ẓāhirī scholars was their presumed "literal" reading of legal texts. Yet neither is the meaning of "literalism" duly discussed, nor is the presumed literalism of Ẓāhirism demonstrated. Therefore, CHAPTER FOUR deals with the meaning of Ẓāhirism, whereas CHAPTER FIVE tackles the subject of literalism. It is then argued on the basis of these two chapters that if we are to seek a modern counterpart to Ẓāhirism, "textualism"—as presented by Justice Antonin Scalia, a contemporary US constitutional judge—is the right candidate. This is not to say that textualism is only a better candidate than literalism. Literalism, in fact, is not a valid description, even if it shares with Ẓāhirism (and textualism, for that matter) some basic views, as will be discussed.

In CHAPTER SIX, five case studies are presented, two extensive and three brief, for further demonstration of some of the arguments made in this study on Dāwūd as well as the nature of the Ẓāhirī juridical thought and its relation to the legal thought of the *Ahl al-Raʾy* and the *Ahl al-Ḥadīth*. My hope is that this study will contribute not only to our understanding of the history and doctrines of the Ẓāhirī *madhhab*, but also to our understanding of Islamic legal history more broadly by revisiting what was characteristic of early Islamic legal trends and offering a new insight as to how the legal theory of the *madhhab* under examination here relates to modern linguistic, legal, and hermeneutical theories.

In the three-year period between the completion of my doctoral dissertation in 2010 and the submission of the manuscript of this book to Brill, a number of works relevant to topics discussed in this book have been published or come to my attention. This latter category includes primarily scholarly articles published in Arabic periodicals. The former category includes David R. Vishanoff's *The Formation of Islamic Hermeneutics: How Sunni Legal Theorists Imagined a Revealed Law* (2011), and Robert Gleave's *Islam and Literalism: Literal Meaning and Interpretation in Islamic Legal Theory* (2012). Readers will immediately notice the similarities between topics discussed and conclusions reached in this book and Gleave's. Therefore, I will limit references to *Islam and Literalism*, first to keep the flavor and originality of my treatment of the subject (noting that tackling the issue of literalism is only one, although very important, of many other issues that I deal with here); secondly, to avoid unnecessary distraction for the purposes of this study by engaging with some of Gleave's conclusions; and thirdly, to give more space to Vishanoff's original work (and also Mohamed Yunis Ali's *Medieval Islamic Pragmatics: Sunni Legal Theorists' Models of Textual Communication*), on which Gleave draws quite heavily.[11]

Finally, the transliteration system used here is that of *Encyclopedia of Islam*, the exceptions being j for dj and q for ḳ. I do not omit the short "a" in Allāh when preceded by a vowel. For Qur'ān translation, I draw freely on the translations of M. Pickthall, Yusuf 'Ali, and M. H. Shakir, taking the liberty to amend them as need be.

---

11 It must be noted here that although no major interpretative revisions have been made to my dissertation, the overall organization has been revised with important stylistic changes that seek to make the book more accessible to a wider readership.

PART 1

The History of the Ẓāhirī Madhhab

CHAPTER 1

Dāwūd al-Ẓāhirī and the Beginnings of the Ẓāhirī *Madhhab*

As a first step toward studying the trajectory of the Ẓāhirī *madhhab*, the purpose of this chapter is to discuss what medieval sources—which sources include biographical dictionaries and works of legal theory (*uṣūl al-fiqh*) and jurisprudence (*fiqh*)—report about the life and doctrines of Dāwūd al-Ẓāhirī.

1 Life and Doctrines

Biographies of Abū Sulaymān Dāwūd ibn ʿAlī ibn Khalaf al-Iṣbahānī al-Ẓāhirī pose a special historiographical difficulty: statements made about his vast knowledge and prominence do not seem to be consistent with the few pieces of information that his biographers report about his life. For example, al-Khaṭīb al-Baghdādī (d. 463/1071) mentions that Dāwūd lived most of his life in Baghdad,[1] but he does not mention where he was born. Abū Isḥāq al-Shīrāzī (d. 476/1083) mentions that Dāwūd was born in Kufa and grew up in Baghdad.[2] Al-Samʿānī (d. 562/1166) reports that he was from Qāshān (a village near Isfahan), but resided in Baghdad.[3] We will see below that the majority of Dāwūd's teachers were either Basran by birth or residents of Basra. It is therefore possible that Dāwūd was born in Kufa, traveled to Basra at an early age, and then possibly to the east where he may have met with Isḥāq ibn Rāhawayh and other traditionists of the time, to finally settle in Baghdad until the end of his life.

Another uncertainty about Dāwūd's basic biographical information is his date of birth. Some of his biographers mention that he was born in the year 200/815; others give the year 202/817.[4] Disagreement over dates of birth of medieval scholars is not uncommon in biographical dictionaries, but information about Dāwūd's death is also uncertain. His biographers were uncertain

1 Al-Khaṭīb al-Baghdādī, *Tārīkh Baghdād*, vol. 8, p. 369.
2 Abū Isḥāq al-Shīrāzī, *Ṭabaqāt al-Fuqahāʾ*, p. 92. Al-Qurashī mentions the same thing in *al-Jawāhir al-Muḍiyyah* (vol. 4, p. 544).
3 Al-Samʿānī, *Ansāb al-Ashrāf*, vol. 4, p. 99.
4 Al-Khaṭīb al-Baghdādī, *Tārīkh*, vol. 8, p. 375.

 | DOI 10.1163/9789004279650_003

about when exactly he died in the year 270/884,[5] and, more importantly, where he was buried in Baghdad.[6] Nothing seems to have been remembered about his funeral.[7]

Other basic biographical information about Dāwūd is missing. For example, the only reference to his family is that his father was a scribe of a certain ʿAbd Allāh ibn Khālid al-Kūfī,[8] and a follower of the Ḥanafī school of law.[9] We do not know what Dāwūd himself did for a living. Only an isolated and ambiguous account suggests that he may have worked as a judge for some time.[10] As for his

---

5 Ibn Khallikān, *Wafayāt al-Aʿyān*, vol. 2, p. 257. Two different months are reported, Ramaḍān and Dhū al-Qaʿdah.

6 Abū Isḥāq al-Shīrāzī (*Ṭabaqāt*, p. 92) and Ibn Khallikān (*Wafayāt*, vol. 2, p. 257) report that Dāwūd was buried in a graveyard in the western part of Baghdad called "al-Shīnūziyyah" (from al-Shīnūzī, a person's name) or *maqābir* Quraysh, where many of Baghdad's scholars and notables were buried, according to al-Khaṭīb al-Baghdādī (*Tārīkh*, vol. 1, p. 122). Elsewhere, Dāwūd is reported to have been buried in his home (*ibid.*, vol. 8, p. 375).

7 Each of these elements is perhaps not of much significance by itself, but they become significant when put together. Biographical dictionaries usually provide far more information about the deaths and funerals of prominent scholars. In *Tārīkh Baghdād*, for example, we are informed of the exact day on which Ibn Ḥanbal died, told who led the funeral prayers over him, and where he was buried, and given an estimation of the number of people who attended his funeral (some 800,000 men and 60,000 women) (al-Khaṭīb al-Baghdādī, *Tārīkh*, vol. 4, p. 422). Likewise, al-Khaṭīb al-Baghdādī reports the date of death of Ibn Ḥanbal's student Abū Bakr al-Marrūdhī (d. 275/888), as well as who led the funeral prayers over him and where he was buried (*ibid.*, vol. 4, p. 424). The funeral of the Sufi al-Junayd (d. 298/910) is reported to have been attended by some 60,000 people, and al-Khaṭīb al-Baghdādī mentions the exact place of his burial (*ibid.*, vol. 7, 248).

8 This is cited by Goldziher (*The Ẓāhirīs*, p. 27) from a manuscript copy of Sirāj al-Dīn ibn al-Mulaqqin's (d. 804/1401) *al-ʿIqd al-Mudhhab fī Ṭabaqāt Ḥamalat al-Madhhab*. I did not find this piece of information in the available edition of *al-ʿIqd*, nor did I find it in al-Samʿānī's *Ansāb al-Ashrāf* (al-Samʿānī, *Ansāb*, s.v. "al-Dāwūdiyya" (vol. 2, pp. 448–449) and "al-Ẓāhirī" (vol. 4, pp. 99–100), where the same piece of information is reportedly mentioned (for this, see Abū ʿĪd, *al-Imām Dāwūd al-Ẓāhirī*, p. 50). Abū ʿĪd also used a manuscript of *al-Ansāb*, but I could not find reference to Dāwūd's father in the edition of *al-Ansāb* available to me. Abū ʿĪd mentions that ʿAbd Allāh ibn Khālid was a judge of Isfahan in the days of the Abbasid Caliph al-Maʾmūn (ruled 198/813–218/833). Be this as it may, what we know about Dāwūd remains marginal.

9 Shams al-Dīn al-Dhahabī, *Siyar Aʿlām al-Nubalāʾ*, vol. 13, p. 98.

10 Seeking to demonstrate how the famous Mālikī judge of Baghdad Ismāʿīl ibn Isḥāq was intolerant of the *ahl al-bidaʿ* (innovators) that they avoided Baghdad out of fear of him, Ibn Farḥūn mentions that Ismāʿīl banished Dāwūd to Basra because of his innovation of rejecting *qiyās* (*li-iḥdāthihi manʿ al-qiyās*) (Ibn Farḥūn, *al-Dībāj al-Mudhhab*, pp. 151–155). According to this, Ismāʿīl used to say: "He who does not have insight (*firāsah*) should not

relationship with the rulers of his time, one report mentions that Dāwūd was a *mawlā* (client) of the Caliph al-Mahdī (r. 158/774–169/785).[11] What is remarkable here is that Dāwūd grew up during the last years of the *miḥnat khalq al-Qur'ān* (an inquisition over the createdness of the Qur'ān) and does not seem to have subscribed to the official state position on this issue.[12] This silence on Dāwūd's relationship with the rulers of his time may indicate that he was not a particularly notable scholar during his life.

Despite this lack of biographical data, Dāwūd's biographers portray him as a scholar who possessed vast knowledge, excelled in reasoning and argumentation, and had many followers. Al-Shīrāzī states that "mastership of knowledge in Baghdad culminated in Dāwūd."[13] Al-Khaṭīb al-Baghdādī reports that Dāwūd was *imām ahl al-Ẓāhir*.[14] Later, Ibn Khallikān (d. 681/1282) mentions that Dāwūd was a scholar with an "independent *madhhab*" that was followed by a large group of people called *al-Ẓāhiriyyah*.[15] Nevertheless, only a few accounts of Dāwūd can substantiate this image. For example, it is reported that his circle of knowledge in Baghdad was attended by some 400 people wearing green *ṭaylasāns*.[16] Among the important people reported to have frequented his

---

work as judge" (*ibid.*, p. 154). It is not clear whether Ibn Farḥūn knew that rejection of *qiyās* was the reason for Dāwūd's alleged banishment or was only a conjecture (we shall see below that rejection of *qiyās* was made the defining characteristic of Ẓāhirism by medieval Muslim scholars). Neither is it clear if Ismāʿīl's comment on insight as a requirement for judgeship was connected to Dāwūd's banishment. This account would only suggest that Dāwūd worked as a judge in Baghdad if there is a connection between these two reports about Ismāʿīl. Ibn Ḥazm probably alludes to this incident in his *Risālah al-Bāhirah*, pp. 38–39, where he mentions that the Abbasid leader al-Muwaffaq (d. 278/891) protected Dāwūd from Ismāʿīl ibn Isḥāq "after what took place between them." These vague accounts and the fact that no other source mentions anything about Dāwūd working as judge in Baghdad make them useless for our purposes here.

11 Al-Dhahabī, *Siyar*, vol. 13, p. 97. Since al-Mahdī ruled and died long before Dāwūd's birth, either it was Dāwūd's father who was his *mawlā*, or a scribe inadvertently changed al-Muhtadī (r. 255/869–256/870) to al-Mahdī. In either case, what this means in terms of Dāwūd's relationship with the Abbasid Caliphate is not definite, of course, given that Dāwūd and his father were non-Arabs anyway and had to have a *mawlā*.

12 On this issue, see M. Hinds, "Miḥna," *EI*², vol. 7, p. 2.

13 *Wa-intahat ilay-hi riʾāsat al-ʿilm fī Baghdād* (al-Shīrāzī, *Ṭabaqāt*, p. 92).

14 Al-Khaṭīb al-Baghdādī, *Tārīkh*, vol. 13, p. 273.

15 Ibn Khallikān, *Wafayāt*, vol. 2, p. 255.

16 *Kāna yaḥduru majlisahu arbaʿumiʾat ṣāḥib ṭaylasān akhḍar* (al-Shīrāzī, *Ṭabaqāt*, p. 92). According to the *Kitāb al-Alfāẓ al-Fārisiyyah al-Muʿarrabah* (p. 113), a *ṭaylasān* is a round green garment that has no bottom and is worn on the shoulders. Mostly made of wool, it was worn by distinguished scholars and notables. Al-Suyūṭī compiled a work on the

circle is the famous Muḥammad ibn Jarīr al-Ṭabarī (d. 310/923).[17] In his *Fihrist*, Ibn al-Nadīm attributes to Dāwūd a large number of works, among which are *Kitāb al-Masāʾil al-Iṣfahāniyyāt, Kitāb al-Masāʾil al-Baṣriyyāt*, and *Kitāb al-Masāʾil al-Khuwārizmiyyāt*.[18] In the absence of evidence that Dāwūd traveled to these places himself, these titles suggest that Muslims from various cities used to send questions to him, pointing to reputation of a notable jurist.

As noted, this image of Dāwūd cannot be easily reconciled with other facts reported about him. We know for example that he did not distinguish himself as a Ḥadīth scholar, at a time when Ḥadīth was becoming more and more the "knowledge" (*al-ʿilm*) that any distinguished jurist must have. Dāwūd does not seem to have made any effort to distinguish himself in the transmission of Ḥadīth;[19] indeed, he figures in only three *isnād*s, two of which are regarded as likely dubious.[20] Ibn al-Jawzī (d. 597/1201) reports that Dāwūd contradicted many traditions.[21] In what could be his earliest biography, Ibn Abī Ḥātim al-Rāzī (d. 327/938) mentions that Dāwūd used to ridicule and offend the *Ahl al-Ḥadīth* on account of their obsessive interest in searching for traditions far

---

merits of *ṭaylasān, al-Aḥādīth al-Ḥisān fī Faḍl al-Ṭaylasān*. And according to Ibn Sīrīn's *Tafsīr al-Aḥlām*, it is felicitous to dream that one is wearing a *ṭaylasān*, for it promises a great status among people or family. But if one's *ṭaylasān* is torn in a dream, this bodes the death of a brother or son (Muḥammad ibn Sīrīn, *Tafsīr al-Aḥlām*, p. 197).

17 Al-Khaṭīb al-Baghdādī, *Tārīkh*, vol. 13, p. 273. Al-Khaṭīb al-Baghdādī adds that al-Ṭabarī later parted company with Dāwūd and started his own circle. It must be noted that a circle of 400 students is not impressive. The circle of one of Dāwūd's own teachers in Basra—Sulaymān ibn Ḥarb—is reported to have been attended by some 40,000 students, and that of ʿAmr ibn Marzūq, also a Basran teacher of Dāwūd, by 10,000 students. In Baghdād, the circles of Abū Yūsuf and later Aḥmad ibn Ḥanbal are said to have gathered thousands of students. While these figures do not have to (and sometimes cannot) be true or accurate, they certainly give an indication of how large or small a circle of knowledge was.

18 Ibn al-Nadīm, *Fihrist*, p. 217.

19 According to al-Khaṭīb al-Baghdādī, transmission of Ḥadīth from Dāwūd was rare (*wa-lākinna ʾl-riwāyah ʿan-hu nādirah jiddan*), although the person who reported this about him also mentioned that his works "contained much Ḥadīth" (al-Khaṭīb al-Baghdādī, *Tārīkh*, vol. 8, p. 370).

20 *Ibid.*, vol. 8, p. 370. The two traditions are described as *munkar*. According to Al-Khaṭīb al-Baghdādī, a tradition is *munkar* or *shādhdh* when it contradicts another tradition transmitted by a number of reliable transmitters (for this, see al-Khaṭīb al-Baghdādī, *al-Kifāyah fī ʿIlm al-Riwāyah*, p. 171). In Dāwūd's case, the traditions were considered *munkar* because their *isnads* contained unreliable transmitters.

21 Ibn al-Jawzī, *al-Muntaẓam fī Tārīkh al-Mulūk wa-l-Umam*, vol. 12, p. 236.

and wide.[22] Furthermore, if references to Dāwūd's engagement in argumentation (see below) are read against the backdrop of what we know about his knowledge, they could also indicate that he was less interested in acquiring knowledge (*al-mudhākarah*) and more interested in engaging in debates (*al-munāẓarah*).[23] That attendees of Dāwūd's circle were relatively few, therefore, is not surprising; in fact, it is not clear what the subject of his lectures was in the first place.

In light of all this, we have to regard al-Shīrāzī's statement about Dāwūd's mastership of knowledge in Baghdad as perhaps an innocent hyperbolic statement that only indicates that his knowledge (probably of legal matters) was more than that of the average scholar of his time. Al-Shīrāzī—who, notably, does not describe Dāwūd as Ẓāhirī and mentions nothing about his Ẓāhirism or his rejection of *qiyās*—seems to have been interested mainly in his admiration for Muḥammad ibn Idrīs al-Shāfiʿī (d. 204/820), a point that allowed later authors of Shāfiʿī biographical dictionaries to include Dāwūd among early Shāfiʿīs.

Dāwūd is also described as having been gifted in disputation and argumentation. The famous Ḥadīth scholar Abū Zurʿah al-Rāzī (d. 264/878) is reported to have said that had he limited himself to what people of knowledge do, Dāwūd would have suppressed people of innovation with his argumentative skills.[24] A famous contemporary of Dāwūd—the grammarian Abū al-ʿAbbās Thaʿlab (d. 291/904)—described him as having had "greater reason than knowledge."[25] In his *Ṭabaqāt al-Shāfiʿiyyah al-Kubrā*, al-Subkī mentions that he had a lengthy treatise which Dāwūd had sent to al-Shāfiʿī's student Mūsā ibn Abī al-Jārūd that indicates Dāwūd's mastery of argumentation and debate.[26] Unfortunately, although some sources refer to some of these debates, they do not preserve sufficient, or even any, details of them. For example, some sources mention that Dāwūd once had a disagreement with Isḥāq ibn Rāhawayh (d. 238/853), a celebrated Ḥadīth scholar of his time, on the subject of the createdness of the Qurʾān.[27] It is also reported that Dāwūd had a debate with the

22 Ibn Abī Ḥātim al-Rāzī, *al-Jarḥ wa-l-Taʿdīl*, vol. 1, p. 410.

23 For how these two activities were characteristic of scholars in Dāwūd's time, see Christopher Melchert, *Formation*, pp. 183–184.

24 *Law iqtaṣara ʿalā mā yaqtaṣiru ʿalay-hi ahl al-ʿilm la-ẓanantu anna-hu yakmidu ahl al-bidʿah bi-mā la-hu min al-bayān wa-l-ālah* (al-Khaṭīb al-Baghdādī, *Tārīkh*, vol. 8, p. 373).

25 *Kāna ʿaqluhu akbar min ʿilmihi* (*ibid.*, p. 371).

26 Tāj al-Dīn al-Subkī, *Ṭabaqāt al-Shāfiʿiyyah al-Kubrā*, vol. 2, p. 290. To my knowledge, Mūsā's date of death is not mentioned in any biographical dictionary.

27 Al-Khaṭīb al-Baghdādī, *Tārīkh*, vol. 8, pp. 370–371.

famous Shāfiʿī scholar Ibn Surayj (d. 306/918),[28] who wrote a refutation of both the *Ahl al-Raʾy* and the *Ahl al-Ẓāhir*.[29] Similarly, al-Zarkashī reports a debate where Dāwūd asks al-Shāfiʿī's student Ismaʿīl ibn Yaḥyā al-Muzanī (d. 264/877) whether *qiyās* was a primary (*aṣl*) or secondary (*farʿ*) source of law, to which al-Muzanī gives a reply that is difficult to construe.[30]

Dāwūd is also reported to have had a debate with a scholar of the *Ahl al-Raʾy*, Ibn al-Ḥusayn al-Bardhaʿī (d. *c.* 317/929),[31] who reportedly decided to remain in Baghdad specifically because of the "predominance" (*ghalabah*) of Ẓāhirī scholars there. According to al-Khaṭīb al-Baghdādī's account, al-Bardhaʿī once saw Dāwūd debating with a Ḥanafī scholar and overcoming him, which prompted al-Bardhaʿī to ask Dāwūd about a legal issue, obviously to refute his view.[32] In addition to these, al-Dhahabī mentions that Dāwūd had a debate with the Muʿtazilī theologian Abū Mukhālid Aḥmad ibn al-Ḥusayn, in the presence of the Abbasid *amīr* al-Muwaffaq (d. 278/891), on the subject of *khabar al-wāḥid*, but al-Dhahabī's account suggests that the debate was probably on the subject of "free will."[33] Muḥyī al-Dīn al-Qurashī reports a debate

28 Al-Khaṭīb al-Baghdādī, *Tārīkh*, vol. 4, p. 290.

29 Ibn al-Nadīm attributes to Ibn Surayj a work in which he responded to Muḥammad ibn al-Ḥasan al-Shaybānī (*al-Radd ʿalā Muḥammad ibn al-Ḥasan*) and ʿĪsā ibn Abān (*al-Radd ʿala ʿĪsā ibn Abān*). Ibn al-Nadīm does not mention any work in which Ibn Surayj refutes the Ẓāhirīs, but he mentions that Ibn Surayj had debates (*munāẓarāt*) with Muḥammad ibn Dāwūd (Ibn al-Nadīm, *Fihrist*, p. 213).

30 Al-Zarkashī, *al-Baḥr al-Muḥīṭ*, vol. 5, p. 26. In his reply, al-Muzanī says that if he says that as a source of law *qiyās* is primary or secondary, primary and secondary, or is neither primary nor secondary, Dāwūd would not be able to refute it. According to al-Zarkashī, the Shāfiʿī scholar Ibn al-Qaffāl (ʿAbd Allāh ibn Aḥmad, d. 417/1026), who transmitted this report, said that al-Muzanī meant that *qiyās* was primary "because it has been commissioned by God." In the same context, the Ḥanafī scholar Abū Bakr al-Rāzī al-Jaṣṣāṣ (d. 370/980) mentions that Dāwūd's question is indicative of his ignorance of the meaning of *qiyās*.

31 Ibn Ḥajar, *Lisān al-Mīzān*, vol. 1, p. 259. For al-Bardhaʿī's biography, see al-Khaṭīb al-Baghdādī, *Tārīkh*, vol. 4, pp. 99–100, where it is reported that al-Bardhaʿī was killed in a Qarmaṭī massacre of pilgrims, most likely in 317/929. See also al-Qurashī, *Jawāhir*, vol. 1, pp. 163–166.

32 al-Khaṭīb al-Baghdādī, *Tārīkh*, vol. 4, pp. 99–100.

33 Al-Dhahabī, *Siyar*, vol. 10, p. 553. According to this report, Dāwūd was debating the subject of the *khabar al-wāḥid* with Abū Mukhālid in front of al-Muwaffaq when Dāwūd looked at al-Muwaffaq and said: "May God put the *amir* on the straight path, Abū Mukhālid has led the people astray (*aṣlaḥa Allāh al-amīr, qad ahlaka Abū Mukhālid al-nās*). Al-Muwaffaq replied: "He has only defeated you by what you have just said, for God, in your view, is the one who has led people astray, so how can Abū al-Mukhālid lead them astray (*qad qaṭaʿaka bi-nafs qawlika hādhā, li-anna Allāh ʿinda-ka huwa ʾlladhī ahlaka ʾl-nās, fa-kayfa*

between Dāwūd and a certain Muḥammad ibn ʿAlī ibn ʿAmmār al-Kurrīnī in the congregational mosque in Baghdad also on the subject of the *khabar al-wāḥid*, which Dāwūd argued, apparently disrespectfully, was a basis for action (*ʿamal*).[34] Al-Qurashī does not report al-Kurrīnī's view here, but he must have had the opposite view on the issue.[35]

This lack of details about the debates that Dāwūd reportedly engaged in does not necessarily indicate that he was not interested in argumentation. It may suggest, however, that he was not especially talented in argumentation—as al-Bardhaʿī's encounter with him may indicate—or that his views were not significant enough for later generations to memorize. In one report, one of Dāwūd's contemporaries used to argue that his view on the question of *khalq al-Qurʾān*—that the Qurʾān of the 'Preserved Tablet' (*al-lawḥ al-maḥfūẓ*) is primordial, whereas that which is in the hands of people is created—was the view of a novice theologian.[36]

Another reported characteristic of Dāwūd was his piety and asceticism. Although Dāwūd's integrity was generally not questioned by the Ḥadīth critics of the age,[37] some reports suggest otherwise. Ibn Abī Ḥātim al-Rāzī called him "deviant and heretical,"[38] and his father is reported to have described Dāwūd in

---

yuhlikuhum Abū Mukhālid)? Al-Muwaffaq's reply, so the anecdote goes, rendered Dāwūd speechless (*ibid.*, p. 553).

34 *Kāna Dāwūd yaḥtajju li-l-ʿamal bi-hi wa-yushanniʿu wa-yubālighu fī thubūtihi* (al-Qurashī, *Jawāhir*, vol. 1, p. 292). Al-Kurrīnī is a toponymic derived from Kurrīn in Ṭabas (al-Samʿānī, *Ansāb*, vol. 5, p. 63), which is between Nishabur and Isfahan (*ibid.*, vol. 4, p. 48). I could not find information on Muḥammad ibn ʿAlī ibn ʿAmmār al-Kurrīnī, nor on Ayyūb ibn Ghassān who transmitted this reported to Ibn Dānkā al-Ṭabarī.

35 Al-Qurashī, *Jawāhir*, vol. 1, pp. 292–293. The rest of the story is unclear. Al-Qurashī mentions that people gathered around Dāwūd and al-Kurrīnī and began throwing one of them with stones until he fled the mosque. When he was asked about the *khabar al-wāḥid* later, that scholar said that if stones were involved in the question, then the *khabar al-wāḥid* is a basis for both or a source of knowledge and a basis for action (*amma bi-l-ḥijārah wa-l-ājurr, fa-inna-hu yūjibu ʾl-ʿilm wa-l-ʿamal jamīʿan*) (*ibid.*, pp. 292–293). While we would imagine that it was Dāwūd who was stoned (since Baghdad was the stronghold of Ḥanafism), the answer indicates that it was al-Kurrīnī rather than Dāwūd, which would suggest that Dāwūd's view on the issue was the more popular. The vagueness of this report does not allow for any such conclusions, however.

36 Al-Khaṭīb al-Baghdādī, *Tārīkh*, vol. 8, p. 374. *Al-lawḥ al-maḥfūẓ* is mentioned in Q 85:21–22, *bal huwa qurʾān majīd, fī lawḥ maḥfūẓ* (Nay! This is a glorious Qurʾan, in a preserved tablet).

37 For this, see, for instance, Ibn al-Jawzī, *al-Muntaẓam*, vol. 12, p. 236.

38 Ibn Abī Ḥātim al-Rāzī, *Jarḥ*, vol. 1, p. 410. A contemporary biographer of Dāwūd—ʿĀrif Abū ʿĪd—believes that al-Rāzī's Dāwūd ibn Khalaf is not our Dāwūd ibn ʿAlī ibn Khalaf

similar terms, describing him as a "deviant who leads people astray" (*ḍāll muḍill*) and warning people against listening to his foolish and absurd talk (*khaṭarātihi wa-wasāwisihi*).[39] After describing him as deviant, Ibn Abī Ḥātim adds that he had seen Dāwūd and listened to his views, of which his father and Abū Zurʿah al-Rāzī did not approve, and mentions his attack on the activities of the *Ahl al-Ḥadīth*.[40] But even if Ibn Abī Ḥātim or his father spoke ill of Dāwūd, their view seems to be isolated and was probably motivated by their rejection of specific views that he held. Generally speaking, however, Dāwūd, to my knowledge, is never impugned on moral or personal grounds.

In brief, whereas the picture of Dāwūd al-Ẓāhirī in medieval sources is that of a distinguished scholar and head of a *madhhab* who had followers in Baghdad, what the same sources mention about him is rather little. Consequently, we must deal with this picture with caution, not necessarily because it cannot be historically true, but because it cannot be corroborated by the sources that make it. What these sources do tell us about Dāwūd is insufficient to allow for definite conclusions about his life and career. While they do indicate that he was not an insignificant scholar, they do not prove that he was regarded in his age as an exceptionally distinguished scholar either.

(Abū ʿĪd, *al-Imām Dāwūd al-Ẓāhirī*, p. 48). Abū ʿĪd, however, does not demonstrate this, nor does he seem to have felt the need to do so. For him, the person about whom Ibn Abī Ḥātim speaks *cannot* be our Dāwūd. Abū ʿĪd apparently did not notice Abū Ḥātim al-Rāzī's view on Dāwūd. Admittedly, there is some confusion in Ibn Ḥajar's account, for he also reports that Ibn Abī Ḥātim had a biography of Dāwūd in which he did well (*ajāda*). It does not seem that Ibn Ḥajar meant that Ibn Abī Ḥātim did well in proving what his father is reported to have said of Dāwūd, for he apparently attributes to Ibn Abī Ḥātim the view that: "He [Dāwūd] transmitted from Isḥāq [ibn Rāhawayh] al-Ḥanẓalī and a group of traditionists. He also followed al-Shāfiʿī in his legal thought (*tafaqqaha li-l-Shāfiʿī*), and then abandoned that and rejected *qiyās*. He then wrote a number of books in which he contradicted earlier authorities (*salaf*) of the *ummah*, and innovated a method on account of which the majority of scholars deserted him. This notwithstanding, he is reliable and honest in his transmission and belief, although his view is the weakest of all views, the farthest from the way of jurisprudence, and the most deviant of all." What Ibn Abī Ḥātim al-Rāzī really thought of Dāwūd, therefore, is not clear. Be this as it may, Abū ʿĪd's assumption about Ibn Abī Ḥātim's biography is not as unfounded as it may sound, for the image of Dāwūd in biographical dictionaries is generally good, especially with regard to his integrity.

39 Ibn Ḥajar, *Lisān*, vol. 2, p. 491. Ibn Ḥajar attributes this to Dāwūd's scribe (*warrāq*), who is probably al-Ḥusayn ibn ʿAbd Allāh ibn Shākir al-Samarqandī (for this, see al-Dhahabī, *Mīzān al-Iʿtidāl*, vol. 1, p. 539). Al-Ḥusayn is reported to have died in 282/895 (Ibn Ḥajar, *Lisān*, vol. 2, p. 290).

40 Ibn Abī Ḥātim al-Rāzī, *Jarḥ*, vol. 1, p. 411.

It is remarkable, however, that if we compare Dāwūd's career with other leading scholars from the 2nd/8th or the 3rd/9th centuries, it appears that he was closer in profile to scholars like Abū Ḥanīfah al-Nuʿmān (d. 150/767) and al-Shāfiʿī than to a scholar like Aḥmad ibn Ḥanbal or other Ḥadīth transmitters or critics. Similar to him, Abū Ḥanīfah, and al-Shāfiʿī to some extent, were not distinguished as Ḥadīth transmitters and were known for their engagement in argumentation. Dāwūd's father was reportedly Ḥanafī, and Dāwūd himself is reported to have been a staunch admirer of al-Shāfiʿī and the first to have compiled works on his virtues (*manāqib*),[41] a report that later Shāfiʿī scholars would make use of to claim that he was Shāfiʿī notwithstanding his rejection of *qiyās*. Ibn Ḥanbal, in contrast, distinguished himself as a leading Ḥadīth transmitter and critic and was known for his extreme abhorrence of argumentation and of those who engaged in it. In fact, Dāwūd's biographers consistently report that Ibn Ḥanbal refused to meet Dāwūd.[42] And whereas Abū Zurʿah al-Rāzī admired his argumentative skills, he lamented the fact that he did not do what "people of knowledge" used to do, namely, transmitting traditions and abstaining from engaging in debates about issues such as the createdness of the Qurʾān.

∴

It is not uncommon for medieval legal works to report Dāwūd's views, either as a source of further support for a particular legal view or as a target of refutation and even ridicule. More often than not, these sources do not mention the bases on which Dāwūd held those views. This problem is compounded by the fact that we do not possess any of Dāwūd's legal works or even any legal works from his immediate students. This continues until Ibn Ḥazm al-Andalusī—writing almost two centuries after Dāwūd's death and thousands of miles away from the birthplace of Ẓāhirism—compiled extensive works of Ẓāhirī legal theory, sources, and methodology (*uṣūl al-fiqh*) and substantive views (*furūʿ*). How representative Ibn Ḥazm is of Dāwūd's legal heritage is a question that we attend to later.

As noted, al-Khaṭīb al-Baghdādī states that Dāwūd was *imām Ahl al-Ẓāhir* and reports that he was the first to hold to *ẓāhir* and reject *qiyās*. The meaning of *ẓāhir* is not explained here, nor is it explained in an explicit way in most medieval sources. Ibn al-Jawzī, probably seeking to explain what this term means, describes Dāwūd's *madhhab* as "rigid" because it fixates on the texts

41 For this, see, for instance, al-Shīrāzī, *Ṭabaqāt*, p. 93.

42 Al-Khaṭīb al-Baghdādī, *Tārīkh*, vol. 8, p. 373.

(*al-naql*), disregarding what could be understood from them (*al-mafhūm*) and focusing only on their wording (*ṣūrat lafẓihi*).[43]

Tāj al-Dīn al-Subkī (d. 771/1370)—who seems keen to bolster Dāwūd's image and defend him[44]—mentions that he received a copy of one of Dāwūd's treatises, including some papers entitled *al-Uṣūl*. According to al-Subkī, these treatises—contrary to al-Subkī's father's belief that Dāwūd rejected only one kind of *qiyās* (*al-qiyās al-khafī*)[45]—demonstrate that Dāwūd rejected all kinds of *qiyās* although he did not say so in an explicit and unambiguous way. In what seems like a quote from Dāwūd, he states that "judging on the basis of *qiyās* is not sound, and adhering to *istiḥsān* is not permitted." Dāwūd goes on to argue that we cannot declare licit what the Prophet had declared illicit and vice versa unless the Prophet himself points out the *ratio legis*, or the cause and rationale (*ʿillah*) of a certain ruling. Other than this, however, the undeclared *ʿillah* of a ruling falls into the category of things that are permitted, or are not prohibited (*ʿufiya ʿan-hā*). Furthermore, Dāwūd rejected *istiḥsān* (generally translated as "equity"), a rather ambiguous term that generally refers to the jurist's consideration of the circumstances of the case at hand when making a legal decision.[46] He also believed in the principle of *al-ibāḥah al-aṣliyyah*, namely, the original, "default" permissibility of whatever the law does not explicitly forbid.[47] Indecisive as this account may be as regards the kind of *qiyās* that he rejected, it gives us first hand access to Dāwūd's writings. Al-Subkī

---

43 Ibn al-Jawzī, *Muntaẓam*, vol. 12, p. 236.

44 Tāj al-Dīn al-Subkī, it should be mentioned, is not the only Shāfiʿī scholar whose discussion of Dāwūd's views betrays this desire to boost his image. We get the same impression from al-Dhahabī, who rejects the view of the famous Shāfiʿī scholar Abū al-Maʿālī al-Juwaynī that Dāwūd's views were worthless. Al-Dhahabī argues instead that Dāwūd was knowledgeable in jurisprudence, Qur'ān, Ḥadīth and legal disagreements, and was also very smart and pious (*Siyar*, vol. 13, pp. 107–108). In his *Tahdhīb al-Asmā' wa-l-Lughāt* (vol. 1, p. 445), the celebrated Shāfiʿī scholar al-Nawawī (d. 676/1277) also argues against the view that Dāwūd's views did not count as a valid legal disagreement. He points out that Dāwūd's merits, piety, and submission to the Sunna are all well-known (*ibid.*, vol. 1, p. 443). In his *ʿIqd al-Mudhhab* (p. 27), Ibn al-Mulaqqin argues that Dāwūd's rejection of *qiyās* does not exclude him from al-Shāfiʿī's students. Al-Subkī also begins his biography of Dāwūd by stating that the latter was one of the leaders and guides of the Muslims (*kāna aḥad a'immat al-muslimīn wa-hudātihim*) (al-Subkī, *Ṭabaqāt*, p. 248).

45 In a nutshell, what distinguishes *al-qiyās al-khafī* from *al-qiyās al-jalī* is the clarity of the *ʿillah* that is identified to compare the two cases in an analogy. If the *ʿillah* is explicitly stated or "obvious," the *qiyās* is *jalī*. But when the *ʿillah* is deduced from a text, the *qiyās* is considered *khafī* (for this, see, for instance, al-Āmidī, *al-Iḥkām*, vol. 3, pp. 95–96).

46 On *istiḥsān*, see *EI*², vol. 4, p. 255.

47 Al-Subkī, *Ṭabaqāt*, vol. 2, p. 290.

argues for the authenticity of the treatise and speculates that it was written in or before 300/912, which would mean that some of Dāwūd's writings were still available until the second half of the 8th/14th century, at least in Egypt.

Another important account for our purposes is Ibn al-Nadīm's list of Dāwūd's works in his *Fihrist*. Ibn al-Nadīm (d. 438/1047) also reiterates that Dāwūd was the first to hold to the *ẓāhir* and that he relied (exclusively?) on the Qur'ān and the Sunnah and rejected *ra'y* (opinion that is arbitrary in this view) and *qiyās*.[48] Ibn al-Nadīm attributes a long list of writings (*kutub*) to Dāwūd. This list (which could include books, epistles, or chapters of books) is indicative only of the scope of Dāwūd's knowledge and the issues in which he was interested, but not necessarily of the size of his written legal heritage. Most of these works are obviously ones that tackled specific substantive legal questions (which are likely to have been chapters in a single work), whereas some are evidently works that dealt with specific theoretical subjects of *uṣūl al-fiqh*. One of these is *al-Uṣūl*, which—if read in view of al-Subkī's statement—must have been a work of *uṣūl al-fiqh* in which Dāwūd dealt with issues like *qiyās* and *istiḥsān*.

After mentioning a few of Dāwūd's works, Ibn al-Nadīm adds that his other works were apparently noted on a piece of paper that had an old handwriting that possibly goes back to Dāwūd's own time.[49] Later, Ibn al-Nadīm mentions that the handwriting was that of a certain Maḥmūd al-Marwazī, whom he suspects may have been a follower of Dāwūd's. Other than *al-Uṣūl*, Ibn al-Nadīm attributes the following works to Dāwūd that probably also dealt with theoretical legal subjects: *Kitāb al-Dhabb ʿan al-Sunan wa-l-Aḥkām wa-l-Akhbār* (which is said to have comprised 1000 folios), *Kitāb al-Ijmāʿ, Kitāb Ibṭāl al-Taqlīd, Kitāb Ibṭāl al-Qiyās, Kitāb Khabar al-Wāḥid, Kitāb al-Khabar al-Mūjib li-l-ʿIlm, Kitāb al-Khuṣūṣ wa-l-ʿUmūm*, and *Kitāb al-Mufassar wa-l-Mujmal*. To these, he adds one work (the title of which is not mentioned) that dealt with two issues on which Dāwūd disagreed with al-Shāfiʿī, and another in which Dāwūd apparently presented some of al-Shāfiʿī's views (*Kitāb al-Kāfī fī Maqālat al-Muṭṭalibī*).[50]

So far Dāwūd is reported to have held what the sources call *al-ẓāhir*, rejected *qiyās, ra'y, istiḥsān*, and *taqlīd*, and held the principle of *al-ibāḥah al-aṣliyyah*. He is also reported to have written on a variety of *uṣūl al-fiqh* issues, including *sunan* and *akhbār, khabar al-wāḥid* and *ijmāʿ*, as well as two linguistic issues,

---

48 Ibn al-Nadīm, *Fihrist*, p. 216.

49 *Ibid.*, p. 216.

50 *Ibid.*, p. 217. Dāwūd's books are probably all lost (for this, see Abū ʿĪd, *al-Imām Dāwūd*, p. 125).

namely, the issues of "generality and restrictedness [of terms]" (*al-ʿumūm wa-l-khuṣūṣ*), and that of "clarified and ambiguous [terms]" (*al-mufassar wa-l-mujmal*).

Remarkably, despite the regular association between Dāwūd and *al-ẓāhir*, there is no solid evidence that he was called al-Ẓāhirī by his contemporaries. However, some evidence suggests that he was referred to as such only a few generations after his death. As noted earlier, Ibn Surayj had written against the *Ahl al-Raʾy* and the *Ahl al-Ẓāhir*. ʿAlī ibn Aḥmad ibn ʿAbd Allāh al-Kūfī (d. 352/963) is said to have written a "Refutation of the *Madhhab* of Dāwūd al-Ẓāhirī," a work that is now probably lost but which explicitly refers to Dāwūd as *al-Ẓāhirī*.[51] While it is possible that *al-Ẓāhirī* was added to the latter title by later scholars (when it became customary to use it as a sobriquet for Dāwūd), it is unlikely that the second title would mention Dāwūd without any sobriquet, either to his father, place of origin, or legal affiliation. There is a good chance, then, that *al-Ẓāhirī* existed in the original title of ʿAlī ibn Aḥmad's work and that Dāwūd was known as such already in the first half of the 3rd century.

2 Teachers and Students

In the 3rd/9th century, Baghdad was a vibrant place where competing theological, legal, and political views were debated, and where plenty of scholars offered their knowledge to interested students. Biographical dictionaries mention many scholars with whom Dāwūd studied. The following presentation of what is known about these scholars seeks to investigate the influence that they may have had on Dāwūd.

1. *ʿAbd Allāh ibn Maslamah ibn Qaʿnab al-Qaʿnabī al-Ḥārithī* (d. c. 220/834)

A resident of Basra who was considered a reliable transmitter of traditions by the Ḥadīth critics of the time,[52] al-Qaʿnabī transmitted from numerous scholars, including prominent jurists and traditionists, such as Ḥammād ibn Salamah (d. 167/783), Ḥammād ibn Zayd (d. 179/795), Mālik ibn Anas (d. 179/795)[53]—whose *Muwaṭṭaʾ* al-Qaʿnabī transmitted—al-Layth ibn Saʿd (d. 175/791), Fuḍayl ibn ʿIyāḍ (187/803), and Wakīʿ ibn al-Jarrāḥ (d. 197/812). Numerous traditionists transmitted from al-Qaʿnabī, including al-Bukhārī

51 Ismāʿīl Pasha al-Baghdādī, *Hadiyyat al-ʿĀrifīn*, vol. 1, pp. 680–681.

52 Ibn Ḥajar, *Tahdhīb al-Tahdhīb*, vol. 16, pp. 136, 139–140.

53 Al-Qaʿnabī appears in one of the various chains of transmission of Mālik's *Muwaṭṭaʾ* (for this see *Thabat al-Balawī*, pp. 119 and 151).

(d. 256/870), Muslim (d. 261/875), Abū Dāwūd (d. 275/889), Abū Zurʿah al-Rāzī (d. 264/878), and Abū Ḥātim al-Rāzī (d. 277/890). Al-Bukhārī is reported to have said that al-Qaʿnabī died in either 220/834 or 221/835. Abū Dāwūd, however, mentioned that he died in 211/826–827, perhaps in Mecca.[54] Since some of al-Qaʿnabī's students died as late as the last quarter of the 3rd century, it is unlikely that he died as early as the date that Abū Dāwūd gives.

2. *Muḥammad ibn Kathīr al-ʿAbdī* (d. 223/837)
Muḥammad ibn Kathīr was a Basran scholar who transmitted from, among others, Sufyān al-Thawrī (d. 161/777), Shuʿbah ibn al-Ḥajjāj (d. 160/776), and Abū ʿAwānah al-Waḍḍāḥ ibn ʿAbd Allāh (d. 176/792). Transmitters from al-ʿAbdī included al-Bukhārī, Abū Dāwūd, al-Dārimī (d. 255/869), ʿAlī ibn al-Madīnī (d. 234/848), Muḥammad ibn Yaḥyā al-Dhuhlī (d. 258/871), Abū Zurʿah al-Rāzī, and Abū Ḥātim al-Rāzī. Although al-ʿAbdī's reliability was questioned by Yaḥyā ibn Maʿīn (d. 233/847), his integrity was vouched for by Abū Ḥātim al-Rāzī and Ibn Ḥibbān (354/965), who reported that Muḥammad died in 223/837 at the age of ninety.[55]

3. *ʿAmr ibn Marzūq al-Bāhilī* (d. 224/838)
ʿAmr ibn Marzūq was a Basran scholar who transmitted from Ḥammād ibn Zayd, Ḥammād ibn Salamah, Shuʿbah ibn al-Ḥajjāj, and Mālik ibn Anas among many others. Al-Bukhārī, Abū Dāwūd, Abū Zurʿah al-Rāzī, Abū Ḥātim al-Rāzī and many other traditionists transmitted from him. He was considered reliable by many Ḥadīth critics, including Yaḥyā ibn Maʿīn and Aḥmad ibn Ḥanbal (d. 241/855), who used to defend him against allegations by ʿAlī ibn al-Madīnī. Some of ʿAmr's contemporaries mention that some 10,000 people or more used to attend his circle in Basra.[56] He is reported to have died in 224/838.

4. *Sulaymān ibn Ḥarb ibn Bajīl al-Azdī al-Wāshiḥī* (d. c. 224/838)
Sulaymān ibn Ḥarb was a Basran scholar who transmitted from Ḥammād ibn Zayd, Shuʿbah ibn al-Ḥajjāj, and Yazīd ibn Ibrāhīm al-Tustarī (d. after 160/776) among many others. From him, al-Bukhārī, Abū Dāwūd, Aḥmad ibn Ḥanbal, Isḥāq ibn Rāhawayh, al-Dārimī, Ibn Abī Shaybah (d. 235/849), Abū Zurʿah al-Rāzī, Abū Ḥātim al-Rāzī, and Yaḥyā ibn Saʿīd al-Qaṭṭān (d. 198/813), to mention but a few, transmitted traditions.[57] Himself a Ḥadīth critic known for

54 Ibn Ḥajar, *Tahdhīb al-Tahdhīb*, vol. 16, p. 141.
55 *Ibid.*, vol. 26, pp. 335–336.
56 *Ibid.*, vol. 22, pp. 225–228.
57 *Ibid.*, vol. 11, pp. 385–386.

his stringency, Sulaymān was trusted by the Ḥadīth critics of his time, and it is reported that some 40,000 students attended his lectures.[58] In 214/829, he was appointed judge of Mecca by the Abbasid Caliph al-Maʾmūn, an appointment that lasted for five years.[59] He died between 223/837 and 227/841, probably in 224/838 in Basra.[60]

5. *Musaddad ibn Musarhad ibn Musarbal (and possibly, ibn Mustawrad, and ibn Muraʿbal) al-Asadī* (d. 228/842)
Musaddad ibn Musarhad was a Basran scholar who transmitted from many traditionists, including Ḥammād ibn Zayd, Sufyān ibn ʿUyaynah (d. 198/813), Fuḍayl ibn ʿIyāḍ, Wakīʿ ibn al-Jarrāḥ, and Yaḥyā ibn Saʿīd al-Qaṭṭān. Transmitters from him included al-Bukhārī, Abū Dāwūd, al-Tirmidhī, al-Nasāʾī, Abū Zurʿah al-Rāzī, and Abū Ḥātim al-Rāzī. Musaddad, who was considered reliable by the Ḥadīth critics of his age, reportedly died in 228/842.[61]

6. *Aḥmad ibn Yaḥyā ibn ʿAbd al-ʿAzīz, Abū ʿAbd al-Raḥmān al-Shāfiʿī* (d. after 230/844)
According to al-Khaṭīb al-Baghdādī, Abū ʿAbd al-Raḥmān al-Shāfiʿī was an associate of al-Shāfiʿī and later a follower of Ibn Abī Duʾād (d. 240/854), the famous Muʿtazilī theologian and *wazīr*.[62] Although al-Khaṭīb al-Baghdādī does not mention Dāwūd among those who transmitted from or studied with him, al-Dhahabī, remarkably, mentions Dāwūd as Abū ʿAbd al-Raḥmān's only student.[63]

7. *Isḥāq ibn Ibrāhīm ibn Makhlad al-Tamīmī al-Marwazī, Ibn Rāhawayh* (d. 238/852)
A renowned scholar of Ḥadīth and jurisprudence in Nishabur, Isḥāq ibn Rāhawayh is probably the only teacher whose encounters with Dāwūd are

58 Ibn Ḥajar, *Tahdhīb al-Tahdhīb*, vol. 11, pp. 387ff.

59 *Ibid.*, vol. 11, p. 389.

60 *Ibid.*, vol. 11, p. 392.

61 *Ibid.*, vol. 27, pp. 445–447.

62 Al-Khaṭīb al-Baghdādī, *Tārīkh*, vol. 5, p. 200. For Ibn Abī Duʾād's biography and reported role in the *Miḥnah*, see al-Dhahabī, *Siyar*, vol. 11, pp. 169–171.

63 Al-Dhahabī, *Siyar*, vol. 10, p. 555. It is worth mentioning here that al-Dhahabī regards Aḥmad ibn Yaḥyā as having been among the smartest scholars (*min kibār al-adhkiyāʾ*) and notable students of al-Shāfiʿī (*ibid.*, vol. 10, p. 555). It is remarkable that al-Dhahabī does not mention any of his other Shāfiʿī students, but his mention of Dāwūd as his student is in line with Dāwūd's image in medieval Shāfiʿī works as has been noted earlier.

mentioned in the sources, although we do not know where exactly they may have met.[64] As noted earlier, he had a debate with Dāwūd on the issue of the createdness of the Qurʾān, and is reported to have assaulted him for his view on this issue. Other accounts indicate that Dāwūd and Ibn Rāhawayh were on good terms.[65]

8. *ʿAbd Allāh ibn Kullāb* (d. after 240/854)
A controversial theologian from Basra, Ibn Kullāb's views brought on him the wrath of theologians belonging to various Islamic sects. According to al-Dhahabī, Ibn Kullāb was Dāwūd's theology teacher.[66]

9. *Ibrāhīm ibn Khālid ibn Abī al-Yamān, Abū Thawr al-Kalbī* (d. 240/854)
Abū Thawr al-Kalbī was a jurist from Baghdad who studied with Sufyān ibn ʿUyaynah, ʿAbd al-Raḥmān ibn Mahdī (d. 198/813), Muḥammad ibn Idrīs al-Shāfiʿī, Wakīʿ ibn al-Jarrāḥ and many others. Among those who transmitted from him are Abū Dāwūd, Ibn Mājah (d. 273/886), Abū Ḥātim al-Rāzī, and Muslim.[67] Abū Thawr wrote a number of legal works that contained both Ḥadīth and jurisprudence.[68] Al-Khaṭīb al-Baghdādī reports that he at first followed the way of the *Ahl al-Raʾy* (more about whom later), preferring the *madhhab* of the Iraqis (the Ḥanafī scholar Muḥammad ibn al-Ḥasan al-Shaybānī (d. 189/805) in particular, as Abū Thawr himself states) until al-Shāfiʿī arrived in Baghdad. According to this account, he abandoned *raʾy* and adhered to Ḥadīth at the hands of al-Shāfiʿī. He is reported to have mentioned that he, along with Isḥāq ibn Rāhawayh, al-Ḥusayn ibn ʿAlī al-Karābīsī (more about whom below) and a number of Iraqi scholars, did not abandon their "innovation" (*bidʿah*, used pejoratively here) until they met al-Shāfiʿī. When al-Shāfiʿī arrived in Baghdad, al-Karābīsī, who also used to frequent the *Aṣḥāb al-Raʾy*, went to Abū Thawr and said: "One of the *Aṣḥāb al-Ḥadīth* has arrived and is teaching jurisprudence (*yatafaqqahu*). Rise up and let us ridicule him." The rest of the anecdote has al-Shāfiʿī respond to each of al-Karābīsī's questions

64 Ibn Rāhawayh, who was from Marw and a resident of Nishabur, visited Iraq, the Ḥijāz, Yemen, and Syria (for this, see al-Dhahabī, *Siyar*, vol. 11, p. 359).
65 In one of these accounts, Dāwūd visits Ibn Rāhawayh in his home, browses his books, and makes jokes with him.
66 Al-Dhahabī, *Siyar*, vol. 11, pp. 174–176.
67 Ibn Ḥajar, *Tahdhīb*, vol. 2, p. 81.
68 Al-Khaṭīb al-Baghdādī, *Tārīkh*, vol. 6, p. 65.

with a Prophetic report. As a result, both men had no choice but to acknowledge his knowledge and follow him.[69]

Abū Thawr does not seem to have been on good terms with the Ḥadīth scholars of his time. Aḥmad ibn Ḥanbal is reported to have disliked his views, although he did not question his reliability. He apparently regarded him as belonging to a group of scholars different from his. When a man asked Ibn Ḥanbal about a legal matter, he repeatedly refused to answer, saying to the man: "Ask the jurists, ask Abū Thawr."[70] In another anecdote, a woman asked a group of Ḥadīth scholars about a certain issue, but they kept looking at each other and did not answer her. When they saw Abū Thawr coming from afar, they instructed the woman to ask him. Abū Thawr replied to her immediately, invoking a Prophetic tradition to support his view. The scholars of Ḥadīth confirmed the authenticity of the tradition and were reportedly happy with Abū Thawr's answer. The woman then looked angrily at them and said: "Where have you been until now?"[71]

10. *Al-Ḥusayn ibn al-Ḥasan ibn Ḥarb* (d. 246/860)

Al-Ḥusayn ibn Ḥarb was a competent Ḥadīth scholar and a reliable transmitter who transmitted from, among others, ʿAbd Allāh ibn al-Mubārak (d. 181/797) and Sufyān ibn ʿUyaynah, in addition to transmitting from Aḥmad ibn Ḥanbal his *Kitāb al-Zuhd*. Many traditionists transmitted from al-Ḥusayn, including al-Tirmidhī, Ibn Mājah, and Dāwūd. Al-Dhahabī mentions that he resided in Mecca,[72] but based on what we know about his teachers and students, there is a good chance that he lived in Baghdad for some time.

11. *Al-Junayd ibn Muḥammad ibn al-Junayd al-Qawārīrī* (d. 298/910)

Mentioned among Dāwūd's teachers by al-Khaṭīb al-Baghdādī and Abū Isḥāq al-Shīrāzī, al-Junayd was a famous Sufi in 3rd/9th-century Baghdad, where he was born to a family that came from Nahawand.[73] He studied Ḥadīth with many scholars and jurisprudence with Abū Thawr al-Kalbī, in whose circle

---

69 *Ibid.*, vol. 6, p. 68. Abū Thawr met al-Shāfiʿī when he went to Baghdad in 195/810 (for this, see al-Shāfiʿī's biography in Ibn Kathīr, *al-Bidāyah wa-l-Nihāyah*, vol. 10, p. 211). Abū Thawr is reported here to have been one of many scholars who attended al-Shāfiʿī's lessons, including Ibn Ḥanbal and al-Karābīsī.

70 *Ibid.*, vol. 6, p. 66.

71 *Wa-ayna kuntum ilā ʾl-ān* (*ibid.*, vol. 6, p. 67).

72 Al-Dhahabī, *Tārīkh al-Islām wa-Wafayāt al-Mashāhīr wa-l-Aʿlām*, vol. 25, p. 238.

73 Al-Khaṭīb al-Baghdādī, *Tārīkh*, vol. 6, p. 345.

he is reported to have started giving *fatwās* when he was only 20 years old.[74] Other than that, all that is mentioned about al-Junayd are anecdotes showing his standing as an ascetic and pious Sufi.

A remarkable observation about Dāwūd's teachers is that many of them were either Basrans or residents of Basra. As noted, Dāwūd likely met these Basran teachers of his in Basra, for their biographies do not indicate that they traveled to Baghdad. What is perhaps more remarkable is that most of these teachers died while Dāwūd was still relatively young in his twenties. The only exception is ʿAbd Allāh ibn Kullāb, whom Dāwūd probably met during his possible visit to Basra in his youth. Furthermore, whether Ibn Rāhawayh was a teacher of Dāwūd in the strict sense is uncertain, for we do not know how long Dāwūd stayed with him and we do know that he used to argue with him (which is more typical of two scholars regarding each other as peers). Al-Junayd was also probably one of Dāwūd's peers in legal matters, for—given that he died in 298/910—he cannot have been much older than him. In addition, al-Junayd was himself a student of Abū Thawr. Finally, the fact that Dāwūd was not interested in Ḥadīth transmission suggests that al-Ḥusayn ibn Ḥarb did not have much influence on him.

Furthermore, unlike his Baghdad teachers whose interests were mainly in jurisprudence, a common feature among Dāwūd's Basran teachers—with the exception of ʿAbd Allāh ibn Kullāb—was their interest in Ḥadīth transmission and criticism, just like typical scholars of their age. All of them seem to have been active in learning traditions from the famous scholars of the time, and all of them transmitted to one or more of the famous 3rd/9th-century compilers of Ḥadīth works. Other than making Dāwūd's apparent lack of interest in transmitting traditions even more striking, this observation suggests that his Basran teachers did not have much influence on him,[75] although the time that he spent there may have had some influence on his thought, especially as far as language and hermeneutics are concerned.[76]

74 Al-Khaṭīb al-Baghdādī, *Tārīkh*, vol. 6, p. 242.

75 Our sources do not mention the exact subjects that Dāwūd studied with each of his teachers, but we can assume that he studied with them whatever they were interested in. If this happened to be predominantly Ḥadīth, this further confirms the conclusion made on their influence on him.

76 Writing about the all-important grammarians of Basra, Vishanoff notes that they "posited a direct correlation between the words and structures of Arabic on the one hand, and the reality that they express on the other. Every word and verbal form is established to express a specific idea, and for every idea there is a normal form of verbal expression. Language is a mirror of reality" (David R. Vishanoff's *The Formation of Islamic Hermeneutics: How*

This leaves us with Abū Thawr al-Kalbī, who was probably Dāwūd's most important teacher, and one who had the longest and strongest influence on him. In fact, Dāwūd is described by some of his contemporaries as one of Abū Thawr's "disciples."[77]

Although Abū Thawr seems to have had some interest in Ḥadīth and reportedly abandoned *ra'y* for Ḥadīth when he met al-Shāfiʿī in Baghdad (when he was probably in his twenties or thirties), anecdotes from a later stage in his life indicate that he was never regarded as part of the *Ahl al-Ḥadīth* of his time. References to Abū Thawr's works that included both Ḥadīth and jurisprudence suggest that his orientation was not like that of typical traditionists, whose works would include only traditions.[78] In fact, Ibn Ḥanbal's reference to him as a *faqīh* suggests that he belonged to a different group of scholars, a group that answered all questions put to them, unlike traditionists who would refrain from answering some questions. Furthermore, Ibn al-Nadīm mentions that Abū Thawr studied with and transmitted from al-Shāfiʿī, but disagreed with him on some issues and developed his own *madhhab* on the basis of al-Shāfiʿī's views.[79] He is also described as an independent scholar who differed with the majority of the scholars on many issues. No wonder, then, that Ḥadīth scholars felt uneasy about Abū Thawr; Ibn Ḥanbal is reported to have

---

Sunni Legal Theorists Imagined a Revealed Law, p. 20). The relevance of this to Dāwūd's understanding of language will be evident in a later context. For an overview of the intellectual milieu and notable scholars of early Basra, see ʿAbd al-Jabbār Nājī, *Min Mashāhīr Aʿlām al-Baṣrah: Dirāsah fī ʾAṭāʾ al-Baṣrah al-Fikrī.*

77 *Min ghilmān Abī Thawr* (al-Dhahabī, *Siyar*, vol. 13, p. 103). It should be mentioned here that the word *ghulām* (singular of *ghilmān*) could indicate that the person who so described Dāwūd meant that he was a blind follower of Abū Thawr, who was thus more than just one of his teachers.

78 This does not mean, of course, that they were not interested in jurisprudence. Some scholars have noted how the very organization of some Ḥadīth compilations indicates support of particular legal views (for this, see, for instance, Mohammad Fadel, "Ibn Ḥajar's Hady al-Sari: A Medieval Interpretation of the Structure of al-Bukhari's al-Jami al-Sahih: Introduction and Translation"). This, however, does not change the fact that those compilations remain Ḥadīth collections in the first place, unlike a work like Mālik's *Muwaṭṭaʾ*, for instance, which is clearly a work of *fiqh* that uses Prophetic and non-Prophetic traditions.

79 In fact, Ibn al-Nadīm—who mentions Abū Thawr among al-Shāfiʿī's followers—says that while Abū Thawr studied with al-Shāfiʿī, he disagreed with him on some issues and developed a new *madhhab* for himself derived from al-Shāfiʿī's views (*aḥdatha li-nafsihi madhhab ishtaqqahu min madhhab al-Shāfiʿī*). Ibn al-Nadīm attributes to Abū Thawr a number of works on specific *furūʿ* issues (Ibn al-Nadīm, *Fihrist*, p. 211).

expressed his dislike of his views, and Abū Ḥātim al-Rāzī described him as a scholar who relied on *raʾy*, thus arriving at right as well as wrong conclusions, but who had no status in Ḥadīth knowledge.[80]

Recall that when Abū Thawr and al-Karābīsī went to al-Shāfiʿī to ridicule him, it was al-Karābīsī and not Abū Thawr who tested him. Sources do not mention any relationship between Dāwūd and al-Karābīsī, who died between 245/859 and 248/863. It is unlikely, however, that the two did not meet, not only because al-Karābīsī was a close friend of Abū Thawr, but also because he was well-known in Baghdad. Fortunately, there is evidence that Dāwūd did meet al-Karābīsī; in one of al-Karābīsī's biographies, there is a transmission of a report by Dāwūd from him.[81]

Similar to Abū Thawr, (Abū ʿAlī) al-Karābīsī followed the methodology of the *Ahl al-Raʾy* until he met al-Shāfiʿī,[82] but he too does not seem to have entirely abandoned *raʾy* when he met al-Shāfiʿī and "converted" to Ḥadīth. Al-Karābīsī was a knowledgeable jurist, and one who wrote many works on both *uṣūl* and *furūʿ* that reveal his "good comprehension and vast knowledge."[83] Tāj al-Dīn al-Subkī—who also included al-Karābīsī among al-Shāfiʿī's followers—describes him as a leading scholar (*imām*) who combined the knowledge of both jurisprudence and Ḥadīth (just as he describes Abū Thawr).[84] This notwithstanding, al-Karābīsī—again, similar to Abū Thawr, did not seem to have much interest in Ḥadīth transmission, which he rarely did.[85] More importantly, he was openly hostile to the *Ahl al-Ḥadīth*, including Aḥmad ibn Ḥanbal who described him as an "innovator"—indeed, the successor of the Murjiʾī heretic Bishr al-Marīsī (d. 218/833) and one of those who abandoned Ḥadīth for their "books"[86]—and warned people against talking to him and to those who talked to him. The reason for this harsh view is that al-Karābīsī was of the opinion that whereas God's speech was not created (i.e., the Qurʾān is not created), our enunciation of the Qurʾān was. When this view reached Ibn Ḥanbal, he spoke ill of al-Karābīsī, who reciprocated in kind. In one report, when al-Karābīsī was told that Ibn Ḥanbal said that his views on the issue of *khalq al-Qurʾān* were heretical innovations, he said: "What should we do with this lad?" When this

80 Al-Subkī, *Ṭabaqāt*, vol. 2, p. 77.
81 *Ibid.*, vol. 2, p. 118.
82 *Ibid.*, vol. 2, p. 117.
83 Al-Khaṭīb al-Baghdādī, *Tārīkh*, vol. 8, p. 64.
84 Al-Subkī, *Ṭabaqāt*, vol. 2, p. 117.
85 Al-Khaṭīb al-Baghdādī, *Tārīkh*, vol. 8, p. 64.
86 *Ibid.*, vol. 8, pp. 64–67. On Bishr al-Marīsī, see *EI*², vol. 1, p. 1241.

happened, al-Khaṭīb al-Baghdādī reports, people (i.e., the Ḥadīth transmitters of the time) abstained from transmitting from al-Karābīsī and Ibn Ḥanbal's associates began to malign him. One of them—Yaḥyā ibn Maʿīn—angrily said: "Who is Ḥusayn al-Karābīsī? May God curse him! Only the equals of people can speak about them."[87] The Shāfiʿī scholar Muḥammad ibn ʿAbd Allāh al-Ṣayrafī used to tell his students to take lesson from al-Karābīsī and Abū Thawr—the former possessed vast knowledge but fell out of favor when Ibn Ḥanbal spoke unfavorably of him; the latter, possessing only a fraction of al-Karābīsī's knowledge, rose in status because Ibn Ḥanbal spoke favorably of him.[88]

It is remarkable that this view of *khalq al-Qurʾān* is almost identical to Dāwūd's view, which is also the case with other views that both scholars held. In *uṣūl al-fiqh*, for instance, al-Karābīsī, held that a report that is transmitted by a single transmitter (*khabar al-wāḥid*) establishes apodictic knowledge, just like reports transmitted through *tawātur*.[89] Ibn Ḥazm attributes this view to al-Karābīsī and Dāwūd, and adds that it differs from the view of Ḥanafī, Shāfiʿī, most Mālikī, Muʿtazilī, and Khārijī scholars.[90]

In sum, Dāwūd's Basran teachers probably had a little influence on him, although the intellectual milieu in Basra itself may have influenced him. If Dāwūd was influenced by any of his teachers, he must have been influenced by Abū Thawr al-Kalbī and probably also by al-Ḥusayn al-Karābīsī.[91] Both men started their careers as scholars of the *Ahl al-Raʾy*, and neither was ever part of the *Ahl al-Ḥadīth* even after they were said to have abandoned *raʾy*. Although it is not clear how long Dāwūd may have studied with these two scholars, it can be surmised that this period was long enough to make their influence on him possible.

∵

The following scholars are reported to have studied with Dāwūd. Unless otherwise noted, these are the scholars that Abū Isḥāq al-Shīrāzī mentions in the first generation of Ẓāhirī scholars in his *Ṭabaqāt al-Fuqahāʾ*.

---

87 Al-Khaṭīb al-Baghdādī, *Tārīkh*, vol. 8, pp. 64–65. He, of course, means that al-Karābīsī was no match of Ibn Ḥanbal.

88 *Ibid.*, vol. 8, pp. 66–67.

89 Al-Subkī, *Ṭabaqāt*, vol. 2, p. 126.

90 Ibn Ḥazm, *al-Iḥkām fī Uṣūl al-Aḥkām*, vol. 1, pp. 97, 107.

91 Later, Ibn Ḥazm would include these two scholars among the early independent scholars (*mujtahids*) who chose to follow in the footsteps of earlier generations in their independence and did not blindly follow other scholars (Ibn Ḥazm, *Iḥkām*, vol. 2, p. 674).

1. *Muḥammad ibn Isḥāq al-Qāsānī* (*fl. c.* second half of 3rd/9th century)[92]
Al-Qāsānī (or al-Qashānī) does not figure in major biographical dictionaries, but references to his views alongside those of Dāwūd in other sources indicate that he was a scholar of considerable weight. Al-Shīrāzī mentions that al-Qāsānī studied with Dāwūd and transmitted his knowledge, but also disagreed with him on many theoretical and substantive legal issues. A later Ẓāhirī scholar—Abū al-Ḥasan ibn al-Mughallis—responded to him in a book that he entitled *al-Qāmiʿ li-l-Mutaḥāmil al-Ṭāmiʿ*.[93] Ibn al-Nadīm mentions that whereas he started his career as a "Dāwūdī" scholar, al-Qāsānī later became a follower of al-Shāfiʿī. He attributes to him two works on *qiyās*, in the first of which al-Qāsānī refutes Dāwūd's rejection of *qiyās* (*Kitāb al-Radd ʿalā Dāwūd fī Ibṭāl al-Qiyās*), and in the second he argued for its validity (*Kitāb Ithbāt al-Qiyās*).[94]

2. *Al-Ḥasan ibn ʿUbayd al-Nahrabānī* (*fl. c.* second half of 3rd/9th century)[95]
Ibn al-Nadīm attributes to al-Nahrabānī (or al-Nahrawānī) a work entitled *Ibṭāl al-Qiyās*,[96] obviously a work against *qiyās*. Later sources make reference to some of al-Nahrabānī's views as a "Dāwūdī" scholar (see below).

3. *Muḥammad ibn ʿUbayd Allāh ibn Khalaf* (*fl. c.* second half of 3rd/9th century)
Muḥammad ibn ʿUbayd Allāh was a student of Dāwūd who nonetheless disagreed with him on some points.[97]

4. *Al-Ḥusayn ibn ʿAbd Allāh al-Samarqandī* (*fl. c.* second half of 3rd/9th century)
According to al-Shīrāzī, al-Ḥusayn ibn ʿAbd Allāh transmitted Dāwūd's books.[98]

---

92 Ismāʿīl al-Baghdādī (*Hadiyyat al-ʿĀrifīn*, vol. 2, p. 12) attributes a work entitled *Uṣūl al-Futyā* to al-Qāshānī and mentions that he died in 280/893–894. I owe references to *Hadiyyat al-ʿĀrifīn* to Māzin al-Buḥṣalī's *Ṭabaqāt Ahl al-Ẓāhir*, where al-Buḥṣalī mentions scholars whose affiliation with the Ẓāhirī *madhhab* cannot be confirmed (and therefore will not appear in our lists of Ẓāhirī scholars). However, when I do not find a date of death that Ismāʿīl al-Baghdādī mentions in any other source, I mention it only in a footnote.

93 Al-Shīrāzī, *Ṭabaqāt*, p. 176.

94 Ibn al-Nadīm, *Fihrist*, p. 213. What is intriguing, however, is that among the works that Ibn al-Nadīm attributes to Ibn al-Surayj is a response to al-Qāsānī (*Kitāb Jawāb al-Qāshānī*) (*ibid.*, p. 213). This title does not indicate the nature of Ibn Surayj's response. In any case, if Ibn al-Nadīm is correct about al-Qāsānī's conversion to Shāfiʿism, Ibn Surayj is likely to have written this work before that conversion.

95 According to Ismāʿīl al-Baghdādī (*Hadiyyat al-ʿĀrifīn*, vol. 1, p. 138), al-Nahrabānī died in 276/889–890.

96 Ibn al-Nadīm, *Fihrist*, p. 318.

97 Abū Isḥāq al-Shīrāzī, *Ṭabaqāt*, p. 176.

98 *Ibid.*, p. 177.

5. *ʿAbbās ibn Aḥmad al-Mudhdhakkir* (*fl. c.* second half of 3rd/9th century)
ʿAbbās is mentioned by al-Khaṭīb al-Baghdādī in Dāwūd's biography as an unreliable transmitter from him.[99] Only one person transmitted from al-ʿAbbās.[100]

6. *Zakariyyā ibn Yaḥyā al-Sājī* (d. 307/919)
Zakariyyā al-Sājī was a famous Basran scholar of Ḥadīth and jurisprudence.[101] He is mentioned by al-Khaṭīb al-Baghdādī as one of Dāwūd's students.[102] Ibn al-Nadīm, however, mentions al-Sājī among al-Shāfiʿī's followers. According to him, al-Sājī studied with the Shāfiʿī scholars Ismāʿīl ibn Ibrāhīm al-Muzanī and al-Rabīʿ ibn Sulaymān al-Murādī (d. 270/884). Al-Sājī's reported works include one on legal disagreement (*Kitāb al-Ikhtilāf fī al-Fiqh*)[103] and another on Ḥadīth defects (*ʿIlal al-Ḥadīth*).[104]

7. *Yūsuf ibn Yaʿqūb ibn Mihrān al-Dāwūdī* (d. *c.* 310/922)
Yūsuf ibn Yaʿqūb is described by al-Khaṭīb al-Baghdādī as a *faqīh*,[105] and by al-Dhahabī as a "Baghdādī *mastūr*," an unknown (or perhaps unreliable) person from Baghdad.[106] Al-Khaṭīb al-Baghdādī mentions only two scholars—one of whom is Dāwūd—from whom Yūsuf transmitted, and attributes to Yūsuf only one report that goes back to ʿAlī ibn Abī Ṭālib.[107]

8. *Ibrāhīm ibn Muḥammad ibn ʿArafah, Nifṭawayh*[108] (d. 323/935)
Nifṭawayh was better known as a grammarian than a legal expert.[109] He is not listed among Dāwūd's students by al-Khaṭīb al-Baghdādī,[110] but al-Dhahabī

99 Al-Khaṭīb al-Baghdādī, *Tārīkh*, vol. 8, p. 370.
100 Ibn Ḥajar, *Lisān*, vol. 3, p. 288.
101 Al-Dhahabī, *Siyar*, vol. 14, p. 198.
102 Al-Khaṭīb al-Baghdādī, *Tārīkh*, vol. 8, p. 370.
103 Ibn al-Nadīm, *Fihrist*, p. 213.
104 Al-Dhahabī, *Siyar*, vol. 14, p. 199.
105 Al-Khaṭīb al-Baghdādī, *Tārīkh*, vol. 8, p. 370.
106 Al-Dhahabī, *Tārīkh*, vol. 31, p. 341.
107 Al-Khaṭīb al-Baghdādī, *Tārīkh*, vol. 8, p. 370.
108 Al-Thaʿālibī explains that this nickname comprises two parts: *nifṭ*, or oil, and *awayh*, a Persian suffix. He mentions that Muḥammad ibn Ibrāhīm was given this nickname for his dark color and ugly face (for this, see Abū ʿĪd, *al-Imām Dāwūd*, p. 105).
109 Al-Dhahabī, *Siyar*, vol. 15, pp. 75–76.
110 Abū Isḥāq al-Shīrāzī, *Ṭabaqāt*, p. 176.

reports that he was a leader (*ra's*) in the *madhhab* of the *Ahl al-Ẓāhir*,[111] and al-Zarkashī mentions him as one of the most noble of Dāwūd's associates.[112]

The only other student of Dāwūd that we know of is his own son Muḥammad, whom we will discuss in more detail below. But to these students we can add some other possible students of Dāwūd who are not listed as such in his available biographies.

9. *ʿAbd Allāh ibn al-Qāsim ibn Hilāl al-ʿAbsī* (d. 272/885)

Al-Dhahabī mentions that Ibn Hilāl al-ʿAbsī was active in seeking and transmitting traditions.[113] Ibn Hilāl was admired by Ibn Ḥazm, who mentions that he was an associate of Dāwūd.[114] Ibn al-Faraḍī reports that Ibn Hilāl started his career as a Mālikī student, but after studying with Dāwūd and learning his books, he adopted his *madhhab* and traveled to Andalus where he actively spread it.[115]

10. *Kunayz ibn ʿAbd Allāh* (*fl.* c. 250/864)

In his *Tārīkh Madīnat Dimashq*, Ibn ʿAsākir mentions that Kunayz transmitted from Dāwūd. Kunayz was born in Baghdad, lived most of his life in Egypt as a client of Aḥmad ibn Ṭūlūn (r. 254/868 to 270/884), and followed the Shāfiʿī *madhhab*.[116]

11. *Aḥmad ibn Muḥammad ibn al-ʿAjannas al-ʿAjannasī* (d. 290/903)

According to al-Samʿānī, al-ʿAjannasī was a scholar from Bukhara who traveled to Iraq and the Ḥijāz and studied with many scholars. Al-Samʿānī also reports that he met with Dāwūd, studied his books with him, and followed his *madhhab*.[117]

---

111 Al-Dhahabī, *Siyar*, vol. 15, p. 76.

112 Al-Zarkashī, *al-Baḥr al-Muḥīṭ*, vol. 2, p. 72.

113 Al-Dhahabī, *Tārīkh*, vol. 30, p. 180.

114 Ibn Ḥazm, *Rasāʾil*, vol. 2, p. 187.

115 Ibn al-Faraḍī, *Tārīkh ʿUlamāʾ al-Andalus*, vol. 1, p. 297. Relying on this account, Mahmud Ali Makki believes that it was indeed Ibn Hilāl who introduced Ẓāhirism to Andalus (Makki, *Ensayo sobre las Aportaciones Orientales en la España Musulaman y su Influencia en al Formación de la Cultura Hispano-Árabe*, p. 205).

116 Ibn ʿAsākir, *Tārīkh Madīnat Dimashq*, vol. 50, pp. 261–262. Ibn ʿAsākir mentions here that Kunayz stayed in Egypt for seven years after Aḥmad ibn Ṭūlūn's death, and then moved to Damascus where he died a few years later.

117 Al-Samʿānī, *Ansāb*, vol. 4, p. 162. According to al-Samʿānī, al-ʿAjannasī is named after ʿAjannas, which is a person's name.

12. *Ruwaym ibn Aḥmad* (d. *c.* late 3rd/9th century)
A story mentioned in most biographies of Muḥammad ibn Dāwūd evidently indicates that Ruwaym used to frequent Dāwūd,[118] and Ibn Ḥazm mentions him among Dāwūd's associates.[119] Ruwaym was also known for being a Sufi master who abandoned Sufism to work in the judiciary and politics.[120]

13. *Mūsā ibn ʿAbd al-Ḥamīd ibn ʿIṣām al-Jurjānī* (d. 300/912)
Al-Dhahabī mentions Mūsā al-Jurjānī as a person who studied with Dāwūd.[121]

14. *Makḥūl ibn al-Faḍl, Abū Muṭīʿ al-Nasafī* (d. 308/920)
Al-Dhahabī mentions that Abū Muṭīʿ al-Nasafī transmitted from Dāwūd.[122]

Mention also should be made here of al-Muʿāfā ibn Zakariyyā al-Nahrawānī, whom al-Shīrāzī includes among Dāwūd's students.[123] However, Ibn al-Nadīm mentions that al-Muʿāfā was the authority of his time in the *madhhab* of al-Ṭabarī, and attributes to him a work in which he evidently argued against Dāwūd (*Kitāb al-Radd ʿalā Dāwūd*).[124] Apparently, al-Muʿāfā was a student of Dāwūd for some time but later joined al-Ṭabarī's circle and became one of his students.

Many of Dāwūd's immediate students do not figure in biographical dictionaries, and only one of them—Zakariyyā al-Sājī, whose relationship with Dāwūd is not even mentioned by al-Dhahabī—seems to have had some significance as a scholar of Ḥadīth and jurisprudence. This is consistent with Dāwūd's apparent lack of interest in Ḥadīth—which he seems to have passed on to his immediate associates. In addition, none of these students were known as Ẓāhirīs, and one of them—Yūsuf ibn Yaʿqūb—was known as "al-Dāwūdī." Disagreements between Dāwūd and some of his students and among these students do not indicate that they shared a fixed doctrinal heritage or had a sense of belonging to one *madhhab*. Thus, what we know about Dāwūd's immediate students is hardly useful either in identifying the main tenets of his

---

118 The story, reported by Ruwaym who was sitting with Dāwūd, mentions that one day Muḥammad ibn Dāwūd went to his father crying because his friends used to call him by a sarcastic nickname (al-Khaṭīb al-Baghdādī, *Tārīkh*, vol. 5, p. 256).

119 Ibn Ḥazm, *Iḥkām*, vol. 2, p. 674.

120 Ibn Kathīr, *Bidāyah*, vol. 11, pp. 303–304.

121 Al-Dhahabī, *Tārīkh*, vol. 30, p. 314.

122 Al-Dhahabī, *Siyar*, vol. 15, p. 33. For more information about Makḥūl ibn al-Faḍl, see al-Qurashī, *Jawāhir*, vol. 3, p. 498.

123 Al-Shīrāzī, *Ṭabaqāt*, p. 93.

124 Ibn al-Nadīm, *Fihrist*, p. 236.

legal thought or in indicating that he left behind a coherent group of students. This leaves us with Dāwūd's own son Muḥammad, to whom we now turn.

3 Muḥammad, Son and Student

Born in 255/869,[125] Muḥammad ibn Dāwūd (d. 297/909) was best known as a litterateur; al-Khaṭīb al-Baghdādī introduces him as the author of the *Kitāb al-Zahrah*,[126] a work most of which he finished while he was very young and his father was still alive.[127] Ibn Dāwūd was a gifted poet, mainly writing about love,[128] which was not always heterosexual. He is reported to have been in love with a certain Muḥammad ibn Jāmiʿ al-Ṣaydalānī, also mentioned as having been his benefactor.[129] Ibn Dāwūd died in 297/909 at the age of 42, leaving behind a son, named Sulaymān, who is reported to have followed in the footsteps of his father and grandfather as a Ẓāhirī scholar.[130]

As a legal scholar, Ibn Dāwūd's biographers report that he succeeded his father in the latter's circle while he was still of young age. An oft-cited anecdote indicates that he proved that he was up to the task and managed to fill his father's position.[131] People used to go to him with legal questions, and he used

125 Al-Khaṭīb al-Baghdādī, *Tārīkh*, vol. 5, p. 262.

126 *Ibid.*, vol. 5, p. 256.

127 *Ibid.*, vol. 5, p. 259. For *Kitāb al-Zahrah*, see Wim Raven, *Ibn Dâwûd al-Iṣbahânî and his Kitâb al-Zahrah* (unpublished PhD dissertation, Leiden University, 1989). I am grateful to Raven's generosity in sending me a bound copy of the dissertation.

128 Al-Khaṭīb al-Baghdādī, *Tārīkh*, vol. 5, pp. 257–258.

129 *Ibid.*, vol. 5, p. 260. Al-Dhahabī gives his name as Wahb ibn Jāmiʿ ibn Wahb al-ʿAṭṭār al-Ṣaydalānī (al-Dhahabī, *Siyar*, vol. 15, p. 115). A tradition that Ibn Dāwūd transmits has the Prophet saying: "The one who loves [another man?], remains silent and patient, and abstains from sin, God forgives his sin and grants him paradise" (*man ʿashiqa wa-ʿaffa wa-katama wa-ṣabara, ghafara Allāh la-hu wa-adkhalahu ʾl-jannah*), al-Khaṭīb al-Baghdādī, *Tārīkh*, vol. 5, p. 262). Yaḥyā ibn Maʿīn is reported to have said that he would kill the transmitter who related this tradition to Muḥammad ibn Dāwūd (al-Dhahabī, *Siyar*, vol. 15, p. 113). Ibn Dāwūd's informant of this tradition was Suwayd ibn Saʿīd (for his biography, see *ibid.*, vol. 4, pp. 228–232, where Ibn Abī Ḥātim is reported to have said that Suwayd was an "honest *mudallis*", viz. an honest person who nonetheless uses deceit to hide defects in the transmission of Ḥadīth). Reports from and about Ibn Dāwūd, however, convey that he abstained from engaging in an illicit relationship with his beloved, thus maintaining his moral integrity (*ibid.*, vol. 5, p. 262).

130 Al-Samʿānī, *Ansāb*, vol. 2, p. 448.

131 The anecdote mentions that a man wanted to test Muḥammad ibn Dāwūd's knowledge so he asked him about the signs that indicate that a person was drunken. Ibn Dāwūd gave a

to give answers in a way that not everyone could understand all the time.[132] According to al-Dhahabī, Ibn Ḥazm greatly admired Ibn Dāwūd and spoke about his knowledge, piety, and beauty. In this report, pointing out that 400 students used to attend Ibn Dāwūd's circle,[133] Ibn Ḥazm gives a list of titles of some of his works. Some titles of these works are not indicative of their content, but others refer explicitly to specific legal issues, such as pilgrimage rituals (*manāsik*) and laws of inheritance (*farāʾiḍ*). One work is apparently devoted to refuting al-Ṭabarī (*al-Intiṣār min Muḥammad ibn Jarīr al-Ṭabarī*), and another deals with differences between the various Qurʾān copies (*muṣḥafs*) of the Companions (*Ikhtilāf Maṣāḥif al-Ṣaḥābah*).[134] Also attributed to Ibn Dāwūd is a work entitled *al-Wuṣūl ilā Maʿrifat al-Uṣūl*.[135] As a Ḥadīth transmitter, al-Dhahabī describes Ibn Dāwūd as reliable and knowledgeable, despite the fact that he did not transmit much. He is also described as having been an expert on the views of the Companions and as an independent scholar who did not just follow anyone's views.[136]

There is evidence that Ibn Dāwūd was a public figure who engaged in the political and intellectual milieu of his time. He is said to have been one of those who condemned al-Ḥallāj.[137] He also used to engage in debates in public and in writing with the Shāfiʿī Ibn Surayj.[138] Al-Ṭabarī is reported to have been a bitter enemy of Ibn Dāwūd, who was responsible for the suffering of al-Ṭabarī's family and associates when they could not bury him on his death. Ibn Kathīr mentions that this tragedy took place because the Ḥanbalī rabble (*ʿawāmm al-Ḥanābilah*) of Baghdad had been told by Ibn Dāwūd that al-Ṭabarī was a *Rāfiḍī*, among other heinous things (*ʿaẓāʾim*).[139]

---

satisfactory rhymed answer, leading people to realize how knowledgeable he was (al-Khaṭīb al-Baghdādī, *Tārīkh*, vol. 5, p. 256).

132 Because of his rhymed answers, some of Ibn Dāwūd's answers were incomprehensible for lay people (for this, see al-Dhahabī, *Siyar*, vol. 13, pp. 114–115).

133 Al-Dhahabī does not cite any source for this report. We can notice here that just as Dāwūd's lectures were attended by 400 students, so also were his son's.

134 Al-Dhahabī, *Siyar*, vol. 13, p. 110. The title of Ibn Dāwūd's *Intiṣār* as appears in his biography in Ibn Khallikān's *Wafayāt* (vol. 4, p. 261) is *al-Intiṣār ʿalā Muḥammad ibn Jarīr wa-ʿAbd Allāh ibn Sharshīr wa-ʿĪsā ibn Ibrāhīm al-Ḍarīr*.

135 Al-Dhahabī, *Siyar*, vol. 13, p. 110.

136 *Ibid.*, vol. 13, p. 109.

137 Ibn Kathīr, *Bidāyah*, vol. 11, p. 118.

138 Al-Khaṭīb al-Baghdādī, *Tārīkh*, vol. 5, p. 259. An example of these debates is preserved in al-Tanūkhī's *Nishwār* (vol. 8, pp. 186–187).

139 Ibn Kathīr, *Bidāyah*, vol. 11, p. 124. This, of course, raises the question of why Ḥanbalīs would take the word of a person whose father was disliked by their *imām*.

Some sources seem to have preserved some of Ibn Dāwūd's legal views.[140] Quotes from and references to some of his works exist in al-Qāḍī al-Nuʿmān's (d. 363/974) *Ikhtilāf Uṣūl al-Madhāhib*, where al-Nuʿmān refers to him by name and mentions that he followed the doctrines of his father.[141] In one passage, al-Nuʿmān attributes to Ibn Dāwūd, his father and those who followed him, the view that consensus (*ijmāʿ*) must be based on an explicit textual evidence from the Qur'ān or Ḥadīth. It is valid only when there is no disagreement whatsoever among scholars on a certain issue. A means by which we know that there

140 For a recent study on Muḥammad ibn Dāwūd's legal views and when they differ from his father's, see Arkān Yūsuf Ḥālub, "Al-Ārā' al-Fiqhiyyah li-Abī Bakr Muḥammad ibn Dāwūd al-Ẓāhirī."

141 For this, see Devin Stewart, "Muḥammad ibn Dāwūd al-Ẓāhirī's Manual of Jurisprudence, *al-Wuṣūl ilā Maʿrifat al-Uṣūl*." On al-Qāḍī al-Nuʿmān, see *EI*², vol. 8, p. 117. Stewart's attempt here should be dealt with with caution. He himself admits that al-Qāḍī al-Nuʿmān's implicit and explicit references to Muḥammad ibn Dāwūd could be accounted for in many different ways other than regarding them as evidence that he was quoting from Ibn Dāwūd's *Wuṣūl*. Stewart, however, believes that "[i]t is simpler and more reasonable to conclude that al-Qāḍī al-Nuʿmān was quoting from a single major work in his possession, and that this work was probably *al-Wuṣūl ilā Maʿrifat al-Uṣūl*" (*ibid.*, p. 121). In endeavors like these, authors always have to stretch their imagination to prove their points, which may not always convince all readers. For instance, Stewart would make use of a comment that al-Qāḍī al-Nuʿmān makes—in which he says that if he had gone on at length in refuting Sunnī views on some *uṣūl al-fiqh* issues, dealing with each of these would require many volumes—to indicate "the immense material on jurisprudence available to him [al-Qāḍī al-Nuʿmān]" (Stewart, "Muḥammad ibn Dāwūd" p. 118). It is very unlikely that al-Qāḍī al-Nuʿmān was speaking "literally" when he mentioned several volumes, and his purpose was clearly to convey to the reader how skillful and knowledgeable he was, rather than to convey that Sunnī views were too complicated to be dealt with in less than several volumes. This, in my view, cannot be marshaled as evidence for the point that Stewart seeks to make. Another example is Stewart's argument on the basis of a minor reference that Muḥammad ibn Dāwūd apparently makes and al-Qāḍī al-Nuʿmān quotes. According to this, *al-Wuṣūl* contained an introduction in which Muḥammad provided a theoretical frame for his work. The reference that Ibn Dāwūd makes is in the context of refuting the proponents of *istiḥsān*, at the end of which Ibn Dāwūd remarks, "as we have stated and explained" (*ibid.*, p. 123). Needless to say, this could be a reference to anything, such as an earlier chapter in his work where he refuted another view on the same basis, or to an entirely different work. In my view, relying on this to infer that the work had an introduction that "must have put forward an argument that served as a frame for the remainder of the book" seems unwarranted. Finally, Stewart does not entertain the possibility that al-Nuʿmān was quoting Ibn Dāwūd from works other than *al-Wuṣūl*, such as his *Intiṣār ʿalā Muḥammad ibn Jarīr wa-ʿAbd Allāh ibn Sharshīr wa-ʿĪsā ibn Ibrāhīm al-Ḍarīr*, which Stewart is aware of (*ibid.*, p. 115), in the context of his rejection of *qiyās*, as al-Nuʿmān explicitly mentions.

is a valid consensus is when God makes something incumbent upon us. "What He is properly shown to have made incumbent is obligatory, and what He is not properly shown to have established as His religion is not valid," al-Qāḍī al-Nuʿmān explains.[142] In other words, there is *ijmāʿ* on what God has made incumbent on us and disagreement indicates lack of obligation.

In another passage, al-Qāḍī al-Nuʿmān presents the view of "one who rejected legal analogy (*qiyās*) and professed inference (*istidlāl*)" for things for which he did not find textual evidence.[143] According to this assault on *qiyās*, those who believe in and practice it often disagree on what they take to be the *ʿillah* in the first case, and which they then use to judge in new cases. Each group of scholars that use *qiyās* only produce evidence that could easily be contradicted by others, and none of them has a better claim to make.[144] In addition, those who accept the validity of *qiyās* justify it on the grounds that God himself has used it, for one can notice that God has assigned similar rulings to things that are similar. This argument is here dismissed as being based on the faulty assumption that God gives similar rulings in similar cases and dissimilar rulings in dissimilar cases. The fact of the matter, however, is that God can and does give different rulings in similar cases, and similar rulings in dissimilar cases. Therefore, since God has given different rulings in similar cases, one can use the same logic as the proponents of *qiyās* to assign different rulings in similar cases that have no textual basis.[145] Furthermore, *qiyās* is practiced only by someone who cannot find an answer for a specific case. How, then, can it be attributed to God?[146]

Qiyās, in this view, is based on another, blasphemous assumption: God *must* rule in a certain way. A true believer, however, would hold that God—exalted as He is—can rule in whatever way he wishes. And this God does, for God has changed things that had been prescribed in the early stages of the Prophet's mission and also things that had been prescribed for earlier nations and prophets,[147] an argument attributed explicitly to Ibn Dāwūd and his father, both described by al-Nuʿmān as "Sunnī."[148] Finally, al-Nuʿmān attributes to Ibn Dāwūd a statement indicating that he did not question the validity of *qiyās*,

---

142 Stewart, "Muḥammad ibn Dāwūd," pp. 138–139. Translation of the relevant passages from al-Nuʿmān's *Ikhtilāf* are Stewart's.

143 *Ibid.*, p. 141.

144 *Ibid.*, pp. 139–141.

145 *Ibid.*, p. 142.

146 *Ibid.*, p. 147.

147 *Ibid.*, pp. 145–146.

148 *Ibid.*, p. 147. This reference is of course dictated by al-Qāḍī al-Nuʿmān's sectarian polemics. However, it is true that despite the Shīʿī or Muʿtazilī leanings of some Ẓāhirīs, they were,

but only opposed using it in religious matters. "The rulings of faith are not to be referred ultimately to the intellects of humans," he explains, "instead, they must be carried out as they were imposed." As for things that God has not commanded us we therefore remain silent.[149]

A subsequent section deals with the refutation of *ijtihād*, which al-Qāḍī al-Nuʿmān defines as a methodology of ruling in matters that are neither found in the Qurʾān nor mentioned by the Prophet. A piece of evidence adduced by those who use *ijtihād* is the oft-cited report in which the Prophet asks his Companion Muʿādh ibn Jabal, who was to serve as a judge in Yemen, how he would judge in each case. Muʿādh replies that he would begin with the Qurʾān, then the Prophet's Sunnah, and then exercise his own *ijtihād*, an answer with which the Prophet was evidently pleased. In the refutation attributed by al-Nuʿmān to a Sunnī jurist who rejected *ijtihād* (possibly Ibn Dāwūd),[150] the jurist rejects this tradition on account of its disconnected (*munqatiʿ*) chain of transmitters and the fact that some of its transmitters are unknown. It is also possible, the jurist continues, that by *ijtihād* here Muʿādh meant exerting effort in finding the answer in the Qurʾān or Sunnah. For if this was a valid methodology, "the truth would lie in two contradictory answers at the same time" since people differ in their *ijtihād*.[151]

These are the views that al-Qāḍī al-Nuʿmān attributes explicitly to Ibn Dāwūd. In a section on *istidlāl* (inference), he attributes to "those who profess *istidlāl*" (who could be Ibn Dāwūd and possibly Dāwūd himself) the view that while the Qurʾān is the ultimate source of authoritative evidence, some of its verses indicate rulings in an implicit way, which requires us to use *istidlāl* to discern them. The same applies to Sunnah, which derives its authority from the Qurʾān where God enjoins believers to obey the Prophet.[152] After giving an example of such *istidlāl*,[153]—which example is reminiscent of Ibn Ḥazm's legal

from a theological point of view, predominantly Sunnīs and regarded as such by other people.

149 Stewart, "Muḥammad ibn Dāwūd," p. 150.

150 At the end of this section, al-Qāḍī mentions that what he had reported was the words of Muḥammad ibn Dāwūd (*ibid.*, p. 158). It is not clear, however, whether this refers to the entire section or only part of it.

151 *Ibid.*, p. 157.

152 *Ibid.*, pp. 153–154.

153 According to this, we know that it is not permitted to do anything at the time of prayers because: (1) God has commanded us to pray, and (2) the Prophet has explained how and when we need to do so. In themselves, these facts do not explicitly say that it is not permitted not to pray during the time of prayer, but we can infer this prohibition from putting these pieces of evidence together.

arguments and textual inference—al-Nuʿmān notes: "[t]his [example] and the like of it are inferences. This is *the* fundamental principle on which [possibly Dāwūd and his son] built their doctrine."[154]

Ibn Dāwūd is presented here as a staunch critic of *qiyās*, seeking to demonstrate that it is contradictory and based on faulty assumptions related to God (the view that God behaves or must behave in a certain way) and reason (the notion that reason can distinguish good from evil independently of revelation). He also rejected *istiḥsān* and (possibly) *ijtihād* in issues on which the law is silent, for like *qiyās*, they rely on faulty notions and lead to disagreement. What is common in this attitude towards *qiyās, istiḥsān* and *ijtihād* is an obvious desire for systematization and consistency that lead to agreement in legal views. Disagreement is here regarded as evil, and a Prophetic tradition is used to demonstrate that when people disagree, only one view is sound. Finally, in the context of this discussion, Ibn Dāwūd refers implicitly to the issue of *al-ibāḥah al-aṣliyyah*, when he argues that we should not compare what God has not mentioned to what He has. The former category falls within the scope of what is permitted as a general rule.

The view on *ijmāʿ* that al-Nuʿmān attributes to Ibn Dāwūd here conveys a circular understanding of this concept that renders it virtually useless. What is agreed upon in this understanding is incumbent upon Muslims, and what is incumbent upon Muslims is what they agree upon. Furthermore, the insistence that valid *ijmāʿ* must be based on a text with an indisputable meaning puts into question the very necessity of *ijmāʿ* in the first place, for the source of the law here becomes the text, not *ijmāʿ*. This argument was made later by Ibn Ḥazm, who charged non-Ẓāhirī scholars of inconsistency when they argue that a certain consensus is based on the meaning of a text. Here, Ibn Ḥazm argues, *ijmāʿ* does not serve any purpose since the text itself provides the answer.

If al-Qāḍī al-Nuʿmān is referring to Ibn Dāwūd and Ẓāhirīs when he mentions *istidlāl*—a hermeneutical tool that seeks to infer meaning from texts—it is indeed remarkable that he describes this as *the* fundamental principles on which their doctrine is based on. Our later discussion of Ẓāhirism may support the possibility that he was indeed referring to them.

∴

154 Stewart, "Muḥammad ibn Dāwūd," p. 154 (emphasis mine).

In addition to al-Qāḍī al-Nuʿmān's *Ikhtilāf Uṣūl al-Madhāhib*, other sources attribute to early generations of Ẓāhirīs views on similar and other issues.[155] For example, whenever *qiyās* is discussed, Dāwūd's and other Ẓāhirīs' views are regularly referred to, mostly to be refuted. Al-Shīrāzī mentions that Dāwūd and the *Ahl al-Ẓāhir* held that *qiyās* is not valid in religious matters, which is also the view of the Muʿtazilī scholar al-Naẓẓām and Imāmī Shiʿīs.[156] However, disagreement is reported among Ẓāhirī scholars concerning the question of whether *qiyās* is valid when the *ʿillah* is explicitly mentioned. Whereas some Ẓāhirīs are said to have sanctioned *qiyās* in such instances, others are reported to have rejected *qiyās in toto*.[157] Considering him "ignorant," al-Sarakhsī mentions that Dāwūd and other *aṣḥāb al-ẓawāhir* rejected *qiyās* by their uncritical reliance on bits and pieces of what earlier scholars—such as Qatādah ibn Diʿāmah, Masrūq, and Ibn Sīrīn—had said about the validity of using *qiyās* in religious matters.[158] In his *Taqwīm al-Adillah*, al-Dabūsī mentions that they relied on reports from the Prophet, his Companions, and some Successors to reject *qiyās* and held that it was based on doubt and did not therefore qualify as evidence. Furthermore, *qiyās* relies on human understanding of the worldly benefits of God's law when it is meant to serve other-worldly purposes that reason cannot necessarily grasp.[159]

Sources also attribute to *Ẓāhirīs* the view that only the consensus of the Companions (*ijmāʿ al-ṣaḥābah*) is valid, a view attributed to Dāwūd himself.[160] This is based on the special status of the Companions—which the Qurʾān and Ḥadīth establish—and the presumption that later generations of Muslims

155 In this section, the following sources have been used: Abū Zayd al-Dabūsī's (d. 430/1038) *Taqwīm al-Adillah fī Uṣūl al-Fiqh*; Abū al-Ḥusayn al-Baṣrī's (d. 436/1044) *Muʿtamad fī Uṣūl al-Fiqh*; al-Sarakhsī's (d. 450/1058) *Muḥarrar fī Uṣūl al-Fiqh*; and Abū Isḥāq al-Shīrāzī's (476/1083) *Tabṣirah fī Uṣūl al-Fiqh*. Given that these contemporaries of Ibn Ḥazm were in Iraq, it can be assumed that they meant Dāwūd and his students when they attributed views to Ẓāhirīs. As a general rule, al-Dabūsī, and to a lesser extent al-Sarakhsī, merely mention different views on a subject without necessarily attributing them to specific scholars (with the exception of Abū Ḥanīfah and other prominent Ḥanafī scholars as well as al-Shāfiʿī at times). To the best of my knowledge, Dāwūd and individual Ẓāhirīs are mentioned only once in both works. In contrast, Abū al-Ḥusayn al-Baṣrī and especially Abū Isḥāq al-Shīrāzī make frequent references to Dāwūd and some Ẓāhirīs in their works.

156 Al-Shīrāzī, *Tabṣirah*, p. 424.

157 Abū al-Ḥusayn al-Baṣrī, *Muʿtamad*, vol. 2, p. 235.

158 Al-Sarakhsī, *Muḥarrar*, vol. 2, p. 92.

159 al-Dabūsī, *Taqwīm*, pp. 260–262.

160 Abū al-Ḥusayn al-Baṣrī, *Muʿtamad*, vol. 2, p. 27, and al-Shīrāzī, *Tabṣirah*, p. 359.

cannot become aware of a matter of which the Companions were not.[161] Furthermore, some Ẓāhirīs held that if scholars of a certain period held two views with regards to a specific question, this does not mean that later scholars are not allowed to introduce a third view.[162] References are made here to instances in which some earlier scholars—such as Sufyān al-Thawrī and Muḥammad ibn Sīrīn—introduced views that differed from two views that earlier authorities had held in specific questions.[163] Also related to consensus is the question of whether it can be valid on the basis of a less certain piece of evidence (*amārah*, contrasted here with the more certain *dalīl*). According to Abū al-Ḥusayn al-Baṣrī, a group of Ẓāhirīs did not approve this kind of *ijmāʿ*.[164] Al-Shīrāzī also attributes to Dāwūd the view that *qiyās* cannot be the object of consensus since the former is not a valid kind of evidence in the first place.[165] Additionally, if a Companion holds a certain opinion that other Companions did not disagree with when they learned about it, this does not necessarily indicates that they had an agreement on the issue (works of *uṣūl al-fiqh* refer to this as *al-ijmāʿ al-sukūtī*, meaning consensus by implied consent or silent endorsement). Valid consensus requires an explicit verbal approval by all Companions.[166]

As regards Ḥadīth, some Ẓāhirīs are said to have held, against the view of most scholars, that a report transmitted by one or a few transmitters in one or more generations (*khabar al-wāḥid*) establishes apodictic knowledge (*yūjibu ʾl-ʿilm*).[167] The basis of this view is that since God has commanded us to act on the basis of such reports and instructed us at the same time to not attribute to him that of which we are not certain, it follows that these reports establish knowledge that does not admit of doubt.[168] Remarkably, al-Shīrāzī attributes to Muḥammad ibn Dāwūd and al-Qāsānī the view that the *khabar al-wāḥid* is not a valid source of *ʿamal* (action), which can only make sense if they had not seen it as a solid source of knowledge.[169] Furthermore, Ẓāhirīs are reported to have held that reports with disconnected chains of transmission did not estab-

---

161 Abū al-Ḥusayn al-Baṣrī, *Muʿtamad*, vol. 2, pp. 27–29.

162 *Ibid.*, vol. 2, p. 44.

163 *Ibid.*, vol. 2, p. 46.

164 *Ibid.*, vol. 2, p. 59.

165 Al-Shīrāzī, *Tabṣirah*, 372.

166 *Ibid.*, pp. 391–392.

167 Abū al-Ḥusayn al-Baṣrī, *Muʿtamad*, vol. 2, pp. 92–93, and al-Shīrāzī, *Tabṣirah*, pp. 298–299.

168 Abū al-Ḥusayn al-Baṣrī, *Muʿtamad*, vol. 2, p. 97.

169 Al-Shīrāzī, *Tabṣirah*, p. 303. In the view of some scholars, a report can be a valid basis of action even if the knowledge that it yields is less than apodictic. In this case, it is said that these reports *tūjibu ʾl-ʿamal wa-lā tūjibu ʾl-ʿilm*.

lish knowledge and consequently did not qualify to be a basis of action.[170] Finally, some Ẓāhirīs rejected a view attributed to Dāwūd according to which when a Companion says that the Prophet has ordered or forbidden something, this does not constitute evidence unless he mentions the exact words of the Prophet.[171]

Also against the view of the majority of non-Ẓāhirī scholars, according to Abū al-Ḥusayn al-Baṣrī, some Ẓāhirīs, including Dāwūd himself and his son Muḥammad, held that the Qur'ān did not contain metaphorical or figurative expressions (*majāz*).[172] In this view, metaphorical language is a degraded form of language that does not befit God, for it indicates that He at times cannot use the language in the proper manner (i.e., non-metaphorically). It also leads to ambiguity that does not befit the Qur'ān.[173] On the issue of *naskh* (abrogation, when a ruling is either annulled or replaced with another), some Ẓāhirīs are reported to have held that the Qur'ān could be abrogated by all kinds of Ḥadīth, including traditions transmitted by one or a large number of individuals (*al-aḥādīth al-mutawātirah*).[174] Ẓāhirīs are also reported to have held that it is not against both reason and revelation that a Qur'ānic ruling or one based on a *mutawātir* report be abrogated by a tradition transmitted by a few people (*āḥād*). This group of Ẓāhirīs cite instances of abrogation of Qur'ānic rulings by *āḥād* traditions and argue that since these traditions are known by definite evidence (*dalīl qaṭʿī*), the rulings that they establish are equal in authority to Qur'ānic rulings and can abrogate them accordingly.[175] Additionally, God can

170 Abū al-Ḥusayn al-Baṣrī, *Muʿtamad*, vol. 2, p. 143.

171 Al-Zarkashī, *al-Baḥr al-Muḥīṭ*, vol. 3, p. 374.

172 For this view of some Ẓāhirīs, see al-Shīrāzī, *Tabṣirah*, p. 177, and al-Zarkashī, *al-Baḥr al-Muḥīṭ*, vol. 2, p. 182. Al-Zarkashī attributes the same view to the important Ẓāhirī scholar Mundhir ibn Saʿīd al-Ballūṭī in his *Aḥkām al-Qur'ān*. In fact, al-Zarkashī mentions that al-Rāzī had noted that Ibn Dāwūd rejected the presence of *majāz* even in Ḥadīth, a view that no other scholar held (*ibid.*, vol. 2, p. 185). This view is indeed consistent with other Ẓāhirī views. If *majāz* does not befit the language used for prescriptions and proscriptions, this should equally apply to Ḥadīth.

173 Abū al-Ḥusayn al-Baṣrī, *Muʿtamad*, vol. 1, pp. 24–25. Dāwūd is reported to have held that the Qur'ān does not contain ambiguous terms (al-Zarkashī, *al-Baḥr al-Muḥīṭ*, vol. 3: p. 455). Abū Isḥāq al-Shīrāzī mentions that in a debate with Ibn Dāwūd, Ibn Surayj demonstrated to him that *majāz* was in fact used in the Qur'ān (al-Shīrāzī, *Tabṣirah*, pp. 178–179). In another context, al-Shīrāzī mentions that there were reports about another debate between Ibn Surayj and Ibn Dāwūd, indicating that memories of these debates were still current in Baghdad a century and a half after they took place.

174 Al-Shīrāzī, *Tabṣirah*, p. 265.

175 Abū al-Ḥusayn al-Baṣrī, *Muʿtamad*, vol. 1, pp. 398–400.

and does replace a duty with a heavier one, a view held by some Ẓāhirīs and rejected by others.[176]

Some Ẓāhirīs are also reported to have held that transmitted texts cover all possible occurrences (*al-ḥawādith*).[177] Some of them regarded the presumption of continuity (*istiṣḥāb al-ḥāl*) as legal evidence,[178] a principle that Dāwūd believed was based on consensus.[179] Related to this is the all-important rule that only things that are statedly forbidden are forbidden. Things that the law has kept silent on are not. For example, things (*al-aʿyān*) that were used before the advent of Islam remain permitted from the religious/legal perspective, a view that Ẓāhirīs shared, remarkably, with the *Ahl al-Raʾy* and Muʿtazilīs.[180] Consequently, if a text says that utensils made of gold and silver are forbidden to drink from, it follows that all their other uses remain permitted according to the general rule that things are all presumably permitted.[181] Other views include one according to which any term (unless it obviously refers to a specific person or thing, such as proper names and pronouns, etc.) indicates the entire genus of all possible referents (*istighrāq al-jins*), absent an indicator suggesting otherwise. Dāwūd reportedly shared this view with, remarkably, Abū Thawr al-Kalbī and al-Ḥusayn al-Karābīsī, in addition to some theologians, including the Muʿtazilī al-Jubbāʾī.[182] Furthermore, according to Ibn Dāwūd and Nifṭawayh, women are included in Qurʾānic or Prophetic statements that use the masculine form, meaning that their rights and obligations are generally similar to men's (unless the context indicates otherwise, of course).[183] Ibn Dāwūd is also reported to have argued that the plural form (*ṣīghat al-jamʿ*) can only be used with reference to two or more persons.[184] Finally, Nifṭawayh, as a Ẓāhirī, according to al-Zarkashī, held that there existed no derivation (*ishtiqāq*)

176 Abū al-Ḥusayn al-Baṣrī, *Muʿtamad*, vol. 1, p. 385.

177 *Ibid.*, vol. 2, p. 228.

178 *Ibid.*, vol. 2, p. 325.

179 Al-Shīrāzī, *al-Tabṣirah*, p. 526. *Istiṣḥāb al-ḥāl* requires two conditions, an earlier one (which is to be assumed or argued for) and a more recent one (e.g., the innocence for a person accused of committing a crime must be assumed). The consensus attributed to Dāwūd here is taken as evidence of the earlier condition.

180 Al-Zarkashī, *al-Bahr al-Muḥīṭ*, vol. 1, p. 154.

181 *Ibid.*, vol. 1, p. 161.

182 *Ibid.*, vol. 3, p. 19. Al-Zarkashī adds to this list—of what we can call the *Ahl al-ʿUmūm*—al-Shāfiʿī, Mālik and Abū Ḥanīfah and their students. Acceptance of *ʿumūm* is important, but what is more significant is how lenient or stringent jurists are in accepting indicators that qualify the generality or default unrestrictedness of terms.

183 Al-Shīrāzī, *Tabṣirah*, pp. 77–78.

184 *Ibid.*, p. 127. In another view, the plural form refers to three or more persons.

in language, meaning that no word is derived from another to refer to different referent,[185] a view that mirrors their rejection of *qiyās*, where a new rule is derived from an existing one to make a judgment on a new case.

4 Conclusion

The previous survey has presented what some medieval Muslim sources mention about the lives and doctrines of Dāwūd al-Ẓāhirī, his teachers, and his immediate students, including his son. Whereas there is much evidence that when he was alive Dāwūd was not insignificant as a scholar, statements about his scholarly status cannot be substantiated on the basis of the information given in the sources that make them. This is hardly surprising: Dāwūd was not engaging in what would have secured him a place among prominent scholars of his time. His was predominantly an age of Ḥadīth transmission and criticism, and those who distinguished themselves in these activities were able to rise to the rank of notable and influential scholars. Neither did Dāwūd do this, nor did he distinguish himself in theology like some prominent theologians in 3rd/9th-century Baghdad. Furthermore, Dāwūd was not on good terms with Ḥadīth scholars who disliked him and his teachers. This must have alienated many people from him and may explain why his lectures were attended by only a relatively small number of students, as well as why his death probably passed unnoticed.

Dāwūd's teachers were mostly the same kind of scholars as he was. Of all his teachers, Abū Thawr must have been the most influential one, not only because he died when Dāwūd was in his forties, but also because there are unmistakable similarities between the two scholars, both in their personal profiles and their doctrines. Abū Thawr probably continued to be regarded as a scholar of *raʾy* even after his meeting with al-Shāfiʿī and reported "conversion" to Ḥadīth. Another scholar whose career resembled Dāwūd's is Abū ʿAlī al-Karābīsī, with whom Dāwūd likely studied. These three scholars were independent, holding views that contradicted those of the majority of scholars around them. They were not interested in Ḥadīth for its own sake, but were interested primarily in legal matters. They used to engage in and seem to have enjoyed legal debates, for which reason they were regarded with suspicion by Ḥadīth scholars.

Dāwūd, however, was not simply following Abū Thawr and al-Karābīsī. The fact that he was regarded as the leader of the Ẓāhirīs indicates that he had something more to say than these two scholars, or that he was more vocal and

185 Al-Zarkashī, *al-Baḥr al-Muḥīṭ*, vol. 2, p. 72.

unequivocal in defending views that they also held. Unfortunately, what was Ẓāhirī about Dāwūd is a question that our sources do not answer. Most medieval works emphasize Dāwūd's rejection of *qiyās* as the doctrine that distinguished him,[186] a (mis)conception that the writings of some Ẓāhirīs on *qiyās* may have confirmed. However, this does not explain why others who rejected *qiyās* were not regarded as Ẓāhirīs. The same applies to the rejection of *taqlīd*, also taken as a hallmark of the Ẓāhirī *madhhab*. Ẓāhirism, therefore, must have meant more than or other than the rejection of *qiyās* and *taqlīd*. The term *ẓāhir* is key here. Adherence to it seem to have been common in the 3rd/9th century, as suggested by al-Khaṭīb al-Baghdādī's reference to Dāwūd as *imām Ahl al-Ẓāhir*, and Ibn Surayj reported works against both the *Ahl al-Raʾy* and the *Ahl al-Ẓāhir*.

It has also been observed that Dāwūd's students and early followers disagreed on some issues. For instance, although we know that Dāwūd and later Ẓāhirīs rejected *qiyās*, other Ẓāhirīs (and possibly Dāwūd himself as well as his son) are reported to have rejected only one kind of it, namely, when *ʿillah* is not explicitly stated. Secondly, although we know that Ẓāhirīs held that the only valid consensus was that of the Companions, al-Qāḍī al-Nuʿmān's *Ikhtilāf* suggests that Muḥammad ibn Dāwūd was willing to acknowledge the validity of the consensus of later generations.[187] Some sources attribute to Dāwūd the rejection of consensus based on implied consent. He is also reported to have accepted the validity of consensus that is based on less decisive evidence, a view with which his son, given his insistence on a solid textual basis for consensus, may have disagreed. Ẓāhirīs also disagreed on *khabar al-wāḥid*; whereas some accepted it as a source of confident knowledge, others, including Ibn Dāwūd, rejected it as a source of knowledge and a basis for *ʿamal*. Nothing is attributed to Dāwūd himself with regards to this issue. Although we know that he had two relevant works (one on *khabar al-wāḥid* and another on the *al-khabar al-mūjib li-l-ʿilm*, i.e., the kind of reports that yields solid knowledge), these titles do not in themselves indicate what the nature of the relationship (if any) between these two kinds of reports may have been in Dāwūd's view. Ẓāhirīs also apparently disagreed on the use of figurative language (*majāz*) in the Qurʾān, on some points related to the issue of abrogation (*naskh*), and even on the principle of the presumption of continuity (*istiṣḥāb*).

---

186 Some modern scholars also seem to believe that rejection of *qiyās* was the defining feature of Dāwūd's legal thought (see, for instance, Camilla Adang, "The Beginning," p. 118).

187 This, of course, does not have to contradict the other view of *ijmāʿ al-ṣaḥābah*, for Ibn Dāwūd may have argued that complete consensus only existed in the age of the Companions.

Medieval sources do not mention any views of Ẓāhirī scholars with regard to some subjects on which Dāwūd reportedly had written. For example, we know that Dāwūd had a work in which he evidently refuted the blind following the views of other scholars (*taqlīd*), and others in which he tackled linguistic issues, such as the scope of application of terms, or the clarity or ambiguity of terms and statements. No Ẓāhirī scholar before Ibn Ḥazm is reported to have had an opinion on these issues. This equally applies to Ibn Dāwūd's rejection of reason as a valid basis for distinguishing good from evil. Exceptionally, views of later Ẓāhirī scholars (although still earlier than Ibn Ḥazm) on some issues—notably *majāz* and *naskh*—are reported.

This exposition suggests that Dāwūd's *madhhab* was still in flux in the century and half after his death, as is probably the case with other *madhhab*s to varying degrees. His immediate students and early generations of Ẓāhirīs seem to have been at liberty to disagree with him. But one important issue remains unresolved; that is, why were Dāwūd and/or his later followers known as Ẓāhirī. In other words, what was Ẓāhirī about Dāwūd's *madhhab*? This question will be tackled in a later chapter. Now the history of the Ẓāhirī *madhhab* continues.

CHAPTER 2

The Spread and Retreat of the Ẓāhirī *Madhhab*

In his *Ṭabaqāt al-Fuqahā'*, al-Shīrāzī lists the first six generations of Ẓāhirī scholars, the second of which has been presented in the previous chapter as Dāwūd's students. Al-Shīrāzī's classification is not only the earliest, but also the only available account of the legal history of early Ẓāhirīs. Mention should be made here, however, of a now lost work by a judge named Muḥammad ibn 'Umar ibn al-Akhḍar (more about him below) entitled *Tārikh Ahl al-Ẓāhir*. Given that al-Shīrāzī apparently had a copy of this book at his disposal,[1] he must have relied on it for his own account. Remarkably, later scholars, including Ibn Ḥazm, do not attempt a similar categorization of Ẓāhirīs.

A goal of the following survey is to examine how Dāwūd's *madhhab* fared after its founder and his students.[2] Attention will be paid to the geographical distribution of Ẓāhirīs and to whether they had any sense of belonging to a *madhhab*, as well as to their scholarly activities and social standing, including government positions that they held. There are two difficulties that must be pointed out at the outset. The first is that the available sources are not always generous with information, as the survey itself demonstrates. The second and perhaps more important difficulty is that the epithet Ẓāhirī was not used exclusively to refer to scholars following the Ẓāhirī *madhhab* (especially in the 8th/14th and 9th/15th centuries), and it is generally difficult to determine whether a given scholar was known to be Ẓāhirī by his contemporaries

1 Al-Shīrāzī, *Ṭabaqāt*, p. 179.

2 The following were particularly useful sources for the research required for this part of the chapter: Tawfīq al-Ghalbazūrī's *Madrasah al-Ẓāhiriyyah*, Māzin al-Buḥṣalī's *Ṭabaqāt Ahl al-Ẓāhir* (although I did not include all the names of Ẓāhirīs that they mention for what I see as lack of enough evidence that they were in fact following the Ẓāhirī *madhhab*), as well as *al-Maktabah al-Shāmilah* (CD-ROM) and *Maktabat Āl al-Bayt* (DVD-ROM). Information obtained from these sources has been checked in the primary sources cited in this monograph. Furthermore, a few Moroccan *Fahrasahs* were used, including the *Fihris* of Ibn 'Aṭiyyah al-Andalusī (d. 541/1146), the *Fahrasah* of Ibn Khayr al-Ishbīlī (d. 575/1179), the *Fihris Shuyūkh al-Qāḍī 'Iyāḍ* (d. 544/1149), the *Barnāmaj Shuyūkh al-Ru'aynī* of Abū al-Ḥasan al-Ru'aynī al-Ishbīlī (d. 666/1267), the *Fahrasah* of Aḥmad ibn Yūsuf al-Lablī (d. 691/1291), and the *Thabat* of Abū Ja'far al-Balawī al-Wādī Āshī (d. 938/1532). These works are useful in mapping Ẓāhirī scholars and the possible circulation of their works. (I am indebted to Michael Cook for bringing these works to my attention.) On these *fahrasahs*, see 'Abd Allāh al-Murābiṭ al-Targhī, *Fahāris 'Ulamā' al-Maghrib*.

 | DOI 10.1163/9789004279650_004

or only so described by his biographers. As will be noted below, some scholars were thought to be Ẓāhirī only on the basis of specific views they held, notably their rejection of *qiyās* or *taqlīd*, and not because they accepted the *madhhab in toto*.[3]

1 Third/Ninth- and Fourth/Tenth-Century Ẓāhirīs

1. *Aḥmad ibn ʿAmr ibn Muḥammad ibn al-Ḍaḥḥāk, Abū Bakr ibn Abī ʿĀṣim* (d. 287/900)
A well-known Ḥadīth scholar and jurist, Abū Bakr ibn Abī ʿĀṣim was probably born in Basra, lived in Isfahan, and traveled frequently. He was known for his rejection of *qiyās*, talent in memorizing traditions,[4] and Sufi leanings.[5] He is

3 For examples of this, Adang refers to Abū ʿUmar Aḥmad ibn Duḥaym (d. 338/949) and argues that although the sources do not mention that he was Ẓāhirī, "this does not necessarily exclude the possibility of his having divulged Dāwūd's writings after his return to his native land [in Andalus]" ("The Beginnings of the Zahiri Madhhab in al-Andalus," p. 119). This remains a speculation that needs demonstration in order to support Adang's aim of proving that "Ẓāhirism in Andalus had a living tradition in the period before Ibn Ḥazm" (*ibid.*, p. 125). Likewise, in his *Madrasah al-Ẓāhiriyyah*, Ghalbazūrī mentions many figures who were considered Ẓāhirīs by medieval scholars mainly on account of their rejection of *taqlīd* (Ghalbazūrī, *al-Madrasah al-Ẓāhiriyyah*, pp. 52, 223ff). Ghalbazūrī himself would include scholars among Ẓāhirīs on unconvincing grounds. For example, he includes the famous grammarian Aḥmad ibn ʿAbd al-Raḥmān ibn Maḍāʾ (d. 592/1195) among Ẓāhirīs primarily on the basis of his appointment as chief judge by Abū Yaʿqūb Yūsuf al-Muwaḥḥidī (d. 580/1184) and his son Yaʿqūb al-Manṣūr who leaned towards the Ẓāhirī *madhhab* (*ibid.*, p. 286). Similarly, Rabīḥ ʿAmmār assumes Ibn Maḍāʾs Ẓāhirism and speaks of his "revolution" in Arabic Grammar (echoing Ibn Ḥazm's revolution in jurisprudence) and "Ẓāhirī" polemics against eastern Grammarians (Rabīḥ ʿAmmār, "Ibn Maḍāʾ al-Qurṭubī: Thawrah fī al-Fiqh, Thawrah fī al-Naḥw"). See also, Kees Versteegh, "Ibn Maḍāʾ as a Ẓāhirī Grammarian," in Camilla Adang *et al.*, *Ibn Ḥazm of Cordoba*, pp. 208–231, where Versteegh argues that Ibn Maḍāʾ—who, he notes, did not call himself a Ẓāhirī and was not referred to as such by biographers—was Ẓāhirī only if Ẓāhirism meant strict adherence to the "obvious meaning" and the rejection of "divergence of opinions" (*ibid.*, p. 229). Considering other evidence, Adang came to the conclusion that Ibn Maḍāʾ can, at best, be considered "semi-Ẓāhirī" (Adang, "*Ẓāhirīs*," pp. 429–432). Given his status as an accomplished grammarian, Ibn Maḍāʾs case is symptomatic of the problem of determining the affiliation of many scholars with the Ẓāhirī *madhhab*.

4 Al-Dhahabī, *Tadhkirat al-Ḥuffāẓ*, vol. 1, pp. 158–159.

5 Al-Dhahabī, *Siyar*, vol. 13, p. 431.

reported to have written on many subjects and worked as a judge in Isfahan for sixteen years after the death of its former judge, Ṣāliḥ ibn Aḥmad ibn Ḥanbal.[6]

Abū Bakr does not appear in al-Shīrāzī's *ṭabaqāt* and al-Dhahabī questions his affiliation with Ẓāhirism on the basis of a work that he is said to have compiled against Dāwūd's acceptance of the authenticity of forty reports.[7] There is no evidence that Abū Bakr and Dāwūd met each other, but he was a student of one of Dāwūd's Basran teachers—ʿAmr ibn Marzūq, and also a teacher of the Ẓāhirī scholar Aḥmad ibn Bundār. Abū Bakr's funeral in 287/900 is said to have been attended by some 200,000 people.[8]

2. *Ibrāhīm ibn Jābir* (d. c. 310/922)

Ibn al-Nadīm mentions that Ibrāhīm was a notable "Dāwūdī" Ḥadīth scholar and jurist. He authored a large work on (possibly legal) disagreements which other Dāwūdī scholars admired.[9] Ibrāhīm probably died in 310/922.[10]

3. *Muḥammad ibn Mūsā al-Wāsiṭī* (d. 320/932)

Muḥammad ibn Mūsā was a Ẓāhirī scholar who became judge of Ramlah. He is reported to have been an expert in jurisprudence and Qurʾān exegesis.[11]

4. *ʿAbd Allāh ibn Aḥmad ibn al-Mughallis* (d. 324/935)

A student of Muḥammad ibn Dāwūd and a transmitter from a number of well-known traditionists of the time—including ʿAbd Allāh ibn Aḥmad ibn Ḥanbal—ʿAbd Allāh ibn al-Mughallis (al-Dāwūdī, according to some scholars)[12] is reported to have compiled several works on Dāwūd's *madhhab* and is credited with spreading it in various places.[13] Al-Shīrāzī mentions him as the first

6 Ibn Ḥajar, *Lisān*, vol. 7, p. 20.

7 Al-Dhahabī, *Siyar*, vol. 13, p. 431.

8 *Ibid.*, vol. 13, p. 431.

9 Ibn al-Nadīm, *Fihrist*, p. 218.

10 For this, see Ghalbazūrī, *al-Madrasah al-Ẓāhiriyyah*, p. 83.

11 Al-Suyūṭī, *Ṭabaqāt al-Mufassirīn*, pp. 117–118.

12 For this, see al-Dhahabī, *Siyar*, vol. 13, p. 110, where he mentions a chain of transmission in which al-Tanūkhī describes Ibn al-Mughallis as "al-Dāwūdī." Al-Dhahabī himself presents Ibn al-Mughallis as "al-Dāwūdī al-Ẓāhirī" (*ibid.*, vol. 15, p. 77). It is possible, of course, that referring to Ibn al-Mughallis as al-Ẓāhirī was done retrospectively, when "Ẓāhirī" replaced "Dāwūdī" for reference to scholars following Dāwūd's *madhhab*.

13 *Wa-ʿan ibn al-Mughallis intashara ʿilm Dāwūd fī-l-bilād* (al-Khaṭīb al-Baghdādī, *Tārīkh*, vol. 9, p. 385). It is not clear what al-Khaṭīb al-Baghdādī means by *bilād* here; this could indicate various regions of the Muslim world at that time or simply various cities in Iraq itself.

in the third *ṭabaqah* of Ẓāhirī scholars.[14] Many works (now lost) are attributed to Ibn al-Mughallis, including *Aḥkām al-Qurʾān, al-Mūḍaḥ fī al-Fiqh, al-Mubhij, al-Dāmigh*.[15] *Al-Mūḍaḥ* was apparently available to the Mālikī scholar Ibn ʿAbd al-Barr (d. 463/1071) in Andalus in the 5th/11th century. Ibn ʿAbd al-Barr refers to it—with the title *al-Muḍaḥ ʿalā Madhhab Ahl al-Ẓāhir*—in which Ibn al-Mughallis apparently reported views of Ẓāhirī scholars.[16] Apparently, Ibn al-Mughallis and al-Ṭabarī were opponents, for Ibn al-Nadīm attributes to the latter a work in which he evidently refutes Ibn al-Mughallis.[17] When he died in 324/935, Ibn al-Mughallis was succeeded in his circle by his student Ḥaydarah ibn ʿUmar al-Zanūdī. Among his other important students were ʿAbd Allāh ibn Muḥammad, a nephew of the Egyptian judge al-Walīd,[18] and Aḥmad ibn ʿAbd Allāh al-Bukhtarī al-Dāwūdī.[19]

5. *Muḥammad ibn Sulaymān ibn Maḥmūd al-Ḥarrānī* (d. after 323/934)
Muḥammad ibn Sulaymān was a merchant from Ḥarrān, Iraq, whence he traveled to Andalus on business in 323/935 or 324/936.[20] Muḥammad was an accomplished Qurʾān reciter and smart scholar who followed Dāwūd's *madhhab* and defended it fervently.[21]

---

14 Al-Shīrāzī, *Ṭabaqāt*, p. 177.

15 Al-Dhahabī, *Tārīkh*, vol. 33, p. 150. Ibn al-Nadīm also attributes to Ibn al-Mughallis a *Kitāb al-Muzanī* (Ibn al-Nadīm, *Fihrist*, p. 218). This title is not indicative in itself of the content of the work. However, among the works that Ibn al-Nadīm attributes to Ibn Surayj is one in which he apparently seeks to reconcile differences between al-Muzanī and al-Shāfiʿī (*Kitāb al-Taqrīb bayna al-Muzanī wa-l-Shāfiʿī*) (*ibid.*, p. 213). There is a possibility, which remains a mere speculation, that the first title is an abridgment of the second.

16 Ibn ʿAbd al-Barr, *al-Istidhkār li-Madhāhib Fuqahāʾ al-Amṣār wa-ʿUlamāʾ al-Aqṭār fī-mā Taḍammanahu al-Muwaṭṭaʾ min Maʿānī al-Raʾy wa-l-Āthār*, vol. 1, p. 106. Ibn ʿAbd al-Barr also makes reference here to a work by a certain Aḥmad ibn Muḥammad al-Dāwūdī al-Baghdādī (whose name, to the best of my knowledge, does not appear in any biographical dictionary) the title of which is *Jāmiʿ Madhhab Abī Sulaymān Dāwūd ibn ʿAlī ibn Khalaf al-Iṣbahānī*, and which evidently had chapters on legal rulings (*ibid.*, vol. 1, p. 213). Al-Zarkashī makes reference to another work by the same Aḥmad entitle *Uṣūl al-Futyā*, which he presents as the most solid work for the Ẓāhirīs on the views of Dāwūd and his son. It seems that al-Zarkashī had a copy of the book which he cites *verbatim* (al-Zarkashī, *al-Baḥr al-Muḥīṭ*, vol. 2, p. 187).

17 *Kitāb al-Radd ʿalā Ibn al-Mughallis*, Ibn al-Nadīm, *Fihrist*, p. 235.

18 Al-Dhahabī, *Tārīkh*, vol. 33, p. 149.

19 For this, see al-Dhahabī, *Siyar*, vol. 13, p. 110.

20 Shams al-Dīn al-Jazarī, *Ghāyat al-Nihāyah fī Ṭabaqāt al-Qurrāʾ*, vol. 2, p. 149. See also Khalaf ibn ʿAbd Allāh ibn Bashkuwāl, *al-Ṣilah*, vol. 2, p. 599.

21 Al-Dhahabī, *Tārīkh*, vol. 43, p. 114.

6. *Muḥammad ibn Yūsuf ibn Yaʿqūb* (d. c. 325/936)
Possibly a son of Yūsuf ibn Yaʿqūb, Dāwūd's student, Muḥammad ibn Yūsuf was an associate of Muḥammad ibn Dāwūd. He worked as a judge, probably in Baghdad.[22]

7. *ʿAlī ibn Bundār ibn Ismāʿīl al-Barmakī* (*fl.* 337/948)
According to al-Maqqarī, ʿAlī ibn Bundār was a student of ʿAbd Allāh ibn al-Mughallis, whose legal works and part of his *Aḥkām al-Qurʾān* he studied. He travelled to Andalus on business in 337/948.[23]

8. *Abd al-Muʾmin ibn Khalaf ibn Ṭufayl al-Nasafī* (d. 340/951)
Al-Dhahabī mentions that ʿAbd al-Muʾmin al-Nasafī was a Ẓāhirī scholar who studied with, among others, Muḥammad ibn Dāwūd. Known for his piety and integrity, he was a staunch critic of the proponents of *qiyās* as well as the Muʿtazilīs.[24] He admired Aḥmad Ibn Ḥanbal and Isḥāq ibn Rāhawayh.[25]

9. *Aḥmad ibn Muḥammad ibn Ziyād, Abū Saʿīd ibn al-Aʿrābī* (d. 340/951 or 341/952)
Abū Saʿīd ibn al-Aʿrābī was highly regarded by the Ḥadīth critics of his age. He transmitted from a certain ʿAlī ibn ʿAbd al-ʿAzīz from al-Qaʿnabī and was a friend of al-Junayd.[26] He was known for his leaning towards the Ẓāhirī *madhhab*[27] as well as the *madhhab* of the *Aṣḥāb al-Ḥadīth*.[28]

10. *ʿAlī ibn Muḥammad al-Baghdādī* (d. c. 350/960)
Mentioned by Abū Isḥāq al-Shīrāzī in the third *ṭabaqah* of Ẓāhirī scholars, ʿAlī ibn Muḥammad was a student of Abū al-Ḥasan ibn al-Mughallis.[29]

11. *Muḥammad ibn al-Ḥasan ibn al-Ṣabbāḥ al-Dāwūdī* (d. c. 350/960)
Muḥammad ibn al-Ḥasan, who probably lived in Baghdad, is reported to have transmitted from Yūsuf ibn Yaʿqūb al-Dāwūdī, Dāwūd's student.[30]

---

22 Al-Khaṭīb al-Baghdādī, *Tārīkh*, vol. 5, p. 258.
23 Aḥmad ibn Muḥammad al-Maqqarī, *Nafḥ al-Ṭīb min Ghuṣn al-Andalus al-Raṭīb*, vol. 3, p. 66.
24 Al-Dhahabī, *Tadhkirat*, vol. 3, pp. 56–57.
25 Al-Dhahabī, *Tārīkh*, vol. 34, p. 354.
26 Ibn ʿAsākir, *Tārīkh*, vol. 5, pp. 353–357.
27 Ibn Ḥajar, *Lisān*, vol. 1, p. 414.
28 *Yamīlu ilā madhhab aṣḥāb al-ḥadīth wa-l-ẓāhir* (Ibn ʿAsākir, *Tārīkh*, vol. 5, p. 355).
29 Al-Shīrāzī, *Ṭabaqāt*, p. 177.
30 Al-Khaṭīb al-Baghdādī, *Tārīkh*, vol. 5, p. 258.

12. *Muḥammad ibn Maʿmar ibn Rāshid* (d. 350/965)
Muḥammad ibn Maʿmar was said to have been a Ẓāhirī scholar who transmitted from many people including the Ẓāhirī judge Yūsuf ibn Yaʿqūb. People of Isfahan, including Abū Nuʿaym al-Iṣbahānī (d. 430/1038), transmitted from him.[31]

13. *Bishr ibn al-Ḥusayn* (d. after 350/960)
Bishr—mentioned in the fourth *ṭabaqah* of Ẓāhirī scholars by al-Shīrāzī as a student of ʿAlī ibn Muḥammad al-Baghdādī—was a chief judge (*qāḍī al-quḍāh*) for the Būyid ʿAḍud al-Dawlah,[32] and master (*imām*) in the *madhhab* of Dāwūd. Bishr traveled to Fars and his students are credited with spreading the *madhhab* to Shiraz and Firozabad. His students included Abū Saʿd Bishr ibn al-Ḥusayn (who may be his brother),[33] who was a Dāwūdī judge in Shiraz.[34]

14. *Mundhir ibn Saʿīd al-Ballūṭī* (d. 355/965)
Mundhir ibn Saʿīd al-Ballūṭī was a famous judge in Cordoba known for his vast scholarly productivity, intelligence, and argumentation skills.[35] He leaned towards Dāwūd's *madhhab* and used to defend it, although it is not clear with whom he studied it.[36] He was also a teacher of one of Ibn Ḥazm's teachers—Aḥmad ibn Muḥammad ibn al-Jasūr.[37] Various works are attributed to Mundhir, including three works on the Qurʾān: *al-Inbāh ʿalā Istinbāṭ al-Aḥkām min Kitāb Allāh*, *Aḥkām al-Qurʾān*,[38] and *al-Nāsikh*

---

31 Al-Dhahabī, *Tārīkh*, vol. 36, p. 132.
32 For this, see Miskawayh, *Tajārib al-Umam*, vol. 6, pp. 399–400.
33 Al-Shīrāzī, *Ṭabaqāt*, pp. 177–178.
34 Al-Tanūkhī, *Nishwār*, vol. 3, p. 227.
35 Al-Dhahabī, *al-ʿIbar fī Khabar man Ghabar*, vol. 2, pp. 302–303.
36 Ibn al-Faraḍī, *Tārīkh*, vol. 2, pp. 181–182, and al-Ḥumaydī, *Jadhwat*, vol. 2, pp. 555–557.
37 For this, see Ghalbazūrī, *al-Madrasah al-Ẓāhiriyyah*, p. 206. Ibn Ḥazm also knew al-Mundhir's son Ḥakam, who may have been Ẓāhirī like his father (for this, see al-Dhahabī, *Siyar*, vol. 16, p. 175).
38 Ḥājī Khalīfah, *Kashf al-Ẓunūn*, vol. 1, p. 56. *Aḥkām al-Qurʾān* is mentioned by Khayr al-Dīn al-Ishbīlī among the books he studied in Andalus. The title of this book does not indicate its exact subject (other than being related to the Qurʾān), and it could very well be the same book as *al-Ibānah*. Al-Ballūṭī studied *Aḥkām al-Qurʾān* with Yūnus ibn Muḥammad ibn Mughīth (d. 532/1138), who had studied it with Aḥmad ibn Muḥammad ibn al-Ḥadhdhāʾ (d. 467/1074), who in his turn had studied it with ʿAbd al-Wārith ibn Sufyān (d. 395/1005). This is the same chain of transmission that links Ibn Khayr to the early great Andalusian traditionist Muḥammad ibn Waḍḍāḥ (d. 287/900) (for this, see, for example, Ibn Kahyr, *Fahrasah*, p. 191). For the contribution of Ibn Waḍḍāḥ to the introduction of Ḥadīth into Andalus, see Isabel Fierro, "Introduction of Ḥadīth to al-Andalus," pp. 79–81. Ibn

wa-l-Mansūkh.[39] The first (and possibly the second too) of these is obviously a work of legal hermeneutics.

15. *Yūsuf ibn ʿUmar ibn Muḥammad ibn Yūsuf ibn Yaʿqūb* (d. 356/966)
Son of Yūsuf ibn Yaʿqūb—Ẓāhirī judge of Baghdad and associate of Ibn Dāwūd—Yūsuf became a judge himself while his father was still alive.[40] According to al-Dhahabī, Ibn Ḥazm had mentioned that Yūsuf converted from Mālikism to Ẓāhirism and compiled many works that defended the Ẓāhirī *madhhab*. Al-Shīrāzī reports that he learned from Ibn al-Akhḍar's *Akhbār Ahl al-Ẓāhir* and finished a work by Ibn Dāwūd entitled *al-Ījāz* (now probably lost).[41] Al-Dhahabī quotes a passage from an epistle attributed to Yūsuf where he converts to Ẓāhirism.[42] In a statement supposedly quoted from this work, Yūsuf states: "We do not hold equal those who begin their writings and arguments with the saying of Saʿīd ibn al-Musayyab, al-Zuhrī, and Zamʿah, and those who begin theirs with the word of God, his Prophet, and the consensus of the masters (*imāms*)."[43]

16. *Ḥaydarah ibn ʿUmar al-Zanūdī* (d. 358/968)[44]
Mentioned by al-Shīrāzī in the third *ṭabaqah* of Ẓāhirīs, Ḥaydrah was a student of ʿAbd Allāh ibn al-Mughallis and is credited with transmitting Dāwūd's knowledge from Ibn al-Mughallis to his own Baghdādī fellows.[45] Ibn al-Nadīm praises Ḥaydarah, who was his friend, and mentions that he had written some works, the titles of which were apparently difficult to read in the available

al-Ḥadhdhāʾ also appears in a chain of transmission of the Ẓāhirī scholar Abū Saʿīd ibn al-Aʿrābī (see above) (Ibn Khayr, *Fahrasah*, p. 390). However, none of the scholars in this chain is reported to have had any Ẓāhirī leanings (for Ibn al-Ḥadhdhāʾ, see al-Dhahabī, *Siyar*, vol. 18, pp. 344–345; for ʿAbd al-Wārith, see *ibid.*, vol. 17, pp. 84–85; and for Yūnus ibn Muḥammad ibn Mugīth, see *ibid.*, vol. 20, pp. 123–124).

39 Adang, "The Beginnings," p. 121.

40 Al-Dhahabī, *Tārīkh*, vol. 36, p. 153, and *Siyar*, vol. 16, p. 77.

41 Al-Shīrāzī, *Ṭabaqāt*, p. 179.

42 In fact, it is not clear here whether al-Dhahabī was quoting this himself from a work of Yūsuf that he had or was just reporting it from Ibn Ḥazm.

43 Al-Dhahabī, *Tārīkh*, vol. 36, p. 154.

44 Al-Buḥṣalī reads "al-Zandawardī", after Zandaward, a neighborhood in Baghdad (al-Buḥṣalī, *Ṭabaqāt Ahl al-Ẓāhir*, p. 56).

45 Al-Khaṭīb al-Baghdādī, *Tārīkh*, vol. 8, p. 273.

manuscripts of *al-Fihrist*.[46] Al-Qurashī mentions that Ḥaydarah wrote a compendium (*mukhtaṣar*), probably containing Ẓāhirī legal views.[47]

17. *Aḥmad ibn Bundār Isḥāq, Abū ʿAbd Allāh al-Shaʿʿār* (d. 359/969)
Abū ʿAbd Allāh al-Shaʿʿār was a competent traditionist and jurist in Isfahan. He transmitted from a number of scholars, including Abū Bakr ibn Abī ʿĀṣim and was affiliated with the Ẓāhirī *madhhab*.[48]

18. *ʿUbayd Allāh ibn Aḥmad ibn al-Ḥusayn* (d. 361/971)
ʿUbayd Allāh was a student of Ibn Dāwūd and reportedly even of Dāwūd himself, although al-Dhahabī, who describes him as "Dāwūdī Ẓāhirī," seems to have doubts about this.[49]

19. *ʿAlī ibn Waṣīf al-Nāshiʾ* (d. 366/976)
According to Muḥammad ibn al-Ḥasan al-Ṭūsī, ʿAlī, who was a theologian and poet, followed the Ẓāhirī *madhhab* in legal matters.[50]

20. *ʿAbd Allāh ibn Aḥmad ibn Rāshid* (d. 369/979)
Known as Ibn Ukht al-Walīd, ʿAbd Allāh ibn Rāshid was a student of Ibn al-Mughallis and a wealthy merchant who became judge of Egypt several times between 329/940 and 334/945, and of Damascus in 348/959. Despite his rather bad reputation and accusations of accepting bribes (it is reported that he bribed Muḥammad ibn Taghj al-Ikhshīd—Egypt's Turkish ruler (r. 321/933 to 334/946)—to appoint him as judge), he is counted among the great Ẓāhirī scholars,[51] and reported to have compiled many works.[52] He traveled frequently between Syria and Egypt where he settled until his death.[53]

---

46 Ibn al-Nadīm, *Fihrist*, p. 219.

47 Al-Qurashī, *Jawāhir*, vol. 2, p. 159. Al-Qurashī adds that Ḥaydarah then became fascinated with the Ḥanafī scholar Muḥammad ibn al-Ḥasan al-Shaybānī (*ibid.*, p. 159).

48 Al-Dhahabī, *ʿIbar*, vol. 2, p. 31. See also al-Dhahabī, *Siyar*, vol. 16, p. 61.

49 Al-Dhahabī, *Tārīkh*, vol. 36, pp. 281–282.

50 Al-Ṭūsī, *Fihrist*, p. 268. I own this reference to Hossein Modarressi.

51 Ibn Ḥajar, *Lisān*, vol. 3, pp. 304–305.

52 Al-Dhahabī, *Tārīkh*, vol. 36, p. 416. To the best of my knowledge, none of ʿAbd Allāh's works has survived.

53 Al-Dhahabī, *Siyar*, vol. 16, pp. 225–226.

21. *Ṭāhir ibn Muḥammad* (d. 369/979)
Ṭāhir ibn Muḥammad was a judge in Jurjan. He was counted among the *Ahl al-Raʾy*, but al-Sahmī mentions that he was Ẓāhirī.[54]

22. *Muḥammad ibn al-Ḥusayn al-Baṣrī* (d. *c.* 375/985)
Al-Khaṭīb al-Baghdādī mentions Muḥammad ibn al-Ḥusayn in his biography of Ibn Dāwūd as a transmitter of an anecdote from Muḥammad ibn al-Ḥasan ibn al-Ṣabbāḥ al-Dāwūdī al-Baghdādī, from the judge Muḥammad ibn Yūsuf ibn Yaʿqūb.[55] According to Ibn Mākūlā, he was known as "al-Ẓāhirī" because he followed Dāwūd's *madhhab*.[56]

23. *Aḥmad ibn ʿAbd Allāh ibn Aḥmad al-Bukhtarī* (d. before 384/994)
According to al-Tanūkhī, Aḥmad was the head of the Ẓāhirīs of his age. He worked as a "Dāwūdī" judge in Baghdad. He is al-Tanūkhī's informant of a debate between Ibn Dāwūd and Ibn Surayj.[57]

24. *Muḥammad ibn Mūsā ibn al-Muthannā* (d. 385/995)
According to al-Samʿānī, Muḥammad ibn al-Muthannā was a noble Dāwūdī scholar who studied with many scholars and taught many students.[58] Al-Ṣafadī mentions that he was a "Baghdādī Ẓāhirī Dāwūdī" jurist and traditionist.[59]

25. *ʿAbd al-ʿAzīz ibn Aḥmad al-Jazarī* (d. 391/1000)
Mentioned by al-Shīrāzī in the fifth *ṭabaqah* of Ẓāhirī scholars, ʿAbd al-ʿAzīz al-Jazarī (or al-Kharazī) was a judge in Baghdad in 377/987.[60] He followed Dāwūd's *madhhab* (which he studied with Bishr ibn al-Ḥusayn)[61] and was known for his argumentative skills.[62] Al-Dhahabī quotes the Ḥanafī scholar al-Ṣaymarī (d. 436/1044) that he never saw a jurist who matched al-Jazarī's sharp intellect.[63] Al-Dhahabī also describes him as a leading Ẓāhirī jurist (*faqīh al-Ẓāhiriyyah*) who taught students in Baghdad. His students included

54 Ḥamzah ibn Yūsuf al-Sahmī, *Tārīkh Jurjān*, p. 102.
55 Al-Khaṭīb al-Baghdādī, *Tārīkh*, vol. 5, p. 258.
56 Ibn Mākūlā, *Ikmāl al-Ikmāl*, vol. 5, p. 281.
57 Al-Tanūkhī, *Nishwār*, vol. 8, p. 186.
58 Al-Samʿānī, *Ansāb*, vol. 2, p. 449.
59 Al-Ṣafadī, *Wāfī*, vol. 5, p. 86.
60 Ibn al-Nadīm, *Fihrist*, p. 219.
61 Al-Shīrāzī, *Ṭabaqāt*, p. 178.
62 Al-Khaṭīb al-Baghdādī, *Tārīkh*, vol. 10, p. 466.
63 Al-Dhahabī, *Tadhkirat*, vol. 3, p. 152, and Al-Dhahabī, *Tārīkh*, vol. 39, pp. 256–257.

Muḥammad ibn ʿUmar al-Dāwūdī, Abū ʿAlī al-Dāwūdī, judge of Firozabad, and his son.[64] Ibn al-Nadīm attributes to him a work on (legal?) disagreements.[65]

26. *Muḥammad ibn Banān* (d. after 400/1009):
Al-Shīrāzī mentions Muḥammad ibn Banān in his fifth *ṭabaqah* of Ẓāhirī scholars.[66] To my knowledge, other biographical dictionaries do not mention him.

∴

These are twenty-six Ẓāhirī scholars who lived in the late 3rd/9th and 4th/10th centuries. Almost half of these lived in Baghdad. Dāwūd's views were transmitted to Ibn al-Mughallis by Dāwūd's son Muḥammad in Baghdad. Ibn al-Mughallis' knowledge passed on to Ḥaydarah al-Zanūdī, the teacher of future generations of Baghdadi Ẓāhirīs. Bishr ibn al-Ḥusayn transmitted Ibn al-Mughallis' teachings to ʿAbd al-ʿAzīz al-Jazarī, after whose students the *madhhab* is said to have disappeared from Baghdad, around the mid-5th/11th century.[67] Furthermore, Iraq is the only region where connected chains of Ẓāhirī teachers and students can be found. One such chain is Muḥammad ibn al-Ḥusayn al-Baṣrī al-Ẓāhirī, from Muḥammad ibn al-Ḥasan ibn al-Ṣabbāḥ al-Dāwūdī al-Baghdādī, from Muḥammad ibn Yūsuf ibn Yaʿqūb. After Muḥammad ibn Yūsuf, the chain can reach Dāwūd through Muḥammad's father Yūsuf ibn Yaʿqūb from Dāwūd directly or through Muḥammad ibn Dāwūd. A second chain is Muḥammad ibn ʿUmar al-Dāwūdī and Abū ʿAlī al-Dāwūdī from ʿAbd al-ʿAzīz al-Jazarī, from Bishr ibn al-Ḥusayn, from ʿAlī ibn Muḥammad al-Baghdādī, from Ibn al-Mughallis, from Muḥammad ibn Dāwūd, from Dāwūd. In other words, although another student of Dāwūd—Yūsuf ibn Yaʿqūb—may have transmitted Dāwūd's knowledge to his (Yūsuf's) son who then transmitted it to future generations of Iraqi scholars, the fact that we do not know much about either Yūsuf ibn Yaʿqūb or his son indicates that Muḥammad ibn Dāwūd was indeed Dāwūd's most important student who preserved his father's teachings. The same can be said about Ibn al-Mughallis in relation to Ibn Dāwūd, for although the latter's knowledge was also transmitted by other students of his, it was Ibn al-Mughallis' chain from Dāwūd that established the *madhhab* in Iraq (through

64 Al-Shīrāzī, *Ṭabaqāt*, p. 178.
65 Ibn al-Nadīm, *Fihrist*, p. 219.
66 Al-Shīrāzī, *Ṭabaqāt*, p. 179.
67 *Ibid.*, p. 179.

Ḥaydarah al-Zanūdī), and it was also Ibn al-Mughallis' students who spread the *madhhab* beyond Iraq.

Outside Iraq, six of these scholars lived in the eastern part of the Muslim world. Dāwūd's *madhhab* is reported to have reached Fars through Bishr ibn al-Ḥusayn, probably in the first half of the 4th century AH. Bishr studied with ʿAlī ibn Muḥammad al-Baghdādī, who was an associate of Ibn al-Mughallis. We will see later that it was also one of Bishr ibn al-Ḥusayn's students—called Abū al-Faraj al-Fāmī—who took the *madhhab* to Shiraz in the 5th/11th century (if it had already not reached it thanks to Abū Saʿd ibn al-Ḥusayn). In fact, al-Muqaddasī mentions that there were many lectures on the "Dāwūdī" *madhhab* in Fars at that time, and that Dāwūdī scholars worked in the judiciary and other professions.[68] The *madhhab* also reached Isfahan at the hands of Muḥammad ibn Maʿmar ibn Rāshid, and as far east as Jurjan at the hands of Ṭāhir ibn Muḥammad.

One Ẓāhirī scholar is reported to have lived in Egypt, another in Palestine, and a third in Damascus. The *madhhab* probably reached Egypt through a slave manumitted by a certain Muḥammad ibn Ṣāliḥ al-Manṣūrī, probably in the mid-4th century AH. He went to Baghdad, studied with Ibn al-Mughallis, went back to Egypt, and transmitted his knowledge to Muḥammad's son, who then continued the tradition there. As for Syria, al-Muqaddasī mentions that there were no Dāwūdī scholars there in the 4th/10th century.[69] This is consistent with our findings here. Only the Syrian Aḥmad ibn Muḥammad ibn Ziyād, in the first half of the 4th century, was known for his Ẓāhirī leanings, but we do not know with whom he studied. Be this as it may, if Dāwūd's *madhhab* ever existed in Syria, it must have reached it at the hands of Aḥmad ibn Muḥammad ibn Ziyād, and probably in the first half of the 4th century.

Three of these twenty-six scholars lived in or travelled to Andalus. We have seen earlier that a direct student of Dāwūd—Ibn Hilāl—was credited with carrying his writings to Andalus and spreading his *madhhab* there. Later, in the second quarter of the 4th century, two other Ẓāhirī scholars—Muḥammad ibn Sulaymān and ʿAlī ibn Bundār—are reported to have brought Dāwūd's teachings to Andalus. Although we do not know with whom the former scholar studied, we know that ʿAlī ibn Bundār was a student of Ibn al-Mughallis. Furthermore, Mundhir ibn Saʿīd al-Ballūṭī, with his knowledge, social status, and argumentative skills, must have boosted the status of the *madhhab* in Andalus around the mid-4th century AH. In other words, although Iraq was the stronghold of

68 Muḥammad ibn Aḥmad al-Muqaddasī, *Aḥsan al-Taqāsīm fī Maʿrifat al-Aqālīm*, p. 334.

69 *Ibid.*, p. 152.

Ẓāhirism in the 4th/10th century, Andalus was one of the few places to which direct students of Dāwūd and Ibn al-Mughallis traveled and settled.

More than half of these scholars—and all scholars whose profession is actually reported—worked as judges, sometimes rising to the rank of *qāḍī al-quḍāh*. Most of these judges lived and worked in Baghdad. Since Ḥanafism was the official *madhhab* of the Abbasid state at that time, it is safe to assume that these judges were trained as Ḥanafī scholars (but also possibly as Mālikī or Shāfiʿī).[70] It is likely that these scholars kept their affiliation with Dāwūd's *madhhab* a private matter, assuming affiliation with other *madhhab*s in public. Whereas approximately six of these scholars are reported to have compiled books, most of these books apparently dealt with specific legal issues, such as refuting *qiyās*, or with exegesis or other Qurʾān-related subjects (such as the case with the Andalusian Ẓāhirī scholar Mundhir ibn Saʿīd al-Ballūṭī). A significant number of these scholars were known for defending Dāwūd's *madhhab*, which suggests that early generations of Ẓāhirī scholars were already on the defensive and felt the need to legitimize their views. We do not know how and against whom they did that, but the Ẓāhirī rejection of *qiyās* and *raʾy* could have caused harm to their relationship with other *madhhab*s.

Remarkably, less than a quarter of these scholars were known for their contribution to Ḥadīth transmission. Whereas some of them were considered reliable, Ḥadīth critics were critical of some others. None of them, however, seem to have authored Ḥadīth compilations or works of Ḥadīth criticism. It could be argued, then, that these scholars seem to have inherited from earlier generations of Ẓāhirīs a general lack of interest in the transmission and criticism of Ḥadīth.

Finally, of these scholars, those who were referred to as "Dāwūdī" outnumber those known as "Ẓāhirī." In fact, al-Muqaddasī mentions that the legal *madhhab*s that were followed in his days (in the 4th/10th century) were the Ḥanafī, Mālikī, Shāfiʿī, and Dāwūdī.[71] In one chain of transmission, a father is known as Dāwūdī while his son is known as Ẓāhirī. This does not necessarily mean that these scholars were known as Ẓāhirī in their lifetime, for it is possible that this epithet was given to them by their biographers later. For example, al-Ṣafadī described Muḥammad ibn Mūsā as "Dāwūdī Ẓāhirī" although al-Samʿānī had described him only as Dāwūdī. But if these were known as such during their

70 This does not exclude the possibility that they may have belonged to other *madhhab*s. For the distribution and percentage of scholars belonging to various *madhhab*s in the first centuries of Islam, see Monique Bernards and John Nawas, "The Geographic Distribution of Muslim Jurists during the First Four Centuries AH."

71 Al-Muqaddasī, *Aḥsan al-Taqāsīm*, p. 44.

lifetime, this could suggest that scholars began to be called Ẓāhirī, rather than Dāwūdī, around the mid-4th century AH. In all circumstances, however, sharing an eponym at a certain point must have given these scholars a sense of belonging to a *madhhab* and of sharing a common legal heritage. The nature of this legal heritage as they understood it, however, is something that we cannot ascertain from their biographies since the sources are generally silent about the works they may have studied and the way they transmitted their knowledge to their students.

To summarize, at the end of the 4th/10th century, Iraq remained the stronghold of Dāwūd's *madhhab*, the majority and most important of which scholars lived there. Andalus, however, was emerging as Iraq's competitor on the strength of hosting immediate students of Dāwūd and Ibn al-Mughallis. A few generations after Dāwūd's death, his *madhhab* had already spread as far as Isfahan in the east and Andalus in the west, with very few representatives in Egypt and possibly Syria. Most Ẓāhirī scholars in Iraq, and some in the east and in Egypt, worked as judges, which suggests that they were Ḥanafīs and on good terms with their rulers. A few of them were known for being active in Ḥadīth transmission and a few of them are reported to have compiled books.

2 Fifth/Eleventh-Century Ẓāhirīs

1. *Dāwūd ibn Aḥmad ibn Yaḥyā ibn al-Khiḍr* (d. 418/1027)
We do not know much about Dāwūd ibn Aḥmad except that he was a Ẓāhirī who died in Baghdad in 418/1027.[72]

2. *Abū al-Faraj al-Fāmī al-Shīrāzī* (*fl. c.* 425/1034)
Abū al-Faraj al-Fāmī is mentioned by al-Shīrāzī in the fifth *ṭabaqah* of Ẓāhirī scholars. He studied with Bishr ibn al-Ḥusayn and was a master in Dāwūd's *madhhab* as well as a Mu'tazilī theologian. He is credited with spreading the *madhhab* in Shiraz. Al-Shīrāzī does not reports Abū al-Faraj's date of death, but mentions that he used to engage in arguments with him when he was young, which suggests that Abū al-Faraj died in the first quarter of the 5th century AH. At this point, al-Shīrāzī states that Dāwūd's *madhhab* died out in Baghdad and that only a handful of Abū al-Faraj's associates in Shiraz were still present.[73]

72 Ibn Ḥajar, Lisān, vol. 2, p. 482.
73 Al-Shīrāzī, *Ṭabaqāt*, p. 179.

3. *Dāwūd ibn Ibrāhīm ibn Yūsuf al-Iṣbahānī* (d. after 425/1033)
Dāwūd ibn Ibrāhīm was a knowledgeable scholar and prolific Ḥadīth transmitter who followed Dāwūd's *madhhab*. He apparently lived in Seville.[74]

4. *Muḥammad ibn ʿAbd Allāh ibn Ṭālib* (d. after 420/931)
Originally from Basra, Muḥammad ibn ʿAbd Allāh traveled frequently to the eastern parts of the Muslim world where he studied with many notable scholars. Ibn Bashkuwāl reports that he followed Dāwūd's *madhhab* and traveled to Andalus on business in 420/931.[75]

5. *Masʿūd ibn Sulaymān ibn Muflit* (d. 426/1035)
A teacher of Ibn Ḥazm, who included him among the independent scholars (*mujtahids*) of his time,[76] Ibn Muflit was known to be a "Dāwūdī" scholar who rejected *taqlīd*, chose from different views, and adhered to *ẓāhir*.[77]

6. *Ibrāhīm ibn Aḥmad ibn al-Ḥasan al-Rubāʿī* (*fl. c.* 438/1046)
Ibrāhīm ibn Aḥmad apparently died not long before Ibn al-Nadīm was writing his *Fihrist*. Ibn al-Nadīm describes him as a Dāwūdī scholar who migrated from Baghdad to Egypt where he died. He also reports that Ibrāhīm wrote a work against *qiyās* (*Kitāb al-Iʿtibār fī Ibṭāl al-Qiyās*).[78]

7. *Ibn al-Khallāl* (*fl. c.* 438/1046)
Ibn al-Nadīm mentions Ibn al-Khallāl among Ẓāhirī scholars and attributes to him a number of works, one of which is a refutation of *qiyās* (*Ibṭāl al-Qiyās*), and another on *uṣūl al-Fiqh* (*Naʿt al-Ḥikmah fī Uṣūl al-Fiqh*).[79]

8. *Abū Saʿīd al-Raqqī* (*fl. c.* 438/1046)
According to Ibn al-Nadīm, Abū Saʿīd followed Dāwūd's *madhhab* and compiled many works, including one on *uṣūl* (most likely of *al-fiqh*) that contained chapters similar to Dāwūd's own work on *uṣūl*.[80]

---

74 Ibn Bashkuwāl, *Ṣilah*, vol. 1, p. 183.

75 *Ibid.*, vol. 2, pp. 598–599. In fact, Ibn Bashkuwāl, who describes Muḥammad as Ẓāhirī, says that he was following *madhhab Dāwūd al-qiyāsī*. As noted earlier, this kind of statements raises questions about the grounds on which scholar were included by medieval biographers and historians among Ẓāhirīs.

76 Ibn Ḥazm, *Iḥkām*, vol. 2, p. 674.

77 Al-Ḥumaydī, *Jadhwat*, vol. 2, p. 558.

78 Ibn al-Nadīm, *Fihrist*, p. 218.

79 *Ibid.*, p. 218.

80 *Ibid.*, p. 218.

9. *Hishām ibn Ghālib ibn Hishām* (d. 438/1046)
Known for his knowledge and intelligence, Hishām ibn Ghālib was a scholar from Granada who, according to Ibn Bashkuwāl, secretly followed Dāwūd's *madhhab*.[81]

10. *Muḥammad ibn ʿUmar al-Dāwūdī* (*fl.* before 450/1058)
Muḥammad ibn ʿUmar al-Dāwūdī is probably Abū Bakr ibn al-Akhḍar whom al-Shīrāzī mentions in the fifth *ṭabaqah* of Ẓāhirī scholars and attributes *Tārīkh Ahl al-Ẓāhir* to him. A judge himself, Abū Bakr was among the witnesses of the chief judge of Baghdad.[82] He appears in the *Tārīkh Baghdād* as al-Khaṭīb al-Baghdādī's source for the dates of death of some Ẓāhirī scholars, including Ibn al-Mughallis and Ḥaydrah al-Zanūdī.[83] Al-Shīrāzī does not report Abū Bakr's date of death, but since he was a student of ʿAbd al-ʿAzīz al-Jazarī, who died in the late 4th/10th century and was an informant of al-Khaṭīb al-Baghdādī, he likely died before or during the first half of the 5th/11th century.

11. *Jābir ibn Ghālib ibn Sālim* (d. before 456/1064)
A contemporary of Ibn Ḥazm who apparently admired him, Jābir ibn Ghālib is reported to have been a Ẓāhirī scholar and traditionist from Seville.[84]

12. *Ibn Ḥazm al-Andalusī* (d. 456/1064)
Ibn Ḥazm's status and influence in the history of the Ẓāhirī *madhhab* is discussed later in this chapter.

13. *Sālim ibn Aḥmad ibn Fatḥ* (d. 461/1068)
According to al-Marrākushī, Sālim ibn Aḥmad, who was from Cordoba, was a friend of Ibn Ḥazm whose *madhhab* he followed and many of whose works he transcribed.[85]

14. *Yūsuf ibn ʿAbd Allāh ibn Muḥammad, Ibn ʿAbd al-Barr* (d. 463/1070)
A famous and prolific Andalusian scholar, Ibn ʿAbd al-Barr is reported to have changed his legal affiliation frequently, starting his career as Ẓāhirī to end up as Mālikī. Ibn Ḥazm admired him as an independent scholar.[86]

---

81 Ibn Bashkuwāl, *Ṣilah*, vol. 2, p. 652.

82 Al-Shīrāzī, *Ṭabaqāt*, pp. 178–179.

83 Al-Khaṭīb al-Baghdādī, *Tārīkh*, vol. 3, p. 38.

84 Muḥammad ibn ʿAbd Allāh ibn al-Abbār, *Takmilat al-Takmilah li-Kitāb al-Ṣilah*, vol. 1, pp. 288–289. Ibn al-Abbār mentions that Ibn Ḥazm wrote an elegy when Jābir died.

85 Al-Marrākushī, *Dhayl*, vol. 4, p. 1.

86 Ibn Ḥazm, *Iḥkām*, vol. 2, p. 674.

15. *Muḥammad ibn Ibrāhīm ibn Fāris* (d. 474/1081)
Muḥammad ibn Ibrāhīm was a bookseller in Baghdad who traveled to Egypt, Shiraz, and Damascus to learn traditions. He was known to be "Dāwūdī Ẓāhirī" and not highly regarded by the Ḥadīth critics of the time.[87]

16. *Abū ʿAlī al-Dāwūdī* (d. before 476/1083)
Abū ʿAlī al-Dāwūdī—whom al-Shīrāzī mentions as his contemporary—was a judge in Firozabad who studied with ʿAbd al-ʿAzīz al-Jazarī.[88]

17. *Al-Faḍl ibn ʿAlī ibn Ḥazm* (d. 479/1086)
As Ibn Ḥazm's son, al-Faḍl, who resided in Cordoba, followed in the footsteps of his father as a Ẓāhirī scholar and completed his *magnum opus* in jurisprudence, *al-Muḥallā bi-l-Āthār*.[89]

18. *Farḥ ibn Ḥadīdah* (d. 480/1087)
A contemporary of Ibn Ḥazm, Farḥ ibn Ḥadīdah is reported to have been a Ẓāhirī scholar and expert on Qurʾān recitation whom al-Muʿtaḍid bi-Allāh (the ruler of Seville from 433/1041 to 461/1068) appointed as Qurʾān reciter in a mosque that he built for his mother.[90]

19. *Muḥammad ibn Futūḥ ibn Ḥumayd al-Ḥumaydī* (d. 488/1095)
A pious, reliable, and studious scholar of Ḥadīth, al-Ḥumaydī studied and taught Ḥadīth in many regions in the Muslim world, including Andalus, Egypt, the Ḥijāz, Syria, and Iraq. He was regarded as Ibn Ḥazm's most important student (and also a student of Ibn ʿAbd al-Barr),[91] but he apparently never openly admitted his Ẓāhirī affiliation. Al-Ḥumaydī is reported to have authored works in various genres, including Ḥadīth, *uṣūl al-fiqh*, history, and "mirrors for princes" (*marāyā ʾl-umarāʾ*). He died in Baghdad and was buried next to the Sufi Bishr al-Ḥāfī in accordance with his will.[92]

20. *ʿAlī ibn Saʿīd al-ʿAbdarī* (d. after 491/1097)
A notable student of Ibn Ḥazm who came from Majorca and later traveled eastwards, al-ʿAbdarī is said to have abandoned Ẓāhirism for Shāfiʿism at the

---

87 Ibn Ḥajar, *Lisān*, vol. 5, p. 36.
88 Al-Shīrāzī, *Ṭabaqāt*, p. 179.
89 Muḥammad ibn Muḥammad al-Marrākushī, *al-Dhayl wa-l-Takmilah li-Kitābayy al-Mawṣūl wa-l-Ṣilah*, vol. 5, part 2, p. 540.
90 *Ibid.*, vol. 5, part 2, pp. 538–539.
91 Al-Dhahabī, *ʿIbar*, vol. 3, p. 323.
92 Ibn ʿAsākir, *Tārīkh*, vol. 55, pp. 77–81.

hands of the Shāfiʿī scholar Abū Bakr al-Shāshī (d. 507/1113). He was a teacher of the Mālikī scholar Abū Bakr ibn al-ʿArabī (d. 543/1148).[93]

21. *Aḥmad ibn Muḥammad ibn Ṣāliḥ al-Manṣūrī* (d. late 5th/11th century)
It has been noted earlier that Aḥmad ibn Muḥammad was a student of a slave that his father had manumitted and who had studied with Ibn al-Mughallis. He also seems to have studied with al-Qāsim ibn Wahb al-Dāwūdī, another follower of Dāwūd.[94] According to Ibn Ḥajar al-ʿAsqalānī (d. 852/1449), he went to Bukhara in the year 460/1067 when al-Ḥākim al-Naysābūrī was there and was appointed judge of Arjan.[95] Apparently, he also resided in Sind for some time.[96] Ibn Ḥajar reports that he was a master who followed Dāwūd's *madhhab*, and he is reported to have fabricated a Prophetic tradition supporting the Ẓāhirī rejection of *qiyās*.[97] Ibn al-Nadīm attributes to him some works, the titles of which are not indicative of their contents.[98]

∴

Biographical dictionaries provide us with these twenty-one Ẓāhirī scholars from the 5th/11th century. It is remarkable that what we know about many of them is very scanty; even their dates of death are not reported at times. Additionally, despite al-Shīrāzī's statement about the extinction of Dāwūd's

---

93 Ibn Bashkuwāl, *Ṣilah*, vol. 2, pp. 422–423.

94 For this, see al-Dhahabī, *Siyar*, vol. 13, p. 115, where al-Dhahabī mentions a chain of transmission of a Prophetic tradition that is apparently predominantly Ẓāhirī, starting with Ibn Dāwūd. I could not find information about al-Qāsim or the intermediary between him and Muḥammad ibn Dāwūd, Wahb ibn Jāmiʿ al-ʿAṭṭār. This Wahb could be al-Qāsim's father or, as al-Dhahabī says, the same Muḥammad ibn Jāmiʿ al-Ṣaydalānī with whom Muḥammad ibn Dāwūd was reportedly in love. Al-Manṣūrī transmitted this tradition to a certain Muḥammad ibn Jaʿfar al-Ẓāhirī, another possible Ẓāhirī scholar. Muḥammad ibn Jaʿfar himself may have been from Shiraz, similar to his grandson (and al-Dhahabī's informant of the Prophetic tradition) ʿAbd al-Karīm ibn Muḥammad ibn Aḥmad al-Shīrāzī.

95 Ibn Ḥajar, *Lisān*, vol. 1, pp. 377–378.

96 Ibn al-Ḥayy al-Ḥasanī refers to Aḥmad as al-Manṣūrī al-Sindī (al-Ḥasanī, *Nuzhat al-Khawāṭir*, p. 65). Al-Ḥasan also mentions that al-Muqaddasī (d. 380/990), in his *Aḥsan al-Taqāsīm*, reported that he had met Aḥmad in Manṣūrah (*Aḥsan al-Taqāsīm*, p. 65). I could not find this reference in the edition of *Aḥsan al-Taqāsīm* that is available to me.

97 Burhān al-Dīn al-Ḥalabī, *al-Kashf al-Ḥathīth ʿamman Rumiya bi-Waḍʿ al-Ḥadīth*, pp. 79–80. In this tradition the Prophet is reported to have said: "Iblīs was the first to have practiced *qiyās*, so do not practice it."

98 Ibn al-Nadīm, *Fihrist*, p. 218. These are *Kitāb al-Miṣbāḥ, Kitāb al-Hādī, Kitāb al-Nayyir*.

madhhab in Baghdad after the students of ʿAbd al-ʿAzīz al-Jazarī, more than one quarter of these scholars still lived in or originated from Iraq (mostly Baghdad, but also Basra). More Ẓāhirī scholars appear in the eastern part of the Muslim world than in the previous century. In Egypt and Syria only two scholars are reported to have followed Dāwūd's *madhhab*. Working as judges remains the profession of those scholars whose occupations are reported to us, and almost a quarter of them were known as having been active in Ḥadīth transmission. Two scholars are reported to have been secretly affiliated with the *madhhab*. And although the eponym "Dāwūdī" continues to be used, the epithet "Ẓāhirī" begins to appear more often. Finally, some of these scholars are reported to have authored some legal works, most of which are about *uṣūl al-fiqh* and the refutation of *qiyās*.

The increasing number of Ẓāhirī scholars associated with Ḥadīth transmission and the displacement of the sobriquet "Dāwūdī" by "Ẓāhirī" in reference to these scholars could be linked to a significant development in the 5th/11th century: the proliferation of Ẓāhirī scholars in Andalus and the advent of Ibn Ḥazm. Most of the Andalusian Ẓāhirī scholars were associated with Ibn Ḥazm, either as friends or students. Furthermore, there is solid evidence of a contact and possibly mutual influence between Andalusian Ẓāhirīs and Iraqi Ẓāhirīs. Iraqi Ẓāhirīs traveled to Andalus, while a student of Ibn Ḥazm—al-Ḥumaydī—moved eastwards and resided in Baghdad. In other words, we can now speak of an extended and connected network of Ẓāhirīs.

Moreover, mention is made for the first time to books that Ẓāhirīs copied and transmitted, including Ibn Ḥazm's substantial writings on various genres of religious studies. Unfortunately, given the lack of any reference to attempt by Ẓāhirīs to present and transmit their knowledge in a systematic and institutionalized way, we are left in the dark regarding how they were transmitted to later generations (with the exception of Ibn Ḥazm's works, of course). This notwithstanding, the distribution of Ẓāhirī scholars in the Muslim world at that time, and Ibn Ḥazm's stature and accomplishments, warrant regarding the 5th/11th century as the golden age of the Ẓāhirī *madhhab*.

3 Sixth/Thwelfth- and Seventh/Thirteenth-Century Ẓāhirīs

1. *Sulaymān ibn Sahl ibn Isḥāq* (*fl.* before mid-6th/12th century)

Nothing is reported about Sulaymān ibn Sahl other than that he was Ẓāhirī.[99]

99 Ibn ʿAsākir, *Tārīkh*, vol. 22, pp. 323–324.

2. *Bakr ibn Khalaf ibn Saʿīd* (d. after 505/1111)
Bakr ibn Khalaf was a Ẓāhirī scholar from Seville. He is reported to have rejected *taqlīd* and *raʾy* and adhered to Ḥadīth.[100]

3. *Muḥammad ibn Ṭāhir ibn ʿAlī ibn Aḥmad, Ibn al-Qaysarānī* (d. 507/1113)
Ibn al-Qaysarānī was from Jerusalem and traveled to many centers of knowledge in the Muslim world in his time. He was active in Ḥadīth transmission and reported to have been "Dāwūdī" (*kāna Dāwūdī ʾl-madhhab*).[101]

4. *ʿAbd Allāh ibn Aḥmad ibn Saʿīd ibn Yarbūʿ* (d. 522/1128)
Al-Ḍabbī, our source on ʿAbd Allāh ibn Aḥmad, only mentions that he was a Ẓāhirī jurist and traditionist.[102]

5. *Muḥammad ibn Saʿdūn ibn Murajjā al-ʿAbdarī* (d. 524/1129)
Ibn Murajjā al-ʿAbdarī was a great Andalusian scholar of Ḥadīth and jurisprudence. A student of Ibn Ḥazm's student al-Ḥumaydī,[103] he followed Dāwūd's *madhhab* and was known for his vast knowledge of Ḥadīth and biting comments on earlier jurists. He traveled eastwards, resided in Syria for a few years, and died in Baghdad. According to Ibn ʿAsākir, he used to give *fatwā*s according to Dāwūd's *madhhab*.[104]

6. *ʿAbd Allāh ibn Mūsā* (d. 526/1131)
ʿAbd Allāh ibn Mūsā was a Cordoban scholar of Ḥadīth reported to have been Ẓāhirī.[105]

7. *Muḥammad ibn al-Ḥusayn al-Anṣārī, Ibn Iḥdā ʿAshrah* (d. 532/1137)
Ibn Iḥdā ʿAshrah was a Ẓāhirī scholar from Almería who was known for his knowledge of Ḥadīth.[106]

---

100 Ibn al-Abbār, *Takmilah*, vol. 1, p. 257.

101 Al-Dhahabī, *Tadhkirat*, vol. 4, p. 29. Al-Dhahabī attributes this information to al-Samʿānī, who learned it from the Shāfiʿī scholar Abū al-Ḥasan al-Karajī (d. 532/1137).

102 Aḥmad ibn Yaḥyā al-Ḍabbī, *Bughyat al-Multamis fī Tārīkh Rijāl Ahl al-Andalus*, p. 294.

103 Al-Dhahabī, *ʿIbar*, vol. 4, p. 57.

104 Ibn ʿAsākir, *Tārīkh*, vol. 53, pp. 59–61.

105 Ibn Bashkuwāl, *Ṣilah*, vol. 1, p. 294.

106 *Ibid.*, pp. 581–582. See also *Biblioteca de al-Andalus*, vol. 3, p. 486.

8. *Muḥammad ibn al-Ḥasan* [*or ibn al-Ḥusayn*] *ibn Aḥmad* (d. 537/1142)
Originally from Majorca, Muḥammad ibn al-Ḥasan travelled to Egypt where he studied with many scholars, then returned to Andalus and resided in Granada until his death. Al-Maqqarī mentions that out of fear of ʿAlī ibn Yūsuf ibn Tashfīn (d. 499/1106) who was Mālikī, Muḥammad did not confess his affiliation with the Ẓāhirī *madhhab* and worked in teaching Ḥadīth.[107] Ibn al-Khaṭīb describes him as "Ẓāhirī Dāwūdī."[108]

9. *Aḥmad ibn Saʿīd ibn Ḥazm* (d. 540/1145)
Grandson of Ibn Ḥazm, Aḥmad ibn Saʿīd was a staunch Ẓāhirī like his own father and grandfather. Al-Dhahabī describes him as an accomplished scholar who knew and defended the pillars and fundamentals (*uṣūl*) of Ẓāhirism.[109] Following his ancestors, he was active in politics, which brought upon him much hardship when he was accused of coordinating a revolt against the ruler of Cordoba at his time.[110]

10. *Aḥmad ibn ʿAbd al-Malik ibn Muḥammad, Ibn Abī Marwān* (d. 549/1154)
A distinguished scholar of Ḥadīth, Ibn Abī Marwān was a Ẓāhirī scholar who resided in Niebla (Arabic Lablah, a town not far from Seville) and followed the teachings of Ibn Ḥazm.[111] He was killed in a revolt by the people of Niebla in 549/1154.[112]

11. *Khiḍr ibn Muḥammad ibn Namir* (d. 571/1175)
Khiḍr ibn Muḥammad was a Ẓāhirī scholar from Seville who used to defend Ẓāhirism.[113] Among his students was Muḥammad ibn ʿAlī ibn ʿUṣfūr, another staunch Ẓāhirī scholar from Seville.[114]

12. *ʿAbd Allāh ibn Muḥammad ibn Marzūq al-Yaḥṣubī* (d. before 576/1180)
ʿAbd Allāh ibn Muḥammad was known as a Ẓāhirī scholar who studied with Ibn Biryāl, a student of Ibn Ḥazm, and took great interest in Ibn Ḥazm's works.

107 Al-Maqqarī, *Nafḥ*, vol. 2, p. 155; Ibn al-Abbār, *Takmilah*, vol. 1, no. 1259.
108 Lisān al-Dīn ibn al-Khaṭīb, *al-Iḥāṭah fī Akhbār Gharnāṭah*, vol. 3, p. 190.
109 Al-Dhahabī, *Tārīkh*, vol. 54, p. 554.
110 Al-Ṣafadī, *Wafayāt*, vol. 6, p. 391.
111 Ibn al-Abbār, *Takmilah*, vol. 1, p. 72; al-Marrākushī, *Dhayl*, vol. 1, pt. 1, p. 266. See also, Adang, "*Ẓāhirīs*," p. 418.
112 Ibn al-Abbār, *Takmilah*, vol. 1, p. 72.
113 *Ibid.*, vol. 1, p. 60.
114 Al-Marrakushī, *Dhayl*, vol. 6, p. 456.

ʿAbd Allāh was from Saragossa, travelled to Egypt, and died in Damascus.[115] Al-Ghalbazūrī believes that it was ʿAbd Allāh who spread Ibn Ḥazm's views in the regions to which he travelled.[116]

13. *ʿAbd al-Raḥmān ibn Yaḥyā ibn al-Ḥasan* (d. 580/1184)
ʿAbd al-Raḥmān was a traditionist from Seville who is reported to have followed Ibn Ḥazm's *madhhab*.[117]

14. *ʿAbd Allāh ibn Abī ʿAmr* (*fl.* 580/1148)
A traditionist from Seville, ʿAbd Allāh was a Ẓāhirī scholar and teacher of Saʿd al-Suʿūd ibn Aḥmad.[118]

15. *Saʿd al-Suʿūd ibn Aḥmad ibn Hishām* (d. 588/1192)
Saʿd al-Suʿūd was known to be a staunch Ẓāhirī who defended his *madhhab*. He was also known for his interest in and adherence to Ḥadīth.[119]

16. *ʿAbd Allāh ibn Bakr ibn Khalaf* (d. *c.* 588/1192)
Son of Bakr ibn Khalaf ibn Saʿīd, ʿAbd Allāh followed in the footsteps of his father as a Ẓāhirī scholar. He was also known for his transmission of Ḥadīth.[120]

17. *Aḥmad ibn Ṭāhir, Ibn Shubrīn* (d. before 595/1198)
Ibn Shubrīn was a teacher of the famous Mālikī scholar and judge ʿIyāḍ ibn Mūsā al-Yaḥṣubī—widely known as al-Qāḍī ʿIyāḍ (d. 544/1149)—who held Aḥmad in high esteem and praised his knowledge and competence in Ḥadīth transmission and criticism. Al-Qāḍī ʿIyāḍ reports that Aḥmad refused to serve as judge and was given to Ẓāhirism in jurisprudence. He does not attribute any works to him.[121]

18. *Sulṭān Abū Muḥammad Yaʿqūb ibn Yūsuf* (d. 595/1198)
According to Ibn Kathīr, Yaʿqūb ibn Yūsuf was a Mālikī scholar who became "Ẓāhirī Ḥazmī" and ended up as a Shāfiʿī.[122]

---

115 Ibn al-Abbār, *Takmilah*, vol. 2, p. 463.
116 Al-Ghalbazūrī, *al-Madrasah al-Ẓāhiriyyah*, p. 272.
117 Ibn al-Zubayr, *Ṣilah*, vol. 3, p. 190.
118 Al-Marrākushī, *Dhayl*, vol. 4, pp. 185–186.
119 *Ibid.*, vol. 4, pp. 18–21.
120 *Ibid.*, vol. 4, pp. 185–187. Al-Marrākushī does not mention ʿAbd Allāh's date of death, but he states that he studied with Saʿd al-Suʿūd ibn Aḥmad (*ibid.*, vol. 4, pp. 18–21).
121 Al-Qāḍī ʿIyāḍ, *Fihrist*, pp. 84–85.
122 Ibn Kathīr, *Bidāyah*, vol. 13, p. 19.

19. *Sufyān ibn Aḥmad ibn ʿAbd Allāh, Ibn al-Imām* (d. before 599/1202)
Ibn al-Imām was a traditionist who was given to Ẓāhirism and resided in Murcia.[123] Among his teachers was Abū al-Qāsim ibn Ḥubaysh, a student of Muḥammad ibn al-Ḥusayn al-Anṣārī.[124]

20. *ʿAbd al-Ṣamad ibn Aḥmad al-Maqbarī* (d. late 6th/12th century)
ʿAbd al-Ṣamad al-Maqbarī was a Ẓāhirī scholar who resided in Granada. He was known for his interest in theology and knowledge of Ḥadīth and jurisprudence.[125]

21. *Ibrāhīm ibn Khalaf ibn Manṣūr* (*fl.* 605/1208)
A scholar of Egyptian origin (from Sanhūr, in northern Egypt) who traveled widely, Ibrāhīm ibn Khalaf had a very bad reputation as a liar, charlatan, and drug user, although some Ḥadīth critics defended him. According to Ibn Ḥajar, he was Ẓāhirī and followed the teachings of Ibn Ḥazm.[126]

22. *ʿAbd Allāh ibn Sulaymān ibn Dāwūd* (d. 612/1215)
ʿAbd Allāh ibn Sulaymān was a judge in many cities in Andalus, including Cordoba, Seville, and Mersile. He was given to Ẓāhirism, studied with many prominent scholars, and was known for his vast and diverse knowledge.[127] Most of the works attributed to him are on Ḥadīth.

23. *Dāwūd ibn Abī al-Ghanāʾim* (d. 615/1218)
Dāwūd ibn Abī al-Ghanāʾim was a Baghdādī scholar who was known for following Dāwūd al-Ẓāhirī in jurisprudence, according to Ibn Ḥajar.[128]

24. *ʿAbd al-ʿAzīz ibn ʿAlī, Ibn Ṣāḥib al-Radd* (d. 621/1224)
Ibn Ṣāḥib al-Radd was a competent Ẓāhirī scholar from Seville. Al-Dhahabī mentions that he transmitted from him.[129]

---

123 Al-Ḍabbī, *Bughyat*, p. 263. See also Adang, "Ẓāhirīs," p. 422.
124 For this, see Adang, "Ẓāhirīs of Almohad times," p. 423.
125 Ibn al-Abbār, *Takmilah*, vol. 2, p. 646.
126 Ibn Ḥajar, *Lisān*, vol. 1, p. 151. Ibn Ḥajar obviously disliked Ibn Diḥyah and regarded him as a liar, whereas he defends Ibrāhīm whom he thought was unjustly humiliated by al-Kāmil (more about him below). Ibn Ḥajar explains that the opinion of people of the Maghrib on Ibn Diḥyah was different from the opinion of the Egyptians.
127 Ibn al-Zubayr, *Ṣilah*, vol. 3, p. 136; Ibn al-Khaṭīb, *Iḥāṭah*, vol. 3, p. 416; and al-Suyūṭī, *Bughyat al-Wuʿāh*, vol. 2, p. 44.
128 Ibn Ḥajar, *Lisān*, vol. 2, p. 492.
129 Al-Dhahabī, *Tārīkh*, vol. 45, p. 65. See also, Adang, "Ẓāhirīs," p. 443.

25. *Aḥmad ibn Yazīd ibn ʿAbd al-Raḥmān* (d. 625/1228)
A descendant of the famous traditionist Baqī ibn Makhlad (d. 276/889),[130] Aḥmad was an influential scholar and judge. He is reported to have inclined to Ẓāhirism.[131]

26. *ʿAlī ibn ʿAbd Allāh ibn Yūsuf, Ibn Khaṭṭāb al-Muʿāfirī* (d. 629/1231)
Known as a scholar who excelled in Ḥadīth and resided in Seville, Ibn Khaṭṭāb al-Muʿāfirī is reported to have had leanings toward Ẓāhirism.[132]

27. *Aḥmad ibn Muḥammad ibn ʿUmar* (d. *c.* 630/1232)
Al-Marrākushī reports that Aḥmad ibn Muḥammad was an Andalusian Ẓāhirī scholar who traveled eastwards, studied with several notable scholars, and returned to Andalus.[133]

28. *ʿUmar ibn al-Ḥasan, Abū al-Khaṭṭāb ibn Diḥyah* (d. 633/1235)
Abū al-Khaṭṭāb Ibn Diḥyah was a scholar of Ḥadīth who was active mainly in North Africa and Andalus. Reportedly born in Sabtah, Andalus, and perhaps worked as a judge there,[134] Ibn Ḥajar found his genealogy suspicious.[135] He was known to be Ẓāhirī, and one of his contemporaries also mentions that he used to speak ill of the "*imāms*."[136]

While in Egypt, Ibn Diḥyah was a mentor to al-Kāmil, who later became ruler of Egypt from 615/1218 to 635/1238. According to this report, Ibrāhīm ibn Khalaf, another Ẓāhirī, told Andalusian scholars that Ibn Diḥyah was an amateur traditionist with dubious genealogy. Ibn Diḥyah complained to al-Kāmil who then humiliated Ibrāhīm and expelled him from Egypt. Later on, his relationship with al-Kāmil deteriorated when it was brought to the latter's attention that Ibn Diḥyah used to confuse traditions.[137]

---

130 On Baqī ibn Makhlad's role in introducing Ḥadīth in al-Andalus, see Fierro, "Introduction," pp. 78–79.

131 Ibn al-Zubayr, *Ṣilah*, vol. 5, p. 348. See also, Adang, "Ẓāhirīs," pp. 444–448.

132 Ibn al-Abbār, *Takmilah*, vol. 2, p. 680; Ibn al-Zubayr, *Ṣilah*, vol. 4, p. 122.

133 Al-Marrākushī, *Dhayl*, vol. 1, pp. 476–477.

134 Ibn Ḥajar, *Lisān*, vol. 4, p. 340.

135 Diḥyah al-Kalbī was a Companion whom the Prophet is reported to have sent to the Byzantine Emperor. It is reported that the angel Gabriel used to assume Diḥyah's shape when he appeared before the Companions. Diḥyah died during the rule of the Umayyad Muʿāwiyah ibn Abī Sufyān (r. 41/661–60/680).

136 Ibn Ḥajar, *Lisān*, vol. 4, p. 336.

137 *Ibid.*, vol. 4, pp. 336 and 338.

29. *Ibrāhīm ibn Muḥammad ibn Yūsuf al-Anṣārī* (d. after 637/1239)
Ibrāhīm ibn Muḥammad was a Ẓāhirī scholar who used to lead the prayers in Seville.[138]

30. *ʿUmar ibn Aḥmad ibn ʿUmar ibn Mūsā* (d. 637/1239)
Al-Marrākushī reports that ʿUmar, who was also from Seville, was a Ẓāhirī scholar who evidently had interests in the Qur'ān and Ḥadīth.[139]

31. *Aḥmad ibn Muḥammad ibn al-Rūmiyyah, Abū al-ʿAbbās al-Nabātī* (d. 637/1239)
According to al-Dhahabī, Ibn al-Rūmiyyah began his career as a Mālikī scholar and then became a staunch "Ḥazmī Ẓāhirī."[140] He was a student of Ibrāhīm ibn Muḥammad al-Anṣārī and studied with Ḥadīth scholars in Spain, the Ḥijāz, Iraq, and Egypt. In addition to piety and uprightness, he was known for his religious knowledge (especially in Ḥadīth), and his vast knowledge of herbs (*aʿshāb*; hence his sobriquet, al-Nabātī).[141] Many works are attributed to Ibn al-Rūmiyyah in various genres of religious and scientific knowledge.[142]

32. *ʿUmar ibn Aḥmad ibn ʿUmar* (d. 637/1239)
A Ẓāhirī scholar from Seville, ʿUmar ibn Aḥmad was a student of Ibn Buryāl, Ibn Ḥazm's student, and a teacher of Ibn Sayyid al-Nās (see below). He was known for his knowledge of Ḥadīth.[143]

33. *Muḥammad ibn Aḥmad ibn ʿAbd Allāh, Ibn Sayyid al-Nās* (d. 659/1260)
A famous Andalusian scholar who received *ijāzah*s to transmit Ḥadīth compilations from scholars in various regions of the Muslim world, Ibn Sayyid al-Nās was known for his vast knowledge of Ḥadīth. Al-Dhahabī, who studied with him, mentions that he was Ẓāhirī, following the method of Abū al-ʿAbbās al-Nabātī (Ibn al-Rūmiyyah).[144] Al-Suyūṭī reports that he was the last great scholar of Ḥadīth in the Maghrib.[145]

138 Ibn al-Abbār, *Takmilah*, vol. 1, p. 159.
139 Cited in Adang, "Ẓāhirīs," p. 460. Ibn al-Zubayr mentions ʿUmar ibn Aḥmad but does not say anything about his Ẓāhirī affiliation (Ibn al-Zubayr, *Ṣilah*, p. 70).
140 Al-Maqqarī, *Nafḥ*, vol. 2, pp. 597–598.
141 Al-Dhahabī, *Tadhkirat*, vol. 4, p. 146.
142 For this, see al-Ghalbazūrī, *al-Madrasah al-Ẓāhiriyyah*, pp. 351–353.
143 Ibn al-Abbār, *Takmilah*, vol. 5, p. 440.
144 Al-Dhahabī, *Tadhkirat*, vol. 4, pp. 161–162.
145 Al-Suyūṭī, *Ṭabaqāt*, p. 534.

34. *Aḥmad ibn Muḥammad, Ibn Ṣābir al-Qaysī* (d. 666/1267)
Ibn Ṣābir al-Qaysī is reported to have begun his career as Ẓāhirī but later abandoned Ẓāhirism. He was also an accomplished Ḥadīth scholar who studied with many scholars in various regions, until he died in Egypt.[146]

35. *Aḥmad ibn Muḥammad ibn Mufarrij* (d. *c.* 666/1267)
Mentioned by Abū al-Ḥasan al-Ruʿaynī among his teachers, Ibn Mufarrij had interest in Ḥadīth and adhered to *ẓāhir*.[147]

36. *ʿAbd al-Muhaymin ibn Muḥammad al-Ashjaʿī* (d. 697/1297)
ʿAbd al-Muhaymin was a Ẓāhirī scholar and poet who used to defend Ibn Ḥazm and Ẓāhirism until his death in Fez.[148]

∴

In the 6th/12th and 7th/13th centuries, there existed thirty-six Ẓāhirī scholars, the majority of whom lived in various cities of Andalus (notably Seville). Others were active in North Africa and Egypt, with a few scholars in Syria and Iraq. Although the professions of most of these scholars are not reported (with the exception of two judges and a herbs seller), some of them were active participants in politics and in direct contact with rulers.

Remarkably, the vast majority of these scholars were known for their activity in Ḥadīth transmission. Two of them are referred to as "Dāwūdī," and one as "Dāwūdī Ẓāhirī." Many are described either as "Ḥazmī Ẓāhirī" (but never "Dāwūdī Ḥazmī"), or were students of either Ibn Ḥazm or one of his students. Furthermore, chains of Ẓāhirī scholars begin to emerge again in these two centuries. Ibn Ḥazm's knowledge was passed on to al-Ḥumaydī who passed it on to Ibn al-Murajjā. Ibn Sayyid al-Nās studied the *madhhab* with Ibn al-Rūmiyyah and with a student of one of Ibn Ḥazm's students, and taught it to Ibn Saʿd al-Anṣārī (more about him below) who then taught it to a certain Aḥmad al-Qaṣīr. These scholars were not confined to Andalus. Al-Ḥumaydī moved to Baghdad, probably after Ibn Ḥazm's death, and his student Ibn al-Murajjā traveled to Syria and Baghdad. ʿAmr ibn Marzūq, who studied with Ibn Ḥazm's student Ibn Buryāl, traveled to Egypt and Syria. Ibn al-Rūmiyyah traveled to Egypt,

---

146 Al-Marrākushī, *Dhayl*, vol. 1, part 2, pp. 437–439.
147 Al-Ruʿaynī, *Barnāmaj*, p. 142.
148 Ibn al-Khaṭīb, *Iḥāṭah*, vol. 4, pp. 18–20.

the Ḥijāz and Iraq.[149] In other words, Ibn Ḥazm's teachings reached the central and eastern parts of the Muslim world almost immediately after his death, and influence of his students continued to infiltrate these regions for some time after his death. Furthermore, it is only at this point that we can speak of a homogeneous group of Ẓāhirī scholars who had a similar profile as transmitters and scholars of Ḥadīth and shared a connection with a common teacher, whose books they copied and transmitted. Finally, cases of Ẓāhirīs hiding their true legal affiliation are reported, together with a report about a Ẓāhirī scholar giving *fatwā*s according to Dāwūd's *madhhab*.

4 Ẓāhirīs after the Seventh/Thirteenth Century

1. *Aḥmad ibn Muḥammad ibn Ḥazm* (d. before 703/1303)
Aḥmad ibn Muḥammad was a skillful scholar of language from Seville who is reported to have authored a book to defend Ibn Ḥazm against allegations made by Ibn al-ʿArabī.[150]

2. *Mufarrij ibn Saʿādah* (d. before 703/1303)
According to al-Marrākushī, Mufarrij ibn Saʿādah was a Ẓāhirī scholar of Ḥadīth.[151]

3. *Muḥammad ibn ʿAlī al-Bayāsī, Abū ʿAbd Allāh al-Gharnāṭī* (d. 703/1303)
Reportedly a scholar of Ḥadīth who adhered to the Ẓāhirī *madhhab*, Abū ʿAbd Allāh al-Gharnāṭī traveled eastwards to study Ḥadīth and died in Egypt.[152]

4. *Muḥammad ibn Muḥammad ibn Sahl* (d. 730/1329)
Known as al-Wazīr ibn Sahl, Muḥammad belonged to a famous family in Granada and traveled eastwards where he met with notable scholars in various places, including Damascus and Cairo. He was active in politics and known for his vast knowledge and social standing.[153]

149 For other possible chains of transmission of Ẓāhirī knowledge, see Adang, "Ẓāhirīs."
150 Al-Marrākushī, *Dhayl*, vol. 1, part 1, pp. 407–408.
151 *Ibid.*, vol. 7, p. 265.
152 Al-Maqqarī, *Nafḥ*, vol. 2, p. 59.
153 Ibn Ḥajar al-ʿAsqalānī, *al-Durar al-Kāminah fī Aʿyān al-Miʾah al-Thāminah*, vol. 4, pp. 296–297.

5. *ʿAbd al-Raḥīm ibn al-Ḥasan al-Tinmālī* (d. 741/1340)
Ibrāhīm ibn al-Ḥasan was a Ẓāhirī scholar who used to defend Ibn Ḥazm. He died in Malaga.[154]

6. *Muḥammad ibn Yūsuf ibn ʿAlī Abū Ḥayyān, Abū Ḥayyān al-Naḥwī* (d. 745/1344)
A famous scholar from Granada, Abū Ḥayyān al-Naḥwī studied with many scholars in Andalus, the Maghrib, and Egypt, where he contacted its rulers and became a teacher in several schools and mosques. He taught many students and authored many books on Qurʾān exegesis, Ḥadīth, language, history, and literature.[155] Al-Maqqarī mentions that he was Ẓāhirī but then abandoned Ẓāhirism for Shāfiʿism.[156]

7. *ʿAlī ibn Ibrāhīm ibn Saʿd al-Anṣārī* (d. 774/1372)
ʿAlī ibn Ibrāhīm was a staunch Ẓāhirī scholar who vigorously defended his *madhhab* and is reported to have copied most of Ibn Ḥazm's works. He was a student of Ibn Sayyid al-Nās and a teacher of a scholar named Aḥmad al-Qaṣīr, who studied the *madhhab* of the *Ahl al-Ẓāhir* with him.[157]

8. *Mūsā ibn Alfāfā* (d. 788/1386)
Mūsā ibn Alfāfā is reported to have been a partisan of the Ẓāhirīs (*kāna yataʿaṣṣabu la-hum*).[158]

9. *Muḥammad ibn Muqbil al-Turkī* (d. 796/1393)
According to Ibn Ḥajar, Muḥammad ibn Muqbil showed interest in legal matters from an early age and admired and supported the Ẓāhirī *madhhab*.[159]

---

154 Al-Ghalbazūrī, *al-Madrasah al-Ẓāhiriyyah*, p. 373. Al-Ghalbazūrī cites a book, edited by ʿAbd al-Salām Shaqqūr, with new entries from Ibn al-Khaṭīb's *Iḥāṭah* (reference is to pp. 233–234 in this book). I could not find this book.

155 For Ibn Ḥayyān's life and career, see al-Maqqarī, *Nafḥ*, vol. 2, pp. 535–584.

156 Al-Maqqarī, *Nafḥ*, vol. 2, p. 541. Ghalbazūrī argues that Abū Ḥayyān remained Ẓāhirī until his death (*al-Madrasah al-Ẓāhiriyyah*, pp. 411ff). For an especially interesting biographical account, see al-Ṣafadī's biography of Abū Ḥayyān (al-Ṣafadī, *Aʿyān al-ʿAṣr*, vol. 5, pp. 325–327). For Ibn Ḥayyān's Ẓāhirism, see Aḥmad Wadīʿ Ṭantāwī, "Shawāhid al-Madhhab al-Ẓāhirī fī al-Dars al-Naḥwī ʿinda Abī Ḥayyān."

157 Ibn Ḥajar al-ʿAsqalānī, *Inbāʾ al-Ghumr bi-Anbāʾ al-ʿUmr*, vol. 1, p. 45.

158 *Ibid.*, vol. 1, p. 330.

159 *Ibid.*, vol. 1, p. 484.

10. *Aḥmad ibn Ṭūghān ibn ʿAbd Allāh al-Shaykhūnī* (d. 808/1405)
Ibn Ḥajar reports that Aḥmad ibn Tūghān used to frequent the *Ahl al-Ẓāhir*.[160]

11. *Aḥmad ibn Muḥammad ibn Ismāʿīl, Ibn al-Burhān al-Ẓāhirī* (d. 808/1405)
Ibn al-Burhān al-Ẓāhirī is reported to have been Shāfiʿī until he met a Ẓāhirī who introduced him to Ibn Ḥazm's views, which he liked so much that he became Ẓāhirī himself. Later, he admired Ibn Taymiyyah, so much so that he came to believe that nobody knew more than Ibn Taymiyyah. Ibn Ḥajar, our source on Ibn al-Burhān, does not indicate his final affiliation, but continues to categorize him as Ẓāhirī and mentions that he was an authority on issues about which *Ẓāhirīs* disagreed with the majority of scholars.[161]

An active participant in politics, Ibn al-Burhān called for seeking a leader from the tribe of Quryash to rule the Muslim world. He argued that this duty was "what Islam demands, and nothing else is valid [as regards this issue]." As a result, together with his religiously-minded followers who abhorred the corruption of the time, he was flogged and jailed for three years. Ibn Ḥajar reports that Ibn al-Burhān was far-sighted, for he once warned Ibn Ḥajar against saving cash, predicting that money was going to lose its value. Shortly after his death, Ibn Ḥajar reports, inflation struck Egypt.[162]

12. *Muḥammad ibn Muḥammad ibn Yaʿqūb al-Jaʿbarī* (d. 810/1407)
A scholar with good reputation who leaned towards the Ẓāhirī *madhhab*, Muḥammad was appointed to several government posts in Syria, including the judiciary.[163]

13. *Muḥammad ibn Ibrāhīm ibn Aḥmad* (d. 832/1428)
Muḥammad ibn Ibrāhīm was a Sufi who worked as a hospital manager (*nāẓir al-māristān*), probably in Egypt. He reportedly admired the Ẓāhirī *madhhab*.[164]

---

160 Ibn Ḥajar al-ʿAsqalānī, *Inbāʾ al-Ghumr*, vol. 2, p. 331.

161 *Ibid.*, vol. 2, pp. 332–333.

162 *Ibid.*, pp. 333–334. For a discussion of Ibn al-Burhān's revolt, see Lutz Wiederhold, "Legal-Religious Elite, Temporal Authority, and the Caliphate in Mamluk Society: Conclusions Drawn from the Examination of a 'Ẓāhirī Revolt' in Damascus in 1386."

163 Ibn Ḥajar, *Inbāʾ al-Ghumr*, vol. 2, p. 393.

164 *Ibid.*, vol. 3, p. 428.

14. *Aḥmad ibn Ṣābir al-Qaysī* (lived before 898/1492)
Aḥmad ibn Ṣābir was a Ẓāhirī scholar who chose to leave Andalus to Egypt when the ruler tried to force him to pray according to the Mālikī *madhhab*. He remained in Egypt until his death.[165]

15. *Burhān al-Dīn ibn Abī Sharīf al-Maqdisī* (d. 923/1517)
Burhān al-Dīn was a Damascene scholar and Sufi with Ẓāhirī leanings.[166]

∴

From the 8th/14th to the 9th/15th centuries, there existed fifteen Ẓāhirī scholars. Andalus remained the stronghold of Ẓāhirism, although Ẓāhirī scholars, including Andalusians, were also active in North Africa and Egypt (and to a lesser extent, Syria). *All* these scholars were referred to as "Ẓāhirī" (and occasionally "Ẓāhirī Ḥazmī"), and the eponym "Dāwūdī" disappears completely. Many of those who were not so described were connected to Ibn Ḥazm through some of his students or took great interest in his views, so much so that they took it upon themselves to defend him.

The little that we know about these scholars indicates that they were public figures who had contacts with their respective rulers, causing them serious troubles at times. They continued the interest of previous generations of Ẓāhirīs in Ḥadīth transmission. Furthermore, many of these scholars are reported to have admired the Ẓāhirī *madhhab* or supported and frequented Ẓāhirī scholars. This rather ambiguous way of reporting their affiliation casts some doubt on their real legal affiliation, for they may have belonged to other *madhhab*s, especially the Shāfiʿī *madhhab* whose scholars, as has been noted earlier, seemed interested in promoting Dāwūd's image as one of al-Shāfiʿī's early followers.

Mention should be made here of the celebrated Sufi Ibn ʿArabī (d. 638/1240). Whereas he is reported to have been Ẓāhirī in legal matters, there is little evidence that he had a significant impact on the legal doctrine of the Ẓāhirī *madhhab*.[167] The same holds true for the Almohads. They are believed to have adopted Ẓāhirism as the official *madhhab* of their dynasty (which lasted from

---

165 Al-Maqqarī, *Nafḥ*, vol. 2, p. 655.

166 Cited in Michael Cook, *Commanding Right and Forbidding Wrong in Islamic Thought*, p. 355, n. 138. I owe this reference to Michael Cook.

167 For Ibn ʿArabī's Ẓāhirism, see al-Ghalbazūrī, *al-Madrasah al-Ẓāhiriyyah*, pp. 377ff, and Adang, "Ẓāhirism," pp. 461–464. This, of course, is not to downplay the importance of studying how Ibn ʿArabī's Ẓāhirism could have affected his views.

514/1120 to 667/1268), but what we actually know about that is rather scanty.[168] Finally, also based on truly scanty evidence, the great historian al-Maqrīzī (d. 845/1442) is similarly believed to have been a Ẓāhirī.[169]

This leaves us with Ibn Ḥazm, generally regarded as the doyen of the Ẓāhirī *madhhab* and the only Ẓāhirī scholar whose legal works have survived.

5 Ibn Ḥazm al-Andalusī (456/1064)

5.1 *Life and Doctrines*

So much has been written about Abū Muḥammad ʿAlī ibn Aḥmad ibn Saʿīd Ibn Ḥazm al-Andalusī (d. 456/1064) that we need only to mention a few brief facts about him. Ibn Ḥazm was born in Liebla in 384/994 to a father of Persian origin. He lived all his life in Andalus with only a few months in Kairouan (al-Qayrawān) in North Africa. He witnessed the fall of the Umayyad Caliphate in Spain—which he supported—in 422/1031 and the subsequent establishment of local dynasties in various parts of Andalus. His father was a *wazīr* of some Umayyad Caliphs, and he himself served the Umayyads as a *wazīr* until their fall from power. While this involvement in politics was a source of power and wealth for Ibn Ḥazm's family in the first part of his life, it later became a source of trouble and suffering for him. Accordingly, he decided to stay away

---

168 For the Ẓāhirism of Almohads, see Adang, "Ẓāhirism," pp. 429ff; Abd al-Bāqī al-Sayyid Abd al-Hādī, "*Al-Madhhab al-Ẓāhiri wa-Nash'atuhu wa-Taṭawwuruhu bi-l-Maghrib wa-l-Andalus ḥattā Nihāyat al-Muwaḥḥidīn.*" pp. 202–214; and Camilla Adang, "Ẓāhirīs," pp. 413–417, and 468. For the Ẓāhirism of Yaʿqūb ibn Yūsuf (d. 595/1199)—the third Almohad ruler—see Ibn al-Athīr, *al-Kāmil*, vol. 10, pp. 161–162, where Ibn Athīr mentions that the many Ẓāhirīs in Maghrib rose in prominence under Yaʿqūb and were known as "al-Jarmiyyah" (or "al-Kharmiyyah," according to another manuscript), after their head Muḥammad ibn Jarm (or Kharm). This is most likely a corruption: these people were probably known as al-Ḥazmiyyah, after Ibn Ḥazm. There is also some evidence that ʿAḍud al-Dawlah al-Buwayhī (d. 372/983) was "Dāwūdī" (for this, see al-Muqaddasī, *Aḥsan al-Taqāsīm*, p. 334), and we have noted that he appointed Bishr ibn al-Ḥusayn as his chief judge. It is also reported that Ẓāhirism was the official *madhhab* of *al-dawlah al-Bihāriyyah*, which ruled in Sind from 247/861 to 417/1026 (For this, see Ṣubḥī al-Maḥmaṣānī, *Falsafat al-Tashrīʿ fī al-Islām*, p. 72 (I owe this reference to Hossein Modarressi). Generally speaking, the available evidence about the status of the Ẓāhirī *madhhab* in these dynasties is too uncertain to allow for solid conclusions. Adang's study of Ẓāhirīs under Almohad rule, for instance, led her to conclude that "[w]e do not find a significantly greater number of Ẓāhirīs in the Almohad period than in the preceding, Almoravid period, when tolerance towards non-Mālikī systems was supposedly limited" (Adang, "Ẓāhirīs," p. 469).

169 For this, see al-Buḥṣalī, *Ṭabaqāt*, pp. 214–215.

from politics and focus entirely on scholarship. As a scholar, his stature and fame were known all over Andalus in his lifetime and he used to engage in debates with notable scholars of the day. He was seen by many scholars as a threat, not only to the Mālikī *madhhab* which was dominant in Andalus, but also to the entire known legal heritage. This fear was motivated by the fact that Ibn Ḥazm was both prolific—writing about numerous genres of religious and non-religious subjects[170]—and skillful in argumentation and disputation. His criticism of other scholars, and more importantly the eponymous founders of other *madhhab*s, was so bitter such that his tongue was compared to the sword of al-Ḥajjāj ibn Yūsuf (d. 95/714), the famous general and governor who restored the Umayyad rule over Iraq and the Ḥijāz in 72/691 and 73/692 by unrelenting brutality and force. Andalusians were thus divided on Ibn Ḥazm: the majority regarded him as a deviant scholar with pernicious teachings, whereas others admired him so much that they believed that he tipped the balance to Andalus (rather than Iraq) as the most prominent center of knowledge in the Muslim world.[171]

Ibn Ḥazm began his life as a Shāfiʿī scholar before converting to Ẓāhirism, which he spent the rest of his life defending and spreading.[172] While Ibn Ḥazm's biographies do not indicate when this conversion took place, it must have been early enough in his life to allow him the time to write those extensive works in which he presented his Ẓāhirī views. As for his legal affiliation,

170 For a list of Ibn Ḥazm's works, see al-Dhahabī, *Siyar*, vol. 18, pp. 193–196. For a chronology of some of these works, see Ljami, *Ibn Ḥazm et la Polémique Islamo-Chrétienne dans L'Histoire de L'Islam*, pp. 43–79.

171 For an 11th/17th-century biography of Ibn Ḥazm, see al-Maqqarī, *Nafḥ*, vol. 2, pp. 77–85. For an overview of Ibn Ḥazm's time, life and works, see Saʿīd al-Afghānī, *Ibn Ḥazm al-Andalusī*, pp. 4–150. Interestingly, the only book of Ibn Ḥazm that Ibn Khayr al-Ishbīlī studied was *Risālah fī Faḍl al-Andalus*, a work that obviously does not tackle any religious issue (Ibn Khayr, *Fahrasah*, p. 194). Al-Ishbīlī also studied works by Ibn Ḥazm's student al-Ḥumaydī: *Jadhwat al-Muqtabis* (on history) and *al-Jamʿ bayna al-Ṣaḥīḥayn* (on Ḥadīth) (*ibid.*, pp. 101 and 195 respectively). Other Ẓāhirī works that Ibn Khayr mentions are not strictly legal in nature, such as *Kitāb al-Ḍuʿafāʾ wa-l-Mansūbīn ilā al-Bidʿah min al-Muḥaddithīn* and *Kitāb al-ʿIlal* (on traditions) by the Ẓāhirī scholar Zakariyyā ibn Yaḥyā al-Sājī (*ibid.*, p. 178) as well as a number of works by Nifṭawayh (*ibid.*, pp. 331, 335, and 366) and one of al-Ḥumaydī's works on Ḥadīth (*ibid.*, p. 101). Similarly, he mentions a number of works by the Ẓāhirī scholar Saʿīd ibn al-Aʿrābī, all of which apparently deal with asceticism and divine love (*ibid.*, p. 251). The chains of transmission of these works do not seem to contain any Ẓāhirī names. For a detailed exposition of Ibn Ḥazm's debates with his contemporaries and anti-Ẓāhirī polemics before and after him, see Samīr Qaddūrī, "Al-Rudūd ʿalā Ibn Ḥazm bi-l-Andalus wa-l-Maghrib min khilāl Mu'allafāt ʿUlamāʾ al-Mālikiyyah."

172 For this, see, al-Maqqarī, *Nafḥ*, vol. 2, p. 78.

Ibn Ḥazm was explicit about his admiration for and affiliation with Ẓāhirism. He speaks about the *aṣḥāb al-ẓāhir* as our fellow Ẓāhirīs (*aṣḥābunā*),[173] and praises their being the ones who followed God's words, refrained from asking Him about what did not concern them, and declared licit or illicit only what He had so declared.[174] Significantly, he seems to have held Dāwūd al-Ẓāhirī in particularly high esteem. He lists Dāwūd among the early independent masters of Islamic law,[175] and maintains that he could not have been more knowledgeable in the sources of the law and legal disagreements, more prolific in his Ḥadīth transmission, or sharper in his intellect.[176] In his *Risālah al-Bāhirah*, he goes so far as to argue that thanks to his adherence to the Sunnah and consensus, refraining from using his *ra'y*, and insistence on remaining independent, Dāwūd was more worthy of the title of jurist (*faqīh*) than the eponymous founders of the other *madhhab*s.[177] Whereas he does not refrain from criticizing other Ẓāhirī scholars, aggressively at times, Ibn Ḥazm, to my knowledge, does not disagree with Dāwūd's views on theoretical legal views of the *uṣūl al-fiqh* and only disagrees with him, quite respectfully, on substantive views.

When disagreeing with Dāwūd on *furū'*,[178] Ibn Ḥazm either keeps silent or appears keen to not allow this to be a ground for questioning Dāwūd's knowledge as he would readily do with other scholars.[179] When it happened that Ibn

173 See, for instance, Ibn Ḥazm, *Iḥkām*, vol. 8, p. 40, and vol. 12, p. 250, where he refers to the Ẓāhirīs as *aṣḥābunā al-Ẓāhiriyyūn*.

174 Ibn Ḥazm, *Iḥkām*, vol. 2, pp. 1146–1147.

175 *Ibid.*, vol. 2, p. 850. Remarkably, Ibn Ḥazm seems to have also held Abū Thawr in high esteem, praising his scholarly independence and excellence in religious knowledge (*ibid.*, vol. 2, p. 674).

176 *Ibid.*, vol. 2, p. 840.

177 Ibn Ḥazm, *Risālah al-Bāhirah*, p. 47.

178 Ibn Ḥazm did disagree with Dāwūd on many issues and said that he erred in many of his *fatwā*s (*ibid.*, pp. 49–50).

179 To demonstrate that Ibn Ḥazm was a truly independent scholar (*mujtahid muṭlaq*) who regarded Ẓāhirism a methodology rather than a school of law, Ibrāhīm Muḥammad 'Abd al-Raḥīm (a contemporary Egyptian scholar) mentions a long list of theoretical and substantive legal views in which Ibn Ḥazm contradicted Dāwūd and other Ẓāhirīs. In most of the theoretical issues that he mentions, Ibn Ḥazm rejects views held by earlier Ẓāhirīs other than Dāwūd, with whom he disagrees on only one issue related to consensus and politely wonders how he could have held it (*wa-mā nadrī kayfa waqa'a li-Abī Sulaymān hādhā 'l-wahm al-ẓāhir*) (Ibrāhīm Muḥammad 'Abd al-Raḥīm, *al-Fikr al-Fiqhī li-Ibn Ḥazm al-Ẓāhirī*, pp. 538–548). (For Ibn Ḥazm's discussion of this issue, see *al-Muḥallā*, vol. 1, p. 577.) Furthermore, when he disagrees with Dāwūd on minor substantial issues, Ibn Ḥazm may refrain from commenting on Dāwūd's view or mention a textual basis on which he could have relied on (for an example of the former case, see Ibn Ḥazm, *al-Muḥallā*,

Ḥazm mentioned a view about which earlier Ẓāhirīs had disagreed while his own view agreed with Dāwūd's, he would highlight that the other view was not the one held by Abū Sulaymān, Dāwūd's *kunyah*.[180] When attributing a view to earlier Ẓāhirīs, he would mention Dāwūd by name if he knows that Dāwūd held it.[181] In brief, not only did Ibn Ḥazm regard Dāwūd as the master of the Ẓāhirī *madhhab*, but he also believed himself to be connected to him through Andalusian scholars who had studied with Dāwūd himself. As a result, Ibn Ḥazm was keen to connect Andalusian Ẓāhirīs to Dāwūd himself. In his epistle on the merits of Andalus and its scholars[182]—where he seeks to show how Andalusian scholars in various fields of knowledge matched or even excelled their counterparts in the east—he compares ʿAbd Allāh ibn Qāsim ibn Hilāl and Mundhir ibn Saʿīd al-Ballūṭī to ʿAbd Allāh ibn al-Mughallis, al-Khallāl, al-Dībājī,[183] and Ruwaym ibn Aḥmad. He adds that unlike these Ẓāhirīs from Iraq, Ibn Hilāl studied with Dāwūd himself.[184] All these points indicate that Ẓāhirism, from the point of view of its most prolific and notable representative, was built on Dāwūd's legal thought. Indeed, the basic core of Ẓāhirism as it was understood by Ibn Ḥazm (as presented below) seems to have been laid down by Dāwūd, except that the textual body it dealt with (particularly Ḥadīth) expanded significantly in the next few generation after his death until it reached its peak at the time of Ibn Ḥazm.

It has been noted earlier that Dāwūd's views found their way to Andalus soon after his death, and that a number of "Dāwūdī" scholars continued to travel between Andalus and other regions of the Muslim world until Ibn Ḥazm's time. Ibn ʿAbd al-Barr apparently had at his disposal legal works by Ẓāhirī scholars in which Dāwūd's views of as well as agreements and disagreements among Ẓāhirīs were reported. It is very likely, then, that Ibn Ḥazm had first-hand access to Dāwūd's views, either through teachers or through legal

---

vol. 1, p. 170, and of the latter, see *ibid.*, vol. 1, pp. 190 and 213). Ibn Ḥazm does not seem to care to be as polite with other Ẓāhirī scholars. But generally speaking, his criticism of other scholars is notably less harsh when he discusses substantive rather than theoretical legal issues.

180 See, for example, Ibn Ḥazm, *Iḥkām*, vol. 8, p. 546. Ibn Ḥazm at times refers to Dāwūd by his name, but more often by his patronymic (*kunyah*), especially where he refers to Dāwūd's views that support his. Reference to someone by his *kunyah* usually indicates respect and closeness.

181 See, for instance, Ibn Ḥazm, *al-Muḥallā*, vol. 8, p. 546, and vol. 12, p. 391.

182 *Risālah fī Faḍāʾil al-Andalus wa-Dhikr Rijālihā.*

183 I could not find information about al-Dībājī in any biographical dictionary.

184 Ibn Ḥazm, *Rasāʾil*, vol. 2, p. 187.

works by Dāwūd and his students.[185] In fact, Ibn Ḥazm seems to have been very familiar with matters of consensus and disagreement among earlier Ẓāhirīs, and he does point out when only some of them held a particular view.[186] What, then, are the views that Ibn Ḥazm believed all Ẓāhirīs shared? In other words, what, in his view, did it mean to be Ẓāhirī? The following is a presentation of what Ibn Ḥazm thought all Ẓāhirīs agreed upon on the basis of his seminal work on *uṣūl al-fiqh, al-Iḥkām fī Uṣūl al-Aḥkām*.[187]

According to Ibn Ḥazm, all Ẓāhirīs agreed on the supremacy of legal texts as the only sound basis of legal rulings.[188] They all agreed that every term is to be interpreted in its widest possible extent unless it is particularized by a valid indicator (*dalīl*).[189] In other words, a term is always assumed to be unrestricted (*ʿāmm*) unless a valid piece of evidence indicates otherwise. They took commands and interdictions (*al-awāmir wa-l-nawāhī*) to indicate absolute obligation (*wujūb*) unless a valid indicator suggests otherwise.[190] They agreed that the actions of the Prophet (*al-sunnah al-ʿamaliyyah*) do not in themselves establish obligation;[191] only a Prophetic statement could establish obligation or qualify a Qurʾānic injunction.

Additionally, Ibn Ḥazm states that all Ẓāhirīs held that every statement tells us only what it says and does not indicate anything beyond this.[192] It may be for this reason that all Ẓāhirīs agreed on the rejection of *argumentum a contrario*, which Ibn Ḥazm takes to be the opposite of *qiyās*.[193] In his view, if this principle is taken to its logical conclusion, "Zayd has died" would mean that everybody other than Zayd has not.[194] It may also be for the same reason that all Ẓāhirīs

185 Among Ibn Ḥazm's works that al-Dhahabī lists in his *Siyar* (vol. 18, p. 194) is *Mukhtaṣar al-Mūḍaḥ*, an abridgement of Ibn al-Mughallis' *Mūḍaḥ*, as al-Dhahabī points out. Ibn Ḥazm also attributes a view to Muḥammad ibn Dāwūd from the latter's *Uṣūl*, and he may well be quoting it from this work (for this, see Ibn Ḥazm, *al-Muḥallā*, vol. 1, p. 167).

186 See, for example, Ibn Ḥazm, *Iḥkām*, vol. 8, p. 130.

187 Abdel-Magid Turki dates *Iḥkām* to the year 430/1038, at least fifteen years after Ibn Ḥazm had devoted his life to religious studies (ʿAbd al-Magid Turki, "Notes sur l'évolution du zâhirisme d'Ibn Ḥazm (456/1063) du *Taqrîb* à l'*Iḥkâm*" pp. 183, and 185).

188 Ibn Ḥazm, *Iḥkām*, vol. 2, p. 931.

189 *Ibid.*, vol. 1, pp. 338–339.

190 *Ibid.*, vol. 1, p. 259.

191 *Ibid.*, vol. 1, p. 422.

192 *Ibid.*, vol. 2, p. 887.

193 In *dalīl al-khiṭāb* (*argumentum a contrario*), instead of ruling on a new case on the basis of a resemblance to an existing one (which *qiyās* does), the opposite ruling of an established case is given in the new case on the basis of a difference noted between the two cases.

194 *Ibid.*, vol. 2, p. 921.

rejected *qiyās* as well as the notion of *ʿillah* on which it is based.[195] Ibn Ḥazm mentions that some scholars affiliated with Ẓāhirism did think that when God or the Prophet informs us of the rationale or cause of a certain ruling, we can use it as a basis for *qiyās*. This, he asserts, was not Dāwūd's view or the view of any other Ẓāhirī scholar, but was the position of people who did not in fact belong to the Ẓāhirīs, such as al-Qāsānī and his likes.[196] Furthermore, Ẓāhirīs were independent scholars who were farthest from the uncritical acceptance of other scholars' views (*taqlīd*). Those among them who were not independent did not belong to Ẓāhirīs and were more blameworthy than scholars of other *madhhabs*.[197] Ibn Ḥazm stresses the centrality of independence and the rejection of *taqlīd* to the extent that he excuses the eponyms of other *madhhabs* and many early scholars with whom he disagreed on the basis of their independent exercise of *ijtihād*. Devoting a chapter in his *Iḥkām* to refuting the notion of *taqlīd*, he argues that it was introduced after the age of these eponyms by lazy students who could not exercise *ijtihād* themselves.[198]

Ibn Ḥazm discusses some other doctrines of earlier Ẓāhirīs without attributing them to all of them. For example, Dāwūd and many Ẓāhirī scholars held that valid consensus was that of the Companions only, for it was the Companions who witnessed what the Prophet said and did, and consensus is only valid when it reflects this.[199] Some Ẓāhirīs held that if consensus contradicted a sound tradition transmitted by one or a few transmitters, this indicates that the tradition has been abrogated, a view that Ibn Ḥazm rejects.[200] He also reports that some Ẓāhirī scholars held that a rule cannot be abrogated by a

---

195 Ibn Ḥazm, *Iḥkām*, vol. 2, p. 1110. In fact, Ibn Ḥazm rejects *ʿillah* also as a basis of studying the etymology of words on the basis of derivation (*ishtiqāq*), as in the view that horses are called *khayl* because of their *khuyalāʾ* (pride), or that al-Raḥmān is a divine name derived from *raḥmah* (compassion and mercy) (*ibid.*, vol. 2, pp. 1123 and 1148). Further on the issue of *qiyās*, Vishanoff has noted a relationship between Roger Arnaldez's (in his *Grammaire et théologie chez Ibn Ḥazm de Cordoue*) characterization of Ibn Ḥazm's linguistic theory as "nominalism" and the Ẓāhirī rejection of *qiyās* (Vishanoff, *The Formation*, p. 88). According to this, if words and names refer to particular things rather than any qualities that they share with other things, then analogy cannot be drawn between things. Vishanoff, however, demonstrates that Ibn Ḥazm did recognize the presence of universals (*kulliyyāt*) and cannot therefore be considered a nominalist (*ibid.*, p. 91). In other words, Ibn Ḥazm rejected *qiyās* on grounds other than being a nominalist.

196 Ibn Ḥazm, *Iḥkām*, vol. 2, p. 1110.

197 *Ibid.*, vol. 1, pp. 233–234.

198 *Ibid.*, vol. 1, p. 539.

199 *Ibid.*, vol. 1, p. 509.

200 *Ibid.*, vol. 1, p. 193.

stricter one,[201] and that their majority held that if two traditions irreconcilably contradicted each other, both traditions fall together and we proceed on the basis that no traditions on the question at hand exist, a view that Ibn Ḥazm also rejects.[202]

These are the views that Ibn Ḥazm attributed to earlier Ẓāhirī scholars. He notes disagreements and indicates the views that he supports, at times refusing to acknowledge that scholars who held other views were Ẓāhirīs in the first place. This is the case with the issues of *taqlīd* and *qiyās*, both of which are to be categorically rejected by any scholar to qualify as Ẓāhirī, Ibn Ḥazm seems to have thought. He also mentions that there are areas of agreement among Ẓāhirīs. Remarkably, almost all of these views have to do with hermeneutics, and we know that Dāwūd himself had an interest in them from the reported titles of his words. Adhering to what a text "says" seems to be the pillar of the *madhhab* here, and this adherence requires that conclusions are not drawn about anything a legal statement does not explicitly refer to (which leads to the rejection of both *qiyās* and *dalīl al-khiṭāb*), that terms are to be construed according to their broadest possible range of potential referents, and that commands and prohibitions are to be taken to indicate absolute and unrestricted obligation.

5.2 *The Ibn Ḥazm Influence: A Mixed Blessing?*

Despite the fact that Ibn Ḥazm does not seem to have introduced new ideas into the Ẓāhirī *madhhab*, the picture of the *madhhab* before and after him is not the same. Unlike earlier eastern and Andalusian Ẓāhirīs who seem to have been interested in the Qur'ān, its exegesis and rulings, Ibn Ḥazm's students and later followers were evidently interested in Ḥadīth study. This was a major shift in the attitude of Ẓāhirī scholars, and it may be because of this that Ẓāhirism came to be regarded as a radical offshoot of the *Ahl al-Ḥadīth* movement (as discussed in CHAPTER THREE). This interest in Ḥadīth was an influence of the milieu in Andalus at that time, and we have seen that some Ẓāhirīs before and during the time of Ibn Ḥazm were already seriously interested in Ḥadīth transmission (such as Dāwūd ibn Ibrāhīm and Jābir ibn Ghālib). However, the role that Ibn Ḥazm has granted to Ḥadīth in his legal theory must have played a significant role in this respect, for Ibn Ḥazm, like the *Ahl al-Ḥadīth*, treated both the Qur'ān and Ḥadīth as authoritatively equal textual sources and accepted the entire body of Ḥadīth literature that was available in his time (which does

201 Ibn Ḥazm, *Iḥkām*, vol. 1, p. 466.

202 *Ibid.*, vol. 1, pp. 166 and 379.

not mean that he did not reject individual traditions).[203] This understanding of the status of Ḥadīth as a textual source seems to have been established in the Ẓāhirī *madhhab* once and for all after Ibn Ḥazm.

Additionally, Ibn Ḥazm provided Ẓāhirī scholars, probably for the first time, with an extensive and *coherent* legal literature, one which they took great interest in preserving and transmitting.[204] Although he mentions earlier disagreements among Ẓāhirīs, he was able to make a coherent theory out of them and reject views that did not fit in it. More importantly, he took much interest in *authenticating* his legal theoretical views by attributing them to the founder of the *madhhab* himself. In fact, Ibn Ḥazm's evident interest in connecting himself to Dāwūd and presenting his views as the authentic Ẓāhirī views that Dāwūd himself had held must have confirmed Dāwūd's status as an exceptional authority whose legal theoretical (but not substantive) views must not be dealt with in the same way that views of other Ẓāhirīs were dealt with. (This notwithstanding, Ẓāhirīs after Ibn Ḥazm were now known for their affiliation with a certain doctrine, Ẓāhirism, rather than with a certain scholar, Dāwūd—as used to be the case earlier—or even Ibn Ḥazm himself.) After Ibn Ḥazm, whose teachings reached the central parts of the Muslim world very quickly, there does not exist any reference to disagreement among Ẓāhirī scholars, for whom his views—which he had linked to Dāwūd and which do not contradict any theoretical views attributed to him in medieval sources—seem to have been regarded as authoritative and final. Ironically, it was after Ibn Ḥazm that rejection of *taqlīd* seems to have been established as the hallmark of Ẓāhirism, just as the rejection of *qiyās* was before him.

---

203 Vishanoff has reached the same conclusion regarding Ibn Ḥazm's role in establishing Ḥadīth as a primary source of law and legal evidence (Vishanoff, *The Formation*, p. 100). However, his statement that Ibn Ḥazm sought to reconcile conflicting texts is problematic. As will be discussed later, Ibn Ḥazm seems to have been more willing than "mainstream" scholars to reject pieces of evidence (notably Prophetic traditions) that could not be easily reconciled with what they identify as the valid evidence in each case. Since he believed that there must exist only one valid piece of evidence in each case, it was difficult for him to reconcile conflicting ones. Therefore, if one piece of evidence did not seem to fit with others, he did not hesitate to question its authenticity or relevance and dismiss it. It was Ḥanbalīs, however, who accepted and sought to reconcile all available pieces of evidence no matter how contradictory they might be.

204 I assume here that if any earlier Ẓāhirī scholar, including Dāwūd, had left behind an extensive legal literature, at least part of it would have survived. In all circumstances, what we know about the works attributed to other Ẓāhirīs does not indicate that any of them was as prolific as was Ibn Ḥazm.

Consequently, the absence of any writings of Ẓāhirīs before Ibn Ḥazm, and his apparent possession of some of Dāwūd's writings and keenness to distinguish Dāwūd's views from views of other Ẓāhirī scholars indicate that while we have no option but to rely on his writings for the study of Ẓāhirism, we can assume that they contain the views of the founder of the *madhhab* as well as the views that ultimately survived as genuinely Ẓāhirī thanks to his prolific and profound scholarship.

Despite the boost that Ibn Ḥazm gave to the *madhhab*, Ẓāhirism appears to have remained a private choice, with no trace of any attempt to institutionalize the transmission of its doctrines. Remarkably, only a few Ẓāhirī fathers and sons or two Ẓāhirī brothers are reported in medieval sources. There does not seem to have been entire families following the Ẓāhirī *madhhab*, as was the case with other *madhhab*s. A natural result of this lack of institutionalization was the gradual decrease in both the quantity and quality of Ẓāhirī scholars. Our survey of Ẓāhirīs after the 5th/11th century does demonstrate the gradual decrease of Ẓāhirīs and their fixation, not on defending the *madhhab* itself, but on defending Ibn Ḥazm. So what does this mean in terms of his influence on the *madhhab*?

Indeed, the changing picture of the Ẓāhirī *madhhab* before and after Ibn Ḥazm may indicate something deeper about his role in the history of the *madhhab*. His accomplishments probably contributed to the failure of Ẓāhirism in various ways. One of these ways was his unconditional conviction of the soundness of his methodology and rulings, and the massive literature that he produced.[205] This is not a reinstatement of the view that Ibn Ḥazm's uncompromising and offensive character—which brought on him the ire and hatred of scholars of his time and afterwards—was behind the failure of his *madhhab*. It is an argument about the effect of Ibn Ḥazm's achievements on the development of Ẓāhirī *madhhab* and how this may be among the reasons for its ultimate demise.

---

205 ʿAbd al-Raḥīm argues that Ibn Ḥazm's legal thought must be understood in light of the political environment in which he lived in Andalus. Witnessing the fall of the Umayyad Caliphate and the emerging states which divided the Muslim community, Ibn Ḥazm thought that uniting Muslims in legal and religious matters was a prerequisite for reuniting them politically. To do this, he shunned all legal views and insisted that the authoritative texts should be the sole basis of any legal issue. If a relevant text is lacking, that legal issue is considered outside the purview of the religious law. In this view, Ibn Ḥazm's polemics against the Jews and Christians was meant, among other things, to show how religious divisions lead to sectarian strife and political division and weakness (ʿAbd al-Raḥīm, *al-Fikr al-Fiqhī*, pp. 537–538).

Adam Sabra has argued that Ibn Ḥazm was against the *madhhab*s because he sought to "assert the individual responsibility of each Muslim to obey God's law as it is clearly revealed in the sacred texts of Islam." Whether Ibn Ḥazm regarded Ẓāhirism as a legal school or was consciously attempting to make it such is difficult to say, although it is worth noting that, to the best of my knowledge, he never speaks of *al-madhhab al-Ẓāhirī* (but rather of the *Ahl* or the *Aṣḥāb al-Ẓāhir*).[206] Two things are certain, however. First, Ibn Ḥazm's character and writings, if anything, only assert his own individuality and scholarly independence as jurist. He was intolerant of disagreement and always questioned the knowledge and integrity of scholars who disagreed with him, including early scholars who had been revered by his time (such as Mālik and Abū Ḥanīfah), which must have been responsible for a great deal of the antagonism that other *madhhab*s had toward Ẓāhirism to the point of discussing whether their views should count in consensus or not.[207] Presenting one's legal findings as absolutely certain and not allowing a minimum degree of disagreement is, arguably, tantamount to claiming possession of an esoteric kind of knowledge. It is difficult to imagine how this attitude could lead to the assertion of each Muslim's individual responsibility to discern and obey God's law.[208]

---

206 ʿAbd al-Raḥīm argues that Ibn Ḥazm and the Ẓāhirīs in general never regarded themselves as belonging to a certain *madhhab*, but rather as *mujtahid*s who only had in common their commitment to a certain methodology (ʿAbd al-Raḥīm, *al-Fikr al-Fiqhī*, p. 545). A similar conclusion was reached by al-Ghalbazūrī, who argues that Ẓāhirism is about *ijtihād* and the rejection of *taqlīd* more than being a legal school (al-Ghalbazūrī, *al-Madrasah al-Ẓāhiriyyah*, p. 338).

207 Many scholars actually held that in cases where all scholars agreed but only Ẓāhirīs dissented, consensus remains valid nonetheless. For a presentation of these views, see, for instance, al-Zarkashī, *al-Baḥr al-Muḥīṭ*, vol. 3, pp. 472–474. Al-Zarkashī himself seems to be among the scholars who did not give much weight to Ẓāhirī disagreement apropos the validity of consensus (*ibid.*, vol. 6, p. 291).

208 It is therefore difficult to accept Vishanoff's statements regarding what he considers "major concessions" that Ibn Ḥazm made to and his "dramatic shift" toward mainstream Sunnī legal paradigm (Vishanoff, *The Formation*, pp. 104–105), even if this only applies to one of the four hermeneutical levels that Vishanoff discusses. It will be noted later that Ẓāhirism only sought to be consistent in applying rules most of which they shared with at least one other *madhhab*. More often than not, therefore, Ibn Ḥazm emphasized the contradictions of the other *madhhab*s in order to demonstrate that they were not faithful to their professed views, which Ẓāhirism shared with them to begin with.

Secondly and more importantly, the reception of Ibn Ḥazm's legal heritage by later Ẓāhirī scholars was definitely going to establish Ẓāhirism as a legal school. This, precisely, may have been the beginning of the failure of the *madhhab*. Once a legal school is established, *ijtihād* is restricted and *taqlīd* sooner or later becomes the norm. This seems to have happened in the case of the Ẓāhirī *madhhab*. It has been noted that after Ibn Ḥazm, Ẓāhirīs took more interest in defending him than in defending Ẓāhirism itself. It is indeed ironic that although rejection of *taqlīd* seems to have been the hallmark of Ẓāhirism after Ibn Ḥazm (as evident in the fact that rejection of *taqlīd* was taken to indicate affiliation with Ẓāhirism),[209] this rejection seems to have been restricted to following the other *madhhab*s, not the *madhhab* to which Ẓāhirīs who rejected *taqlīd* belonged. We do not, of course, have positive evidence to support this point, but, to the best of my knowledge, no disagreements among Ẓāhirīs after Ibn Ḥazm are ever reported. The Almohads themselves are said to have tried to force Ẓāhirī views on the scholars of the time without enough preparation of their methodology of deducing legal rules from the authoritative texts.[210]

Ibn Ḥazm's accomplishments, in other words, froze Ẓāhirism.[211] If he managed to do without legal analogy and notions like *istiḥsān* and *maṣlaḥah*, he was able to do so because he was a true *mujtahid* who was able to produce what he took to be relevant and decisive textual evidence in each legal question. His followers, however, were definitely less ingenious and more dependent on him than he on earlier Ẓāhirī scholars. It is unlikely, therefore, that they would have succeeded as jurists while remaining true to their *madhhab*. Arguing that there is an inherent inconsistency between the rejection of *taqlīd* and the notion of a school of law, de Bellefonds writes: "Du moment que chaque auteur Ẓāhirīte n'est pas lié par l'enseignement de ses prédécesseurs, it serait préférable de parler d'enseignement Ẓāhirīte ou de mêthode Ẓāhirīte, et d'éviter l'expression d'Ecole Ẓāhirīte."[212] The view that Ibn Ḥazm's doctrine would rid Islam of "tout

---

209 In his Forward to ʿAbd al-Raḥmān ibn ʿAqīl's *Ibn Ḥazm khilāl Alf ʿĀmm*, p. 8, Iḥsān ʿAbbās argues that "at its core, Ẓāhirism is a revolt against *taqlīd*." ʿAbd al-Raḥmān ibn ʿAqīl is a contemporary Saudi Ẓāhirī scholar who is the most prominent among contemporary Ẓāhirīs.

210 Al-Ghalbazūrī, *al-Madrasah al-Ẓāhiriyyah*, pp. 729–30.

211 A similar conclusion was reached by Y. Linant de Bellefonds in "Ibn Ḥazm et le Ẓāhirisme juridique."

212 De Bellefonds, "Ibn Ḥazm," p. 7.

instrument d'adaptation et toute possibilité d'évolution,"[213] therefore, seems accurate, even if only because later Ẓāhirī scholars "followed" him.

213 Cited in Sabra, "Ibn Ḥazm," p. 9. Admittedly, Sabra does not reject Arnaldez's view categorically, but rather seeks to qualify it by asserting that since Islamic law in Ibn Ḥazm's view is "finite in scope," what it covers in his understanding was much less than what it covers for other jurists. It has been noted, however, that Ibn Ḥazm does allow a degree of doubt in his jurisprudence. His certainty is conditional on the assumption that he had all the relevant evidence on a given case. What is beyond the scope of the law (i.e., what the sources do not seem to be tackling) according to the evidence available to him could easily come under its purview should additional textual evidence—a Prophetic tradition, for instance—be brought to his attention, which always remains a theoretical possibility.

PART 2

Ẓāhirism: A Critical Review

CHAPTER 3

Jurisprudence in Third/Ninth-Century Baghdad

It has been noted that what we know about Dāwūd al-Ẓāhirī indicates that he was closer in profile to scholars like Abū Thawr al-Kalbī and Ḥusayn al-Karābīsī, and that he did not maintain good relationships with prominent traditionists of his time, notably Aḥmad ibn Ḥanbal. In 3rd/9th-century Baghdad there existed two main legal trends, the *Ahl al-Raʾy* and the *Ahl al-Ḥadīth*.[1] Building on biographical information about him, this chapter discusses these two legal trends in order to examine the extent to which what we know about Dāwūd's juridical thought is consistent with what the biographical evidence suggests, that is, that if he belonged to either of these two trends, he must have belonged to the *Ahl al-Raʾy* and not to the *Ahl al-Ḥadīth* as has been generally assumed.

1 The *Ahl al-Raʾy* and the *Ahl al-Ḥadīth*

Notable among the scholarly trends in 3rd/9th-century Baghdad, medieval Muslim sources report, are two, the *Ahl al-Raʾy* and the *Ahl al-Ḥadīth*.[2] Scholars, particularly jurists, belonged to either of these two trends that had many significant disagreements on their understanding of the law. Modern

1 The 3rd/9th century is generally considered key to understanding the development of Islamic law. For most modern Muslim scholars, it witnessed the crystallization of the main doctrines and methodologies of the existing schools of law. For this, see, for instance, ʿAlī al-Khafīf, *Muḥāḍarāt fī Asbāb Ikhtilāf al-Fuqahāʾ*, pp. 269–284, where the author argues that the basics of the four Sunnī schools of law go back to their eponymous founders and their immediate students in the late 2nd century AH (the Ḥanafī and Mālikī schools), or the 3rd century AH (the Shāfiʿī and Ḥanbalī schools). (Al-Khafīf notes that Abū Bakr al-Khallāl (d. 311/923) was to Aḥmad what Muḥammad ibn al-Ḥasan al-Shaybānī was to Abū Ḥanīfah and al-Rabīʿ ibn Sulaymān al-Murādī to al-Shāfiʿī (p. 280), meaning that whereas the Ḥanafī and Shāfiʿī schools took shape in the 3rd century AH, the Ḥanbalī school did that in the 4th century.) See also Muḥammad ibn al-Ḥasan al-Fāsī, *al-Fikr al-Sāmī fī Tārīkh al-Fiqh al-Islāmī*, where the author makes a similar argument about the Ḥanafī (pp. 424ff), Mālikī (pp. 453ff.) and Shāfiʿī (pp. 468ff.) schools. For some Western views on the same subject, see Wael Hallaq, "From Regional to Personal Schools of Law: A Reevaluation," and Christopher Melchert, "The Formation of the Sunnī Schools of Law." For an idea about the legal affiliation (or the lack thereof) of scholars in the early Muslim centuries, see Monique Bernard and John Nawas, "The Geographical Distribution of Muslim Jurists during the First Four Centuries AH."

2 *Aṣḥāb al-Raʾy* and *Aṣḥāb al-Ḥadīth* are also used occasionally.

 | DOI 10.1163/9789004279650_005

scholarship has accepted this distinction, regarding the two trends as distinct and perhaps diametrically opposed to each other. The following discussion of some medieval and modern treatments of these two trends seeks to contribute to our understanding of the characteristic features of each.

1.1 *Medieval and Modern Literature*

More often than not, medieval discussions of the difference between the *Ahl al-Ḥadīth* and the *Ahl al-Raʾy* are succinct and at times indeterminate.[3] For example, seeking to defend the *Ahl al-Ḥadīth* against their detractors, the famous scholar Ibn Qutaybah al-Dīnawarī (d. 276/889) begins with the *Ahl al-Kalām* (theologians, mostly Muʿtazilīs). These accused the *Ahl al-Ḥadīth* of accepting traditions that contradicted reason, revelation, and the consensus of the community, of arbitrariness in accepting the reliability of transmitters, and of ignorance of the meaning of what they transmitted.[4] Ibn Qutaybah responds to this by pointing out that whereas the *Ahl al-Ḥadīth* had full agreement on the fundamentals of religion,[5] the tools of reason (*ālāt al-naẓar*) that the *Ahl al-Kalām* used (*qiyās* in particular) did not save them from disagreement and contradiction on both legal and theological issues, and from holding absurd interpretations of some Qurʾānic passages.[6]

Similarly, the *Ahl al-Raʾy*, the other enemy of the *Ahl al-Ḥadīth*, disagreed among themselves, were contradictory and inconsistent even in their use of *qiyās*, and used (whimsical) *istiḥsān* in their constantly changing legal rulings,

---

3 This presentation of some medieval Muslim views avoids some early works—such as al-Shāfiʿī's *Risālah*, al-Shaybānī's *al-Radd ʿalā Siyar al-Awzāʿī*, *al-Ḥujjah ʿalā Ahl al-Madīnah*, *Ikhtilāf Abī Ḥanīfah wa-Ibn Abī Laylā*, as well as some early biographical works such as Ibn Saʿd's *al-Ṭabaqāt al-Kabīr*. Whereas there is no assumption here that later scholars did not have their own biases, the polemical nature of some of these early sources would unnecessarily complicate the picture for our purposes here.

4 Ibn Qutaybah al-Dīnawarī, *Taʾwīl Mukhtalif al-Ḥadīth*, pp. 114–120. Responding to these charges was Ibn Qutaybah's basic concern in this work. For some examples of these traditions, see *ibid.* pp. 107–114. Remarkably, regarding himself a member of the *Ahl al-Ḥadīth*, Ibn Qutaybah was aware of how his *Taʾwīl* could be easily considered polemical, and he promises the reader at its beginning that his exposition of the views of the *Ahl al-Ḥadīth* and the *Ahl al-Kalām* would not involve deliberate conceit or misrepresentation (*ibid.*, p. 120).

5 *Ibid.*, pp. 122–126. The *Ahl al-Ḥadīth* that Ibn Qutaybah mentions include ʿAbd al-Raḥmān al-Awzāʿī, Sufyān al-Thawrī, al-Layth ibn Saʿd, Mālik ibn Anas, and Aḥmad ibn Ḥanbal (*ibid.*, pp. 127–128). Notably, Ibn Qutaybah's attack on analogy here is similar to al-Naẓẓām's, which was also used later by Ibn Ḥazm (and possibly by Dāwūd himself). For an overview of al-Naẓẓām's and some other critiques of analogy, see Aaron Zysow, *The Economy of Certainty: An Introduction to the Typology of Islamic Legal Theory*, pp. 167–173.

6 Ibn Qutaybah, *Taʾwīl*, pp. 197–205.

leading at times to catastrophic results. This is what their foremost representative, Abū Ḥanīfah al-Nuʿmān, used to do, Ibn Qutaybah explains. He changed his mind about legal opinions that he had given to people, and ignored Prophetic traditions and held views that contradicted them even when they were brought to his attention.[7] Isḥāq ibn Rāhawayh, the harshest critic of the *Ahl al-Raʾy*, according to Ibn Qutaybah, believed that the *Ahl al-Raʾy* "abandoned the Qurʾān and Prophetic Sunnah and adhered to *qiyās*," which led them to contradictions and absurdities. In a revealing report, a discussion took place between Saʿīd ibn al-Musayyab (d. *c.* 94/715) and Rabīʿah ibn Abī ʿAbd al-Raḥmān (known as Rabīʿat al-Raʾy, d. 136/753) about the compensation that a woman gets if someone causes her to lose her fingers. When Rabīʿah asked Ibn al-Musayyab how much she would get for a finger, he said ten camels; for two, twenty camels; and for three, thirty. When Rabīʿah asked about four fingers, Ibn al-Musayyab replied that the compensation would be twenty camels. Rabīʿah then wondered: "When her injury is greater, and her calamity worse, her compensation decreases?" Ibn al-Musayyab replied decisively: "It is the Sunnah, my brother."[8]

On the other hand, the *Ahl al-Ḥadīth* are those who followed the Sunnah of the Prophet, spent their lives collecting and transmitting his Ḥadīth, distinguished between sound and unsound traditions, and kept an eye on jurists who contradicted and abandoned the Sunnah for their own opinions and warned people against them. Thanks to them, the truth became obvious, and those who were negligent and indifferent to the Sunnah came back to it and judged on its basis and abandoned following the opinions of so and so.[9] It is remarkable that when defining the *Ahl al-Ḥadīth*, Ibn Qutaybah focuses on a particular aspect of their career, that is, their great interest in collecting, verifying, transmitting Ḥadīth and reports in order to follow the Prophet's Sunnah, as well as warning people against those who contradicted it. This focus on the Ḥadīth-related activities of the *Ahl al-Ḥadīth* echoes the contention of their enemies that they were primarily Ḥadīth transmitters but not competent jurists or theologians.

---

7 *Ibid.*, pp. 174–180. Al-Awzāʿī's statement says: "We do not hold it against Abū Ḥanīfah that he uses his opinion, for we all do so. What we hold against him, however, is that when a tradition from the Prophet reaches him, he abandons it for something else." For a fuller account of Abū Ḥanīfah's reported rejection of traditions, see Ibn Abī Shaybah's chapter on "The cases in which Abū Ḥanīfah contradicted some Prophetic traditions" in his *Muṣannaf* (vol. 13, pp. 80–195).

8 Ibn Qutaybah, *Taʾwīl*, pp. 180–185.

9 *Ibid.*, p. 206.

Ibn Qutaybah's presentation distinguishes explicitly (but not always carefully) between two enemies of the *Ahl al-Ḥadīth*: the *Ahl al-Kalām*, and the *Ahl al-Ra'y*, the most notorious representative of whom is Abū Ḥanīfah. While the latter are censured for a number of reasons, Ibn Qutaybah puts significant emphasis on their use of *qiyās*. The problem that the *Ahl al-Ḥadīth* had with *qiyās* was that it led to abandoning some traditions that obviously contradicted it.

The great Andalusian Ibn 'Abd al-Barr provides us with many early anecdotes and reports about disagreements among early religious authorities, including the Prophet's Companions, regarding the use of *ra'y* and Ḥadīth, the interpretation of some Qur'ānic verses and Prophetic traditions, and the acceptance and rejection of traditions.[10] Reports about the *Ahl al-Ra'y* here generally refer to their use of *ra'y*, but there is a special emphasis on *qiyās*. In one anecdote, 'Āmir ibn Sharāḥīl al-Sha'bī (d. *c.* 105/723) referring to some people in the mosque in Baghdad, is reported to have once said, "By God, these people have made the mosque abhorrent to me, such that it has become more repulsive to me than the rubbish of my house." When he was asked about whom he was talking, he said: *al-ara'ayyūn*, i.e., those used to saying *ara'ayta* ("what if," "consider") in their deliberations. These people included Ḥammād ibn Abī Sulaymān (d. 120/737), a teacher of Abū Ḥanīfah's.[11] In another report, al-Sha'bī warns people against using *qiyās*, insisting that it leads to permitting that which is not, as well as forbidding that which is permissible.[12] Shurayḥ (d. *c.* 178/794), a famous judge in Kufa, argued with users of *qiyās* that because the Sunnah had preceded their *qiyās*, they should follow it and abandon their "innovation," for no one would be led astray by following the reports from and about the Prophet.[13] Mālik ibn Anas remarked that Islam was on the straight path until *Abū Ḥanīfah* appeared and spread the use of *qiyās*. A similar statement is attributed to the famous traditionist Sufyān ibn 'Uyaynah (d. 198/814).[14]

10 In his *A'lām al-Muwaqqi'īn*, Ibn Qayyim al-Jawziyyah offers a similar presentation of the reports that Ibn 'Abd al-Barr mentions in his *Jāmi'*, for which reason *A'lām al-Muwaqqi'īn* is not discussed here.

11 Ibn 'Abd al-Barr, *Jāmi' Bayān al-'Ilm wa-Faḍlihi*, vol. 2, p. 1074.

12 *Iyyākum wa-l-muqāyasah, fa-wa-'lladhī nafsī bi-yadihi, la-in akhadhtum bi-l-muqāyasah la-tuḥillunna 'l-ḥarām wa-la-tuḥarrimunna 'l-ḥalāl* (*ibid.*, vol. 2, p. 1047).

13 *Inna 'l-sunnah sabaqat qiyāsakum, fa-ittabi'ū wa-lā tabtadi'ū, fa-innakum lan taḍillū mā akhadhtum bi-l-athar* (*ibid.*, vol. 2, p. 1050).

14 *Ibid.*, vol. 2, p. 1079. Despite his Mālikī affiliation, Ibn 'Abd al-Barr seems rather keen to defend Abū Ḥanīfah. Maintaining that the *Aṣḥāb al-Ḥadīth* exceeded in censuring him, he points out that Abū Ḥanīfah mixed *ra'y* and *qiyās* with traditions (*idkhālihi 'l-ra'y wa-l-qiyās 'alā 'l-āthār*). However, whereas the majority of scholars assessed the

The excessive use of *qiyās* is presented here again as the main feature of the jurisprudence of the *Ahl al-Raʾy*. The *Ahl al-Ḥadīth* are those who avoided all forms of *raʾy*, including *qiyās*, and relied exclusively on traditions. Aḥmad ibn Ḥanbal is reported to have said that for him, it did not matter whether the *raʾy* was that of al-Awzāʿī (d. *c.* 157/773), Mālik, or Sufyān (al-Thawrī), as all this was merely *raʾy*. What mattered were the traditions (*al-āthār*).[15] This interest in Ḥadīth is echoed more explicitly by al-Shahrastānī (d. 548/1153) in his *Milal wa-l-Niḥal*, where he presents a clear distinction between the *Ahl al-Raʾy* and the *Ahl al-Ḥadīth*. The religious leaders of the Muslim community (*aʾimmat al-ummah*), he points out, are of two kinds: the *Aṣḥāb al-Ḥadīth* and the *Aṣḥāb al-Raʾy*. The former are the people of the Ḥijāz, the companions of Mālik, al-Shāfiʿī, Sufyān al-Thawrī, Aḥmad ibn Ḥanbal, and *Dāwūd ibn Khalaf*. They were called the *Ahl al-Ḥadīth* because of the great care that they gave to

---

soundness of traditions on the basis of its chain of transmitters, he rejected them on the basis of "plausible interpretations" (*bi-taʾwīl muḥtamal*), following the example of the Companion ʿAbd Allāh ibn Masʿūd and the Successor Ibrāhīm al-Nakhaʿī (d. 96/714). There was hardly any scholar, Ibn ʿAbd al-Barr notes, who did not abandon a tradition for another or by a plausible interpretation. Similar charges of abandoning Prophetic traditions were made against no less an authority than Mālik himself; al-Layth ibn Saʿd is reported to have said that he counted 70 cases in which Mālik contradicted the Sunnah of the Prophet. Furthermore, it is true that Abū Ḥanīfah and his ilk were excessive in using *raʾy* and *istiḥsān*, disagreeing in many of these with the forebears. This notwithstanding, it was the *Ahl al-Ḥadīth*'s envy of Abū Ḥanīfah in Ibn ʿAbd al-Barr's view that dominated them so much as to allege that he held heretical Murjʾī views. This defense of Abū Ḥanīfah is followed by the testimonies of a number of Ḥadīth scholars in his favor. In one significant report, Yaḥyā ibn Maʿīn, the famous Ḥadīth critic and associate of Ibn Ḥanbal's, concedes: "Our companions have exaggerated in what they say about Abū Ḥanīfah and his followers." When asked if Abū Ḥanīfah was a liar, he replied emphatically that he was more honorable than that (*kāna anbal min dhālika*). In another report, Ibn Maʿīn mentions that he did not like al-Shāfiʿī's traditions, and would not transmit from Abū Yūsuf (d. 182/798)—Abū Ḥanīfah's famous disciple—although he was not a liar. When asked about Abū Ḥanīfah, he said: "Good people have transmitted from him." Ibn ʿAbd al-Barr takes these disagreements about Abū Ḥanīfah as indicative of his intelligence (*wa-yustadallu ʿalā nabāhat al-rajul min al-māḍīn bi-tabāyun al-nās fī-hi*), comparing him to ʿAlī ibn Abī Ṭālib (d. 40/661), "with regard to whom two [groups of] people went astray: an excessive lover, and an excessive detractor." (*ibid.*, pp. 1080–1084). In a chapter on "The judgment on what the scholars say about each other," Ibn ʿAbd al-Barr mentions that when Ibn Ḥanbal learned that Yaḥyā ibn Maʿīn was speaking ill of al-Shāfiʿī, he accused him of having been ignorant of al-Shāfiʿī, adding that "one is antagonistic toward that of which one is ignorant" (*wa-man jahila shayʾ ʿādāhu*) (*ibid.*, p. 1114).

15 *Ibid.*, vol. 2, p. 1082. Note that these are the Ḥadīth scholars that Ibn Qutaybah had mentioned.

learning and transmitting Ḥadīth, their relying on religious texts (*al-nuṣūṣ*) in their jurisprudence, and their refraining from using *qiyās* when a tradition is available.[16] On the other hand, the *Aṣḥāb al-Raʾy* are the people of Iraq, Abū Ḥanīfah's associates who used *qiyās*—at times giving one of its forms, *al-qiyās al-jalī*, precedence over traditions—and relied on the "meaning that can be deduced from legal rulings" (*al-maʿnā ʾl-mustanbaṭ min al-aḥkām*).[17]

In this account, *qiyās* and *istinbāṭ* (deduction) are presented as characteristic of the jurisprudence of the *Ahl al-Raʾy*, who are explicitly and exclusively associated with Abū Ḥanīfah and his followers. However, it presents the *Ahl al-Ḥadīth* as a label that referred to various and disparate scholars who perhaps had more differences than similarities. Ibn Khaldūn (d. 808/1406), however, is more precise in identifying them as well as the origins of their differences. The *Ahl al-Ḥadīth*, he says, were the Ḥijāzīs, particularly Mālik and al-Shāfiʿī, and the *Ahl al-Raʾy wa-l-Qiyās* were the Iraqis, particularly Abū Ḥanīfah, a jurist whose unmatched status in jurisprudence was acknowledged by Mālik, al-Shāfiʿī and others. The disagreement between these two groups was old, for it had to do with 1) the nature of the language of the Arabs whose terms (*alfāẓ*) can be construed in multiple ways, and 2) the differences in the criteria used to test the authenticity of the Prophet's and Companions' reports. Furthermore, since the authoritative texts do not cover all new cases, *qiyās* is indispensable, which inevitably produces disagreement. Later, the Arabs mastered literacy and deduction, jurisprudence became a craft (*ṣināʿah*) and a matter of knowledge (*ʿilm*), and the jurists came to be divided into the *Ahl al-Raʾy wa-l-Qiyās* and the *Ahl al-Ḥadīth* according to their methodologies.

Possessing few traditions, the *Ahl al-Raʾy wa-l-Qiyās* mastered *qiyās* and used it excessively, which gave them their label. On the other hand, Mālik was distinguished by his consideration of the practice of the Medinese (*ʿamal ahl al-Madīnah*), which he believed originated in the practice of the Prophet himself. Mālik was followed by al-Shāfiʿī, who went to Iraq after his death and met with Abū Ḥanīfah's followers and learned from them. He then mixed the

16 Al-Shahrastānī, *al-Milal wa-l-Niḥal*, vol. 1, p. 243.

17 *Ibid.*, vol. 1, p. 245. Scholars of Islamic law distinguish between two kinds of *qiyās*. In *al-qiyās al-jalī*—which is usually what is meant when *qiyās* is mentioned—the *ʿillah* (*ratio legis*) used to draw analogy between an existing ruling and a new case is deemed "obvious." In *al-qiyās al-khafī* (also called *qiyās al-shabah*), however, the analogy between the two cases is based on a certain resemblance (hence *shabah*) between them (for the various kinds of *qiyās*, see Muḥammad Abū Zahrah, *Uṣūl al-Fiqh*, pp. 237–239). Ḥanafī scholars argued that *istiḥsān* meant abandoning a more obvious analogy for a more nuanced one for "good reasons" (for this, see, for example, al-Jaṣṣāṣ, *al-Fuṣūl*, vol. 2, pp. 344ff., and Abū Zahrah, *Abū Ḥanīfah*, pp. 342–344).

methodologies of the two regions and developed his own *madhhab*. Then came Aḥmad ibn Ḥanbal, who was among the most notable traditionists (*wa-kāna min ʿilyat al-muḥaddithīn*) whose followers learned from Abū Ḥanīfah's students despite their large stock of traditions.[18] Ibn Ḥanbal's *madhhab*, however, had few followers, for it was far from the use of *ijtihād* and was dependent on his originality in weighing traditions against each other.[19] His followers thus learned traditions more than anybody else, but were the least inclined to using *qiyās*.[20]

Remarkably, Ibn Khaldūn does not seem to have regarded Ibn Ḥanbal as a jurist. He attributes the formation of his *madhhab* to his students, who actually learned from Abū Ḥanīfah's students. But because they were rigid in rejecting *qiyās* altogether, they failed relative to other *madhhab*s. Earlier, Ibn Khaldūn had mentioned another group of scholars who also rejected *qiyās*, considered all understandings (*madārik*) to be "restricted to the texts and consensus," and related the *qiyās jalī* and the *ʿillah* that has a textual basis (*al-ʿillah al-manṣūṣah*) to the text from which it is derived on the ground that stating it is nothing other than a statement of the ruling itself. The leader of this *madhhab* was Dāwūd ibn ʿAlī, followed by his son and their disciples. Their Ẓāhirī *madhhab*, Ibn Khaldūn reports, perished, except for some books in which some students developed an occasional interest, bringing on themselves the animosity of the rest of the Muslim community. One of these students was Ibn Ḥazm in Andalus; despite his stature as a Ḥadīth expert, he excelled in the *Ẓāhirī madhhab* and ridiculed many of the "masters," which brought upon him widespread resentment and caused his books to be neglected and banned.[21]

Medieval Muslim scholars do not thus present coherent views on the identity and distinctive features of the *Ahl al-Raʾy* and the *Ahl al-Ḥadīth*. Generally speaking, the *Ahl al-Ḥadīth* are presented as having been, first and foremost, Ḥadīth scholars, such that there is some reluctance on the part of some medieval scholars to regard them as jurists. However, this reluctance appears to apply primarily to a particular group of the *Ahl al-Ḥadīth* that included Aḥmad ibn Ḥanbal and similar traditionists. Their other members included scholars like Mālik ibn Anas, whose interest in jurisprudence was certainly no less than his interest in Sunnah. Mālik's legal interests notwithstanding, medieval accounts of the *Ahl al-Ḥadīth* are obviously especially interested in

---

18 ʿAbd al-Raḥmān ibn Khaldūn, *al-Muqaddimah*, pp. 416–418.

19 *Fa-ammā Aḥmad ibn Ḥanbal fa-muqallidūhu qalīlūn li-buʿd madhhabihi ʿan al-ijtihād wa-aṣālatihi fī muʿāḍadat al-riwāyāt wa-l-akhbār baʿḍihā bi-baʿḍ* (*ibid.*, p. 419).

20 *Ibid.*, p. 419.

21 *Ibid.*, pp. 417–418.

highlighting a particular aspect of their career when *contrasting* them with the *Ahl al-Raʾy*. It is probably in this context that the attitude of the *Ahl al-Raʾy* toward Ḥadīth is emphasized. Not only were they not active in transmitting traditions, but they also ignored or rejected some of them on various grounds.

If the *Ahl al-Hadīth* engaged in something—learning and transmitting Ḥadīth—that the *Ahl al-Raʾy* were not interested in, the *Ahl al-Raʾy* in their turn engaged in something that the *Ahl al-Ḥadīth* avoided, that is, the use of *qiyās*. It is particularly this rejection of *qiyās* that made it possible for al-Shahrastānī to include Dāwūd among the *Ahl al-al-Ḥadīth*. Al-Shāfiʿī is included here because he is believed to have used *qiyās* only when no textual evidence existed in a given case. Ibn Khaldūn explicitly links the use of *qiyās* to the shortage of the texts that the *Ahl al-Raʾy* either had or accepted as authentic. As noted earlier, however, the use of *qiyās*, no matter how it is defined, seems to have aimed to produce coherent jurisprudence where new rulings are consistent with established ones. This interest in consistency and coherence is evident in the interlocution between Rabīʿat al-Ra'y and Ibn al-Musayyab. Ibn al-Musayyab did not argue that what Rabīʿat al-Ra'y said about the correlation between the extent of the injury and the compensation did not make sense. However, he ended the discussion by just asserting that that was how the Sunnah was, meaning that it should be followed irrespective of what "reason" has to say.

It is possible to conclude, therefore, that the underlying feature of the jurisprudence of the *Ahl al-Raʾy* was their keenness to be consistent and for their jurisprudence to be coherent, whereas for the *Ahl al-Ḥadīth*, following traditions (contradictory as they may be) was crucial.

∵

Modern scholarship that tackled the subject of the origins of and differences between the *Ahl al-Raʾy* and the *Ahl al-Ḥadīth* have generally tended to accept one of the views of medieval scholars. Aḥmad Amīn, for example, accepts the regional dichotomy (the Ḥijāz vs. Iraq) that some sources made and accounts for it on the basis of the cultural differences between the two regions and the Companions who happened to reside there. The *Ahl al-Raʾy*, for instance, thrived in Iraq where ʿAbd Allāh ibn Masʿūd (d. 32/653) lived. Ibn Masʿūd did not refrain from using his opinion in the absence of relevant textual evidence. He also abstained from transmitting much Ḥadīth "out of piety." Therefore, the Iraqis inherited a fear of fabricating Ḥadīth, which led them to lay down very stringent conditions for the acceptance of traditions, resulting in accepting only very few of them. The relatively sophisticated life in Iraq, however, required solutions that this limited stock of traditions could not provide. This generated their interest in debating even hypothetical cases that were unrealistic (in the sense of being highly unlikely to take place) at times. On the other hand, the Ḥijāz was the stronghold of the school of the *Ahl al-Ḥadīth* (who also had some representatives in Iraq) because of the abundance of traditions there, which were sufficient for the simple life of the Ḥijāzīs. Therefore, the *Ahl al-Ḥadīth* relied on Prophetic traditions, including ones that were deemed "weak," and abhorred dealing with hypothetical questions. Some of them went to such an extreme as to give Ḥadīth and Sunnah precedence over the Qur'ān itself, Amīn notes.[22]

Similarly, the Moroccan scholar Muḥammad al-Ḥijwī holds that the legal thought in the Ḥijāz and Iraq was colored by the views of the Companions who happened to live there, especially after the death of ʿUmar ibn al-Khaṭṭāb (d. 23/644), when ʿUthmān ibn ʿAffān (d. 35/656) allowed the Companions to "disperse" to various regions. Later, each group of students of these Companions in Iraq and the Ḥijāz insisted that what they learned represented the true (Prophetic?) Sunnah. As early as the second half of the 1st century AH, scholars of both regions were already split. The *Ahl al-Ḥadīth* were led by Saʿīd ibn al-Musayyab in the Ḥijāz, whereas the *Ahl al-Ra'y* were led by Ibrāhīm al-Nakhaʿī in Iraq. From the former group originated the Mālikīs, Shāfiʿīs, Ḥanbalīs, *Ẓāhirīs*, and others. The latter were mainly represented by the school of Abū Ḥanīfah.[23] Comparing Saʿīd ibn al-Musayyab and Ibrāhīm al-Nakhaʿī, al-Ḥijwī argues that the latter maintained that legal rulings were based on fixed rules and rationales (*qawāʿid wa-ʿilal thābitah*) that were meant to serve the interests of the people. These rationales were discernible from the Qur'ān and Sunnah, in addition to "reason" which is able to distinguish between good and evil. In contrast, Saʿīd ibn al-Musayyab was searching more for texts and less for their underlying rationales. He used *ʿillah* only where there existed no relevant text.[24]

Sālim al-Thaqafī, notably a contemporary Saudi scholar, reiterates Ibn ʿAbd al-Barr's contention that while it is true that the *Ahl al-Ra'y* contradicted some Prophetic traditions that reached them, they were not the only group of scholars who did that. Even among the Companions there were those who

22 Aḥmad Amīn, *Fajr al-Islām*, pp. 240–244.

23 Muḥammad ibn al-Ḥasan al-Ḥijwī, *al-Fikr al-Sāmī fī Tārīkh al-Fiqh al-Islāmī*, pp. 378–383. Al-Ḥijwī points out that whereas some Iraqi scholars, such as al-Shaʿbī, rejected *ra'y*, some Medinese scholars accepted and used it, such as Rabīʿat al-Ra'y. But to reconcile this with the strict dichotomy he draws between the two regions, al-Ḥijwī suggests that Rabīʿat al-Ra'y was most likely influenced by the Iraqis when he served as *wazīr* to Abū al-ʿAbbās al-Saffāḥ (the first Abbasid Caliph, d. 136/754).

24 *Ibid.*, pp. 385–386.

contradicted Prophetic traditions, and there is hardly any legal school of law which, in one instance or another, did not act in disagreement with one or more Prophetic tradition.[25] Apart from making such a sweeping generalization about the Companions and early Muslim scholars, al-Thaqafī does not appear to think that the rejection of Prophetic traditions is a valid criterion on the basis of which we can distinguish between the early *madhhab*s. We shall return to this point in a later context.

When discussing the views presented in medieval Muslim sources about the two legal trends of the *Ahl al-Raʾy* and the *Ahl al-Ḥadīth*, Western treatments of this subject displays some hesitancy. Goldziher, for example, holds that whereas the *Ahl al-Ḥadīth* were "concerned with the study of transmitted sources," the *Ahl al-Raʾy* were concerned with "the practical aspects of the law." In the same breath, however, he seems to agree that both designations "referred to branches of legists occupied with the investigation of Islamic law." The *Ahl al-Raʾy* had a "method of dealing with Islamic jurisprudence [that was based on the belief that] ... *not only the written and orally transmitted sources* are authoritative—namely, the Koran and the traditions of Muḥammad and his companions—but also ... what is valid according to *the principles of Islam*, what the individual insight of a legist or judge, in real or apparent dependence on those indisputable sources, recognizes as the truth emanating from their *spirit*."[26] In other words, he agrees that the *Ahl al-Raʾy* paid some attention to the "orally transmitted sources," but also holds that much subjectivity was involved in their legal thinking in general and their treatment of the transmitted materials in particular. "The exponents of *raʾy* derived the legal basis for the introduction of *subjective* motives in the deduction of law from the *spirit* of the transmitted divine law," he states.[27] This understanding is based on Goldziher's view that early Muslim jurists differed from one another "in the extent to which they permit *raʾy* to be a determining factor in establishing Islamic law in a given case."[28] Thus, while there may not have been sharp dichotomy between *raʾy* and tradition in early Islam, each scholar was more given towards one of them. In other words, there was a continuum, at one end of which was *raʾy*; at the other traditions. On this continuum, Goldziher places

25 Sālim ibn ʿAlī al-Thaqafī, *Asbāb Ikhtilāf al-Fuqahāʾ*, pp. 79–81.

26 Goldziher, *The Ẓāhirīs*, p. 3 (emphasis mine). I rely here on Goldziher's *Ẓāhirīs* because it was among his latest contributions to the field of Islamic legal history. Furthermore, given its subject, his discussion of the doctrines of the *Ahl al-Raʾy* and the *Ahl al-Ḥadīth* here should be more nuanced than in his other works.

27 *Ibid.*, p. 7 (emphasis mine).

28 *Ibid.*, p. 3.

Abū Ḥanīfah and Dāwūd at two opposite ends; the former made "considerable concessions" to the use of *raʾy*, whereas the latter completely shunned it.[29]

While this seems to be a balanced view of the relation between *raʾy* and traditions in early Islam, the contrast that Goldziher draws between the *Ahl al-Ḥadīth*'s concern for the study of traditions and the *Ahl al-Raʾy*'s interest in the "practical aspects" of the law suggests that he did not regard the former as full-fledged jurists like the latter.[30] Furthermore, he associates the "spirit of the law" and the "principles of Islam" with the *Ahl al-Raʾy*, which suggests that these were not among the tools of the *Ahl al-Ḥadīth*. Making legal judgments according to the "spirit" and "principles" of Islam was thus a criterion on the basis of which Goldziher believes that we can distinguish between the two trends.

Joseph Schacht's discussion of this subject is more nuanced. He pays attention to how polemics between the two trends may have shaped some of our information on them. He argues that the distinction between the *Ahl al-Raʾy* and the *Ahl al-Ḥadīth* was "to a great extent artificial" since the *Ahl al-Raʾy* was coined and used pejoratively by the *Ahl al-Ḥadīth* to defame their opponents.[31] Yet, he too seems hesitant to accept the *Ahl al-Ḥadīth* as legal scholars. They were "naturally specialists in the transmission and study of traditions and in the criticism of their *isnāds*,"[32] and only "*occasionally* interested in purely legal issues."[33] Their "most important activity [was] the creation and putting into circulation of traditions from the Prophet," he says. Nonetheless, because of

---

29 Goldziher, *The Ẓāhirīs*, pp. 3–4. Motzki argues that the sharp distinction that Goldziher made between the *Ahl al-Raʾy* and the *Ahl al-Ḥadīth* was central in his overall theory about the development of Islamic law, and particularly the idea that Prophetic traditions only came into existence and gained wide and authoritative use in the late 2nd century AH. Therefore, Goldziher failed to realize that we cannot categorize some early works, such as Mālik's *Muwaṭṭaʾ*, as belonging solely to either camp, for these were works of "Tradition," in the broader sense of not being limited only to the Prophetic traditions like later compilations of Ḥadīth (Harald Motzki, *The Origins of Islamic Jurisprudence: Meccan Fiqh before the Classical Schools*, p. 16).

30 Goldziher must have been aware that some medieval scholars—such as al-Ṭabarī—did not recognize people like Ibn Ḥanbal as jurists. Any treatment of this issue of whether the *Ahl al-Ḥadīth* were also jurists or only Ḥadīth scholars, therefore, should be rather nuanced, giving equal attention to the *Ahl al-Ḥadīth*'s jurisprudence, just as they often do when discussing the *Ahl al-Raʾy*.

31 Schacht, "Aṣḥāb al-Ra'y," *EI*², vol. 1, p. 691. In Schacht's view, the *Ahl al-Ḥadīth* movement emerged in the second half of the 2nd century AH in opposition to the use of *raʾy* in the ancient schools of law (Schacht, *The Origins of Muḥammadan Jurisprudence*, p. 253).

32 Schacht, *Origins*, p. 254.

33 Schacht, *An Introduction to Islamic Law*, p. 35 (emphasis mine).

the traditions they "created and put into circulation" to replace the "living tradition" used by the ancient *madhhabs*, "[t]heir activity [was] an integral part of the development of legal theory and positive legal doctrine during the first half of the second century A.H."[34]

So, unlike the early *madhhabs* and their "extensive use of human reasoning and personal opinion," Schacht argues, the *Ahl al-Ḥadīth* sought to establish the Prophetic Sunnah as the only valid source of law (besides the Qur'ān, of course) and detested all forms of human reasoning and personal opinion.[35] This approach was accepted later by the other *madhhabs* which also maintained their inherited legal doctrine.[36] Furthermore, "[t]he main material aim of the traditionists," he adds, "was the same as that of the ancient schools, that is, to subordinate the legal subject-matter to *religious and ethical* considerations."[37] Schacht seems to regard religiosity and morality (which could be "strict and rigid") as having been characteristic of the *Ahl al-Ḥadīth*, if not their *raison d'être*: "The movement of the traditionists was the natural outcome and continuation of a movement of *religiously and ethically inspired* opposition to the ancient schools of law," which schools "represented, in one aspect, an Islamic opposition to popular and administrative practice under the later Umayyads."[38] Alluding to al-Shāfi'ī's reference to the traditionists' "lack of systematic reasoning," he argues that their "standards of reasoning" were generally inferior to the early *madhhabs*.[39] Accordingly, Schacht—for whom the only doctrine that was "purely traditionist" remained that of Aḥmad ibn Ḥanbal's—was

34 Schacht, *Origins*, p. 253.

35 In commenting on their acceptance and rejection of traditions, Schacht held that traditionists rejected some traditions "for reasons of their own." It is not clear whether this means subjective reasons or reasons that had to do with their career as Ḥadīth critics, who, at least in theory, only accepted and rejected traditions according to their *isnāds*. While others did not consider this method sufficient, the fact that traditionists had a methodology means that their overall assessment was intended to be objective. Arguably, the subjectivity involved in assessing transmitters' reliability is not significantly different from that involved in accepting and rejecting traditions on the basis of their contents.

36 Schacht, "Aṣḥāb al-Ra'y," *EI*², vol. 1, p. 691. The *Ahl al-Ḥadīth* must have held that subordinating legal issues to moral and religious considerations was not as subjective an exercise as it sounds. These considerations, they maintained, were not their own product but were rather based on principles that, in their view, were integral to Islam and thus binding to all Muslims.

37 Jeseph Schacht, "Aṣḥāb al-Ḥadīth," *EI*², vol. 1, p. 258 (italics added).

38 Schacht, *Introduction*, p. 34 (emphasis mine).

39 Schacht, *Origins*, p. 254.

hesitant to regard them as jurists, for they were concerned with law only to the extent to which it served their religious and moral agenda.

For his part, G. H. A. Juynboll builds his discussion of this subject on a sharp distinction that he thinks has afflicted Islam from the very beginning between *raʾy* (individual judgment or "common sense," in his understanding), and *ʿilm*, namely, knowledge of the Tradition (in a wide sense that includes views of people other than the Prophet). To illustrate the difference, he argues that when a Companion was asked about an issue and gave his view, he was acting like a jurist (*faqīh*) who exercised *raʾy*. However, when he mentioned the view of another Companion or a precedent of the Prophet,[40] he was acting as a learned man (*ʿālim*) who knew precedents and refrained from expressing his own view. "[D]uring the earliest years, say the first century of the Hijra," Juynboll contends, "*fiqh* and *ʿilm* were only *occasionally* combined in one and the same person."[41] Elsewhere, he concedes that some figures were able to combine *fiqh* and *ʿilm*: "It is a generally accepted *fact* that the first four caliphs set their own standards. They ruled the community in *the spirit of the prophet*, thinking of their own solutions to problems rather than meticulously copying his actions."[42] Juynboll carries the same dichotomy to the second century. Speaking of Abū Ḥanīfah, he suggests that most of the traditions in whose *isnād* he figures, and all the accounts that mention a relationship between him and Ḥadīth, were later fabrications by his followers aiming to bolster his image that was tainted by Ḥadīth scholars.[43] At that time, much of the *raʾy* of the

40 G. H. A. Juynboll, *Muslim Tradition: Studies in Chronology, Provenance, and Authorship of Early Ḥadīth*, p. 33. I am following Juynboll's order here. If made consciously, this would suggest that, for one reason or another, what would come to a Companion's mind first would be an opinion from another Companion, and then a precedent from the Prophet.

41 *Ibid.*, p. 33 (emphasis mine). When talking about Abū Ḥanīfah's circle elsewhere, Juynboll states that "if on some occasions it so happened that a tradition was readily at hand to be adduced, it *was not disregarded altogether* but it never seemed to play a crucial part in the decision making" (*ibid.*, p. 120, italics mine). This statement, of course, remains an unsubstantiated speculation.

42 *Ibid.*, p. 15 (emphasis mine). Juynboll makes a reference here to a later part of the book where he shows that most of the rulings of the first four Caliphs were not based on Prophetic traditions, but were mostly their own *raʾy* and judgment.

43 Juynboll seems to endorse the *Ahl al-Ḥadīth*'s view regarding Abū Ḥanīfah. In another context, he argues that "[t]here are several reports in which Abū Ḥanīfah appears to ridicule prophetic sayings, especially those which have taken the form of legal maxims or slogans" (*ibid.*, p. 121). However, if Abū Ḥanīfah "ridiculed" those sayings, it stands to reason that he must not have considered them Prophetic in the first place. According to Juynboll, by the time of Abū Ḥanīfah, one could reject a saying attributed to the Prophet

early jurists was already assuming the shape of *ʿilm*, which, in its turn, would echo what used to be the personal views of early scholars.[44]

Juynboll's sharp and arguably exaggerated distinction between *raʾy* and *ʿilm* is problematic, both historically and theoretically.[45] For our purposes here, it suggests that we cannot compare the *Ahl al-Raʾy* and the *Ahl al-Ḥadīth* who represented two completely distinct categories of people who did not have much in common.[46]

In Christopher Melchert's view, starting from the late 8th and throughout the 9th centuries CE, there was a heated controversy between "those who would found their jurisprudence exclusively on *Ḥadīth, Aṣḥāb al-Ḥadīth* or traditionalists, and those who reserved a leading place for *common sense, Aṣḥāb al-Raʾy.*"[47] The former group of scholars "defined itself by its loyalty to the *Sunnah*; that is, to normative precedent"[48] and condemned *qiyās* because it "could evidently be used to evade the strict requirements indicated by *Ḥadīth.*"[49] They refrained from privileging some of the traditions (Prophetic and otherwise) that they collected. Aḥmad ibn Ḥanbal, for instance, relied on reports from the Prophet as well as from Companions and Successors.[50] When he did not give his personal opinion, he "adduced a great many different sorts of evidence in support of his opinions, including examples and dicta from Followers, Companions, the Right-Guided Caliphs and the Prophet."[51] Melchert compares Abū Ḥanīfah, as representative of the *Ahl al-Raʾy*, with Sufyān al-Thawrī (d. 161/778), a representative of the *Ahl al-Ḥadīth*, to demonstrate that the "conscious enmity" between the two groups dates to the 2nd/8th century. Remarkably, however, he notes that the distinction between the two groups was not as sharp as is assumed, for there were occasions when they agreed with each other, and even had followers in common.[52]

---

only on the basis of its *isnād*, or by dismissing its authenticity on account of its presumed contradiction with the Qurʾān or another tradition that is considered authentic.

44 Juynboll, *Muslim Tradition*, p. 67.

45 It is not clear, for instance, how a jurist would use the "spirit" of any legal system absent enough precedents that illustrate it.

46 Incidentally, when defining them, Juynboll states unreservedly that the *Ahl al-Ḥadīth* were an "early Islamic faction propagating *the transmission and promotion of traditions*" (*ibid.*, p. 257; emphasis mine). Jurisprudence is not even alluded to here.

47 Melchert, *Formation*, p. 1. Emphasis on "common sense" mine.

48 Melchert, *Ahmad ibn Hanbal*, p. 62.

49 Melchert, *Formation*, pp. 9–10.

50 *Ibid.*, p. 16. This particular feature of the *Ahl al-Ḥadīth* will be brought up in a later context.

51 Melchert, *Ahmad ibn Hanbal*, p. 77.

52 Melchert, *Formation*, pp. 3–4.

Finally, Wael Hallaq distinguishes between the rationalists (the *Ahl al-Raʾy*) and the traditionalists (the *Ahl al-Ḥadīth*) on the basis of *how* they came to their legal conclusions. "Rationalism," he argues, "signifies a perception of an attitude toward legal issues that is dictated by rational, pragmatic, and practical considerations." It is "a substantial legal reasoning that, for the most part, does not directly ground itself in what came later to be recognized as the valid textual sources." In contrast, traditionalists "held that law must rest squarely on Prophetic Ḥadīth, the Qurʾān being taken for granted by both rationalists … and traditionists." This, however, does not tell us much about "the methodology" of the *Ahl al-Ḥadīth* which Hallaq believes crystallized in the second half of 2nd century AH;[53] however, the attention that he gives to the *process* of reasoning by each group is indeed useful

2 The *Ahl al-Raʾy* and the *Ahl al-Ḥadīth* Revisited

Probably due to the varied reports that medieval sources mention about the *Ahl al-Raʾy* and the *Ahl al-Ḥadīth*, modern discussions of the origins of and differences between them exhibit some problems. There is a latent assumption that both trends were represented by two coherent groups of scholars, the line of demarcation between whom was their attitude toward the traditions. Whereas the *Ahl al-Ḥadīth* relied exclusively on them, the *Ahl al-Raʾy* relied instead on *qiyās*. Historically, the situation seems more complex. The *Ahl al-Raʾy* never made a formal statement about their rejection of any textual evidence *when they accepted its authenticity*. There *is*, in fact, evidence that it was not the outright rejection of traditions that they were mostly accused of (although this accusation was made by a few scholars, such as al-Awzāʿī); it was primarily their *inconsistency* in accepting some traditions and rejecting others for no obvious or good reasons (from the point of view of their detractors, of course). For instance, to prove his inconsistency (rather than his presumptuous rejection of Ḥadīth), some of his Ḥadīth detractors accused Abū Ḥanīfah of accepting traditions that they considered "weak."[54] There is no reason to

53 Hallaq, *Origins*, pp. 74–75. Two other modern Muslim views on our present subject will be discussed in a separate section later in this chapter.

54 See, for instance, Abū Zahrah, *Abū Ḥanīfah*, pp. 299–303. The traditions mentioned here are *mursal*, traditions in the chain of transmitters of which a transmitter is missing, mostly the Companion. These were accepted by Ḥanafīs, but remarkably rejected by most traditionists (for this, see, for instance, al-Khaṭīb al-Baghdādī, *al-Kifāyah fī ʿIlm al-Riwāyah*, p. 423).

believe that Abū Ḥanīfah would use a tradition that he did not believe was authentic, or reject another that he thought was. The fact that he used traditions at all indicates that he regarded them as the most authentic textual evidence that existed on certain issues, let alone that he accepted the authority of Ḥadīth in principle. The rejection of traditions, as Ibn ʿAbd al-Barr notes, was not specific to the *Ahl al-Raʾy*. Furthermore, the use of *qiyās*, presented in all medieval accounts as having been characteristic of the *Ahl al-Raʾy*, actually indicates that they sought to relate their legal views to textual evidence, even if indirectly. Al-Thaqafī, therefore, has good reasons to hold that the acceptance and rejection of Ḥadīth should not be taken as the criterion by which we characterize any of the early legal schools, even if they differed on the degree to which they did that. Likewise, Motzki is right in asserting that "[i]t is not reference to traditions of the Prophet which is the innovation [of the *Ahl al-Ḥadīth*], but their demand for recognition," adding that "[t]he enmity toward newly appearing *ḥadīth*s which were not compatible with the existing doctrines says nothing about the role which *ḥadīth*s per se played in the schools of law."[55]

Some scholars have rightly questioned the link that some medieval and modern discussions make between the *Ahl al-Ḥadīth* and the Ḥijāz, on the one hand, and the *Ahl al-Raʾy* and Iraq, on the other hand. They note that the Companions who are thought to have laid the foundations of the Ḥijāzī jurisprudence and their followers who developed and spread it were also jurists as well as traditionists.[56] Mālik used *raʾy* no less than Abū Ḥanīfah and his predecessors,[57] however different the underlying principles that governed

55 Motzki, *Origins*, p. 20.

56 That ʿUmar ibn al-Khaṭṭāb used his discretionary opinion frequently is beyond doubt, although some scholars account for this on the basis of his prerogatives and responsibilities as Caliph (see, for instance, Abū Zahrah, *Tārīkh al-Madhāhib al-Islāmiyyah*, vol. 2, pp. 16–17). On the contrary, his son, ʿAbd Allāh ibn ʿUmar, is reported to have been conservative in giving his opinion if he did not recall a relevant Prophetic tradition. Some scholars hold that ʿUmar's approach was carried to Iraq by ʿAbd Allāh ibn Masʿūd (who is said to have been a staunch admirer of ʿUmar), while Ibn ʿUmar's was maintained by the Ḥijāzīs, whose head among the Successors was Saʿīd ibn al-Musayyab. Ibn ʿUmar's conservatism, however, does not necessarily mean that he never used *raʾy*. This is even more so in the case of Ibn al-Musayyab who did not hesitate to give his own opinion even when no text existed and felt at liberty to choose from among various pieces of evidence (for this, see, for example, Abd al-Majīd Maḥmūd Abd al-Majīd, *al-Ittijāhāt al-Fiqhiyyah li-Ahl al-Ḥadīth fī al-Qarn al-Thālith al-Hijrī*).

57 See, for instance, Muḥammad Yousuf Gouraya, *Origins of Islamic Jurisprudence* (*with Special Reference to Muwatta' Imam Malik*), making a strong case that Mālik never bound

their use of *raʾy* were.[58] Some Iraqi scholars, on the other hand, were known for their hatred of *raʾy* and *qiyās*. This means that what existed in the first two or three centuries of the Islamic history were "personal" scholarly circles that differed on their willingness to use their own discretionary views and the traditions available to them.[59] Consequently, instead of focusing on *what* legal evidence each side used, it would perhaps be more useful if discussions focus on *how* they used it. This will be dealt with in CHAPTER FOUR.

The following is a presentation of the views of two other modern scholars whose critical treatment of the issues discussed in this chapter is noteworthy. These are the Sudanese Khalīfah Bābakr al-Ḥasan and the Egyptian ʿAbd al-Majīd Maḥmūd ʿAbd al-Majīd. Seeking to take into consideration most of what medieval sources mention about them, al-Ḥasan's and ʿAbd al-Majīd's historical investigation of the origins of the *Ahl al-Raʾy* and the *Ahl al-Ḥadīth* has avoided the harmful assumption that each of these two terms referred a coherent group of the scholars, or referred to any one group in one particular time. They have also entertained the possibility that the thought and activities of each group may have changed over time.[60]

In his *Ijtihād bi-l-Raʾy fī Madrasat al-Ḥijāz al-Fiqhiyyah*, al-Ḥasan accepts the view that the Ḥijāz and Iraq were the stronghold of the *Ahl al-Ḥadīth* and the *Ahl al-Raʾy* respectively. However, he rejects the argument that this was "natural" for both regions. Jurisprudence in each region depended on the Companions who resided there and on their personal views which their followers adopted, expanded and handed over to next generations.[61] At this stage,

himself either by the consensus of the scholars of Medina or even the practice of the Medinese (*ʿamal ahl al-Madīnah*), and that his *fatwās* reflected only his own personal views. See also Khalīfah Bābakr al-Ḥasan, *al-Ijtihād bi-l-Raʾy fī Madrasat al-Ḥijāz al-Fiqhiyyah*, pp. 463ff, and *passim*. This may actually account for the bitterness of the confrontation between Ẓāhirīs and Mālikīs in Andalus, whereas the former's confrontation with the Ḥanafīs in Iraq was apparently less intense. Arguably, Ẓāhirīs may have regarded Mālikīs more arbitrary and less consistent than Ḥanafīs.

58 Abū Zahrah, for example, argues that *raʾy* in Iraq, which was influenced by ʿAbd Allāh ibn Masʿūd and ʿAbd Allāh ibn ʿAbbās, was mostly inclined toward *qiyās*, whereas *raʾy* in the Ḥijāz, which relied on ʿUmar's juridical legacy, was based on considerations pertaining mostly to personal and social interests (*maṣāliḥ*) (*Tārīkh al-Madhāhib al-Islāmiyyah*, pp. 31–34).

59 For this, and for the various views on this issue, see, Wael Hallaq, "From Personal to Doctrinal Schools of Law: A Reevaluation."

60 It is unfortunate that al-Ḥasan's and ʿAbd al-Majīd's writings have not received attention in Western scholarship. I owe reference to ʿAbd al-Majīd's work to Hossein Modarressi.

61 Al-Ḥasan, *al-Ijtihād*, pp. 253–254.

the difference was not between two distinct trends or disagreement over the use of *raʾy* and traditions as such. It only had to do with different teachers who were active as both jurists and Ḥadīth transmitters (such as ʿAbd Allāh ibn ʿUmar in Medina and ʿAbd Allāh ibn Masʿūd in Iraq), but had different doctrines and knew different traditions.[62] The Companions who went to Iraq happened to be more disposed to issuing *fatwā*s than those who remained in Medina.[63] Because these Companions were themselves competing with each other,[64] competition between the two regions was natural and did occur at a very early stage when each region took much pride in its Companions and adhered to their legal doctrines.[65]

At the time of Abū Ḥanīfah, the *Ahl al-Raʾy* emerged as a *distinct* group with a *distinct* methodology, al-Ḥasan argues. Almost *concomitant* with that was the emergence of the "movement" of the *Ahl al-Ḥadīth* in several regions of the Muslim state at the hands of people like Mālik ibn Anas, al-Awzāʿī, ʿAbd Allāh ibn al-Mubārak, and Sufyān al-Thawrī.[66] It so happened, however, that the leadership of that movement passed into the hands of scholars who were taught by Ḥijāzī teachers (such as al-Shāfiʿī, Ibn Ḥanbal, Isḥāq ibn Rāhawayh, and Abū Thawr), whereas the movement of the *Ahl al-Raʾy* passed from Abū Ḥanīfah to his students and thus remained in Iraqi hands.[67] In Iraq, the *Ahl al-Ḥadīth* were basically those scholars who rejected the juridical thought and practice of Abū Ḥanīfah and his likes.[68] Additionally, while in their early career in the Ḥijāz the *Ahl al-Ḥadīth* were suspicious of the traditions of the Iraqis, in a later stage they developed criteria by which they assessed the reliability of transmitters and the authenticity of traditions regardless of their provenance.[69]

At this point, the basis of the competition ceased to be regional. Instead, there existed two distinct trends side by side in the same region, Iraq. Only then, in the second half of the 2nd and throughout the 3rd centuries AH, did the two camps begin to attack each other with accusations regarding the use of *raʾy* and traditions. The *Ahl al-Ḥadīth* accused the *Ahl al-Raʾy* of being ignorant of Ḥadīth and giving their own opinions precedence over it. The *Ahl al-Raʾy*

---

62 Al-Ḥasan, *al-Ijtihād*, p. 268.

63 *Ibid.*, p. 270.

64 *Ibid.*, pp. 261–263. For a good presentation of this, see Ibn ʿAbd al-Barr, *Jāmiʿ Bayān al-ʿIlm*, vol. 2, pp. 1100ff., where the author mentions many anecdotes and reports of what the Companions used to say about and against each other.

65 Al-Ḥasan, *al-Ijtihād*, p. 320.

66 Al-Ḥasan draws here on Ibn Taymiyyah's *Ṣiḥḥat Uṣūl Madhhab Ahl al-Madīnah*.

67 *Ibid.*, pp. 268–269.

68 *Ibid.*, pp. 263–264.

69 *Ibid.*, p. 269.

reciprocated by accusing them of rigidity and mental deficiency.[70] During the *Miḥnah* in the first decades of the 3rd century AH, however, the struggle between the two groups reached its peak. The *Ahl al-Ḥadīth*, who relied only on reports from the Prophet and his Companions, fought on two fronts: against the theologians (*al-mutakallimūn*, the *Ahl al-Kalām*) who used *ra'y* in theology, and the Iraqi jurists (*al-fuqahā'*) who used it in jurisprudence.[71]

The *Ahl al-Ra'y*, then, were the Iraqis, notably Abū Ḥanīfah and his followers. They adhered to the doctrines of the Companions who had moved to Iraq in the early decades of Islam and made a practice of issuing *fatwā*s.[72] Their distinguishing feature was their largescale and frequent use of *qiyās* and their giving it precedence over traditions transmitted by single transmitters. The term *Ahl al-Ra'y*, al-Ḥasan argues, was invented by the *Ahl al-Ḥadīth* to refer to scholars who had these particular features, as evinced by al-Awzāʿī's statement that the problem with Abū Ḥanīfah was not his use of *ra'y per se*, but rather his abandoning Prophetic traditions brought to his attention for it. Ibn Abī Shaybah devoted a long chapter in his *Musnad* to listing more than a hundred cases in which Abū Ḥanīfah gave opinions that contradicted what the *Ahl al-Ḥadīth* considered sound traditions.[73] Al-Ḥasan rejects this accusation, arguing that Abū Ḥanīfah's criteria for accepting traditions were simply more stringent than required by the *Ahl al-Ḥadīth*.[74] In reality, he contends, Ḥanafīs were the target of the *Ahl al-Ḥadīth* for a number of reasons in addition to the use of *qiyās*. These included their excessive engagement in hypothetical jurisprudence and use of legal stratagems (*ḥiyal*), their holding theological views that the *Ahl al-Ḥadīth* found heretical, and their maintaining strong ties with rulers.[75] By contrast, the *Ahl al-Ḥadīth*, both in the Ḥijāz and in Iraq, were more reluctant to give *fatwā*s and preferred to remain silent when they did not have a relevant text to rely on in a particular case. In the second stage of their development, however, they developed technical skills that dealt with the verification of Ḥadīth and its status vis-à-vis the Qur'ān.[76]

Making a similar effort to situate the subject in its historical context, ʿAbd al-Majīd notes that the confusion about the identity of the *Ahl al-Ra'y* and the *Ahl al-Ḥadīth* is old. Examining a large number of reports from and about the

70 Al-Ḥasan, *al-Ijtihād*, pp. 266–267.
71 *Ibid.*, p. 265.
72 *Ibid.*, pp. 269 and 272.
73 *Ibid.*, pp. 272–273.
74 *Ibid.*, pp. 279–280.
75 *Ibid.*, pp. 290–295.
76 *Ibid.*, p. 300.

Companions as well as the Successors and their followers,[77] he argues that we can speak meaningfully about a distinction between the *Ahl al-Raʾy* and the *Ahl al-Ḥadīth* as two distinct legal trends only in the 3rd/9th century. He begins by narrowing down the focus of the two regions which these two trends are believed, erroneously in his view, to have emerged in the early decades of Islam. The discussion should be about Medina and Kufa. These two cities figured more than any others in early Islam. Medina was the city of the Prophet and the capital of the Muslim state where most of the Prophet's Companions spent their lives. Kufa was the pure Islamic establishment *par excellence* which many Companions built and settled therein.[78]

The problem of regarding the *Ahl al-Ḥadīth* and the *Ahl al-Raʾy* as having emerged and developed in Medina and Kufa respectively is that this assumes that there was no communication between the two cities, ʿAbd al-Majīd points out. This is historically not true, for people used to go back and forth between the two cities (if only to make the pilgrimage) and their scholars had in common many teachers from among the Companions.[79] Scholars in both cities used both Ḥadīth and *raʾy almost equally*. In Medina, there were scholars who were more given to the use of *raʾy*, such as Saʿīd ibn al-Musayyab—who was influenced by ʿUmar ibn al-Khaṭṭāb and Zayd ibn Thābit, in whose juridical thought *raʾy* played an important role—and Rabīʿat al-Raʾy, Mālik's teacher.[80] In Iraq, some scholars were less inclined to use *raʾy*, such as al-Shaʿbī who was very critical of some fellow Iraqis—such as Ḥammād ibn Abī Sulaymān—on account of their extensive use of it.[81] Yet even those scholars of Medina who were known for their detestation of *raʾy* did not fully refrain from using it. Similarly, Iraqi scholars who used *raʾy* detested the unrestrained use of it in religion and did use traditions in their jurisprudence.[82] In both cities, there existed controversies between those who were more and those who were less disposed to using *raʾy* and issuing *fatwās*.[83]

---

77 ʿAbd al-Majīd is not skeptical about what medieval sources attribute to early authorities, nor does he try to reconcile these seemingly contradictory attributions. Rather, in line with his theory, he tends to take them to indicate that early scholars were still in the process of working through various views and that we should not expect them to have had a coherent juridical thought at that point.

78 ʿAbd al-Majīd, *al-Madrasah al-Fiqhiyyah li-l-Muḥaddithīn*, pp. 20–21.

79 *Ibid.*, pp. 21–22.

80 *Ibid.*, pp. 39–40.

81 *Ibid.*, pp. 49–50.

82 *Ibid.*, pp. 29–30 and 33–36.

83 *Ibid.*, pp. 47–48.

The main difference between the two cities in ʿAbd al-Majīd's view had mostly to do with the cultural requirements of each. What turned these differences into open rivalry was the excessive zeal to defend the teachings of the particular Companions from whom they learned.[84] For personal, psychological, and intellectual reasons, the Companions differed on the weight that each of them gave to *raʾy* and to traditions.[85] For example, among the most prolific Companions in the transmission of Ḥadīth are ʿĀʾishah (d. 57/676), the Prophet's widow; ʿAbd Allāh ibn ʿAbbās (d. 68/687), his cousin; ʿAbd Allāh ibn ʿUmar (d. *c.* 73/693) and Abū Hurayrah (d. 57/676), two of his famous Companions. Nonetheless, they were significantly different. ʿĀʾishah and Ibn ʿAbbās were critical, rejected some traditions that reached them, and did not take reports at face value. On the other hand, Ibn ʿUmar and Abū Hurayrah accepted all the traditions that they heard and were hesitant to use reason to interpret them in a way that changed their apparent meaning. Ibn ʿUmar, for instance, was so scrupulous that he would still act on the basis of a tradition even if he had doubts about its authenticity.[86] Additionally, there existed a "natural" competition between the scholars of the Ḥijāz and Iraq and between the Arabs and non-Arabs in each region, but predominantly in Iraq.[87] Their loyalty to their teachers intensified with the passage of time and continued until the late 2nd century AH, when the *madhhab*s began to crystallize and distinguish themselves from others. It was this regional competition and not doctrinal differences that led to the split between the two regions at this stage. This also holds true as far as the second half of the 2nd century AH is concerned, when the Ḥanafī and Mālikī *madhhab*s—which inherited the old regional rivalry between Medina/the Ḥijāz and Kufa/Iraq—were taking shape.[88] While both *madhhab*s used *raʾy* equally, the Ḥanafīs tended to use *qiyās* as the basis for *raʾy* (which led them to increasingly pose hypothetical questions to test what they identified as *ʿillah* in each case),[89] whereas the Mālikīs were more

---

84 ʿAbd al-Majīd, *al-Madrasah al-Fiqhiyyah*, pp. 31–33.

85 *Ibid.*, p. 110. This is an interesting reference to how these personal features may have affected the willingness of different Companions to give *fatwā*s.

86 *Ibid.*, pp. 146–184.

87 For example, the dire statements attributed to Shaʿbī against *raʾy* and scholars who used it probably resulted from his competition with Ḥammād, who was not Arab, rather than with Ḥammād's teacher Ibrāhīm al-Nakhaʿī, who was, like al-Shaʿbī, an Arab (*ibid.*, pp. 37–39).

88 *Ibid.*, pp. 43–45.

89 *Ibid.*, p. 48. This connection between *qiyās* and the need to pose hypothetical questions to test *ʿillah* was made by other scholars (see, for instance, Abū Zahrah, *Abū Ḥanīfah*, pp. 229–234). However, it does not seem to have caught the attention of some scholars

inclined to search for the interest (*maṣlaḥah*) in each case and establish their opinion on its basis.[90]

When the process of collecting Prophetic traditions from various regions in the early 2nd century AH began, a group of traditionists emerged. Because of their limited argumentation skills, they accused the Ḥanafīs of ignorance and of rejection of traditions.[91] The situation was exacerbated by the emergence and popularity of the Muʿtazilīs in Iraq, some of whom happened to be Ḥanafīs in jurisprudence.[92] Abū Ḥanīfah himself held theological views that the traditionists regarded as deviant. This intensified the suspicion of the *Ahl al-Ḥadīth* who began to be conscious of themselves as a distinct group, although *not yet* as legal experts. Thus, it is only in the second half of the 2nd century AH that we can speak of the *Ahl al-Ḥadīth* vis-à-vis the *Ahl al-Raʾy*,[93] although the former had not yet developed legal thought and followed the *madhhab*s of the Ḥijāzīs (like Ibn Jurayj) or the Kufīs (like Sufyān al-Thawrī, Yaḥyā ibn Saʿīd al-Qaṭṭān, and others.[94]

In the 3rd/9th century two developments took place. The first was the attack on the use of *qiyās* in jurisprudence. Significantly, this attack was led by, not only the traditionists, but also by theologians who held that rituals (*al-ʿibādāt*) were not the domain of reason. The second development was the power that the Muʿtazilīs acquired and their attempts to impose their views on people either through argumentation or by force if necessary.[95] This brought the hostility between the *Ahl al-Ḥadīth* and the Muʿtazilīs into the open, and the popularity that some traditionists—notably Ibn Ḥanbal—gained for their refusal to submit to the government that backed the Muʿtazilīs increased their consciousness of their distinct identity as well as their confidence in their understanding of Islam, including its law. Therefore, while Ibn Ḥanbal was willing to accept some opinions of scholars like Mālik and al-Shāfiʿī before the *Miḥnah*,

---

who wrote about the early Ḥanafī school of law and its casuistry. For the Ḥanafī casuistry, see Baber Johansen, "Casuistry: Between Legal Concept and Social Praxis," p. 149, where Johansen describes it as a useful tool in "reconciling the requirements of practical life with those of legal doctrine."

90 ʿAbd al-Majīd, *al-Ittijāhāt*, p. 47. For a similar view on the difference between the use of *raʾy* in the Ḥijāz and Iraq, and the Ḥanafī and Mālikī notions of *istiḥsān*, see Abū Zahrah, *Tārīkh al-Madhāhib al-Islāmiyyah*, pp. 31–34, and 342.

91 ʿAbd al-Majīd, *Ittijāhāt*, pp. 57–58.

92 *Ibid.*, pp. 78–80.

93 *Ibid.*, pp. 59–61.

94 *Ibid.*, pp. 116–117.

95 *Ibid.*, pp. 65–66.

he totally rejected all *ra'y* after it and adhered only to Ḥadīth.[96] He thus paved the way for his fellow traditionists to develop their own legal school. Ḥadīth collections and works of Ḥadīth criticism produced at that time were all due to these events, and so was the total rejection of *ra'y* by the traditionists who did not distinguish between the use of *ra'y* in jurisprudence and its use in theology, or between sound *ra'y* and bad *ra'y*.[97] This development forced the *Ahl al-Ra'y*, for their part, to pay more attention to Ḥadīth.[98]

Next, 'Abd al-Majīd embarks on studying the *Ahl al-Ḥadīth*'s works (such as their Ḥadīth compilations) with the aim of uncovering the characteristics and underlying principles of their jurisprudence,[99] of which the very arrangement of these works can be indicative.[100] His research on their legal methodology[101] led him to determine two important aspects of their jurisprudence: their strong tendency toward comprehensiveness—in the sense

96 'Abd al-Majīd, *Ittijāhāt*, p. 120. In 'Abd al-Majīd's view, this explains the fact the more often than not, more than one view were attributed to Ibn Ḥanbal (*ibid.*, pp. 125–126).

97 *Ibid.*, pp. 100ff.

98 *Ibid.*, p. 126.

99 *Ibid.*, p. 7.

100 'Abd al-Majīd studied the opening chapters of these compilations, the kinds of reports that they include (Prophetic only or also include opinions of the Companions and Successors), the titles of their chapters, the comments made on some traditions and their authenticity, and the Qur'ānic verses mentioned and how they are ordered (*ibid.*, pp. 291–331). Ibn Ḥajar al-'Asqalānī engaged in a similar exercise to study al-Bukhārī's jurisprudence relying on the headings and sub-headings in his *Ṣaḥīḥ* (for this, see Mohammad Fadel, "Ibn Hajar's Hady al-Sari").

101 The first of these features is the *Ahl al-Ḥadīth*'s attitude toward the Qur'ān and Ḥadīth. Despite their disagreement on the hierarchy of the Qur'ān and Ḥadīth as two textual sources (Ibn Ḥanbal and al-Bukhārī held that both were on a par with each other whereas others gave Ḥadīth precedence over the Qur'ān on the ground that it can qualify it in various manners), they agreed that both were two independent yet inter-connected kinds of revelation and must therefore be used in conjunction with each other ('Abd al-Majīd, *Ittijāhāt*, p. 191). Secondly, they refused to judge Ḥadīth on the basis of the Qur'ān, which could lead to the rejection of many traditions (*ibid.*, pp. 205–207). Thirdly, Ḥadīth could and did establish rulings that did not exist in the Qur'ān (*ibid.*, p. 213). Fourthly, each of the Qur'ān and Ḥadīth could abrogate each other (*ibid.*, p. 227). Fifthly, while they differed on the question of whether *khabar al-wāḥid* established solid knowledge (the majority of them thought that it did not), they were agreed that it provided a sufficient basis for action (*'amal*) (*ibid.*, p. 242). Sixthly, they did not accept *mursal* traditions—except when the missing transmitter in the *isnād* was a Companion—due to the disconnectedness of its *isnād* (*ibid.*, pp. 260–262). Seventhly, they gave much weight to the opinions of the Companions when they agreed, and selected from their views when they differed (*ibid.*, p. 269). Furthermore, they abstained from giving an opinion when they did not find a

of using all available textual evidence in each case, including evidence on which authenticity they had some doubt[102]—and their "moral-psychological bent" (*al-ittijāh al-khuluqī al-nafsī*). This latter aspect is the key to understanding their thought and activities as Ḥadīth scholars as well as jurists. The *Ahl al-Ḥadīth* proceeded on the basis of a moral and religious worldview regarding the nature of human beings, the rules that govern their behavior, and the final judgment of their deeds.[103] This worldview led them to give much weight to intentions and have more interest in the practical aspects of religious knowledge.[104] Their focus, therefore, was on moral (rather than purely legal) traditions that epitomized the "spirit" of Islam.[105] It is this moral worldview that explains their total abhorrence of notions like legal stratagems,[106] as well as their adherence to principles like *sadd al-dharāʾiʿ*, according to which they would avoid something, not because it is forbidden in itself, but only because it may lead to something that is.[107]

ʿAbd al-Majid's views can give a lead in search for the underlying principles and characteristic features of the *Ahl al-Ḥadīth*. Most of the misgivings that the *Ahl al-Ḥadīth* reportedly had against the *Ahl al-Raʾy* can be seen as moral and religious in nature, such as their relationship with rulers (whom they did not consider pious enough), their holding "heretical" views, as well as their use of legal stratagems (which they regarded as deceitful) and excessive confidence in reason (which should only follow revelation). Likewise, the main feature that distinguished them could also be seen as moral in nature, namely, their

---

tradition in a certain case. Finally, they rejected *qiyās* and "hypothetical jurisprudence" (*al-fiqh al-taqdīrī*), and refused to put their legal opinions into writing (pp. 284ff.).

102 While the rejection of *mursal* traditions by the Ḥadīth scholars does not seem to support this view, it could only be taken to refer to a tension that existed between being Ḥadīth scholars as well as jurists at the same time. This notwithstanding, traditionists managed to find ways to incorporate many *mursal* traditions (for this, see al-Khaṭīb al-Baghdādī, *al-Kifāyah*, pp. 423ff.).

103 ʿAbd al-Majīd, *Ittijāhāt*, p. 413.

104 *Ibid.*, p. 431.

105 *Ibid.*, pp. 421–422. When they discussed charity (*zakāh*), for example, the *Ahl al-Ḥadīth* were not primarily concerned with its value or beneficiaries, or how a person refusing to pay it should be dealt with. Instead, they placed greater emphasis on how to encourage people to love the poor, have the desire to give them, and hate to be stingy, selfish, and careless about others. They linked charity to social and moral dimensions in a way that would motivate people to think of their communities and the value of cooperation and solidarity, rather than thinking only of their own self-interest, ʿAbd al-Majīd argues (*ibid.*, pp. 224–225). These statements needed further demonstration, nonetheless.

106 *Ibid.*, p. 451.

107 *Ibid.*, pp. 444–445.

excessive scrupulous fear that they may inadvertently attribute to religious law what did not belong to it. It is for this reason that they abstained from giving opinions in the absence of relevant textual evidence. In ʿAbd al-Majīd's view, it was this moral bent that shaped the *Ahl al-Ḥadīth*'s jurisprudence and distinguished them from others.

Other modern scholars have come to a similar conclusion. Commenting on Ibn Ḥanbal's views concerning issues like marriage and divorce, Susan Spectorsky writes:

> It... becomes clear, despite inconsistencies, that there is a moral dimension to Ibn Ḥanbal's responses: he gives preference to doctrines that protect women from exploitation, condemns the use of *ḥiyal* (legal stratagems), and requires actions and words to have consequences for which the doers and speakers are responsible.[108]

For example, according to the Qur'ān, a man cannot marry a woman that his father has once married,[109] but it is not clear if this prohibition covers women with whom the father had only an illicit sexual relationship. Most scholars, including Isḥāq ibn Rāhawayh, held that, regardless of whether he *should* do that or not, a son can legally marry a woman with whom his father had fornicated. Ibn Ḥanbal, however, argued that for that purpose, "illicit sexual relations equal marriage."[110] In fact, even lustful behavior suffices "to produce an affinity between a man and a woman that acts as an impediment to future sexual relations between either of them and the other's lateral descendants."[111] An obvious way to explain this view is to relate it to Ibn Ḥanbal's moral orientation that always—but not without exceptions as Spectorsky rightly observes—governed his legal thought. In agreement with this, Melchert argues that "[f]or the most part, the pious concern to do right and not impose his own reasoning

108 Susan Spectorsky, *Chapters on Marriage and Divorce: Responses of Ibn Ḥanbal and Ibn Rahwayh*, p. 7.

109 Q. 4:22 reads: "And marry not (*wa-lā tankiḥū*) women whom you father married." Most scholars (jurists and Qur'ān exegetes) take the word *nikāḥ* here to refer to marriage, although it is a homonym that refers to marriage as well as sexual intercourse. Obviously, Ibn Ḥanbal restricted the meaning of *nikāḥ* to marriage. For a discussion of the various views on this issue, see Ibn Ḥazm, *al-Muḥallā*, vol. 9, pp. 147–151, where he discusses whether involving in illicit sexual relationship can generally invalidate some kinds of marriage.

110 Spectorsky, *Chapters*, p. 23.

111 *Ibid.*, p. 24.

shines through Aḥmad [Ibn Ḥanbal]'s doctrine more than almost any comparable body of quotations from any other early Muslim jurisprudent."[112] There is indeed plenty of references in medieval sources to the *Ahl al-Ḥadīth*'s—and particularly Ibn Ḥanbal's[113]—piety and morality.[114]

It is noteworthy that when Spectorsky discusses Ibn Ḥanbal's juridical thought, she judged it in terms of two elements: consistency and morality. There is no attempt here to suggest that a jurist had to choose between morality and consistency, for it is obviously possible for a jurist to be "consistently moral" (or "morally consistent") in his legal thinking. However, jurists may frequently be compelled to privilege one element over the other in a particular case, or be consistent in privileging this particular element every time he has to. Elements that jurists take into consideration are numerous, including morality, individual and social interests, consistency etc. Whereas the particular consideration that influences a certain legal view is not always easy to discern, in the kind of jurisprudence that seeks to enforce moral principles, we can expect a natural emphasis on the actual *outcome* of legal rulings rather than on *how* this outcome is achieved. For example, in the case of his rejection of a marriage between a man and a woman with whom his father had an affair without an obvious textual basis, the immediate concern that appears to have triggered this view is Ibn Ḥanbal's moral bent, and he would maintain this view even if he failed to substantiate it on the basis of the available textual evidence. On the other hand, jurists for whom consistency is important seek to apply the same principles and methodology consistently irrespective of the final outcome. The excessive use of *qiyās* by the *Ahl al-Ra'y* is indicative of their concern for consistency, whereas Ibn Ḥanbal's concern for morality would lead him to abandon consistency if need be. This point, among others, will be taken up in CHAPTER FOUR.

112 Melchert, *Ahmad ibn Hanbal*, p. 78.

113 For this, see, for instance, Abū Zahrah, *Aḥmad ibn Ḥanbal*, pp. 64ff; Melchert, *Ahmad ibn Hanbal*, pp. 103–120; and Nimrod Hurvitz, *The Formation of Ḥanbalism: Piety into Power*, pp. 147–149.

114 For this, see Eerik Dickinson, *The Development of Early Sunnite Ḥadīth Criticism: The Taqdima of Ibn Abī Ḥātim al-Rāzī*, pp. 68–78. This may have been an influence of the *Ahl al-Ḥadīth*'s engagement in Ḥadīth criticism. They assessed and disqualified Ḥadīth transmitters on moral grounds, at times for reasons that other scholars found trivial and surpassing "reasonable" limits of observing the behavior of transmitters. For Ḥadīth critics, however, these reasons sufficed to question their morality and integrity (for an overview of the various notions and practices of the Ḥadīth critics, see al-Khaṭīb al-Baghdādī, *al-Kifāyah*, pp. 138–142, and *passim*).

3 Dāwūd's Ẓāhirism between the *Ahl al-Raʾy* and the *Ahl al-Ḥadīth*

Naturally, the way modern scholars understand the nature of the *Ahl al-Raʾy* and the *Ahl al-Ḥadīth* has shaped the way they conceive of Dāwūd and his Ẓāhirism in relation to them. Most of these scholars tend to regard Dāwūdism as a radical form of the thesis of the *Ahl al-Ḥadīth* who flourished in the 3rd/9th century. "In the rigorous interpretation of the judicial sources," Goldziher argues, "Aḥmad ibn Ḥanbal's school approaches most closely the method of the Ẓāhirite school." He made this argument on the basis of some cases which he discusses in an earlier chapter in his work on the Ẓāhirīs, which cases demonstrated to him that "the founder of the Ḥanbalite school decides according to the same *principles* which guide the Ẓāhirite school."[115] In this view, Ẓāhirīs and Ḥanafīs, the rivals of Ḥanbalīs, stood at two opposite extremes in Islamic law. Joseph Schacht followed suit, describing Dāwūd as "an extreme representative of the tendency hostile to human reasoning and relying exclusively on Kur'ān and Ḥadīth."[116] He believed that Dāwūd was a "traditionalist," one whose "doctrine represents a one-sided elaboration and development of that of al-Shāfiʿī and his school." Despite his total rejection of *qiyās* which al-Shāfiʿī endorsed, Dāwūd admired al-Shāfiʿī—who was a traditionalist himself[117]—and agreed with many of his doctrines.[118] Noel Coulson unequivocally regarded Ḥanbalism and Ẓāhirism as two schools of law that originated as extremist advocates of the traditions.[119] Likewise, in Wael Hallaq's view, Aḥmad ibn Ḥanbal and Dāwūd al-Ẓāhirī belonged to the same camp and held the same doctrine, which he describes as "restrictive and rigid." The only difference between them is that whereas the former detested *qiyās* and only used it in exceptional circumstances, the latter rejected it categorically as arbitrary and flawed. Among other things, this attitude toward *qiyās* accounts for the failure of Ẓāhirīs and the subsequent success of Ḥanbalīs. The former remained unwilling to join the "Great Synthesis" (i.e., adopting a middle stance between extreme "rationalism" and extreme "traditionalism," which original

---

115 Ignaz Goldziher, *The Ẓāhirīs: Their Doctrine and their History*, p. 81.

116 Joseph Schacht, "Dāwūd B. ʿAlī B. Khalaf al-Iṣfahānī, Abū Sulaymān," *EI*², vol. 2, p. 182.

117 *Ibid.*, vol. 2, p. 182. Schacht held that al-Shāfiʿī was a traditionalist whose main concern was to assert the overriding authority of Prophetic traditions against the living traditions and the "opinions of men" that were dominant at that time. For this, see Schacht, *Origins*, pp. 6–20.

118 Schacht, "Dāwūd B. ʿAlī," *EI*², vol. 2, p. 182.

119 N.J. Coulson, *A History of Islamic Law*, p. 71.

Ḥanbalism represented), whereas the latter managed to "meet rationalism halfway," Hallaq argues.[120]

Abdel Magid Turki places Ẓāhirism "at the furthest limit of orthodoxy."[121] He describes Dāwūd as a "disciple of al-Shāfiʿī, *albeit an indirect one*."[122] Turki does not associate Dāwūd's legal thought with the *Ahl al-Ḥadīth* explicitly, but he argues that "opposing the free use of opinion (*raʾy*) and hence the imitation of those who practised it," *Ẓāhirīs* "called for an effort of search (*idjtihād*) which, far from being identified with Ḥanafī *raʾy* or with Shāfiʿī reasoning by analogy (*ḳiyās*), could only be involved with the search for a text." Furthermore, they followed a methodology that "sought to rid *fiḳh*, as far as is possible, of any trace of subjectivity, confining it within the narrow limits of the evident meaning of the sacred text."[123] In this view, Dāwūd's acceptance of the general consensus of the Muslim community while rejecting the consensus of the ancient schools of law is revealing, for this acceptance "could only be realized on the basis of a body of *Tradition* which could not be overlooked by everybody."[124]

---

120 Hallaq, *Origins*, pp. 124–127.

121 Abdel Magid Turki, "al-Ẓāhiriyya," *EI*², vol. 11, p. 394. This in itself only means that Dāwūdism was traditionalist if "orthodoxy" means traditionalism, which is most likely what Turki had in mind. Orthodoxy here refers to both theological as well as legal beliefs. For the relationship between Muslim orthodoxy and law, see George Makdisi, "Ḥanbalite Islam," p. 264, where Makdisi argues that "[i]t is now time to rethink our idea of Muslim Orthodoxy. For the only orthodoxy which is certified in Islam by the consensus of the community (*ijmāʿ*) is Sunnī orthodoxy, represented since the third/ninth century by the four schools of Sunnī law . . . In the realm of [the] religion [of Islam], everything must be legitimized through the schools of law. For Islam is nomocratic and nomocentric." On the relationship between Aḥmad ibn Ḥanbal in particular and various aspects of "orthodox" (Sunnī) Islam, see Hurvitz, *Formation*. Remarkably, Hurvitz believes that "traditionalism" was introduced to jurisprudence by al-Shāfiʿī and maintained by Ibn Ḥanbal and Dāwūd, although the former delegated *qiyās* to the last position among the sources of the law, whereas Dāwūd rejected it altogether (Hurvitz, *Formation*, pp. 103, 186). Hurvitz's discussion of Ibn Ḥanbal's jurisprudence leads him to say that it was his acceptance of views of Companions and Successors (which Dāwūd did not do) and his giving them precedence over *qiyās* that characterized his thought (*ibid.*, p. 156).

122 *EI*², vol. 11, p. 395 (emphasis mine). Remarkably, Turki relies here entirely on Ibn Ḥazm, holding that this is "inevitable" for lack of other sources on Ẓāhirism. He also relies, at times uncritically, on modern studies on Ẓāhirīs, particularly Abū Zahrah's, Goldziher's, Brunschvig's, and Schacht's.

123 *Ibid.*, vol. 11, p. 395.

124 *Ibid.*, vol. 11, p. 395 (emphasis mine). The assumption here is that this "Tradition" was the one the cause of which the *Ahl al-Ḥadīth* were supporting, since this was the Tradition that differed from that of the ancient schools of law.

When read together, these statements indicate that the Ẓāhirīs in Turki's view were only interested in texts and opposed the use of other sources, primarily reason, in religious matters, an attitude characteristic of the *Ahl al-Ḥadīth* as most scholars understand them.[125]

The 14th/20th-century Ḥanbalī scholar Muḥammad al-Shaṭṭī counts Ibn Ḥanbal among the *imām*s of the *Ẓāhirīs*, alongside Dāwūd and Ibn Ḥazm, as evinced by the commitment of some early Ḥanbalīs to report Dāwūd's views in their legal works.[126] Al-Shaṭṭī himself collected Dāwūd's legal views and pointed out instances in which he agreed with Ibn Ḥanbal and other prominent Ḥanbalīs like Ibn Taymiyyah. Similarly, Muḥammad Abū Zahrah stresses Dāwūd's early admiration of al-Shāfiʿī—the upholder of the cause of the Prophetic Sunnah (*nāṣir al-sunnah*)—and his studying with some scholars of the *Ahl al-Ḥadīth*. Dāwūd's was "transmitted jurisprudence" (*fiqh marwī*) that was based primarily on transmitted traditions. He did not use *raʾy* in his jurisprudence, and in the few instances that he did, he did not do this on the same basis of the *Ahl al-Raʾy* who used to search for *ʿillah*s and used them in new cases. Dāwūd's jurisprudence, Abū Zahrah concludes, was the jurisprudence of texts in general, and of Ḥadīth in particular.[127]

In his doctoral dissertation on Dāwūd, Abū ʿĪd subscribes fully and rather uncritically to these views. He too emphasizes Dāwūd's admiration for al-Shāfiʿī as well as his adherence to Ḥadīth and avoidance of *raʾy*.[128] His studying with al-Shāfiʿī's students and other famous traditionists like Isḥāq ibn Rāhawayh were all factors that lead him to think in the same fashion as the *Aṣḥāb al-Ḥadīth*. He became a Ḥadīth student himself, and spent his life opposing the use of *raʾy* in religion.[129] Even ʿAbd al-Majīd—despite his

---

125 Mahmud Makki's view on the origin of Ẓāhirism is similar to Turki's in its indirect but evident association of Ẓāhirism with "Traditionalism". In his view, "El šāfiʿismo—ya lo hemos señalado—era un término medio entre el Razonamiento y la Tradición. Pero los ʿiraqíes partidarios de la Tradición, no se sintieron satisfechos de la forma en que al-Šafiʿī intentaba conciliar los dos principios. Hubo algunos exremistas que exigieron basarse más en la Tradición. Claro que el gran florecimiento de lose studios tradicionistas en ʿIrāq, a fines del siglo III, favorecía mucho a este partido, que acabó por formar una nueva escuela: la zāhirí, que reclamó unareforma jurídical a base de limitarse a la utilización del Corán y la Tradición y restringir la Unanimidad, al-Iŷmāʿ, concelando por completo el Razonamiento y la Analogía" (Makki, *Ensayo*, p. 205).

126 Muḥammad al-Shaṭṭī, "Risālah fī Masāʾil al-Imām Dāwūd al-Ẓāhirī," in *Majmūʿ yashtamilu ʿalā Risālatayn*, p. 3.

127 Muḥammad Abū Zahrah, *Ibn Ḥazm: Ḥayātuhu wa-ʿAṣruhu, Ārāʾuhu wa-Fiqhuhu*, p. 264.

128 Abū ʿĪd, *al-Imām Dāwūd*, p. 102.

129 *Ibid.*, pp. 133–135.

originality in understanding the origins of the *Ahl al-Raʾy* and the *Ahl al-Ḥadīth* and the features of the latter's jurisprudence—argues that all Ẓāhirīs belonged to the *Ahl al-Ḥadīth*, but the opposite was not necessarily true. It was from the *Ahl al-Ḥadīth*, who were inclined to adhere to the "apparent" meaning of the words and texts, that Ẓāhirism emerged and distinguished itself, for Ẓāhirīs admired traditionists and learned from them to respect texts and not neglect any of them without solid evidence. Furthermore, the *Ahl al-Ḥadīth* provided Ẓāhirīs with their raw materials, and Ẓāhirīs built on their offense against *qiyās* to exclude it completely from their jurisprudence. This notwithstanding, Ẓāhirīs had their own distinct identity and jurisprudence. They made a coherent *madhhab* out of the *Ahl al-Ḥadīth*'s general approach and followed it to the letter, even when this led them into absurdities (*ighrāb wa-shudhūdh*). Unlike the *Ahl al-Ḥadīth*, they refused to accept the opinions of the Companions (unless they all agreed on one thing) and the Successors as authoritative and binding.[130] They categorically rejected *qiyās*, *istiḥsān*, and the consideration of *maṣlaḥah* in jurisprudence, whereas the *Ahl al-Ḥadīth* only detested but occasionally used them.[131]

Remarkably, however, other differences that ʿAbd al-Majīd notes between Dāwūd and the *Ahl al-Ḥadīth* also constitute similarities between him and the *Ahl al-Raʾy*. Whereas the *Ahl al-Ḥadīth*, due to their scrupulousness, were generally reluctant to give *fatwā*s, Ẓāhirīs and the *Ahl al-Raʾy* never abstained from giving opinions when asked. Unlike the *Ahl al-Ḥadīth* who avoided stating that something was categorically religiously permitted or forbidden,[132] Ẓāhirīs and the *Ahl al-Raʾy* used to do this. Furthermore, unlike the *Ahl al-Ḥadīth*, both groups of scholars agreed that "intention" (*niyyah*) had no legal use or

---

130 ʿAbd al-Majīd, *Ittijāhāt*, pp. 350–359.

131 *Ibid.*, pp. 361–362. Other differences that ʿAbd al-Majīd mentions are technical. For instance, when a Companion says "we were commanded" or "we were prohibited," Ẓāhirīs would not accept this as valid textual and legal evidence. The *Ahl al-Ḥadīth*, however, treated this as a kind of *marfūʿ* traditions that are Prophetic in origin even if the Prophet himself is not explicitly mentioned (for *marfūʿ* traditions, see al-Khaṭīb al-Baghdādī, *al-Kifāyah*, p. 10). Secondly, whereas the imperative mood (*al-amr*) denotes obligation for both sides, Ẓāhirīs would take it to establish recommendation or permission only when there is solid textual evidence, while the *Ahl al-Ḥadīth* would change its default sense on other grounds that are not strictly textual in nature (ʿAbd al-Majīd, *Ittijāhāt*, pp. 366–367).

132 *Ibid.*, p. 417. According to this, it would therefore be rather hasty to say that Ibn Ḥanbal was "careless" in not always distinguishing between what was "required" and "recommended," as Melchert argues (Melchert, *Ahmad ibn Hanbal*, p. 76), for this was done on purpose and not without good reasons in Ibn Ḥanbal's view.

relevance.[133] Both agreed that nothing should be prohibited only because it could lead to something that is. Thus, the principle of *sadd al-dharāʾiʿ*, a main features of the jurisprudence of the *Ahl al-Ḥadīth*, had no place in the jurisprudence of both Ẓāhirīs and the *Ahl al-Raʾy*. Finally, juridical coherence and consistency were two obvious goals of the two groups, although they were at two opposite ends of the spectrum, ʿAbd al-Majīd notes.[134]

In a thoughtful discussion of Dāwūd's place in 3rd/9th-century jurisprudence, however, Christopher Melchert begins to entertain other possibilities. He follows the useful distinction between a "traditionist" who transmits Ḥadīth, and a "traditionalist" who holds certain beliefs antagonistic to the use of personal opinion, as represented by people like Ibn Ḥanbal. Despite his similarities with the traditionalists—such as their rejection of *raʾy, qiyās*, and *taqlīd*, acceptance of the *khabar al-wāḥid*, and understanding of *ijmāʿ*—Melchert seems to have some discomfort with considering Dāwūd one of them.[135] In fact, he is even able to entertain the possibility that, as least in some aspects of his career, Dāwūd was closer to the *Ahl al-Raʾy*. He observes that Dāwūd does not figure as a prominent traditionist and may even have a bad reputation in some biographical dictionaries. Furthermore, Dāwūd had little interest in *mudhākarah* (Hadith memorization and transmission), an activity that characterized the *Ahl al-Ḥadīth*, and engaged in *munāẓarah* (disputation), a common practice of the *Ahl al-Raʾy*. In addition to this personal profile, "Dāwūd's position concerning Ḥadīth was in some respects ... very far from Aḥmad's, much closer [to] the position of the rationalistic adherents of *raʾy*." He was close to al-Shāfiʿī's legal thought, which sets him apart from "the main body of Iraqi traditionalists," Melchert argues. Finally, Dāwūd disagreed with some of the fundamental theological doctrines of the *Ahl al-Ḥadīth*, as in the case of the nature of the Qurʾān.[136] In short, Dāwūd's jurisprudence was not traditionalist and may have been similar to the *Ahl al-Raʾy*'s.

---

133 ʿAbd al-Majīd, *Ittijāhāt*, p. 447.

134 *Ibid.*, p. 357.

135 Christopher Melchert, *Formation*, pp. 179–180. As noted earlier, in their view, valid *ijmāʿ* was only the consensus of the Prophet's Companions.

136 *Ibid.*, pp. 180–184. The issue of *khalq al-Qurʾān* dealt with the question of whether or not the Qurʾān was "created." This issue was raised in the late 2nd century and continued to be controversial for most of the first half of the 3rd. During that time, Ibn Ḥanbal and some other scholars refused to subscribe to the "official" view (influenced by Muʿtazilī connections with the Caliph) on the created nature of the Qurʾān. Ibn Ḥanbal is thought to have emerged from this *Miḥnah* (inquisition) as the champion of what became orthodox Sunnī Islam (for Ibn Ḥanbal's life and status in the aftermath of *Miḥnah*, see, Hurvitz, *Formation*, pp. 145ff. For the view that *Miḥnah* did not play such a significant role

Speaking of "Scripturalists," Vishanoff has recently argued that unlike traditionalists who relied only on Prophetic traditions, they "limited law to the dictates of the Qurʾān, literally interpreted, and left unregulated other aspects of life that were not directly addressed by the Qurʾān."[137] These Scripturalists included Muʿtazilīs and Ẓāhirīs.[138] Based on this, Vishanoff is able to argue that "[t]he vision characteristic of the preclassical Ẓāhiriyya had its roots primarily in early Muslim scripturalism, *not* in traditionalism."[139] As noted earlier, there is indeed strong evidence that Dāwūd and other early Ẓāhirīs had little interest in the study and transmission of Ḥadīth. However, this does not necessarily mean that they ignored Ḥadīth in principle as a source of legal and theological views, just as was the case with Ḥanafīs. In fact, we have seen that some of the works attribute to him suggests that Dāwūd was interested in Ḥadīth, and it is indeed remarkable that despite all the reported disagreements among early Ẓāhirīs, there is no reference to any disagreement over the authoritativeness of Ḥadīth. This notwithstanding, Vishanoff is confident that the Ẓāhirīs were not "traditionalists" and even notes that most of Dāwūd's and Ẓāhirī views in many hermeneutical issues are similar to the views of Muʿtazilīs and Ḥanafīs, although he asserts in the same breath that they "were indeed opposed to the rationalist jurisprudence of the Ḥanafiyya."[140]

With the exception of Melchert and Vishanoff, there seems to be an agreement among scholars of Islam's legal history that Dāwūd and Ẓāhirism originated within the camp of the *Ahl al-Ḥadīth*. Admittedly, Goldziher, Schacht, and Turki appear to have had some doubt about this, but they never spelled it out. They noted some differences between Dāwūdism and traditionalism, but failed to note any similarities between Dāwūdism and legal "rationalism" that is associated with the *Ahl al-Raʾy*. They do not therefore entertain the possibility that Dāwūd may have been more influenced by the *Ahl al-Raʾy* and perhaps one of them.

In her discussion of some views of Ibn Ḥanbal and Isḥāq ibn Rāhawayh, the famous traditionist and Ibn Ḥanbal's associate (and a possible teacher of Dāwūd's, as noted in CHAPTER ONE), Spectorsky has noted that there were particular differences between both of them. While the moral aspect in Ibn Ḥanbal's thought is evident, Ibn Rāhawayh's jurisprudence reveals a "*concern*

---

in the intellectual history of Islam, see Scott Lucas, *Constructive Critics: Ḥadīth Literature and the Articulation of Sunnī Islam*, pp. 192–202).

137 Vishanoff, *The Formation*, p. 37.

138 *Ibid.*, pp. 66ff.

139 *Ibid.*, p. 68 (emphasis mine).

140 *Ibid.*, p. 68.

for consistency and systematic thinking and exhibits *little interest in the human or moral dimensions* of a particular problem."[141] On the question of marriage with a women that a man's father had sexual relationship with, for instance, Ibn Rāhawayh did not share Ibn Ḥanbal's view that illicit sexual relationships had the same effect of marriage. Consequently, a man can perfectly marry a woman with whom his father had illicit sexual relationship.[142] Remarkably, Ibn Rāhawayh's jurisprudence manifests many of the features of the *Ahl al-Ẓāhir*, and some of his views could only come from a staunch Ẓāhirī, as ʿAbd al-Majīd notes.[143] This does not necessarily mean that he was a Ẓāhirī (although the possibility that he was should not be dismissed out of hand),[144] but it does suggest that if Ibn Ḥanbal was representative of the *Ahl al-Ḥadīth* (which we will assume here), we have to either accept that the *Ahl al-Ḥadīth* never developed into a coherent trend, or that some scholars regularly assumed as having belonged to them did actually not. Both Ibn Rāhawayh and Dāwūd may have been among these. We will now discuss this possibility apropos the latter.

---

141 Spectorsky, *Chapters*, p. 7 (emphasis mine).

142 *Ibid.*, p. 23.

143 Ibn Rāhawayh, for instance, would argue that not using *siwāk* (a piece of wood that the Prophet used to brush his teeth with before the prayers) and washing in between the hair of the beard (*takhlīl al-liḥyah*) void the prayers, on the basis that the Prophet said that a Muslim should?/must? do these before praying (ʿAbd al-Majīd, *Ittijāhāt*, p. 349). It is, of course, clear that what is at stake here is whether the Prophet, when he issued that command, meant that it was obligatory or only praiseworthy. Ibn Rāhawayh's views here are based on the notion that the imperative denotes obligation, a central notion in the jurisprudence of both Ẓāhirīs and the *Ahl al-Raʾy*, as will be discussed in CHAPTER FIVE.

144 ʿAbd al-Majīd notes aspects of similarity between al-Bukhārī's and Ẓāhirīs' legal methodology.

CHAPTER 4

Ẓāhirism between the *Ahl al-Raʾy* and the *Ahl al-Ḥadīth*

It has been noted earlier that medieval sources are not clear on why Dāwūd was referred to as *al-Ẓāhirī*, focusing primarily on his rejection of *qiyās*.[1] Likewise, modern scholars assume that *ẓāhir* is the "literal," "apparent," "plain" or "evident" meaning.[2] This chapter seeks to investigate what *ẓāhir* may have meant in the 3rd/9th century. In conjunction with what the biographical evidence suggests about Dāwūd's affiliation (CHAPTER ONE), the question of the relationship between his Ẓāhirism and the two legal trends of the *Ahl al-Raʾy* and the *Ahl al-Ḥadīth* (CHAPTER FOUR) will be revisited. It will be argued that, contrary to what has been assumed about him, both the biographical and doctrinal evidence strongly indicates that Dāwūd was closer to the *Ahl al-Raʾy* than to the *Ahl al-Ḥadīth*.

1 The only exception to this may be al-Qāḍī al-Nuʿmān. As noted in CHAPTER ONE, he mentioned that *istidlāl*, a clearly hermeneutical tool, was the pillar of the jurisprudence of a certain group of jurists whom Stewart takes to be the Ẓāhirīs. This chapter will demonstrate that this could in fact be a reference to them.

2 For examples of scholars who define the *ẓāhir* meaning as the "apparent" or "evident" meaning, see Abdel Magid Turki, "al-Ẓāhiriyya" (*EI*², vol. 11, p. 395), where he argues that Ẓāhirīs sought to confine jurisprudence "within the narrow limits of the evident meaning of the sacred text". See also, Arnaldez, *Grammaire et théologie*, p. 26. To identify "le sens apparent," Arnaldez argues, one does not need to search "en dehors de la définition nominale, lexicographique." These scholars do not explain what the apparent or evident meaning is. Nor do they demonstrate that this was the understanding of *ẓāhir* by Ẓāhirīs. "Literal," of course, is also widely used, which will be discussed in the next chapter. To my knowledge, the only modern scholar who attempted to explain the meaning of *ẓāhir* is Tawfīq al-Ghalbazūrī. He, however, only mentions that *ẓāhir* for the scholars of *uṣūl al-fiqh* is any term or word the meaning of which does not require an indicator other than itself (*an yakūna al-lafẓ bi-ḥaythu yadullu maʿnāh bi-ṣīghatihi min ghayr tawaqquf ʿalā qarīnah khārijiyyah*). He does not, however, demonstrate that this is how Ẓāhirīs understood it, nor does he argue that this was the sense of the term as it was used in the 3rd/9th century. In fact, he admits that it is one of "the most ambiguous terms" (*akhfā ʾl-muṣṭalaḥāt*) in Ibn Ḥazm's writings (al-Ghalbazūrī, *al-Madrasah al-Ẓāhiriyyah*, p. 549).

 DOI 10.1163/9789004279650_006

1 *Ẓāhir* in the Muslim Tradition

1.1 *Arabic Lexica*

The root *ẓ-h-r*, from which *ẓāhir* is derived, is quite rich in meaning. Its first and basic meaning is "[i]t was, or became, outward, exterior, external, extrinsic, or exoteric; and hence, it appeared; became apparent, overt, open, perceptible or perceived, manifest, plain or evident."[3] *Ẓāhir al-jabal*, thus, refers to a mountain peak,[4] and *ẓuhūr*, the verbal noun of *ẓahara*, means for something hidden to become apparent. This basic meaning of *ẓ-h-r* is always contrasted with *b-ṭ-n*, which refers to what is hidden. Ibn Manẓūr mentions a tradition in which the Prophet is reported to have said that every verse in the Qurʾān has a *ẓahr* and a *baṭn*, which some scholars took to mean the verbal expression of the Qurʾān (*lafẓ*) and its interpretation respectively. Other scholars held that *ẓahr* referred to what is "apparent" of the meaning of the Qurʾān, and *baṭn* to what is hidden of its interpretation. According to this view, the *ẓāhir* of Qurʾānic stories, for example, are the records of their events; their *bāṭin* is the lessons that they seek to convey.[5] Other senses of *ẓ-h-r* denote dominance, such as in *ẓahara ʿalā*, meaning for a person to have dominated or subdued another, or for something to have prevailed. *Taẓāharat al-akhbār*, thus, means that numerous accounts have reported such and such. Additionally, *ẓahara ʿalā* can mean to become cognizant or knowledgeable of something.[6] Thus, *ẓahara ʿalā ʾl-shayʾ* means for someone to become aware or knowledgeable of something, and *aẓharahu ʿalā ʾl-shayʾ* means for a person to have informed another or made him aware of something.[7]

---

3 Lane, *An Arabic-English Lexicon*, vol. 5, p. 1926.

4 For this, see al-Khalīl ibn Aḥmad, *Kitāb al-ʿAyn*, pp. 505–506, and Ibn Manẓūr, *Lisān al-ʿArab*, vol. 8, p. 277. I will refer to Ibn Manẓūr for the other derivatives of *ẓ-h-r*. Other lexica, such as *Kitāb al-ʿAyn* of al-Khalīl ibn Aḥmad al-Farāhīdī (d. 175/774), *Jamharat al-Lughah* of Ibn Durayd (Abū Bakr Muḥammad ibn al-Ḥasan al-Azdī) (d. 321/933), *al-Ṣiḥāḥ* of Ismāʿīl ibn Ḥammād al-Jawharī (d. 400/1010), *al-Qāmūs al-Muḥīṭ* of Majd al-Dīn Muḥammad al-Fīrūzābādī (d. 816/1414), and *Tāj al-ʿArūs* of Muḥammad Murtaḍā al-Zabīdī (d. 1205/1791) do not add much to what Ibn Manẓūr mentions.

5 Ibn Manẓūr, *Lisān*, vol. 8, p. 274.

6 *Ibid.*, vol. 8, pp. 277–279.

7 *Ibid.*, vol. 8, pp. 278–279. Other meanings of *ẓāhir* have to do with *ẓahr*, meaning back. Ironically, the Arabs used *ẓahr* for back, not face, which suggests that it was coined in reference to animals, whose *ẓahr* is usually more apparent than their bellies (*baṭn*), especially for those mounting them. For human beings, however, *baṭn* rather than *ẓahr* is what people usually see of each other when they interact.

Paradoxically, *ẓahara*, when used in certain contexts and expressions, can mean the opposite of what is presented as its basic senses. For instance, *al-ẓahr* refers to what is hidden from one or of something.[8] *Takallama bi-l-shayʾ ʿan ẓahr al-ghayb* means that someone has talked about something that he has not witnessed. Other derivatives also suggest concealment, in the sense of pretending something that is not real.[9] Here the meanings of *ẓahr* and *baṭn* conflate. For example, to refer to what appears of the sky, the Arabs used to say *ẓahr al-samāʾ* or *baṭn al-samāʾ*.[10] *Ẓahara la-hu* thus means "it seemed to him," and *aẓhara la-hu* means for a person to have pretended something to another.[11] Common among these derivatives is an element of hiddenness or uncertainty about what appears to the eyes. Furthermore, whereas *ẓahara ʿalā* means "to have prevailed," it can also mean just the opposite: to support someone, such as *ẓahartu ʿalay-hi*, meaning "I have assisted or supported him" (*aʿantuhu*).[12] In brief, the productivity of the root *ẓ-h-r* is potentially misleading. The basic meaning of the root indicates something that is obvious and evident, or one that prevails over others. Other meanings, however, indicate just the opposite, such that *ẓāhir* and *bāṭin* could indicate just the same thing.

Some legal scholars were inspired by lexical senses of *ẓāhir*. In a section on "the *ẓāhir* and its interpretation" (*fī ʾl-ẓāhir wa-taʾwīlihi*) in his *Iḥkām fī Uṣūl al-Aḥkām*, Sayf al-Dīn al-Āmidī presents two views on the meaning of *ẓāhir*. According to the first, *ẓāhir* is the "obvious or apparent" meaning, or that which readers take to be the most likely meaning.[13] The other view, which al-Āmidī supports, is that *ẓāhir* is the "conventional" meaning. A meaning can be conventional when it is assigned to a certain word *ab initio* (*al-waḍʿ al-aṣlī*), or when a certain group of people agree to use a certain word in a certain sense (*al-waḍʿ al-ʿurfī*). Referring to a lion by the word *asad* is an example of the former, but using *ghāʾiṭ* (a word that refers to a small hole in the ground in which people relieve themselves) to refer to human defecation is an example of the second.[14] The first view on the meaning of *ẓāhir* here raises the question of how the "obvious" meaning can be determined, or why a reader would take a certain meaning to be the most likely one intended by a certain word or

8 *Al-ẓahru mā ghāba ʿan-ka* (Ibn Manẓūr, *Lisān*, vol. 8, p. 279). In al-Zabīdī's view, this is a figurative use of *ẓahara* (al-Zabīdī, *Tāj al-ʿArūs*, vol. 7, p. 170).

9 Lane, *An Arabic-English Lexicon*, vol. 5, p. 1930.

10 Ibn Manẓūr, *Lisān*, vol. 8, p. 274.

11 Lane, *An Arabic-English Lexicon*, vol. 5, p. 1927.

12 Ibn Manẓūr, *Lisān*, vol. 8, p. 277.

13 This view is attributed to the Shāfiʿī scholar al-Ghazzālī (for this, see Abū Ḥāmid al-Ghazzālī, *al-Mustaṣfā min ʿIlm al-Uṣūl*, vol. 2, pp. 713–714).

14 Sayf al-Dīn al-Āmidī, *al-Iḥkām fī Uṣūl al-Aḥkām*, vol. 2, pp. 197–198.

sentence. The second view, however, can be helpful. What is *ẓāhir* is conventional rather than self-evident. In other words, the *ẓāhir* sense of a word is not inherent in the language, but is rather a matter of convention among its users. Put differently, language does not have an ontological existence separate from those who *use* it in communication. If this is the case, then *ẓāhir* is open to interpretation; indeed, al-Āmidī argues that *ẓāhir* is less certain than other modes of *bayān* (expression), particularly *naṣṣ*.[15]

Ẓāhir in al-Āmidi's account and in all other accounts in *uṣūl al-fiqh* is thus a linguistic term. Yet it has not yet been established that Dāwūd was labeled *al-Ẓāhirī* on account of linguistic views that he held. Accordingly, we now turn to the question of how *ẓāhir* was used in selected works written in the first three centuries AH, starting with the Qurʾān, followed by al-Shāfiʿī's *Risālah* and al-Ṭabarī's *Jāmiʿ al-Bayān*.

1.2 *The Qurʾān*

Various derivatives of the root *ẓ-h-r* appear some 59 times in the Qurʾān.[16] Nearly one third of these are related to *ẓahr* (meaning the back of something),[17] and one quarter indicates prevailing over someone or something (*ẓahara ʿalā*),[18] or siding with someone against another (*ẓāhara ʿalā*).[19] Other derivatives that appear frequently in the Qurʾān are *ẓahara*, meaning "to appear," *aẓhara*, "to cause to appear," and *aẓhara ʿalā*, to "reveal to."[20] All these derivatives do not seem to have posed special difficulty for Qurʾān exegetes, indicating

15 *Ibid.*, vol. 2, pp. 199–207. A *naṣṣ* is any statement the meaning of which does not need any further indication beyond itself. For various meanings and uses of this term, see A. J. Wensinck (and J. Burton), "Naṣṣ," *EI*², vol. 7, p. 1029.

16 For a complete list of this root and its derivatives in the Qurʾān, see Muḥammad Fuʾād ʿAbd al-Bāqī, *al-Muʿjam al-Mufahras li-Alfāẓ al-Qurʾān al-Karīm*, pp. 559–560.

17 See, for instance, Q. 6:94, Q. 6:138, Q. 35:45, and Q. 42:33. Some of these instances have to do with *ẓihār*, a declaration by a husband that his wife is to him like the back (*ẓahr*, hence *ẓihār*) of his mother (for this, see Q. 33:4, Q. 58:2, and Q. 58:3). (For *zihār*, see Ibn Qudāmah al-Maqdisī, *al-Mughnī*, pp. 54ff.)

18 See, for instance, Q. 9:8: "How [can there be any treaty for the others] when, if they prevail over you (*kayfa wa-inn yaẓharū ʿalaykum*)." See also Q. 18:20, Q. 40:20, and Q. 48:28.

19 See, for instance, Q. 9:4: "Except those of the idolaters with whom you [Muslims] have a treaty, and who have since abated nothing of your right nor have supported anyone against you (*wa-lam yuẓāhirū ʿalay-kum aḥadan*)." See also Q. 33:26 and Q. 60:9.

20 For example, all exegetes take *ẓahara* in Q. 30:41 (Corruption has appeared (*ẓahara*) on land and sea) to mean "to appear," and in Q. 40:26 (... he will make mischief to appear (*yuẓhir*) in the land) to mean "to cause to appear." Furthermore, all exegetes take *aẓhara ʿalā* in Q. 66:3 (... and God made it known to him (*aẓharahu ʿalā*) [i.e., the Prophet Muḥammad]" and Q. 72:26 ([He is] the Knower of the Unseen and he does not reveal

that their various senses were quite clear. However, these exegetes had disagreements over the Qur'ānic use of *ẓāhir* itself, used as a noun and adjective in some Qur'ānic verses. The following discussion of four instances of Qur'ānic usages of this word seeks to examine how this could be helpful in contributing to our understanding of what the term *ẓāhir* may have meant in early Islam. Two early commentaries on the Qur'ān (*tafsīrs*) are used here—those attributed to Mujāhid ibn Jabr (d. *c.* 102/720) and Muqātil ibn Sulaymān (d. 150/767), and some other *tafsīrs* written between the late 3rd/9th and the 8th/14th centuries and generally considered authoritative.[21]

In Q. 6:120, "Forsake the outwardness of sin (*ẓāhir al-ithm*) and the inwardness thereof (*wa-bāṭinahu*)," *ẓāhir* is distinguished from, indeed contrasted with, *bāṭin*.[22] Medieval scholars had various views as to what *ẓāhir al-ithm* and *bāṭin al-ithm* mean. Muqātil ibn Sulaymān held that *ithm* in this and similar verses refers to fornication; whereas *ẓāhir* refers to committing it openly, *bāṭin* refers to doing it secretly.[23] Attributing Muqātil's view to many earlier authorities (Companions and Successors), al-Ṭabarī does not accept this restriction of the meaning of *ithm* to a particular sin (for reasons that a later discussion will reveal). Supporting his view by reports from earlier authorities, he nevertheless accepts the view that *ẓāhir* refers to sins committed in public and *bāṭin* to sins committed secretly.[24] Later scholars generally accept this element of publicity regarding the difference between *ẓāhir al-ithm* and *bāṭin al-ithm*, but they also provide more views about the kind of sins to which the verse refers. Fakhr al-Dīn al-Rāzī, for instance, mentions a view that whereas *ẓāhir al-ithm* refers to physical sins, *bāṭin al-ithm* refers to spiritual and doctrinal sins, such as holding wrong beliefs, hatred, envy, haughtiness, wishing harm for others, etc.[25] Al-Qurṭubī accepts this view,[26] but Ibn Kathīr is more inclined to

---

(*yuẓhiru ʿalā*) His secret to any) to mean "to reveal to" or "to inform someone" or "to make someone aware of something."

21 These are *Jāmiʿ al-Bayān fī Taʾwīl Āy al-Qurʾān* of Muḥammad ibn Jarīr al-Ṭabarī (d. 310/922), *al-Tafsīr al-Kabīr* of Fakhr al-Dīn al-Rāzī (d. 606/1209), *al-Jāmiʿ li-Aḥkām al-Qurʾān* of Abū ʿAbd Allāh al-Qurṭubī (d. 671/1272), and *Tafsīr al-Qurʾān al-Aẓīm* of Ismāʿīl ibn ʿUmar ibn Kathīr (d. 774/1372).

22 Other Qurʾānic verses that contrast *ẓāhir al-ithm* and *bāṭin al-ithm* include Q. 7:33, ("Say: My Lord forbids indecencies, *mā ẓahara min-hā wa-mā baṭana*"), Q. 6:151, and Q. 7:33. For other verses that contrast *ẓāhir* and *bāṭin*, see, for instance, Q. 57:3 and Q. 31:20.

23 Muqātil ibn Sulaymān, *Tafsīr Muqātil*, vol. 1, p. 586.

24 Al-Ṭabarī, *Jāmiʿ al-Bayān*, vol. 8, pp. 13–15.

25 Fakhr al-Dīn al-Rāzī, *al-Tafsīr al-Kabīr*, vol. 13, pp. 167–168.

26 Al-Qurṭubī, *al-Jāmiʿ*, vol. 7, p. 74.

al-Ṭabarī's views on the unrestrictedness of the term *ithm* and the view that for a sin to be *ẓāhir* or *bāṭin* depends on whether it is done publicly or privately.[27]

In Q. 13:33, "Is He Who is aware of the deserts of every soul as he who is aware of nothing? Yet they ascribe partners to Allah. Say: Name them. Is it that you would inform Him of something which He does not know in the earth? Or is it but a way of speaking (*am bi-ẓāhir min al-qawl*)?," the meaning of *ẓāhir* appears to be problematic. According to Mujāhid ibn Jabr, *ẓāhir* here means *ẓann*, something of which one has no definite knowledge.[28] For Muqātil, *ẓāhir min al-qawl* means a false matter (*amr bāṭil kadhib*),[29] a view that al-Ṭabarī supports with several reports.[30] In agreement with this, al-Rāzī explains that this means that they [those who ascribe partners to Allāh, presumably the Meccan polytheists] propagate falsehood to deceive others.[31] For his part, al-Qurṭubī connects this to the previous part of the verse, where God is asking polytheists if they would inform him of something that he did not know (other deities in this context). In al-Qurṭubī's view, *am bi-ẓāhir min al-qawl* means that they would inform him of known deities like those they used to worship in the Ḥijāz, while *bāṭin* would be referring to deities of whom they would not inform Him.[32] Ibn Kathīr adopts Mujāhid's view and explains that this part of the verse means that they worshiped their false deities on the basis of *ẓann*, or the false belief that they could do them good or harm.[33]

A third verse is Q. 30:7, "They know only some appearance of the life of the world (*yaʿlamūna ẓāhir min al-ḥayāt al-dunyā*) and are heedless of the Hereafter." According to Muqātil, the "knowledge" (*ʿilm*) meant in this verse refers to their—presumably Persians living in the time of the Prophet—mastery of worldly activities and skills in gaining worldly benefits, although they were otherwise heedless of the Hereafter.[34] Al-Ṭabarī agrees with this understanding, supporting it with reports from earlier authorities. In one such report, what these people knew were the worldly and material matters, but they were ignorant in matters of religion,[35] a view that al-Qurṭubī and Ibn Kathīr supports.[36] In al-Rāzī's view, this means that the knowledge of these people

27 Ibn Kathīr, *Tafsīr*, vol. 6, pp. 145–146.
28 Mujāhid ibn Jabr, *Tafsīr Mujāhid*, vol. 1, p. 329.
29 Muqātil ibn Sulaymān, *Tafsīr Muqātil*, vol. 2, p. 381.
30 Al-Ṭabarī, *Jāmiʿ al-Bayān*, vol. 12, p. 359.
31 Al-Rāzī, *al-Tafsīr al-Kabīr*, vol. 19, p. 56.
32 Al-Qurṭubī, *al-Jāmiʿ*, vol. 9, p. 323.
33 Ibn Kathīr, *Tafsīr*, vol. 8, p. 154.
34 Muqātil ibn Sulaymān, *Tafsīr Muqātil*, vol. 3, p. 407.
35 Al-Ṭabarī, *Jāmiʿ al-Bayān*, vol. 21, pp. 22–23.
36 Al-Qurṭubī, *al-Jāmiʿ*, vol. 14, pp. 7–8; Ibn Kathīr, *Tafsīr*, vol. 11, p. 15.

was superficial, focusing only on certain aspects of worldly life—indulgence in pleasurable activities and material satisfaction—and ignoring the *bāṭin* part of it, i.e., its troubles and harms. He also reports the view that *ẓāhir* here refers to the existence of life, of which the Persians were aware, whereas *bāṭin* refers to its end, of which they were negligent.[37]

Finally, Q. 57:13, "On the day when hypocritical men and women will say to those who believe: Look on us that we may borrow from your light! It will be said: Go back and seek for light! Then there will separate them a wall wherein is a gate, the inner side whereof (*bāṭinuhu*) contains mercy, while the outer side thereof (*ẓāhiruhu*) is toward the doom," distinguishes again between *ẓāhir* and *bāṭin*. Muqātil explains that the "wall" in this verse refers to a wall separating Paradise and Hellfire, and *ẓāhir* and *bāṭin* refer to the two sides of this wall (*bāṭin* to the side of Paradise and *ẓāhir* of Hellfire).[38] In addition to this view, al-Ṭabarī reports another one according to which the wall mentioned in the verse is a wall in *al-Aqṣā* mosque in Jerusalem. Known as the Eastern Wall, it separates the mosque and a place called *wādī jahannam* (or the Valley of Jahannam or Hellfire). *Bāṭin* refers to the side facing the mosque (or the interior of the mosque) and *ẓāhir* to the side facing the valley.[39] Al-Rāzī prefers Muqātil's view,[40] but al-Qurṭubī, following al-Ṭabarī, only reports all various views.[41] Ibn Kathīr believes that since Paradise and Hellfire are in two different places, the wall here is only used figuratively (by those holding that it refers to a specific wall between Paradise and Hellfire) to clarify the meaning. This wall, he argues, is a wall that leads to Paradise. When all believers have passed through it on the Day of Judgment, it will be closed, leaving hypocrites behind in bewilderment, darkness and torment.[42]

To recapitulate, when used verbally, derivatives of *ẓ-h-r* in the Qur'ān refer to prevailing over, supporting someone, appearing or causing to appear, and spreading. Nouns and adjectives derived from this root, however, bear a generally negative sense, such that *ẓāhir* refers to something that is uncertain, false, misleading, superficial and materialistic. This is hardly useful in providing a satisfactory answer as to the meaning of *ẓāhir* in early Islam or why would someone be labeled "al-Ẓāhirī." While it is possible that Dāwūd was labeled *al-Ẓāhirī* because his understanding of the Qur'ān was deemed superficial and

37 Al-Rāzī, *al-Tafsīr al-Kabīr*, vol. 25, p. 97.

38 Muqātil ibn Sulaymān, *Tafsīr Muqātil*, vol. 4, p. 240.

39 Al-Ṭabarī, *Jāmiʿ al-Bayān*, vol. 27, pp. 225–227.

40 Fakhr al-Dīn al-Rāzī, *al-Tafsīr al-Kabīr*, vol. 29, p. 226.

41 Al-Qurṭubī, *al-Jāmiʿ*, vol. 17, p. 246.

42 Ibn Kathīr, *Tafsīr ibn Kathīr*, vol. 13, pp. 419–420.

misleading, the fact that Ibn Ḥazm used this epithet himself and referred to Dāwūd and other Ẓāhirīs as such indicates that it cannot have been used in this Qurʾānic sense. Therefore, we now turn to 3rd/9th-century writings to explore other possibilities of the meaning of *ẓāhir* and how it pertains to jurisprudence.

∴

Al-Shāfiʿī's *Risālah* and al-Ṭabarī's *tafsīr* seem potentially useful for our purposes of identifying what *ẓāhir* may have meant in Dāwūd's time. The former discusses various theoretical legal issues, whereas the latter is the earliest comprehensive Qurʾān commentary that has reached us.[43] Both works have the advantage of having been written just before and just after Dāwūd's time. *Al-Risālah* was written in the late 2nd or the early 3rd century AH, whereas al-Ṭabarī wrote his *tafsīr* in the late 3rd century AH. Furthermore, we have noted earlier the relationship of Dāwūd with these two scholars. Dāwūd began his career as a follower of al-Shāfiʿī's legal thought and met with al-Shāfiʿī's immediate students, whereas al-Ṭabarī is reported to have attended Dāwūd's lectures in Baghdad. Finally, both works do use the term *ẓāhir*. In other words, if there exists some consistency in the way both scholars use this term in their writings, we should be able to assume that that was how it was understood in Dāwūd's time.

1.3 *Al-Shāfiʿī's* Risālah

The term *ẓāhir* appears frequently in al-Shāfiʿī's *Risālah*.[44] The first extensive use of this term there is in a chapter that discusses various methods of expression (*bayān*) that the Qurʾān uses:

---

43 Earlier Qurʾān commentaries are usually succinct, only give the "meaning" of Qurʾānic verses without much discussion. Indeed, the term *ẓāhir* does not appear in other early *tafsīr*s such as those of Mujāhid ibn Jabr and Muqātil ibn Sulaymān.

44 Not all instances in which *ẓāhir* appears in *al-Risālah* are discussed here. Some of these do not seem to have a particular relevance to or significance for this discussion. In his discussion of *qiyās*, for instance, al-Shāfiʿī speaks about our knowledge of *ẓāhir* and *bāṭin*. Khadduri—mistakenly, in my view—translates this as the "literal" and "implicit" meaning respectively (*al-Risālah* (1961), pp. 288ff). Al-Shāfiʿī's discussion, however, strongly indicates that *ẓāhir* here means that of which we are certain (through a *mutawātir* text or *ijmāʿ*), whereas *bāṭin* refers to what is real, even if we do not know it for certain—i.e., what is hidden from us (for this, see *al-Risālah* (1938), pp. 476ff, §§1321ff). For example, when jurists draw a certain analogy between a new case that resembles more than one existing case and the *ʿillah* of which is disputed among scholars, each jurist's *qiyās* in

> God addressed the Arabs in His Book in a way consistent with what they know about their language's features. Among those features of their language with which they are familiar is their language's broad scope, and [the Arab] knows by nature that he could be addressed with a sample of language which is *ʿāmm ẓāhir* which is in fact intended as *ʿāmm ẓāhir*, such that one can dispense with bringing something else to bear on it; or which is *ʿāmm ẓāhir* and is intended as *ʿāmm*, but also contains something which is *khāṣṣ*, which is indicated by some of what is mentioned in it [*al-ʿāmm al-ẓāhir*]; or which is *ʿāmm ẓāhir* but is intended as *khāṣṣ*; or which is *ẓāhir* that the context indicates that what is intended by it is not, in fact, the *ẓāhir*. Knowledge of all this could be at the beginning of the speech, the middle, or the end thereof.[45]

In this rather difficult passage, al-Shāfiʿī stresses that the Qurʾān was revealed in a specific language to a specific people who used it. Accordingly, under-

---

this case is "apparently" (*fī ʾl-ẓāhir*) correct. Whether it is truly correct in reality (*fī ʾl-bāṭin*), however, is beyond our certainty (*al-Risālah* (1938), p. 479, §1332). The same point applies to testimonies. Testimonies are valid on the basis of what appears to us of the reliability of the witnesses (*al-ẓāhir min ḥāl al-shuhūd*), but their *bāṭin* (i.e., the truth about their testimonies and integrity) is beyond our ability to ascertain (*ibid.*, pp. 478–479, §1330). A third example is when a man unknowingly marries his sister. In the unknown (*fī ʾl-mughayyab*), she is his sister. But in what appears to us and what we know (*fī ʾl-ẓāhir*), she can perfectly be his wife (*ibid.*, pp. 499–500, §§1430–1439). See also *ibid.*, pp. 481–482, §§1350–1354, for a similar discussion and use of *ẓāhir* in reference to *ʿadālah* (integrity and reliability).

45 *fa-inna-mā khāṭaba Allāh bi-kitābihi ʾl-Arab bi-lisānihā ʿalā mā taʿrifu min maʿānīhā, wa-kāna mimmā taʿrifu min maʿānīhā ittisāʿ lisānihā, wa-anna fiṭratahu an yukhāṭaba bi-l-shayʾ min-hu ʿāmm ẓāhir yurādu bi-hi ʾl-ʿāmm al-ẓāhir, wa-yustaghnā bi-awwal hādhā min-hu ʿan ākhirihi, wa-ʿāmm ẓāhir yurādu bi-hi ʾl-ʿāmm wa-yadkhuluhu ʾl-khāṣṣ, fa-yustadallu ʿalā hādhā bi-baʿḍ mā khūṭiba bi-hi fī-hi, wa-ʿāmm ẓāhir yurādu bi-hi ʾl-khāṣṣ, wa-ẓāhir yuʿrafu fī siyāqihi anna-hu yurādu bi-hi ghayr ẓāhirihi. Fa-kull hādhā mawjūd ʿilmuhu fī awwal al-kalām aw wasaṭihi aw ākhirihi. Al-Risālah* (1938), §173, pp. 51–52. For the translation of the quoted passages from *al-Risālah*, I use the translations of Khadduri (*al-Risālah*, 1961) and Joseph Lowry (*Early Islamic Legal Theory*) with at times significant changes. For example, in this passage, Lowry translates *ẓāhir* as "appears to be" (Lowry, *Early Islamic Legal Theory*, p. 73). Obviously, Lowry does not hold that *ẓāhir* is used technically here. I also take *fiṭrah* in this passage to be a reference to an Arab, and not to God. The evidence is a reference later in the passage to an addressee (*mukhāṭab*, in *bi-baʿḍ mā khūṭiba bi-hi*), which cannot be God if He is the speaker (*mukhāṭib*). Therefore, I do not follow Shākir's vocalization of the verb in the third line of this paragraph as *yukhāṭiba*, which is translated accordingly by both Khadduri and Lowry.

standing it requires knowledge of how these people used their language. This requirement further suggests that there existed rules of their understanding. Believing that these rules are knowable, al-Shāfiʿī sets out to list them, and it is within this framework that he discusses what the Arabs considered *ẓāhir* or otherwise. In other words, al-Shāfiʿī held that the *ẓāhir* meaning is not self-evident or inherent in the language itself; rather, it must be defined from the perspective of the people who *use* the language.

On the face of it, this passage may suggest that al-Shāfiʿī's held that many forms of *bayān* can equally be *ẓāhir*. Other instances of his use of the term *ẓāhir*, however, do not support this understanding. In numerous other passages, he seems to use the term *ẓāhir* to refer to the general, unrestricted (*ʿāmm*) scope of Qurʾānic terms and verses. *Ẓāhir* in these instances refers to the widest possible extension or the broadest range of referents of a verse or term. The term *bāṭin*, in contrast, is used to refer to just the opposite: the restricted meaning of some Qurʾānic references.[46] For example, "traditions from the Messenger should be accepted as 'general' as they apparently are (*ʿalā ʾl-ẓāhir min al-ʿāmm*) unless an indicator suggests otherwise … or unless there is an agreement of the Muslim [scholars] that their meaning is *bāṭin* but not *ẓāhir*, and that it is *khāṣṣ* (restricted) and not *ʿāmm* (general, unrestricted)."[47]

Al-Shāfiʿī applies this understanding of *ẓāhir* and *bāṭin* meanings to some legal issues. For instance, discussing the issue of the number of times one is required to wash his head during ablution, he argues that "the *ẓāhir* meaning of God's statement: 'Wash your faces' is that the minimum requirement for

---

46 For the various translations of the terms *ʿāmm* and *khāṣṣ*, see Lowry, *Early Islamic Legal Theory*, p. 69. Arguing that other translations could be clumsy at times, Lowry suggests translating *ʿāmm* as unrestricted, and *khāṣṣ* as restricted. Arguably, however, for those who maintain that "*all* texts appear at first to be, or in fact are at one level, *ʿāmm*, but some are then shown to have an import that should be described as *khāṣṣ*" (*ibid.*, p. 70), it is redundant to qualify any term by descrbing it as *ʿāmm*. Any term should be presumed to be *ʿāmm* unless there is a valid indicator that suggests otherwise, in which case it undergoes restriction or particularization (*takhṣīṣ*) and becomes restricted (*khāṣṣ*). This, of course, does not apply to terms that are restricted or specific by their nature, such as proper names as well as personal and demonstrative pronouns (for this, and for an overview of this subject, see Bernard Weiss, "ʿUmūm wa-Khuṣūṣ," *EI*², vol. 10, p. 866).

47 *Al-Risālah* (1938), p. 322, §882. Lowry translates *bāṭin* here as the "objectively correct meaning," and *ẓāhir* as the "apparent meaning," a translation he seems to consider standard (Lowry, *Early Islamic Legal Theory*, p. 328). Lowry argues, rightly, in my view, that the *ʿāmm*/*khāṣṣ* dichotomy deals with the scope of application of rules. In this view, a rule is *ʿāmm* when it "applies to the entirety of a class," and is said to be *khāṣṣ* when it "applies only to a subset of the class" (Lowry, *Early Islamic Legal Theory*, p. 69).

washing is once, but it may [also] mean more [than once]." The *ẓāhir* meaning of washing here is one that is inclusive of any one single performance of what can be described as washing. "[T]he apostle decreed that ablution must be performed by washing once, in conformity with the *ẓāhir* [meaning] of the Qur'ān," al-Shāfiʿī adds.[48] In another instance, he discusses *zakāt* (charity) and its amount or value for various assets and commodities. Quoting Q. 9:103, "Take of their goods a freewill offering to cleanse and purify them," he notes the various values of *zakāt* and concludes that "[i]f it were not for the evidence of the *Sunnah*, all goods would have been treated on an equal footing on [the basis of] the *ẓāhir* meaning of the Qur'ān, and *zakāt* would have been imposed on all, not on some only."[49] What al-Shāfiʿī says here is that the *ẓāhir* meaning of the verse is its meaning that is inclusive of everybody and everything without restriction. It is only the *Sunnah* that restricts this unrestricted, *ẓāhir* meaning of the verse and limits its scope of application.[50]

Al-Shāfiʿī also uses the term *ẓāhir* in another context. On the subject of "forbidden women" (women whom a man cannot marry, temporarily or categorically), he comments on the list of such women given in Q. 4:23 by stating: "This communication may have two meanings: [it may mean] that the women whom God has [specifically] forbidden shall be [regarded as] forbidden, and that those whom He has not specifically forbidden shall be lawful on the

48 *Al-Risālah* (1938), p. 29, §87.

49 *Ibid.*, p. 196, §534.

50 It befits here to mention an additional example of al-Shāfiʿī's use of *ẓāhir* that demonstrates what appears to be a corruption in both the wording of *al-Risālah* and the translation of Khadduri. "Had it not been for the evidence of the *Sunnah* and our decision on the [basis of the] *ẓāhir* [meaning of the Qur'ān]," al-Shāfiʿī argues, "we should have been in favor of punishing everyone to whom the term stealing applies by the cutting off [of the hand]" (*al-Risālah* (1961), p. 107; (1938), pp. 72–73, §235). Apparently, both Shākir and Khadduri did not notice that this passage, as it stands, contradicts the points that al-Shāfiʿī seeks to make here. What al-Shāfiʿī must be saying here is: "Had it not been for the evidence of the *Sunnah*, and if we decide on the basis of the *ẓāhir* meaning of the Qur'ān, we should have been in favor of punishing everyone to whom the term stealing applies by the cutting off [of the hand]." This passage as it is in Shākir's edition of *al-Risālah* would make sense only if al-Shāfiʿī held that *al-khāṣṣ* rather than *al-ʿāmm* was the *ẓāhir* meaning, which nothing else that he mentions indicates. In fact, in another context, al-Shāfiʿī argues that "the term 'theft' is binding upon whoever steals, regardless of the value of the stolen article or of its security" (*al-Risālah* (1938), pp. 112–113, §333). This means that without the *Sunnah* evidence—which identifies the minimum value of the stolen article and the circumstances of the theft that warrants cutting off the hand—any person who steals anything in any circumstance would be treated as a thief whose hand must be amputated.

ground that He is [both] silent about them and [also] according to His saying (Q. 4:24): 'And [it is] lawful for you to seek what is beyond that'." This, he states, "may be regarded as the *ẓāhir* meaning of the communicated message."[51] Remarkably, in reading this verse, al-Shāfiʿī made conclusions not only about women whom one *cannot* marry, but also about women whom one *can* marry. The verse, as it is, does not say anything about the other category of women, but this, he believes, we can reasonably understand or infer from the verse. Even more remarkable is al-Shāfiʿī's reference to another verse where the Qurʾān declares a general rule, namely, that it is permitted to marry any category of women beyond those listed in Q. 4:23. The significance of this will be discussed later.

In another context, al-Shāfiʿī discusses the various kinds of food that Muslims are not allowed to eat. Quoting Q. 6:146, "Say, I do not find, in what is revealed to me, anything forbidden to one who eats of it, unless it be a dead animal, or blood outpoured, or the flesh of swine, for it is an abomination, or an impious thing over which the name of a god other than God has been invoked," he notes that it could be understood in two different ways. The first meaning, which concerns us here, is that "nothing is forbidden except that which God has [specifically] excluded. This is the *aẓhar* [superlative of *ẓāhir*] most common and prevalent of all meanings (*aʿammahā wa-aghlabahā*), and anyone presented with it would immediately understand that nothing is forbidden except that which God has specifically forbidden."[52] This statement shows the strong relationship that al-Shāfiʿī saw between the *ẓāhir* meaning and the assumption that what is explicitly mentioned with regards to a particular case represents the only exception to any general rule under which it could be subsumed. In this case, the general rule is: everything is permissible. Q. 6:146 mentions some exceptions that restrict the scope of this otherwise general rule. The unrestricted meaning of the verse is the *ẓāhir* meaning, and it is the default meaning that users of the language understand with immediacy as soon as they read or hear this or similar verses. The use of *ẓāhir* in other contexts in *al-Risālah* similarly relates to the issue of *ʿumūm/khuṣūṣ* (the generality and restrictedness of the scope of terms). Speaking of the relationship of the Prophetic *Sunnah* to the Qurʾān, an interlocutor asks al-Shāfiʿī: "If we find in the Qurʾān a *ẓāhir* meaning which a certain *Sunnah* may either make specific [i.e., restrict] or to which it may give a *bāṭin* meaning that is contradictory, do you [not] agree that the *Sunnah* [in such a case] is abrogated by the

51 *Al-Risālah* (1938), pp. 201–202, §547.

52 *Ibid.*, pp. 206–207, §557.

Qur'ān?"[53] Al-Shāfiʿī replies by explaining that the role of the *Sunnah* is to explain the Qur'ān, not to abrogate it, but he was obviously in agreement with this use of *ẓāhir*.[54]

Ẓāhir also appears in al-Shāfiʿī's *Risālah* in a way that is reminiscent of another usage of it indicating something that differs from that which is real, even if it is the obvious, self-evident, or prevalent meaning. For example, in a section on the "category [of declaration] the wording of which indicates the *bāṭin*, not the *ẓāhir*,"[55] the *ẓāhir* meaning is rejected because it cannot be possibly intended by the speaker. The example mentioned here is that of Jacob's sons when they say to him: "Ask the town in which we have been, and the caravan with which we have come" (Q. 12:82). Al-Shāfiʿī asserts that what Jacob's sons obviously mean here is not the *ẓāhir* meanings of "town" and "caravan," but rather an implicit meaning, namely, the "people of the town" and the "travelers in the caravan."[56] Thus, the *ẓāhir* meaning here is *not* the intended meaning. This particular example of Q. 12:82 will be brought up again in another context.

A last context in which al-Shāfiʿī uses *ẓāhir* is the context of the imperative mood. For example, the Prophet is reported to have said that washing (*ghusl*) on Fridays is *wājib* (obligatory/highly commended).[57] Although this tradition does not use the imperative as such, many Muslim scholars, including al-Shāfiʿī in this and other instances,[58] take similar kinds of expression (in which the Prophet states that a certain act is *wājib*) to indicate that it is *obligatory* (and not just meritorious) for Muslims to perform it. Elsewhere, he addresses a question that arises from another tradition in which the Prophet is reported to have prohibited Muslims from seeking to marry women who are engaged to

53 *Al-Risālah* (1938), pp. 222ff, §§610ff, and (1961), p. 185.

54 This is consistent with Lowry's argument that, more often than not, al-Shāfiʿī uses the *ʿāmm/khāṣṣ* dichotomy to reconcile the Qur'ān and *Sunnah*. The Qur'ānic text is usually *ʿāmm*, and evidence from the *Sunnah* restricts its generality (Lowry, "The Legal Hermeneutics," p. 10). For a detailed discussion of the issue of the *ʿāmm/ khāṣṣ* dichotomy, see Lowry, *Early Islamic Legal Theory*, pp. 69–87. Lowry's discussion of this issue is important, but what renders it less relevant for us here is his interest in the *ʿāmm/khāṣṣ* dichotomy itself, while we are interested in it insofar as it relates to what al-Shāfiʿī regards as the *ẓāhir* meaning. Otherwise, Lowry does not say anything about this issue that seems to contradict what is mentioned here.

55 *Al-Risālah* (1938), p. 64; (1961), p. 103.

56 *Ibid.*, p. 64, §§212–213.

57 *Ghusl yawm al-jumuʿah wājib* (*al-Risālah* (1938), p. 303, §841).

58 *Al-Risālah* (1938), p. 303, §841.

others.[59] He mentions here various views on what this tradition means, but argues that if we do not have an indication from the Prophet that it meant one thing and not another (*ʿalā maʿnā dūna maʿnā*), its *ẓāhir* indicates that a Muslim cannot, in *all* circumstances, seek to marry a woman already engaged to another.[60] What is remarkable about these two instances in which *ẓāhir* appears in *al-Risālah* is that they provide cases of a command (*amr*) and a prohibition (*nahy*). *Ẓāhir* in both cases is presented as the absolute, unconditional obligation of either carrying out the command or avoiding that which is prohibited.

This presentation of al-Shāfiʿī's use of *ẓāhir* suggests that it is used technically in a specific context, namely, the context of the scope of application of terms and statements. A *ẓāhir* meaning is one that allows for the broadest scope of terms and statements in a way that is inclusive of all its possible referents. This use of *ẓāhir* is obviously (if still implicitly) connected by al-Shāfiʿī to another notion, *al-ibāḥah al-aṣliyyah*, namely, the presumption that everything is permissible unless proven otherwise. This is evident in the example of the "prohibited women." What is noteworthy here is that al-Shāfiʿī's reading attributes to this verse what it does not actually say, that is, women who are *not* included in the Qur'ānic list of prohibited women must be lawfully available for marriage. Al-Shāfiʿī, however, seems to have felt the need to adduce another verse that is more *explicit* about the permissibility to marry all other women in order to justify his reading. It is difficult to determine whether al-Shāfiʿī would have made the same argument absent this second verse. What is useful for our purposes here, however, is that the notion of *al-ibāḥah al-aṣliyyah* provides scholars with a very important general rule that they can always refer to, viz. everything that is not explicitly forbidden is, it must be presumed, permissible. Prohibition is thus an exception to this general rule.

In a section that deals with analogy with reference to *Sunnah*, al-Shāfiʿī argues if the Prophet mentions the rationale (*maʿnā*) of a divine ordinance, it can be used to draw analogy with other cases. If the same rationale applies to another case that is not mentioned by the Prophet, jurists can apply to the new case the same ruling of the *Sunnah* case. This is the most productive method of drawing analogy with *Sunnah*.[61] A second method of such analogy is when the Prophet declares something lawful using a general expression, but then prohibits a specific part of it. What jurists (should) do in this case is consider

59 *Lā yakhṭub aḥadukum ʿalā khiṭbat akhīhi* (*al-Risālah* (1938), p. 307, §847).

60 *Al-Risālah* (1938), pp. 307–308, §849.

61 *Al-Risālah* (1938), pp. 217–218, §594. This passage in *al-Risālah* is difficult to construe, but Khadduri's translation is obviously inaccurate here.

unlawful only the specific part that the Prophet had so declared. No analogy to this specific part is permissible, al-Shāfiʿī stresses, for drawing an analogy to a general rather than a specific rule is more reasonable.[62] The same logic applies to the opposite case, i.e., when the Prophet declares something to be generally unlawful but makes exception of a specific part of it.

We have noted earlier that scholars of *ūṣul al-fiqh* distinguished between *al-qiyās al-jalī* and *al-qiyās al-khafī*. In the former kind, the *ʿillah* is known or evident, whereas in the second it has to be inferred from other statements.[63] This second kind of *qiyās* interests us here, for it was reported that Dāwūd rejected this particular kind of *qiyās*, despite later Ẓāhirī rejection of all forms of it. The problem with this kind of *qiyās* is twofold. First, it relies on a mere assumption that a certain case is governed by a particular rationale (a view that al-Qāḍī al-Nuʿmān attributes to Muḥammad ibn Dāwūd).[64] Secondly, it restricts the generality (*ʿumūm*) of both permissions and prohibitions. Al-Shāfiʿī's discussion of it, in other words, suggests that for him *qiyās* qualified the default, unrestricted scope of a given general rule by drawing analogy to its exception, a method that he explicitly rejects. Arguably, if a scholar does not seek to include something under a *khāṣṣ*, restricted statement (i.e., include it under the exception), it necessarily remains under the general, unrestricted rule with no need of *qiyās*. It is in fact unclear how one can draw an analogy to a general rule, and it seems that al-Shāfiʿī only mentions this to show the absurdity of drawing analogy to an exception *unless* the rationale or the basis of a given ruling is explicitly indicated by the Prophet.

1.4 *Al-Ṭabarī's* Tafsīr

In a prolegomenon with which he begins his *tafsīr*, al-Ṭabarī, similar to al-Shāfiʿī, stresses that the Qurʾān was written in the language of a specific people and that full mastery of this language and how the Arabs used it is essential for understanding its literary styles. God's wisdom requires that he address people in a way that they understand and send messengers to people in the language that they use.[65] Therefore, the Prophet Muḥammad's message "had to conform to the rules of the Arabic language, and its *ẓāhir* should match the *ẓāhir* of this language, although we acknowledge that the Qurʾānic language is superior to the language that the Arabs used."[66] Al-Ṭabarī notes, however, that

62 *Al-Risālah* (1938), p. 218, §595.

63 For this, see al-Āmidī, *al-Iḥkām*, vol. 3, pp. 95–96.

64 For this, see chapter one above.

65 Al-Ṭabarī, *Jāmiʿ al-Bayān*, vol. 1, p. 7.

66 *Ibid.*, vol. 1, p. 7.

the way the Arabs used their language was "multiple and diverse," for they expressed the same thing in ways that varied in length or in brevity. The Arabs may have referred to a specific idea or thing by what appears as a general statement, or to a general idea by what appears to be a statement with a specific or restricted reference.[67] Elsewhere, al-Ṭabarī argues that the Qurʾānic *ẓāhir* terms or statements can indicate either general or restricted reference (*muḥtamil khuṣūṣan wa-ʿumūman*). The only way to figure out what each term or statement indicates is through the person whom God trusted with explaining the Qurʾān, viz. the Prophet Muḥammad.[68] He mentions numerous versions of the well-known tradition in which the Prophet says that the Qurʾān was revealed "in seven *aḥruf*." The meaning of *aḥruf* here is debatable, but one version of this tradition mentions that each of these *aḥruf* has a *ẓahr* and a *baṭn*.[69] According to al-Ṭabarī, *ẓahr* here refers to people's recitation of the Qurʾān (*tilāwah*), whereas *baṭn* refers to the hidden part of its interpretation (*bāṭin al-taʾwīl*).[70] Next, he states that Qurʾānic statements are of two kinds: statements the interpretation of which only comes from the Prophet, and statements the *taʾwīl* (here, meaning) of which can be discerned by anyone with knowledge of Arabic. Ibn ʿAbbās once said that the explanation (*tafsīr*) of the Qurʾān is of four kinds: one that the Arabs know according to their tongue (*wajh taʿrifuhu ʾl-ʿArab min kalāmihā*), another that a Muslim is not excused for being ignorant of, a third that only scholars know, and a fourth that is only known to God.[71]

Al-Ṭabarī thus held that while the meaning of some Qurʾānic statements is clear for those who know the rules of Arabic, others are ambiguous and open to various interpretations. Without Prophetic guidance in the case of these ambiguous statements (which probably Ibn ʿAbbās's second and possibly third kinds of *tafsīr* refer to), it is not possible to determine God's intent. Al-Ṭabarī's view that *ẓāhir* refers to the recitation of the Qurʾān and *bāṭin* to its interpretation is problematic, however. If we assume that he does not mean the mere recitation of the Qurʾān (which would be useless without any attention to the meaning), we can infer that for him *ẓāhir* meant that which is understandable from the Qurʾān without interpretation that requires specialized knowledge. In other words, *ẓāhir* is what is not hidden of the Qurʾān and only requires

67 *Al-khabar ʿan al-khāṣṣ fī al-murād bi-l-ʿāmm al-ẓāhir, wa-ʿan al-ʿāmm fī al-murād bi-l-khāṣṣ al-ẓāhir* (al-Ṭabarī, *Jāmiʿ al-Bayān*, vol. 1, p. 7).

68 *Ibid.*, vol. 1, p. 11.

69 *Ibid.*, vol. 1, p. 12. For a presentation of various views on this tradition, see *ibid.*, pp. 11ff.

70 *Fa-ẓahruhu ʾl-ẓāhir fī ʾl-tilāwah, wa-baṭnuhu mā baṭana min taʾwīlihi* (*ibid.*, vol. 1, p. 32).

71 *Ibid.*, vol. 1, pp. 33–34.

knowledge of the Arabic language to understand. It is not clear, however, if this means that all Arabs should understand (or indeed have understood) the Qur'ān's *ẓāhir* statements similarly. Other statements, however, potentially have more than one possible meaning and it is only through Prophetic guidance that we can determine their intended meaning. It is not clear, however, whether this kind of statements does not have *ẓāhir* in the first place, or has more than one potential *ẓāhir*. What follows, therefore, discusses how al-Ṭabarī uses *ẓāhir* in approximately the first 100 verses of Q. 2 (*sūrat al-Baqarah*).[72]

In his commentary on Q. 2:1, al-Ṭabarī presents several explanations of the "disjointed letter" (*al-ḥurūf al-muqaṭṭaʿah*), *alif, lām, mīm*, with which Q. 2 begins. In one view, these letters are abbreviations of *anā, Allāh, aʿlamu* respectively. In other words, the verse intends to say: "I, God, know." It is prevalent (*ẓāhir mustafīḍ*) in the usage of the Arabs, al-Ṭabarī points out, to use only a few letters of a word as long as the remaining letters are indicative of what the shortened version is, a practice that he illustrates by citing a number of poetry verses.[73] *Ẓāhir* here, then, refers to a certain convention of using the language. A similar use of *ẓāhir* appears in al-Ṭabarī's commentary on verse 31, "And He taught Adam all the names..."[74] He mentions various theories as to what "names" in this verse means. Whereas some early religious authorities held that this refers to the names of a specific category of things, others held that it refers to everything. Al-Ṭabarī does not rule out the plausibility of this latter explanation, yet he believes that the use of the pronoun *-hum* in *ʿaraḍa*hum (showed them) later in the verse suggests that "names" refers to the names of the angels as well as Adam's entire progeny. The Arabs, he explains, only use the pronoun *-hum* with reference to the angels and human beings, and *-ha* or *-hunna* when referring to other things. This is what the *ẓāhir al-tilāwah* suggests, and it is the more common and prevalent (*al-ghālib al-mustafīḍ*) in the use of the Arabs. In fact, he finds an excuse for those who held that "names" referred to everything—including no less an authority than Ibn ʿAbbās—in a report that mentions that Ubayy ibn Kaʿb did read the verse

---

72 *Ẓāhir* and its variants appear in al-Ṭabarī's entire *tafsīr* approximately 500 times. I will focus on the first half of *sūrat al-Baqarah*, avoiding some instances of the use of *ẓāhir* which would require lengthy and hair-splitting discussions that are not relevant to our purposes here.

73 Al-Ṭabarī, *Jāmiʿ al-Bayān*, vol. 1, p. 91.

74 The complete verse reads: "And He taught Adam all the names (*al-asmāʾ kulla-ha*), then showed them to the angels, saying: Inform Me of the names of these, if you are truthful."

with *ʿaraḍa*hā, which is more inclusive than *ʿaraḍa*hum, for it can be used to refer to everything, including the angels and humans.[75]

It is noteworthy that al-Ṭabarī needed to argue against the view that sought to extend the scope of "names" to its fullest possible reference, which only suggests that the general, unrestricted rather than the restricted or particularized sense of terms and statements was the default assumption. Indeed, he appears reluctant to categorically dismiss the view of the term's unrestrictedness and seems to have felt the need to justify his restricting construal of it, which he did on the basis of the prevalent use of pronouns by the Arabs. This prevalent use, according to him, is the *ẓāhir al-tilāwah*, apparently what readers can understand by the mere recitation of the Qurʾān without much reflection. In the same vein, he argues against the view that "hard" in Q. 2:45, "Seek help in patience and prayers, and truly it is hard save for the humble-minded," refers to accepting Islam.[76] In his view, what is being referred to here is the prayers. This is *al-ẓāhir al-mafhūm* (the *ẓāhir* that is understood) of the verse, which should not be abandoned for a *bāṭin* the soundness of which is not verifiable.[77] The *ẓāhir* meaning here is taking the pronoun to refer to something that is explicitly mentioned in the same verse.

In commenting on Q. 2:38, al-Ṭabarī mentions a disagreement on the reference of one part of it, "and whoso follows my guidance ..."[78] In one view, this is an address to all humanity. In his view, however, God is only addressing those whom the first part of the verse mentions: Adam, Eve, and Iblīs. This is closer to the *ẓāhir al-tilāwah* (the *ẓāhir* of the recitation) and is the *ẓāhir al-khiṭāb* (the *ẓāhir* of the communication). Nonetheless, he does not categorically dismiss the view that this part of the verse could refer to all the progeny of Adam and Eve. In fact, he says that this *is* a possible interpretation of the verse.[79] He, therefore, feels the need to provide evidence for limiting what appears to be the unrestricted reference of the verse, and the evidence in this instance is the first part of the verse. In other words, al-Ṭabarī seems to argue that the

---

75 Al-Ṭabarī, *Jāmiʿ al-Bayān*, vol. 1, pp. 261–267. Ubayy ibn Kaʿb was an early Medinan Companion known for his mastery in reading the Qurʾān. His date of death is disputed, but he certainly died before 35/655 and possibly in 19/640 (for his biography, see, for example, Jamāl al-Dīn al-Mizzī, *Tahdhīb al-Kamāl fī Asmāʾ al-Rijāl*, vol. 2, pp. 262–273).

76 The verse reads: "Seek help in patience and prayers; and truly it is hard (*kabīrah*) save for the humble-minded."

77 Al-Ṭabarī, *Jāmiʿ al-Bayān*, vol. 1, p. 261.

78 The verse reads: "We said: Go down, all of you, from hence; but verily there comes unto you from Me a guidance; and whoso follows My guidance, there shall no fear come upon them neither shall they grieve."

79 Al-Ṭabarī, *Jāmiʿ al-Bayān*, vol. 1, p. 247.

ẓāhir of a given verse can only be understood on the basis of its entirety and not a fragment of it.

Al-Ṭabarī uses *ẓāhir* in another, significant context. In commenting on Q. 2:27,[80] he mentions several explanations of what "… and sever that which God has ordered to be joined" means. Some have understood "sever" here to refer only to *ṣilat al-raḥim*, viz. maintaining good ties with one's kindred. Others held that the intended referent is the ties with the Prophet and the believers, as well as the blood ties. This view, he reports, relies on the unrestrictedness of the verse (*ẓāhir* ʿumūm *al-āyah*) and the lack of indication that it meant to refer to only one part of what God has ordered to be joined and not another. Al-Ṭabarī himself does not hold this view, but he comments on it by saying that it is not far from the sound understanding of the verse,[81] although the fact that there are Qur'ānic verses that speak about the hypocrites and their severing of their blood ties specifically indicates, in his view, that the verse can be speaking about this particular form of severing things that God has ordered to be joined.[82] Similarly, al-Ṭabarī argues against the view that "sin" in Q. 2:81, "… whoever has done evil and his sin surrounds him …"[83] refers to any sin, notably grave sins (*al-kabā'ir*). He states that this understanding of the unrestrictedness and all-inclusiveness of sin here is the *ẓāhir* of the verse, but argues at the same time that its *bāṭin* exclusively refers to polytheism (*shirk*) only. Since no one holds that even minor sins could lead to eternal damnation, he points out, there is an agreement that "sin" here does not refer to all its referents. Furthermore, even grave sins (other than *shirk*, namely, associating partners with God) are not included in the reference of this verse because believers, according to Prophetic traditions, will not abide in Hellfire eternally.[84]

In these examples, *ẓāhir* refers to the unrestricted scope of application or the broadest range of referents (*ʿumūm*) of terms, and when he rejects their *ẓāhir*, al-Ṭabarī finds himself compelled to argue against it but never feels that he can simply ignore or reject it. There are numerous other instances in which he mentions that *ẓāhir* indicates the understanding of a given term or verse in

---

80 The verse reads: "Those who break the covenant of Allāh after ratifying it, and sever that which Allāh ordered to be joined, and (who) make mischief in the earth: Those are they who are the losers."

81 Al-Ṭabarī, *Jāmiʿ al-Bayān*, vol. 1, p. 185.

82 *Ibid.*, vol. 1, p. 185.

83 The verse says: "Nay, but whosoever has done evil and his sin (*khaṭī'atuhu*) surrounds him; such are rightful owners of the Fire; they will abide therein [forever]."

84 Al-Ṭabarī, *Jāmiʿ al-Bayān*, vol. 1, pp. 386–387.

a way that does not restrict or limit its scope of possible referents, but he mentions this explicitly in his commentary on verse 70.[85] Listing many reports from Companions and Successors according to which the Jews who were ordered to slaughter a cow would have fulfilled their duty by slaughtering any cow, he points out that their repeated questioning about the cow led to more restrictions from God and thus increased the hardship of their duty. The Companions and Successors held that whatever God commands or prohibits should be understood according to the apparent generality (*al-ʿumūm al-ẓāhir*) of his speech, and not in a restricted, uncertain sense (*al-khuṣūṣ al-bāṭin*). This restriction of the scope of terms or verses could only be made by reference to another statement from God or from the Prophet, in which case what is mentioned by them is *excluded* from their otherwise unrestricted scope and all-inclusiveness.[86] These reports, he adds, demonstrate that his own view conformed to the view of the Companions and Successors, and that his *madhhab* (here, view) was identical with theirs. They also prove the *erroneous belief* in the restricted meanings of terms (*al-khuṣūṣ*), or the view that when a specific aspect of a term is excluded from its scope of referents, all its other aspects necessarily lose their all-inclusive nature.[87]

Furthermore, al-Ṭabarī uses *ẓāhir* in the context of arguing against the figurative explanation of some Qurʾānic verses. For example, in his commentary on Q. 2:65,[88] he rejects Mujāhid's view that this verse does not mean that God did actually transform the Jews who violated the Sabbath into real apes, but rather means figuratively that God transformed their hearts because of their transgression. This understanding, al-Ṭabarī argues, contradicts what the *ẓāhir*

---

85 The verse reads: "They [Moses' people] said: Pray for us unto your Lord that He make clear to us what (cow) it is. Lo! Cows are much alike to us; and Lo! If Allāh wills, we may be led aright."

86 Al-Ṭabarī mentions that he discussed this at length in a work of his entitled *al-Risālah*.

87 Al-Ṭabarī, *Jāmiʿ al-Bayān*, vol. 1, pp. 348–349. Al-Ṭabarī believes that when the scope of a *ʿāmm* statement is restricted, this restriction applies only to that particular part of the statement that is subject to that restriction. For example, when the Jews asked God about the cow, he gave them some description. According to al-Ṭabarī, they would have obeyed the order had they slaughtered any cow with the new description only (*ibid.*, p. 349). In other words, the first command (slaughter any cow) lost only one part of its unrestrictedness, and that is the part that is being specifically identified as restricting the generality of the statement. If the description has to do with the color of the cow, for instance, any cow with the specified color would do. If it has to do with age, any cow of any color that meets the age criterion would do.

88 The verse says: "And you know of those of you who broke the Sabbath, how We said to them: Be you apes, despised and hated!"

of the Qur'ān indicates, that is, God *did* transform them into real apes.[89] *Ẓāhir* here is used to reject the figurative and metaphorical understanding of the Qur'ān.

Finally, al-Ṭabarī's use of *ẓāhir* in some instances is difficult to discern. For example, in a lengthy commentary on Q. 2:30,[90] he mentions a view that has no support from the *ẓāhir al-tanzīl* in his view, namely, that the angels wondered about God's intention to create human beings because He Himself had given them permission to do so.[91] The meaning of *ẓāhir al-tanzīl* here is not clear, but it is reminiscent of al-Ṭabarī's distinction of *ẓāhir* and *bāṭin* in his prolegomenon. *Ẓāhir* is that which people actually read, while *bāṭin* is the meanings that can be uncovered only through interpretation. Another example is his argument for *ẓāhir* in his commentary on Q. 2:41,[92] where there is disagreement on the reference of "therein." Whereas some scholars held that the reference is to the Prophet Muḥammad, others believed that it was to the Scripture of the Jews (whom God addresses in this verse). Al-Ṭabarī rejects these two explanations on the ground that they are far from what *ẓāhir al-tilāwah* indicates. He argues that the verse begins by referring to what God has revealed, and this is *not* the Prophet Muḥammad, but the Qur'ān itself. It is not customary in communication to end a verse by enjoining people to not disbelieve in something other than what the verse begins by calling them to believe in. This is *al-ẓāhir al-mafhūm*, even if it is possible to refer to something not mentioned explicitly in a verse by way of metonymy (*kināyah*). In other words, while he does not categorically reject the possibility that "therein" could be referring to the Prophet Muḥammad or the Jewish Scripture and implies that *ẓāhir al-kalām* allows for this kind of understanding, al-Ṭabarī still believes that a safer explanation is to take it to be referring to what the verse itself begins by mentioning.[93] If we rule out the possibility that al-Ṭabarī's use of *ẓāhir* here is haphazard, it is difficult to determine what he means by it in the context of this verse, for at the same time of accepting that the reference to the Jewish Scripture here is possible according to *ẓāhir al-kalām*, he argues that it is far from what *ẓāhir al-tilāwah*

---

89 Al-Ṭabarī, *Jāmiʿ al-Bayān*, vol. 1, pp. 331–332.

90 The verse reads: "And when your Lord said to the angels, I am going to place in the earth a *khalīfah*, they said: Will you place therein one who will do harm therein and will shed blood, while we, we hymn Your praise and sanctify You? He said: Surely I know that which you know not."

91 Al-Ṭabarī, *Jāmiʿ al-Bayān*, vol. 1, p. 209.

92 The verse reads: "And believe in that which I have revealed, confirming that which you possess already (of the Scripture), and be not first to disbelieve therein, and part not with My revelations for a trifling price, and keep your duty unto Me."

93 Al-Ṭabarī, *Jāmiʿ al-Bayān*, vol. 1, pp. 234–235.

wa-l-tanzīl indicates. The use of the superlative form of *ẓāhir* (*al-aẓhar*) here, however, can suggest that there can be more than one, but not necessarily equal, *ẓāhir* meanings of a given statement.

Al-Ṭabarī, then, uses *ẓāhir* in a variety of contexts, one of which is the common use of the Arabic language by the Arabs. Using a certain pronoun to refer to certain objects is one such instance. In other contexts, *ẓāhir* is used to refer to the non-figurative meaning of a term or a statement. *Ẓāhir* is also used to refer to the meaning understood with certainty in a given verse, in which case *bāṭin* refers to a hidden meaning that needs to be uncovered with the help of extra-textual evidence, such as Ḥadīth.[94] At other times, what al-Ṭabarī means by *ẓāhir* is not clear, such as when he speaks about *ẓāhir al-tanzīl* or *ẓāhir al-tilāwah*, which, if taken at face value, could suggest that he held that some Qurʾānic statements can be understood without the need for any interpretation. Finally, some instances of his use of *ẓāhir* suggest that there exists various layers of *ẓāhir*, i.e., some meanings can be more *ẓāhir* than others or even the most *ẓāhir* (*al-aẓhar*).

These instances notwithstanding, *ẓāhir* seems to appear in al-Ṭabarī's *tafsīr* more often in the context of the *ʿumūm/khuṣūṣ* dichotomy. Here, the broadest meaning or the fullest scope of a term or a statement is its *ẓāhir* meaning, whereas *bāṭin* refers to the restricted meaning. It is evident that al-Ṭabarī had a real concern about not jeopardizing the generality of any term or statement without justification based on a textual or a non-textual indicator. Textual indicators, which al-Ṭabarī seems to prefer, can be obtained from the same verse in which a term is mentioned, or from another verse in the same text. Non-textual or external indicators include theological views that scholars hold, such as the case with minor sins. Although he does use them himself, al-Ṭabarī seems hesitant about their weight. For example, relying on what he regarded as the *ẓāhir* meaning of Q. 2:30, he rejected the view that the angels only expressed their inability to apprehend God's decision because God Himself had permitted them to do so, a view that is probably based on certain theological views concerning the nature of the angels and their relationship with God. Finally, al-Ṭabarī's discussion also indicates that there was an assumption that the *ẓāhir* meaning should be taken to reflect the intention of the speaker (God, in the case of the Qurʾān), and that any deflection from this meaning requires justification.

---

94 See, for instance, al-Ṭabarī, *Jāmiʿ al-Bayān*, vol. 1, p. 537, where al-Ṭabarī says: *wa-dhālika anna ʾl-kalām maḥmūl maʿnāh ʿalā ẓāhirihi ʾl-maʿrūf dūna bāṭinihi ʾl-majhūl ḥattā yaʾtiya mā yadullu ʿalā khilāf dhālika mimmā yajibu ʾl-taslīm la-hu.*

∵

That *ẓāhir* is used by al-Shāfiʿī and al-Ṭabarī in the context of hermeneutics is evident, and this is in perfect agreement with al-Qāḍī al-Nuʿmān's identification of *istidlāl*, obviously a hermeneutical tool, as the defining feature of Ẓāhirīs, if these were indeed whom he was referring to. But what aspect of hermeneutics does Ẓāhirism relate to? Arguably, nothing in what al-Shāfiʿī says in his *Risālah* and al-Ṭabarī in his *tafsīr* proves the view that the *ẓāhir* was taken to mean the "obvious" or "apparent' meaning. Their understanding of how to interpret a text proceeds on the assumption that the Arabic language has rules that we can identify by investigating how the Arabs used it. The *ẓāhir* meaning is one such linguistic aspect that needs reference to the common use of the Arabic language by its speakers when the Qurʾān was revealed. Both scholars seem to use the term *ẓāhir* consistently in two contexts. The first is the context of the figurative vs. non-figurative use of language. The *ẓāhir* meaning is the non-figurative meaning of a certain term or a statement, although al-Shāfiʿī (possibly inspired by a Qurʾānic use of *ẓāhir*) adds to this that the figurative meaning can in some instances be the intended meaning. Accordingly, the *ẓāhir* meaning here is what is understood (or what is recited, as al-Ṭabarī puts it), but it is not what is communicated, so to speak.

The other context in which both scholars use *ẓāhir* is the context of the scope of application or range of referents of terms (the *ʿumūm vs. khuṣūṣ* dichotomy). According to this, any term must be taken to refer to all its potential referents without exception, i.e., without particularization or restriction. In other words, the *ẓāhir*, general meaning of a term or a statement is one which allows it to encompass all its referents in an all-inclusive manner. This view, however, does not seem to have been the only view about how to interpret a term or statement. We have seen that in one instance of using *ẓāhir* in this context, al-Ṭabarī attributes this view (that the *ẓāhir* meaning is the general, unrestricted meaning of a term or verse) to earlier generations of Muslims, and his discussion here strongly indicates that this was a disputed issue in or before his time, for which reason he may have written his own *Risālah* to discuss this issue and defend his viewpoint which he attributes to the Arabs and early Muslim authorities. Evidently, some people in or before al-Ṭabarī argued against the presumption of *ʿumūm*, which may explain why he was keen to argue for any restriction he makes with respect to the scope of application of a term or statement.[95] In all circumstances, the *ʿumūm/khuṣūṣ* dichotomy seems

95 Roger Arnaldez came to a similar conclusion regarding the meaning of *ẓāhir*. He argues that "pour le penseur ẓāhirite [Ibn Ḥazm], un terme doit d'abord être pris dans toute

to be the context in which the term *ẓāhir* was used technically in the 3rd/9th century, and we know that this is a subject to which Dāwūd and his son Muḥammad devoted chapters in their works on *uṣūl al-fiqh*.

Is it possible, then, that Dāwūd was labeled al-Ẓāhirī because of his vehement defense of the *ʿumūm* presumption? There is no reason why this cannot be the case, but if we can establish links between this notion of *ʿumūm* and other views of Dāwūd's, we can be more confident that this notion was central to his legal thought. It is remarkable that some of al-Shāfiʿī's discussions in *al-Risālah* suggest possible relationship between the notion of *ʿumūm* and other tenets of Dāwūd's legal thought. These include the rejection of *qiyās* and the presumption that everything is permissible unless proven otherwise (the principle of *al-ibāḥah al-aṣliyyah*). *Qiyās*, in al-Shāfiʿī's view, meant additional qualification or restriction of a general rule (e.g., any intoxicating beverage is forbidden by analogy to grape wine), which therefore can only be valid if the *ʿillah* is explicitly indicated by a Prophetic tradition (it is usually a tradition because the function of Sunnah/Ḥadīth is to explain the Qurʾān). If the *ʿillah* is not mentioned, however, no analogy to the exception can be drawn. In addition, since the *ẓāhir* meaning for al-Shāfiʿī meant that what is listed in the Qurʾān as forbidden indicates that other things (that are not mentioned) are not forbidden, this can only work out if a particular general rule is assumed, and this rule is: everything is permissible unless proven otherwise.

Dāwūd started his career as an admirer of al-Shāfiʿī, and it is not unlikely that he drew on many of his views to develop a distinct legal thought. But apparently, he did not draw only on al-Shāfiʿī. Much of what we know about Dāwūd's life suggests that he had a strong relationship with the *Ahl al-Raʾy* of his time. Additionally, much of his legal views on *uṣūl* are almost identical with legal views that the *Ahl al-Raʾy* held. In what follows, therefore, the question of

---

l'étendue de ses significations, c'est-à-dire dans son ẓāhir" (Arnaldez, *Grammaire et théologie*, p. 128). His keenness to demonstrate Ibn Ḥazm's consistency and the universality of his Ẓāhirism (in that it permeates his legal and non-legal thinking, such as his linguistic, psychological, logical and metaphysical) (*ibid.*, p. 226), however, has distracted him from focusing on the meaning of *ẓāhir* itself. This notwithstanding, he points out that "ce qui sépare Ibn Ḥazm des autres ẓāhirites, c'est qu'il a systématizé la doctrine, et qu'il en a étendu le principe à tous les domains de la spéculation. Or la question logico-grammaticale de la nature du sens général, est chez lui à la base de son interprétation des texts et de sa théologie." In any case, Arnaldez does not seek to determine how Dāwūd himself have understood *ẓāhir*, although he does examine al-Shāfiʿī's use of it and discusses the relationship between "le sens général" and "le sens immédiatement manifeste (*ẓāhir*)" (*ibid.*, p. 225).

the relationship of Dāwūd's juridical thought with the two legal trends that existed in 3rd/9th-century Baghdad will be pursued.

2 Ẓāhirism between the *Ahl al-Raʾy* and the *Ahl al-Ḥadīth* Revisited

It has been noted earlier that the complicated picture of the legal scene in early Islam and the sharp differences among scholars regarded as members of either the *Ahl al-Raʾy* or the *Ahl al-Ḥadīth* requires that we choose a representative of both legal trends. Abū Ḥanīfah was evidently a, or *the*, master of the *Ahl al-Raʾy* and is obviously the best candidate to represent them. Ibn Ḥanbal is a good representative of the *Ahl al-Ḥadīth*, which designation actually ended up referring especially to him and to his followers. However, there is no assumption here that all scholars belonging to either group were thinking similarly, or that each of these two scholars was invariably consistent in his legal thought.[96]

2.1 *Ẓāhirism and the* Ahl al-Raʾy

Dāwūdism and Ḥanafism shared some fundamental views on the nature and philosophy of Islamic law, as well as many legal and linguistic assumptions. "The great dividing line in Islamic law," writes Aaron Zysow, "is between those legal systems that require certainty in every detail of the law and those that will admit probability. The latter were historically dominant and include the

96 It must be pointed out that investigating the authenticity and historicity of views attributed to Abū Ḥanīfah, Aḥmad ibn Ḥanbal, and Dāwūd al-Ẓāhirī in medieval sources is beyond the scope of this study. While we do not have specific statements on *uṣūl* attributed to them, it is here assumed that if medieval sources are *consistent* in attributing a certain view to any of them, there is a reasonable chance that that was his view if he ever had one. This may perhaps be the only possible way we can speak meaningfully about their legal thought. Without ruling out the obvious possibility that medieval scholars may have retrospectively read some of their own views on *uṣūl* into the *masāʾil* (cases, rulings, and views) that reached them from the founders of their schools, only views that they attribute unanimously to these founders or presented as being a matter of consensus among earlier scholars will be referred to. For our purposes here, even if these *uṣūl* rules were deduced from the *masāʾil* of earlier scholars, we should be able to proceed on the reasonable assumption that if later scholars were able to deduce similar principles from these *masāʾil*, they probably deduced the right principles. After all, if these scholars agree on any principle, it becomes *the* principle of their school, regardless of what the founder himself may have thought. In brief, what this part seeks to demonstrate is that if we assume that there existed jurists named Abū Ḥanīfah and Ibn Ḥanbal who held particular legal views, it is erroneous to perceive Dāwūd as having been intellectually closer to the latter than to the former.

leading legal schools that have survived to our own day. Ẓāhirism and, for much of its history, Twelver Shīʿism are examples of the former."[97] Later on, Zysow distinguishes between two groups of Muslim legal scholars. Formalists, like Ḥanafīs, believed in the validity of and practiced *ijtihād*, the results of which were deemed valid "by the fact that the framework within which he [the Muslim jurist] practices is known with certainty," even if there was some probability in the actual outcome. The second group is the materialists, such as Ẓāhirīs, for whom "probability has no place in the formulation of the rules of law."[98]

On the face of it, this makes exactly the opposite argument of what is being argued here, but this is only so if this argument were that Dāwūdism/Ẓāhirism was identical to Ḥanafism. As discussed shortly, Ẓāhirism shared a particular view of knowledge that was itself only part, albeit significant, of the Ḥanafī understanding of knowledge. Secondly, the received wisdom about the place and role of certainty in the Ẓāhirī legal thought is not accurate. Ibn Ḥazm *does* admit a degree of uncertainty in his jurisprudence and acknowledges the possibility of changing some of his conclusions in cases where contradictory evidence or traditions with disputed authenticity exist.[99] In this kind of cases, we only know *to the best of our knowledge* that our conclusions are sound, but we cannot pretend that we know them for certain.[100] He is even willing to give the benefit of the doubt to scholars who abandoned the *ẓāhir* of a text on the basis of an interpretation that they thought was sound.[101] Whether what Ibn Ḥazm mentions here was only a theoretical possibility that did not materialize or that he knew would not take place is a question that requires further investigation. However, it does not change the fact that he did not claim that probability had no place whatsoever in his jurisprudence.

In a chapter on "The meaning of *dalīl, ʿillah, qiyās*, and *ijtihād*" in his *Fuṣūl fī al-Uṣūl*, the leading Ḥanafī scholar, and one of the earliest scholars to write about the Ḥanafī *uṣūl al-fiqh* following the "method of the jurists,"[102] Abū Bakr

97 Aaron Zysow, *Economy*, pp. 2–3.

98 *Ibid.*, pp. 2–4.

99 Ibn Ḥazm, *Iḥkām*, vol. 1, p. 21.

100 *Ibid.*, vol. 1, p. 67 and vol. 2, p. 657.

101 *Ibid.*, vol. 2, p. 829.

102 Some medieval scholars, like Ibn Khaldūn, distinguished between two methods of writing on *uṣūl al-fiqh*. The first is the "the method of the jurists" (*ṭarīqat al-fuqahā'*), which was mostly the method of Ḥanafī scholars. Here, the rules of *uṣūl al-fiqh* are deduced from the *furūʿ* (or the legal rulings on individual cases) that were inherited from the founder(s) of the school (such as Abū Ḥanīfah and his two famous disciples, Abū Yūsuf and Muḥammad ibn al-Ḥasan al-Shaybānī in the Ḥanafī *madhhab*). In the "method of the

al-Jaṣṣāṣ (d. 370/980) distinguishes carefully between two forms of deduction (*istidlāl*),[103] the first of which leads to [apodictic] knowledge (*al-ʿilm bi-l-madlūl*), while the other only establishes high probability (*yūjibu ghalabat al-raʾy wa-akbar al-ẓann*). The former includes the "rational" proofs (*dalāʾil al-ʿaqliyyāt*), and *many* of the rulings of cases (*aḥkām al-ḥawādith*) for which there is only *one indicator*, and in which we are required to find the *correct* ruling.[104] The second category of knowledge is that of the rulings that are deduced through *ijtihād* (*aḥkām al-ḥawādith allati ṭarīquhā ʾl-ijtihād*), and in which we are not required to determine the ruling with certainty, for God Himself has not provided us with a conclusive indicator (*dalīl qaṭʿī*) that leads to determining it with certainty (for which reason, al-Jaṣṣāṣ adds, we call it [the indicator] *dalīl* only figuratively (*ʿalā wajh al-majāz*)).[105] This distinction between these two categories of knowledge seems central to the Ḥanafī jurisprudence as presented by al-Jaṣṣāṣ. Although he does not attribute it to Abū Ḥanīfah or his earlier disciples, there is nothing surprising about this distinction after all. Any scholar would probably agree that if there is one valid indicator in a certain case, we can be confident that a ruling based on it is certain. So irrespective of whether this distinction goes back to Abū Ḥanīfah's time or was a later development, the argument that is made here is that Dāwūd shared with (or perhaps drew on) Ḥanafism's first category of knowledge. He sought to demonstrate that in each case there existed one, and only one, valid indicator, and the duty of jurists it was to search for and determine this indicator to reach the *right* ruling. While this practically eliminates the need for the second

---

dialecticians/theologians" (*ṭarīqat al-mutakallimīn*), mostly developed and followed by Shāfiʿī scholars, the rules of *uṣūl* are expounded in a more theoretical and dialectical manner, with relative independence from the *furūʿ* (for this, see, ʿAbd al-Raḥmān ibn Khaldūn, *al-Muqaddimah*, pp. 426–427). Al-Jaṣṣāṣ's work is a good example of the first method, as he seeks to demonstrate how his theoretical discussions are built on or related to specific rulings that were attributed to the early masters of his *madhhab*.

103 Al-Jaṣṣāṣ defines *istidlāl* as "the search for the evidence" (*ṭalab al-dalālah*) and studying it (*wa-l-naẓar fī-hā*), to reach the knowledge of what is referred to (*li-l-wuṣūl ilā ʾl-ʿilm bi-l-madlūl*). Thus, *istidlāl* here is used in a general way that refers to the process of identifying legal rulings (*aḥkām*). As will be discussed later, "obvious" or "literal" meanings of a term or a text are inseparable from the linguistic convictions of the reader. Nothing in the law, we can understand from al-Jaṣṣāṣ, is not in need for evidence, although pieces of evidence differ in their clarity, and, consequently, how much certainty they can yield (Abū Bakr al-Jaṣṣāṣ, *al-Fuṣūl fī al-Uṣūl*, vol. 2, p. 200).

104 This category of *istidlāl* deals with, in al-Jaṣṣāṣ's words, *kathīr min dalāʾil aḥkām al-ḥawādith allatī laysa ʿalay-hā illā dalīl wāḥid qad kullifnā fī-hā iṣābat al-maṭlūb*.

105 *Ibid.*, p. 200.

category of knowledge, it requires a number of "tools" that jurists can use in the process of identifying the valid indicator in each case in order to attain the required certainty. Many of the tools that Dāwūd relied on were used, and possibly developed, by Ḥanafī jurists.

One such tool that was particularly useful for Ḥanafīs in achieving certainty was their belief in the principle of *istiṣḥāb al-ḥāl*, or the presumption of continuity. Al-Jaṣṣāṣ mentions the question of whether touching the male sexual organ (usually of oneself) invalidates ritual purity (meaning that a Muslim who does so has to perform ablution (*wuḍūʾ*) before praying). He attributes to Abū Ḥanīfah the view that it does not, for we *know* that the Prophet would have had to make this (that touching the penis invalidates ritual purity) known to everybody so that his Companions (who must have experienced that) would not pray while ritually impure. The Prophet did that with other things that invalidated ritual purity, and they were transmitted to us through *tawātur* (the concurrence of large number of reports).[106] In other words, the presumption is that what counts here is only what the Prophet explicitly specified as invalidating ritual purity. If there is dispute over one thing, this presumption, which we know for certain, overrides any doubtful source of ritual impurity. Integral to this principle of *istiṣḥāb*, therefore, is the principle of *al-ibāḥah al-aṣliyyah*, according to which Muslims can assume that anything and everything is permissible unless there is a valid indictor that invalidates this assumption in a particular case. Dāwūd and other Ẓāhirīs accepted both principles and used them extensively in their jurisprudence.

Another tool, also related to the issue of certainty, is setting carefully the relationship between the Qurʾān and the Prophetic *Sunnah*. We have noted that a notion that the *Ahl al-Ḥadīth* sought to establish was that the *Sunnah* was independent of the Qurʾān, in the sense that it can establish rules that did not exist in the Qurʾān, or modify some of those that exist in it. Although the dominant view among them was that the *akhbār al-āḥād* (traditions transmitted by individual transmitters) did not yield apodictic knowledge even if they were solid enough to establish obligation, they did not allow this issue to interfere with the way they perceived the relationship between the Qurʾān and Sunnah. The *Ahl al-Raʾy*, including Ḥanafīs, on the other hand, did not give such weight to *akhbār al-āḥād*, whose authenticity was lacking the level of certainty of the Qurʾān, the authenticity of which did not need any investigation due to its transmission through a large number of people in each stage in its chain of transmitters (*tawātur*). When it comes to the relationship between the Qurʾān and Sunnah, therefore, al-Jaṣṣāṣ mentions that Ḥanafīs did not

106 For this and for some examples on it, see al-Jaṣṣāṣ, *al-Fuṣūl*, vol. 1, pp. 14–15.

approve the possibility of the Qur'ān being abrogated except by traditions that were transmitted by way of *tawātur*. A *khabar al-wāḥid*, he points out, cannot abrogate either the Qur'ān or another Sunnah that was transmitted by *tawātur*. The reason for this is that that which is proven in a way that yields apodictic knowledge (*bi-ṭarīq yūjibu 'l-ʿilm*) can be abrogated only by a piece of evidence that yields similar certainty, and not by one the authenticity of which is disputed and cannot accordingly be a source of certainty.[107]

This logic must have had a significant influence on how Ḥanafīs identified the indicator that could be used to achieve certainty in each case. Whereas the *Ahl al-Ḥadīth* had to take the *akhbār al-āḥād* into consideration, resulting in establishing their entire juridical system on probability, Ḥanafīs simply rejected them, especially when they contradicted the Qur'ān in their view. Dāwūd, however, had another way in dealing with this issue. Seeking to avoid abandoning the *āḥād* traditions or his interest in certainty, he held that these traditions, in fact, did yield apodictic knowledge and were therefore a solid ground of obligation.[108] In other words, both Ḥanafism and Dāwūdism held that certainty was attainable in legal issues, although they differed on how that was possible. Ideally, if certainty is the goal of any jurist, he would likely prefer to have as many pieces of textual evidence as possible. But if we are dealing with a legal system the textual evidence of which is, more often than not, diverse at best and contradictory at times, certainty would be better served with as few pieces of textual evidence as possible, as well as with a clear categorization of the weight of each kind of evidence on the basis of how much certainty it yields. Ḥanafīs were able to reject many pieces of evidence on the basis of their lack of certainty in their view, and were thus able to have many of their rulings fall in the first category of knowledge that al-Jaṣṣāṣ mentions. For his part, Dāwūd managed to find a way to incorporate categories of evidence that Ḥanafism rejected (such as *akhbār al-āḥād*) without causing damage to the principle of certainty itself.

Goldziher had noticed that while most schools of Islamic law have accepted a tradition in which the Prophet is reported to have said: "Disagreement in my community is a kind of mercy" (*ikhtilāf ummatī raḥmah*), both Ẓāhirīs and Muʿtazilīs rejected it. Ḥanafīs, he added, also rejected this tradition on the basis of its content.[109] Ibn ʿAbd al-Barr attributes to Abū Ḥanīfah himself the view that when jurists disagree on a given issue, only one of their differing

107 *Ibid.*, vol. 1, p. 449.

108 For this, see Ibn Ḥazm, *Iḥkām*, vol. 2, pp. 132ff. On the possibility of the Qur'ān being abrogated by the *Sunnah* and the *Sunnah* by the Qur'ān, see *ibid.*, vol. 1, pp. 617ff.

109 Goldziher, *The Ẓāhirīs*, pp. 89ff.

views could be correct.[110] He also mentions that two views were attributed to Abū Ḥanīfah apropos disagreement among the Companions on a given issue. According to the first view, Abū Ḥanīfah, in accordance with a Prophetic report that praises disagreement among the Companions, would choose (randomly?) from among the various opinions attributed to them.[111] In the second view, he held that when two Companions disagreed, one of them must have been right and the other wrong.[112] Al-Jaṣṣāṣ's categorization of knowledge could be the key to solving this apparent contradiction. It is possible to imagine that Abū Ḥanīfah's first view was related to the second category of knowledge (which is only "probable"), while the second view referred to the first category of knowledge, which is "certain." Similarly, Ẓāhirīs believed that the "truth is one," and that all other views were categorically wrong.[113] It is remarkable, but not coincidental or surprising, that the *Ahl al-Ḥadīth* embraced the *ikhtilāf ummatī raḥmah* tradition as well as the other tradition that sanctions all differing views of the Companions. Thus, unlike Ḥanafīs and Ẓāhirīs, they regularly had to deal with conflicting evidence based on contradictory views attributed to Companions, which may have made it impossible for them to argue that their own rulings, which were more often than not in apparent contradiction with one or two items of the relevant legal evidence, were certain.

Another significant resemblance between Ḥanafism and Ẓāhirism relates to the issue of the "wisdom" and higher goals of the law, an issue that later came to be known as *maqāṣid al-sharīʿah.* Muslim scholars generally agree that God's law must be based on some wisdom (*ḥikmah*) and is meant to serve

---

110 Ibn ʿAbd al-Barr, *Jāmiʿ Bayān al-ʿIlm wa-Faḍlihi*, vol. 2, p. 886.

111 Ibn ʿAbd al-Barr, *Jāmiʿ*, p. 908. Ibn ʿAbd al-Barr argues that Abū Ḥanīfah probably held that opinion on the basis of the *ẓāhir* of the tradition in which the Prophet says: "My Companions are like the stars" (*aṣḥābī ka-l-nujūm, ibid.*, p. 909). The rest of the tradition reads: "whomever of them you follow you will be rightly guided" (*bi-ayyihim iqtadaytum ihtadaytum*).

112 It is worth noting here that in his letter to the Basran scholar ʿUthmān al-Battī, Abū Ḥanīfah argued with regards the civil wars between the Companions that only one side must have been right and the other wrong, even if we cannot know for certain who was right and who was wrong (for this, see Amr Osman, " *ʿAdālat al-Ṣaḥāba*: The Construction of a Religious Doctrine," pp. 297–298 and *passim*). Whereas this does not necessarily have to reflect his view on the juridical opinions of the Companions, it could be an indication that Abū Ḥanīfah thought that there existed always one right view, even if determining it was not necessarily attainable. The *Ahl al-Ḥadīth*, for their part, held that all the Companions on both sides in each conflict followed what they sincerely believed was right and in the interest of Islam, for which they will be rewarded.

113 For this, see Ibn Ḥazm, *Iḥkām*, vol. 2, pp. 845ff.

some higher goals. However, they differ on the *verifiability* of this wisdom and its *practical relevance* to the actual jurisprudence. A large number of scholars believe that some immediate legal purposes can be discerned and used to judge cases not covered by the law. These legal purposes or causes of rulings (*ʿilal*, plural of *ʿillah*) are at times obvious and determinate enough to be used to draw analogy between cases. In contrast, the wisdom of the law is its general and higher goals, which ultimately relies on each jurist's understanding of its overall nature. For example, the *ʿillah* of forbidding alcoholic beverages is their intoxicating effect (by analogy, then, an intoxicating substance is forbidden). But why the law seeks to avoid intoxication in the first place—viz. the *ḥikmah* of the law—is a question that jurists answer variously according to their religious worldview. Historically, Mālikīs and Ḥanbalīs were willing to accept some *ʿillah*s that were less exact and objective than the requirements of Ḥanafīs and Shāfiʿīs, who insisted that a valid *ʿillah* must be both exact (well-defined) and objective.[114]

The Ḥanafī *qiyās* only accepts *ʿillah*s that have specific features, which features betray their concern for both consistency and objectivity. In this respect, al-Jaṣṣāṣ makes a fine distinction between two kinds of *ʿillah*. The first is *ʿilal al-aḥkām* (causes and rationales of rulings), which can be determined and used in *qiyās*, and the second is *ʿilal al-maṣāliḥ* (bases and sources of interests), which are known *only* through revelation. The former are features (*awṣāf*) of an existing ruling (*al-aṣl al-maʿlūl*), whereas the latter pertain to the subjects of law (*al-mutaʿabbadūn*) and their interests. In this latter case, we do not necessarily know God's wisdom in each case, but we do know that He must have one.[115] By way of example, the majority of Muslim scholars held that God—even if He can in theory abrogate any ruling by any other according to His will—would abrogate a ruling with another that is equal to it in terms of hardship or even lighter and less demanding (*akhaff*). This belief is based on their understanding of divine mercy that takes people's interests into consideration and would not therefore inflict more hardship on them.[116] Al-Jaṣṣāṣ, however, rejects this notion, pointing out that Ḥanafīs held that God can abrogate any

114 For this, see, Abū Zahrah, *Uṣūl al-Fiqh*, pp. 227–233 and pp. 339–341.

115 Al-Jaṣṣāṣ, *al-Fuṣūl*, vol. 2, p. 291.

116 For this, see, for instance, al-Āmidī, *Iḥkām*, vol. 2, pp. 261–263; Ibn Ḥazm, *Iḥkām*, vol. 1, pp. 602ff. Remarkably, Ibn Ḥazm mentions that even some Ẓāhirīs had subscribed to the view that God would not abrogate a ruling (mostly a duty to either do or avoid doing something) by imposing a heavier one (*ibid*., vol. 1, pp. 602ff).

ruling with another without being bound with the issue of hardship, for God's law is meant to "serve our interests," which are known only to God.[117]

Al-Jaṣṣāṣ's view here seems inconsistent with the assumption of many medieval and modern scholars that the notion of *maṣlaḥah*, which is related to the overall wisdom and purposes of the law, was fundamental to Ḥanafī jurisprudence. The Ḥanafī notions of *istiḥsān* and *ḥiyal*, among other things, are considered indicative of the Ḥanafī interest in and use of *maṣlaḥah*. Although it is not our purpose here to argue for or against consistency in the Ḥanafī jurisprudence, three points could help reconcile what al-Jaṣṣāṣ presents as the Ḥanafī rejection of the *verifiability and usability* of *maṣlaḥah* with other Ḥanafī notions such as *istiḥsān*. Firstly, it has been surmised that Abū Ḥanīfah adopted this notion of *maṣlaḥah* from Ibrāhīm al-Nakhaʿī through Ḥammād.[118] It is argued that Ibrāhīm held that the rulings of the law were both reasonable (in terms of being identifiable by reason), and purposeful (in the sense of seeking to realize individual and public interests).[119] Proceeding on the assumption of homogeneity in the Ḥanafī jurisprudence, this argument rules out the possibility that there may have been a difference between Abū Ḥanīfah and his teachers, on the one hand, and between him and his students, on the other hand. That Abū Ḥanīfah was an uncritical follower (*muqallid*) of Ibrāhīm al-Nakhaʿī is unlikely, and so is the contention that he himself was an exponent of the notion of *maṣlaḥah*.[120] Secondly, the actual role of *istiḥsān*—at times perceived as a defining feature of Ḥanafism—in Abū Ḥanīfah's jurisprudence may have been over-emphasized.[121] This holds equally true to the notion of the legal stratagems[122]—also considered important tools that Ḥanafīs used to serve individual and social interests as they understood them—despite frequent references to Abū Ḥanīfah in works on *ḥiyal*.[123] The question here is not

117 Al-Jaṣṣāṣ, *al-Fuṣūl*, vol. 1, p. 368. For Ẓāhirīs' similar argument, see Ibn Ḥazm, *Iḥkām*, vol. 1, p. 602.

118 See, for instance, Abū Zahrah, *Abū Ḥanīfah*, pp. 224–227, where Abū Zahrah mentions this view to refute it, although he agrees that Abū Ḥanīfah inherited Ibrāhīm al-Nakhaʿī's legal thought through Ḥammād.

119 Al-Fāsī, *al-Fikr al-Sāmī*, p. 386.

120 Muḥammad Mukhtār al-Qāḍī, *al-Raʾy fī al-Fiqh al-Islāmī*, p. 131. Al-Qāḍī argues that all Ḥanbalīs, including Aḥmad ibn Ḥanbal himself, not only recognized the notion of *al-maṣāliḥ al-mursalah*, but also used it extensively (*ibid.*, pp. 154–155).

121 Abū Zahrah, for instance, argues that Abū Ḥanīfah used *istiḥsān* "too often" (Abū Zahrah, *Abū Ḥanīfah*, p. 342). Further research is needed to investigate how significantly *istiḥsān* actually contributed to Abū Ḥanīfah's juridical thinking.

122 On the relation between *ḥiyal* and *maṣlaḥah*, see al-Fāsī, *al-Fikr al-Sāmī*, pp. 433–435.

123 Muḥammad ibn al-Ḥasan al-Shaybānī, *Kitāb al-Makhārij fī al-Ḥiyal*.

whether Abū Ḥanīfah made use of *istiḥsān* and *ḥiyal* or not; it is a question of how frequently he did that and how significant they were in his jurisprudence.

Finally, if we lend more credence to medieval Ḥanafī scholarship—such as al-Jaṣṣāṣ's views presented above—we would be able to consider the possibility that Abū Ḥanīfah himself may have distinguished between two categories of knowledge, each with its own rules and assumptions.[124] The assumption here is that even if he had believed that the wisdom of the law was recognizable and usable, Abū Ḥanīfah did not use this notion when there existed textual evidence that he accepted. If it is agreed that he had a genuine interest in consistency, objectivity, and certainty, he must have been seeking to apply his linguistic assumptions without trying to read into authoritative texts considerations of any nature. In fact, systematization and consistency do not serve flexibility, a basic requirement of a legal system that seeks to give itself enough room to respond to the surrounding reality and take the changing interests of people into account. In the second category of knowledge, however, he may take the benefit and interests of the parties involved into account.

Ẓāhirīs were notorious for their rejection of the notion that the wisdom of the law was knowable and accordingly relevant to the actual application of the law, a view that they categorically rejected as both arbitrary and baseless.[125] Furthermore, their uncompromising rejection of the notion of *ʿillah*, as attributed to Muḥammad ibn Dāwūd by al-Qāḍī al-Nuʿmān, is a recurrent theme in the writings of a Ẓāhirī scholar like Ibn Ḥazm, to the extent that this particular notion has been identified by many scholars, erroneously in my view, as the defining feature of Ẓāhirism.[126] In brief, both Ḥanafīs and Ẓāhirīs operated on the same principle regarding the overarching goals of the law. They all held that jurists and believers should focus on what they are required to do, not on the wisdom of the religious law which is beyond our knowledge and, therefore, has no practical relevance to jurisprudence.

Another major common feature in the juridical thought of both Ẓāhirīs and the *Ahl al-Raʾy*/Ḥanafīs is their hermeneutics. A basic view on language that Ẓāhirism and Ḥanafism shared was their understanding of the nature and

124 This distinction, of course, does not have to be sophisticated, but the view that Abū Ḥanīfah may have regarded cases differently on the basis of the available evidence is not unlikely.

125 For this, see Ibn Ḥazm, *Iḥkām*, vol. 2, pp. 1426ff.

126 See, for instance, Abū Zahrah, *Ibn Ḥazm*, pp. 261–262, and 394ff.

workings of language.[127] "The classical Ḥanafī *uṣūl* doctrine," Zysow argues, "stands out from that of other legal schools in the consistency with which it defends a view of language that permits *confident, secure* interpretation. In this respect, it stands close to the doctrine of Ẓāhirīs such as Ibn Ḥazm and that of certain Ḥanbalīs such as Ibn Taymiyya." Zysow goes on to explain that "[w]hat all these systems of interpretation have in common is that they seek to explain the workings of language, or at least the language of the sacred texts, in such a way as to exclude uncertainty from the process of interpretation."[128] Thus, for Ḥanafīs, "a valid interpretation of discourse cannot be expected to go beyond the evidence. In this respect, the Ḥanafī position on interpretation may be seen to represent a clinging to the *ẓāhir* of the text, its apparent meaning, and historically the Ḥanafīs were partisans of the natural reading of the texts against those who claimed to be pursuing a more sophisticated analysis of language."[129]

It is worth noting that textual evidence falls within the first category of knowledge that al-Jaṣṣāṣ mentions, which is how this statement by Zysow could be reconciled with what he says earlier about the difference between formalist and materialist scholars of Islamic law and their different notions of how much certainty is attainable in law. But to give concrete examples of this perception of language, it suffices to mention two issues that demonstrate how Ḥanafīs and Ẓāhirīs shared essential linguistic postulates in dealing with textual sources. The first is the issue of the imperative mood (*al-amr*) and what it entails. To illustrate the paramount importance of this issue in Islamic law, it suffices to take a look at introductory chapters in works of *uṣūl al-fiqh* by the Shāfiʿī scholar Abū Isḥāq al-Shīrāzī, the Ḥanafī scholar Abū Bakr al-Sarakhsī, and the Ḥanbalī scholars of the Āl Taymiyyah, which chapters deal with the imperative.[130] Al-Sarakhsī points out that knowledge of this subject allows Muslims to distinguish between what is lawful and what is not, for which reason knowledge of it completes knowledge of religion.[131] Therefore, this issue was a subject of much controversy among Muslim scholars.[132] We will focus here on three points, all of which have to do with the question of whether the

---

127 For the importance of the Arabic language for Islamic law, see, for instance, Bernard Weiss, "Language and Law: the Linguistic Premises of Islamic Legal Science," p. 15.

128 Zysow, *Economy*, p. 58. (italics added).

129 *Ibid.*, p. 59.

130 Abū Isḥāq al-Shīrāzī, *al-Tabṣirah*; Al-Sarakhsī, *al-Muḥarrar*; and *al-Musawwadah fī Uṣūl al-Fiqh* of Majd al-Dīn, Shihāb al-Dīn, and Taqī al-Dīn ibn Taymiyyah.

131 Al-Sarakhsī, *al-Muḥarrar*, vol. 1, p. 6.

132 For a brief discussion of the issue of the imperative, see Weiss, "Language and Law," pp. 19–20.

imperative form (*ifʿal*, in the Arabic language) signifies in and of itself—"as its sole *literal* sense," as Bernard Weiss puts it[133]—more than the mere calling for an act. The first issue is the degree of obligation that the imperative establishes: absolute obligation (*wujūb*), recommendation (*nadb*), or permissibility (*ibāḥah*). The second is the time framework that the imperative allows: whether it requires the immediate performance of what is commanded (*ʿalā ʾl-fawr*), or allows more time for its performance (*ʿalā ʾl-tarākhī*). The third is whether the imperative, in and of itself, requires the repetition (*tikrār*) of what is commanded, or only one single performance of it.

Muslim legal scholars have differed on each of these issues. Many scholars held that the imperative has an original, default sense that could be changed only when a strong indicator (*dalīl*) exists. Other scholars were hesitant, denying that the imperative, in and of itself, carried any sense beyond the calling for the action to be performed, which means that in all circumstances we have to search for an indicator to know what the imperative signifies and entails. The imperative, they argued, does not tell us, in and of itself, whether the act it calls for must, should, or only could be performed, whether or not the performance must be immediate or could be delayed, and whether the person commanded need to perform it only once or has to keep repeating it. If we discuss this issue from the angle of certainty, we can say that scholars who are hesitant about that which the imperative conveys (in other words, they do not hold that it has any default sense) do not aspire to achieve absolute certainty in their jurisprudence (if, of course, they do not make the argument that in each case they can identify clear-cut evidence that indicates what the imperative signifies with complete certainty). On the other hand, scholars who hold that the imperative has an inherent sense are in a much better position to claim certainty for the legal views that they derive from textual sources.

Both Ḥanafīs and Ẓāhirīs belonged to this last group of scholars. Both *madhhabs* held that the imperative in and of itself carried more meaning than the mere calling for an act. Both held that this inherent sense of the imperative can only be changed when a solid indicator can be determined with complete certainty; otherwise, the imperative form retains its original sense. They, admittedly, differed on the evidence they considered certain and definite, although this was also done on principles that both shared. That is, Ḥanafīs, as discussed earlier, did not acknowledge the *khabar al-wāḥid* as a valid and solid indicator, whereas Ẓāhirīs accepted it as such and held accordingly that it was able to change the sense of Qurʾānic commands, for instance. The Ẓāhirī acceptance of the validity of *khabar al-wāḥid* as indicator is, of course, in complete consis-

133 Bernard Weiss, *The Search for God's Law*, p. 350 (italics added).

tency with their acceptance of it as a source of apodictic knowledge. It is equally remarkable that Ḥanafism and Ẓāhirism made similar arguments as for why they held this view on the signification of the imperative. They argued that the imperative that signified obligation *must* have a form out of necessity (*ḍarūratan*); otherwise we, as the ones who are commanded and required to perform the command (*al-mukallafūn*), would be left in complete confusion, since there would be no way anyone could indicate to another that he *must* do what he commands him to do. Al-Sarakhsī argued that the centrality of the issue of the imperative (that requires obligation) makes it indispensable that it have a peculiar form, the sense of which could change only on the basis of a solid indicator.[134] Similarly, Ibn Ḥazm argues that if there were no form for the imperative that establishes absolute obligation, communication would be impossible and God's message to us would be meaningless. Language, he adds, is meant to clarify, not to confuse.[135]

What is even more pertinent to our purposes here, however, is that both Ḥanafīs and Ẓāhirīs shared the same views on the default senses of the imperative form. Both believed that the imperative, in and of itself, and when no indicator exists that suggests otherwise, establishes obligation.[136] Both believed that the imperative established an obligation of the immediate performance of the act it commands.[137] Furthermore, both believed that the subjects of the command (*al-mukallafūn*, in our case) fulfilled their duty and were spared further obligation to perform the act commanded the very first time they perform it, unless there is a certain indicator that suggests otherwise.[138]

Another linguistic issue that demonstrates a significant resemblance between Ḥanafī and Ẓāhirī juridical thought is the issue of the scope of applicability of terms, the issue that may have given Ẓāhirīs their name as discussed earlier. Some scholars held that any term should be assumed to be general, meaning that it encompasses its entire range of referents, i.e., everything to which it can be used to refer. Other scholars, on the other hand, held that

---

134 Al-Sarakhsī, *al-Muḥarrar*, pp. 8–13.

135 Ibn Ḥazm, *al-Muḥallā*, vol. 1, p. 330. This view on language is consistent with another important Ẓāhirī view, that is, God is not testing us on whether we would be able to determine the right ruling in each case, but on whether or not we would abide by his rulings which, by following the right methodology, we should be able to determine.

136 For the Ḥanafī view, see al-Jaṣṣāṣ, *al-Fuṣūl*, vol. 1, p. 283. For the Ẓāhirī view, see Ibn Ḥazm, *Iḥkām*, vol. 1, p. 329.

137 For the Ḥanafī view, see al-Jaṣṣāṣ, *al-Fuṣūl*, vol. 1, p. 295. For the Ẓāhirī view, see Ibn Ḥazm, *Iḥkām*, vol. 1, p. 375.

138 For the Ḥanafī view, see al-Jaṣṣāṣ, *al-Fuṣūl*, vol. 1, p. 314. For the Ẓāhirī view, see Ibn Ḥazm, *Iḥkām*, vol. 1, p. 401.

terms, in and of themselves, do not indicate their range of referents, which range we constantly have to search for indicators to determine. The first group of scholars knew, or so they thought, what terms encompassed; the second was hesitant. The importance of this issue stems from the fact that, more often than not, textual sources, especially the Qur'ān, use terms that, if always taken to refer to the entire range of their possible referents, this can lead to catastrophic results. For example, the Qur'ān mentions the amputation of a thief's (*al-sāriq*) hand as a prescribed punishment. *Al-sāriq* can be used to refer to any person who steals anything. If the reference of this term is not restricted, a person who steals a penny or an egg is considered a *sāriq* whose hand must be cut off according to the Qur'ānic verse. This term, however, was restricted by the Prophet, who determined a minimum value that a person must steal to be considered a thief and thus deserves the Qur'ānic prescribed punishment for theft. A problem could arise if a scholar were to dismiss this tradition as being of dubious authenticity, for instance. In this particular case, since this tradition was transmitted by individual transmitters rather than by way of *tawātur*, it is thus short of absolute certainty and cannot therefore restrict a term the range of referents of which we know with certainty.[139]

Zysow writes: "the problem of the general term stands ... at the heart of the Ḥanafī exegetical tradition, for the mainstream Ḥanafīs were almost alone in regarding the general term as a source of absolute certainty."[140] He goes on to say that even if the possibility of restriction or specialization (*takhṣīṣ*) was readily admitted, the majority of Ḥanafīs were of the opinion that "each general term was to be taken in its fullest extension unless there was an accompanying indication."[141] Abū Bakr al-Jaṣṣāṣ—who confirms that this was the opinion of *all* Ḥanafī scholars[142]—adds that we know the range and scope of application of general terms with absolute certainty, which is why it is treated as a source of solid, apodictic knowledge.[143] He rejects the view that since Ḥanafīs allow some traditions to limit the applicability of some general Qur'ānic terms, they should do the same on the basis of the *akhbār al-āḥād*, for they accept only traditions that, while being transmitted by one person, have

139 While falling in the category of the *akhbār al-āḥād*, this tradition was accepted almost unanimously by Muslim scholars.

140 Zysow, *Economy*, p. 78.

141 *Ibid.*, p. 79. As noted earlier, it is redundant to describe a term as "general." If scholars agree that a certain term is general (meaning unrestricted), they would not disagree on its scope of application.

142 Al-Jaṣṣāṣ, *al-Fuṣūl*, vol. 1, p. 40.

143 *Ibid.*, vol. 1, p. 79.

become so well-known that they now carry the same epistemological weight of *mutawātir* traditions.[144] This, we recall, is also the opinion of all Ẓāhirīs (*jamīʿ aṣḥāb al-ẓāhir*) as Ibn Ḥazm points out. All terms should be taken to include all its possible referents unless a valid or "true" indicator (*dalīl ḥaqq*) changes that.[145] Restricting the scope of application of any term is similar to holding that the imperative does not establish absolution obligation, or that performing commanded acts could be delayed. These are all cases of unjustifiable tampering with the inherent, default senses of terms (*naql al-asmāʾ ʿan musammayātihā*).[146] Ḥanafīs, therefore, were not alone in this.

2.2 *Ẓāhirism and the* Ahl al-Ḥadīth

In his *ʿUddah fī Uṣūl al-Fiqh*, the famous Ḥanbalī scholar Ibn Abī Yaʿlā al-Farrāʾ (d. 458/1066) mentions that the *ẓāhir* (here, most probable or likely) of Ibn Ḥanbal's views on the default sense of the imperative is that it establishes absolute obligation (*wujūb*) absent the presence of an indicator that suggests otherwise. This was inferred from a statement attributed to Ibn Ḥanbal in which he says: "If [the authenticity of] a report from the Prophet is established, it must be followed."[147] However, al-Farrāʾ also mentions, in a rather enigmatic way, that Ibn Ḥanbal "suspended his view" in the version (*riwāyah*) of ʿAbd al-Malik al-Maymūnī who collected some of Ibn Ḥanbal's cases. The basis of this suspension is a Prophetic tradition that says: "When I command you to do something, do as much of it as you can; and when I prohibit you to do something, avoid it!"[148] Commenting on this tradition, Ibn Ḥanbal is reported to

144 Al-Jaṣṣāṣ, *al-Fuṣūl*, vol. 1, p. 84.

145 Ibn Ḥazm, *al-Muḥallā*, vol. 1, p. 431.

146 *Ibid.*, vol. 1, p. 471. Significantly, targeting the Ḥanafīs with his bitter polemics in his *Iʿrāb ʿan al-Ḥayrah wa-l-Iltibās al-Mawjūdayn fī Madhāhib Ahl al-Raʾy wa-l-Qiyās*, Ibn Ḥazm censures them primarily for their inconsistency and arbitrariness in applying their rules rather than rejecting the rules themselves.

147 *Idhā thabata ʾl-khabar ʿan al-nabī wajaba ʾl-ʿamal bi-hi* (Ibn Abī Yaʿlā al-Farrāʾ, *al-ʿUddah*, vol. 1, p. 224). Obviously, Ibn Ḥanbal may not have had the issue of the imperative in mind when he made this statement. But to put al-Farrāʾs discussion here into perspective, specific statements from Aḥmad ibn Ḥanbal on *uṣūl* issues did not exist. Later Ḥanbalī scholars, who must have been influenced by views of other *madhhab*s, sought to infer what Ibn Ḥanbal may have thought about various *uṣūl* issues. More often than not, however, more than one view were reached by studying his cases. We will discuss what this suggests about his juridical thinking, but it must be pointed out here that if we regard Ibn Ḥanbal as a legal scholar, it is unlikely that he did not have at least some theoretical views, even if rudimentary.

148 The tradition in Arabic: *mā amartukum bi-hi fa-iʾtū min-hu mā istaṭaʿtum, wa-mā nahaytukum ʿan-hu fa-ijtanibūhu.*

have said that "commands in my view are less stringent than prohibitions."[149] Al-Farrā' argues against the view that this statement could be taken to mean that commands, in Ibn Ḥanbal's view, only established recommendation. In their *Musawwadah fī Uṣūl al-Fiqh*,[150] the Āl Taymiyyah also reject this understanding, which, they argue, contradicts other statements (*manṣuṣāt*) attributed to Ibn Ḥanbal. Accordingly, they reinterpreted this statement in a way that would reconcile it with their view that the imperative established absolute obligation, which was Ibn Ḥanbal's own view.[151]

What is noteworthy here is that later Ḥanbalī scholars were uncomfortable with the possibility, or perhaps the reality, that Ibn Ḥanbal may have had a different view on what they regarded as the default sense of the imperative. Abū Yaʿlā is in fact the only scholar who actually sought to produce evidence, in the form of a statement attributed to Ibn Ḥanbal, for his contention that he did not differ from the view of most [later] scholars on this issue. The statement that he produces, however, does not serve his purpose here. Ibn Ḥanbal's statement about the reports of the Prophet does not, even indirectly, tackle the question of the imperative and the level of obligation that it establishes. It may be for this reason that no other Ḥanbalī scholar of *uṣūl* used it, and, in fact, the Āl Taymiyyah considered it a "weak indication" of Ibn Ḥanbal's opinion.[152] Furthermore, Ibn Ḥanbal's other comment on the Prophet's tradition of commands and prohibitions suggests that he was hesitant between two possibilities of the denotation of the imperative—either absolute obligation or mere recommendation. In this comment, he seems to be distinguishing between prohibitions, which establish absolute obligation to abstain from certain acts, and commands, which could have a similar degree of obligation (to do something), or a lesser degree (which is the case with recommendations).

Scholars who held that the imperative had a certain default or primary meaning argued that when it is used to indicate another degree of obligation (or complete lack thereof, such as in the case of permissibility), it does so figuratively. For example, as we have seen, al-Jaṣṣāṣ mentions that the imperative in and of itself indicates absolute obligation. It could, however, be used figuratively (*majāzan*) to indicate any other level of obligation (i.e.,

149 *Al-amr ashal ʿindī min al-nahy* (al-Farrā', *al-ʿUddah*, vol. 1, p. 228).

150 This work is attributed to three scholars of the Taymiyyah family: Majd al-Dīn (ʿAbd al-Salām ibn ʿAbd Allāh, d. 652/1254), Shihāb al-Dīn (ʿAbd al-Ḥalīm ibn ʿAbd al-Salām, d. 682/1283), and Taqī al-Dīn (Aḥmad ibn ʿAbd al-Ḥalīm, or the celebrated scholar Ibn Taymiyyah, d. 728/1328).

151 Āl Taymiyyah, *al-Musawwadah*, p. 5.

152 *Ibid.*, p. 15.

recommendation).[153] Ḥanbalī scholars of *uṣūl al-fiqh*, however, attributed to Ibn Ḥanbal the view that when the imperative is used to indicate recommendation, it does so *ʿalā ʾl-ḥaqīqah* ("factually," "literally"?), not figuratively (which is the case when it is used to indicate permissibility).[154] This confirms the impression that Ibn Ḥanbal was probably hesitant about this issue. If the same imperative form (*ṣīghat ifʿal* here) can be used to indicate, *ʿalā ʾl-ḥaqīqah*, two degrees of obligation, this renders less certain our understanding of the degree of obligation that any imperative establishes. On the other hand, the other view that the imperative form indicates one thing *ʿalā ʾl-ḥaqīqah* but could indicate another only *ʿalā ʾl-majāz* allows for certainty.

Ibn Ḥanbal was evidently hesitant about other issues too. On the question of whether the imperative indicates that the act requested must be done immediately or could be delayed, the Ḥanbalī scholar ʿAlī ibn ʿAqīl (d. 513/1119) attributes to him the view that the imperative, in and of itself, and if no indicator suggests otherwise, carries the requirement of the immediate performance of the commanded act.[155] Reporting other views that indicate that Ibn Ḥanbal did not actually think that the imperative carried the requirement of the immediate performance of the act, al-Farrāʾ agrees that what Ibn ʿAqīl says is the *ẓāhir* of Ibn Ḥanbal's views.[156] Ibn ʿAqīl, however, criticizes al-Farrāʾ for concluding this on the basis of some of Ibn Ḥanbal's *masāʾil*,[157] arguing that the masters of *uṣūl* do not deduce the *uṣūl* principles from the *furūʿ*, but rather establish the *furūʿ* on the *uṣūl*.[158] In Ibn ʿAqīl's view, Ibn Ḥanbal *must* have held the view that the imperative required the immediate performance of the command because this was more "precautionary," and precaution (*iḥtiyāṭ*) in the *uṣūl* and *furūʿ* "is the heart of Ibn Ḥanbal's *madhhab*," he contends.[159] In addition to demonstrating the difficulty of determining the principles that guided his juridical thought (which was probably due to his own hesitancy), this statement is a strong indication of the moral dimension of Ibn Ḥanbal's jurisprudence as Ḥanbalī scholars themselves understood it, and it contrasts sharply with the beliefs of both Ḥanafīs and Ẓāhirīs who insisted that a certain act cannot be declared forbidden on any basis other than a text (or analogy thereto

153 Al-Jaṣṣāṣ, *al-Fuṣūl*, vol. 1, p. 281. For a complete list of the uses of the imperative form, see *ibid.*, vol. 1, pp. 280–281.

154 For this, see al-Farrāʾ, *al-ʿUddah*, vol. 1, p. 248, and Āl Taymiyyah, *al-Musawwadah*, pp. 6–7.

155 Ibn ʿAqīl, *al-Wāḍiḥ fī Uṣūl al-Fiqh*, vol. 2, p. 17.

156 Al-Farrāʾ, *al-ʿUddah*, vol. 1, p. 281.

157 Most works on Ḥanbalī *uṣūl al-fiqh* follow the *ṭarīqat al-fuqahāʾ* (see p. 149, fn. 102 above) and rely on Ibn Ḥanbal's *masāʾil* to infer his legal principles.

158 Ibn ʿAqīl, *al-Wāḍiḥ*, vol. 3, p. 17.

159 *Ibid.*, vol. 3, p. 17.

for Ḥanafīs), the authenticity and meaning of which we have full confidence in. Precaution, which is based on the same logic that governs the *sadd al-dharāʾiʿ* principle (where an act is avoided not because it is wrong in itself, but because it may lead to a forbidden act), is not a principle they would consider for declaring an act forbidden. Remarkably, while works of Ḥanbalī *uṣūl* affirm that for Ibn Ḥanbal the imperative denoted the requirement to carry out the commanded act repeatedly (*ʿalā ʾl-tikrār*),[160] the Muʿtazilī scholar Abū al-Ḥusayn al-Baṣrī (d. 436/1044) mentions that those who held the view that the imperative indicated the necessity to repeat the act did so on the basis of *iḥtiyāṭ*.[161]

On the issue of the scope of application of terms, however, Ḥanbalī *uṣūl* works attribute to Ibn Ḥanbal the view that any term is to be interpreted as broadly as possible unless an indicator suggests otherwise.[162] Yet the authors of *al-Musawwadah* mention that many of Ibn Ḥanbal's associates held other views regarding this issue.[163] Arguably, this contention (that Ibn Ḥanbal's view on the issue of *ʿumūm* was similar to that of Abū Ḥanīfah and Dāwūd) is inconsistent with Ibn Ḥanbal's moral agenda and with his hesitation, and the case studies discussed in chapter six will demonstrate that he was more concerned with reconciling various pieces of evidence that he had on a certain issue rather than following the *ʿumūm* of a particular textual evidence.

It is worth noting that Abū al-Ḥasan al-Ashʿarī (d. 324/936) figures as the most important scholar of *waqf* (suspension of opinion), not only on the issue of the imperative, but also on the issue of the scope of application of terms. Al-Ashʿarī is reported to have argued that the imperative that required absolute obligation has no specific form, and that the *ifʿal* form, in and of itself, does not have any inherent sense.[164] In every single case, therefore, we have to search for clues that indicate what the imperative suggests.[165] What is remarkable here is that this is not the view of the Muʿtazilīs, who held that the imperative denoted recommendation unless proven otherwise.[166] Similarly, al-Ashʿarī

---

160 Al-Farrāʾ, *al-ʿUddah*, vol. 2, pp. 264–265; Ibn ʿAqīl, *al-Wāḍiḥ*, vol. 2, pp. 545–546.

161 Abū al-Ḥusayn al-Baṣrī, *al-Muʿtamad fī Uṣūl al-Fiqh*, vol. 1, p. 102.

162 Al-Farrāʾ, *al-ʿUddah*, vol. 2, p. 485; Āl Taymiyyah, *al-Musawwadah*, p. 89.

163 Āl Taymiyyah, *al-Musawwadah*, p. 89.

164 For this, see, for instance, al-Farrāʾ, *al-ʿUddah*, vol. 2, p. 489, and al-Shīrāzī, *al-Tabṣirah*, vol. 1, p. 22.

165 The same opinion was attributed to al-Shāfiʿī by the Shāfiʿī scholar Ibn Surayj, but is rejected by all other Shāfiʿīs (for this, see, for instance, al-Sarakhsī, *al-Muḥarrar*, p. 11).

166 Ibn ʿAqīl, *al-Wāḍiḥ*, vol. 2, p. 495. This is the view that most scholars of *uṣūl* attribute to Muʿtazilīs. In *al-Muʿtamad*, however, Abū al-Ḥusayn al-Baṣrī argues that the imperative establishes absolute obligation, but he also mentions that Abū ʿAlī al-Jubbāʾī (d. 303/915)

also denied that *al-lafẓ al-ʿāmm* had a specific form in the language in the first place. Therefore, every term could be of broad or limited scope of application depending on the clues available, which we need to seek in every single case.[167] On the other hand, Muʿtazilīs had the same view of Ḥanafīs and Ẓāhirīs regarding the scope of application of terms.[168] This suggests that al-Ashʿarī, who converted from Muʿtazilism to Ḥanbalism, may have thought that his views on these two issues were those of Ibn Ḥanbal himself, which is more consistent with what we know about Ibn Ḥanbal. If Ibn Ḥanbal thought that all the Companions were correct, the fact that they disagreed on many issues—many of which must have been related to the imperative and scope of application of terms—must have made it difficult for him to take a definite position on any of these issues. In other words, Ibn Ḥanbal's inconclusiveness is consistent with other things that we know about him, and the conflicting *uṣūl* views that later Ḥanbalīs concluded on the basis of his *masāʾil* are only indicative of this.

3 Conclusion

This chapter has sought to determine the meaning of *ẓāhir* and, accordingly, why Dāwūd was labeled *al-Ẓāhirī* (i.e., what was defining of his juridical thought) and how this relates to the question of the relation of his juridical thought to the two legal trends of his time. Examining some Qurʾanic uses of *ẓāhir* was not particularly helpful in this respect. Some ambiguities and inconsistencies notwithstanding, however, discussion of the uses of *ẓāhir* in al-Shāfiʿī's *Risālah* and part of al-Ṭabarī's commentary on the Qurʾān suggests that it was employed in the context of hermeneutics and used extensively and frequently, and most likely technically, in a specific context, that of the scope of application—or the generality/restrictedness (*ʿumūm/khuṣūṣ*)—of terms. *Ẓāhir* is the most comprehensive sense, or the broadest and fullest possible scope of application or range of referents of a certain word or statement. Al-Ṭabarī's discussion strongly suggests that there was an assumption that the *ẓāhir* meaning should be taken to reflect the intention of the speaker (God, in the case of the Qurʾān), and that any deflection from this meaning required a valid indicator, one both the authenticity and indication of which is beyond

held the view that it only suggested recommendation. In both circumstances, however, it is noteworthy that every Muʿtazilī scholar held one view or another on the degree of obligation that the imperative establishes. None of them was hesitant about it.

167 See, for instance, *al-Tabṣirah*, vol. 1, p. 105.

168 Al-Baṣrī, *al-Muʿtamad*, vol. 1, p. 189.

doubt. Deviating himself from the *ẓāhir* meaning at times, al-Ṭabarī had an evident concern to not jeopardize the all-inclusiveness of any Qurʾānic term or statement without valid evidence. This use of *ẓāhir* was implicitly, but obviously, connected by al-Shāfiʿī to the principle of *al-ibāḥah al-aṣliyyah*, or the presumption that any act is permissible from the religious point of view unless proven otherwise. In other words, what is forbidden is only what God has explicitly forbidden, and that on which He has been silent is not forbidden. Therefore, when God or the Prophet prohibit something, this particular thing is regarded as an exception to this general rule of permissibility, but that which is not prohibited remains covered by the general rule, viz. it remains permissible. This principle has provided scholars with a very important general rule with which they can begin thinking of new cases.

Furthermore, from this discussion of *ẓāhir* as it was used in the 3rd/9th century, we can infer a relation between the subject of *ʿumūm* and Dāwūd's rejection of *qiyās*. *Qiyās*, as al-Shāfiʿī explains, qualifies (here, restricts) general rules by drawing analogy between what it textually prohibited and other things deemed similar to it but are not textually prohibited. For example, if we assume, for the sake of the argument, that jurists agree that the Qurʾānic word *khamr* refers only to grape wine, a Ẓāhirī scholar would consider grape wine to be the only exception to the general rule of the permissibility of all beverages. A scholar who draws analogy between grape wine and some other beverages, declaring thereby these other beverages forbidden, violates *al-ibāḥah al-aṣliyyah* rule by reducing its range of referents or increasing the exceptions to it.[169] This, of course, does not apply to scholars who do not subscribe to the principle of *al-ibāḥah al-aṣliyyah*, and for whom *qiyās* is a valid tool to demonstrate that something is permissible (by drawing analogy between it and something else that we know to be permissible). In other words, *qiyās*, in this case, seeks to demonstrate that something that is *not* explicitly mentioned by the law is not permissible because of a presumed similarity between it and another thing that is known to be forbidden. This is a further expansion of the exception to the general rule of *al-ibāḥah al-aṣliyyah*, or, reversely, a further restriction of its scope. Scholars who hold the principle of *al-ibāḥah al-aṣliyyah*, however, do not need to argue for the permissibility of anything in the first

169 A modern scholar who sought to find a connection between the principle of *istiṣḥāb al-ḥāl*, on the one hand, and the rejection of *qiyās*, on the other hand, is Y. Linant de Bellefonds. He argues that from the Ẓāhirī point of view, since permissibility (*ibāḥah*) is the rule and prohibition is the exception, only a clear text can establish prohibition. This view is thus inconsistent with *qiyās* which is not direct textual evidence yet is nonetheless used to prohibit that which is not textually forbidden (de Bellefonds, "Ibn Ḥazm," p. 18).

place, for they presume that everything and anything is permissible unless a valid piece of evidence proves otherwise.

This means that if *ẓāhir* had multiple applications in different linguistic contexts, it was particularly associated with the subject of *ʿumūm/khuṣūṣ*. There is solid evidence that Ibn Ḥazm understood the *ẓāhir* meaning to be the *ʿāmm* sense of words and statements. For example, commenting on various views on the meaning of "those who are in authority among you" (*ūlī ʾl-amr min-kum*) in Q. 4:59,[170] he rejects the view that *ūlī ʾl-amr* here refers exclusively to scholars rather than to other Muslims. Since there is no textual evidence from the Qurʾān or Ḥadīth that it refers to one part of the Muslim community rather than another, it must be interpreted according to its *ẓāhir*, the restriction (*takhṣīṣ*) of which requires evidence (*burhān*). The *ẓāhir* meaning of the *ūlī ʾl-amr* here is obviously its unrestricted meaning that is inclusive of the entire possible range of its potential referents. Furthermore, the relationship between *ʿumūm* and *qiyās* is also evident in some of Ibn Ḥazm's discussions. On the question of the punishment of a male slave who engages in an illicit sexual relationship while he is or had been married (*muḥṣan*), Ibn Ḥazm argues against the view, attributed to Abū Ḥanīfah, Mālik, al-Shāfiʿī, and Ibn Ḥanbal, that he is not to be stoned to death as is the case with free men, but should rather receive fifty lashes similar to slave girls who engage in a similar relationship. Ibn Ḥazm relies on a Prophetic tradition to argue that stoning to death is the rule in the case of adultery.[171] The only exception to this rule is female slaves, according to Q. 4:25.[172] It is not to anyone, he asserts, to challenge the *ʿumūm* of this tradition without evidence. *Qiyās*, which is used to include male slaves in the exception, is therefore invalid. Accordingly, a male slave is to be stoned to death just like free men according to the general rule on this matter.[173]

In addition to the subject of *ʿumūm*, *ẓāhir* appears in the context of the imperative. The *ẓāhir* meaning of a command, according to al-Shāfiʿī, is that it is meant to establish absolute obligation to do something, a view that Ibn Ḥazm fully endorses.[174] What is remarkable here is that a relationship between the two issues of *ʿumūm* and the imperative is conceivable. That is, just as it is

170 This part of the verse reads: "O you who believe, obey God and obey the Messenger and those in authority among you."

171 *Al-thayyib bi-l-thayyib, jald miʾah wa-l-rajm*. Ibn Ḥazm, *Iḥkām*, vol. 1, pp. 497–498.

172 *Fa-idhā uḥṣinna fa-in atayna bi-fāḥishah fa-ʿalay-hinna niṣf mā ʿalā ʾl-muḥṣanāt min al-adhāb* (and if when they [slave girls] are married they commit lewdness, their punishment is half that of free women).

173 Ibn Ḥazm, *al-Muḥallā*, vol. 12, pp. 181–182. It is remarkable here that it Ḥadīth that provides the general rule and the Qurʾān the restriction.

174 Ibn Ḥazm, *Iḥkām*, vol. 1, pp. 85–86.

the case that any term is presumed to refer *unconditionally* (i.e., without restriction) to *any* thing or person that falls or can potentially fall within its reach, the imperative is presumed to establish an *unconditional* obligation on *everyone* in *all* circumstances to do something, or, in the case of prohibition, to avoid doing something. There is then an element of *unconditionality, unrestrictedness*, and *absoluteness* in this understanding of commands and prohibitions, an element that is central to the belief in the supremacy and immediacy of the all-comprehensiveness of words and statements. In both cases, challenging the absoluteness of a statement requires a valid, solid indicator. Furthermore, out of the desire to defame Ẓāhirīs, medieval scholars have typically focused on cases that demonstrate how their presumption that all commands established absolute obligation led them to many "absurdities." For example, in Q. 2:282, Muslims are commanded to write down a note when they borrow money or any other item.[175] Ẓāhirīs insisted that the imperative in this verse (*fa-iktubūhu*) established absolute, unconditional obligation, which means that the value of the debt is irrelevant to the duty to put it in writing. However, if rather than focusing on the command itself and how Ẓāhirīs construed it, we focus on the *object* of the command, the relationship between the imperative and the issue of *ʿumūm* would be evident. In this case of debt, what really distinguished Ẓāhirīs was their contention that writing was obligatory regarding *any* debt and regardless of its object or value.[176] In the *lā yakhṭub* tradition mentioned earlier, the general rule that it establishes is that no Muslim is allowed *under any circumstance* to ask *any* woman who is already engaged to another for marriage. The views that al-Shāfiʿī mentions in this context do not seek to mitigate the degree of obligation of this prohibition, but rather to qualify the apparently absolute, unconditional, and unrestricted rule that this tradition establishes.[177] Thus, presuming the imperative to establish less than absolute obligation that applies "across the board," so to speak, threatens its *ʿumūm* or *ẓāhir*.

---

175 *Yā ayyuhā ʾlladhīna āmanū idhā tadāyantum bi-dayn ilā ajal musammā fa-iktubūhu* (O you who believe, when you contract a debt to a fixed term, record it in writing).

176 The views that al-Ṭabarī attributes to earlier authorities on the meaning of this verse suggest that there existed an attitude that sought to restrict it to certain items (*ḥinṭah*, or wheat), or to certain values (hence, the view that all debts, be they significant or otherwise (*ṣaghīran aw kabīran*), should be written down).

177 In al-Shāfiʿī's view, the prohibition applies only when a woman accepts a marriage offer from a man. In this case, no other Muslim should seek to marry her. If, however, a man offers to marry a woman and she does not give him a word, other men can ask her for marriage (al-Shāfiʿī, *al-Risālah* (1938), pp. 308–309, §§851–859).

Remarkably, it is not uncommon for non-Ẓāhirī scholars to make conclusions about the purpose of the law on the basis of exceptions to general rules. For example, al-Ṭabarī mentions a number of scholars who held that the command in the verse of the debt is for absolute obligation and not just recommendation (which is the Ẓāhirī view). Others held that this command was in fact abrogated by Q. 2:283, "And if you are in a journey and cannot find a scribe, then a pledge in hand [shall suffice]. And if one of you trusts another, he who is trusted should deliver his trust."[178] In their view, this textual evidence mitigates the command, for it spares people of the requirement of writing their debts or have witnesses when they are traveling and do not find a scribe. When this is done, however, the gate is wide open, not only for mitigating the obligatoriness of the first verse, but also for adding new exceptions to the general rule that it establishes on the basis of each scholar's understanding of the "spirit" of the law and the purposes that it seeks to serve. It is not therefore surprising that the majority of scholars, including those who held that the command in and of itself established absolute obligation, agreed that this command to write debts cannot be taken to establish absolute obligation.[179] For Dāwūd, the unrestrictedness of terms and rules can only be qualified by the lawgiver. The logic behind a certain exception or qualification of a rule is one that we (the interpreters of the law as well as its followers) do not know and are not required to seek to begin with. Therefore, we cannot use an exception to make conclusions about the purpose of the law.

Dāwūd shared the belief in *ʿumūm* with the *Ahl al-Raʾy*, as well as their understanding of the nature of divine law. Both believed that certainty in not only required in the law, but was also attainable if the right methodology is used. Accordingly, there must exist one correct reading of any legal text, and this correct reading is within our reach with complete confidence. To achieve certainty, the *Ahl al-Raʾy*/Ḥanafīs and Dāwūd/Ẓāhirīs emphasized the centrality of legal texts and the importance of interpreting them on the basis of well-defined assumptions and rules, such as the notion of *istiṣḥāb al-ḥāl*, the assumption that restricting the full scope of application of a text requires a valid evidence, and the assumption that the imperative in and of itself established absolute obligation. It is important to note that Dāwūd evidently had more textual evidence to deal with than the *Ahl al-Raʾy*, for which reason he was able to argue that in most cases, there existed one, and only one, valid evidence, unlike the *Ahl al-Raʾy* who felt more at liberty to use their own

178 The verse reads: *wa-in kuntum ʿalā safar wa-lam tajidū kātib fa-rihān maqbūḍah, fa-in amina baʿḍukum baʿḍ fa-l-yuʾaddī ʾlladhī iʾtumina amānatahu.*

179 For this, see al-Ṭabarī, *Jāmiʿ al-Bayān*, vol. 3, pp. 117–119.

judgment where no valid textual evidence existed in their view, or when conflicting pieces of evidence existed on one issue. What is significant is that Dāwūd and the *Ahl al-Raʾy* dealt similarly with the textual evidence that they *accepted* without emphasizing notions such as the wisdom and higher goals of the law.

On the other hand, Aḥmad ibn Ḥanbal does not seem to have been interested in abiding by specific assumptions and rules in his jurisprudence. His evident hesitancy made later Ḥanbalī scholars unable to infer one view on the issues of the scope of application of terms and the imperative, for instance, from his legal cases. Hesitancy appears as a hallmark of Ibn Ḥanbal, and this is consistent with the view that he was more concerned for the morality rather than the legality of acts and practices. To serve his moral agenda, and also to be able to reconcile and synthesize various pieces of evidence from the Qurʾān, the Prophetic Sunnah, and Companions' views, he needed to be at liberty to deal with the evidence without abiding by rigid and restrictive rules. The case studies discussed in CHAPTER SIX will seek to demonstrate these views on Dāwūd and Ẓāhirīs, the *Ahl al-Raʾy* as represented by Abū Ḥanīfah and later Ḥanafīs, and the *Ahl al-Hadīth*, as represented by Aḥmad ibn Ḥanbal and his later followers. Now we attend to the question of the nature of Ẓāhirism as a hermeneutical and legal theory.

CHAPTER 5

Ẓāhirism, Literalism and Textualism

Modern Islamicists, and perhaps some medieval Muslim scholars, have regarded Ẓāhirism as a literalist approach, assuming that the *ẓāhir* meaning is the "literal" meaning.[1] They, however, do not examine how the term *ẓāhir* was used in the Muslim tradition, nor do they take into account the controversy in modern linguistics on the validity of the very notion of "literalism," or the possibility of identifying a literal meaning for a given word or sentence. The

---

1 For modern scholars, see, for instance, Goldziher, *The Ẓāhirīs*, p. 117; Turki, "al-Ẓāhiriyya," in *EI*², vol. 11, p. 394, and his *Polémiques entre Ibn Ḥazm et Bāǧi sur les principes de la loi musulmane: Essai sur le littéralisme zahirite et la finalité malikite*, p. 72; Coulson, *History*, p. 71; Melchert, *Formation*, p. 179; Adang, "The Beginning of the Ẓāhirī Madhhab in al-Andalus," p. 116, and her "Ibn Ḥazm on Homosexuality," p. 13, where Adang says that "[a]s their name indicates, the Ẓāhirīs advocate the *literal* interpretation of the revealed sources" (italics added); and al-Shehabi, "Illa and Qiyas," p. 29. More recently, Adam Sabra ("Ibn Ḥazm's Literalism," p. 7) has discussed how Ibn Ḥazm was misunderstood because of his "insistence that the Qur'ān and Sunnah be interpreted *literally*" (italics added). Likewise, Saʿīd al-Afghānī (*Ibn Ḥazm al-Andalusī*, p. 66) speaks of Ibn Ḥazm's fixation on the "letter" of texts (*wuqūfihi ʿalā ḥarfiyyat al-nuṣūṣ*). Even Mohamed Yunis Ali, who uses modern pragmatics theory to study some aspects of Ibn Taymiyyah's juridical thought in his *Medieval Islamic Pragmatics*, continues to use "surface" and "literal" for *ẓāhir*, assuming that the *ẓāhir* statements can yield meaning without the need for contextual clues, which only change the surface meaning: "The *surface* meaning of a given utterance must be taken in principle as the intended meaning of the utterance unless there is some contextual ... evidence to the contrary" (Ali, *Medieval Muslim Pragmatics*, p. 5). Vishanoff (*The Formation*, p. 5) translates ẓāhir as "apparent." As has been noted earlier, medieval Muslim scholars are not clear as to their understanding of the meaning of Ẓāhirism. However, some of their views about it suggest that they regarded it as "literalist" if by literalism we mean fixation on the wording of a text (assuming that focus on the text is sufficient to make a certain reading literalist, an issue that is dealt with below) without consideration to non-textual factors. Ibn al-Jawzī, for instance, contends that Dāwūd "abandoned what could be understood of a tradition for the form of its words" (*yaltafitu ʿalā mafhūm al-ḥadīth ilā ṣūrat lafẓihi*) (Ibn al-Jawzī, *al-Muntaẓam*, vol. 12, p. 236). Speaking of the *aṣḥāb al-alfāẓ wa-l-ẓawāhir* and citing some Ẓāhirī legal views, Ibn Qayyim al-Jawziyyah argues that their focus on the (literal?) meaning made their understanding fall short of the intended objectives of the lawgiver (*qaṣarū bi-maʿānī* [*ʾl-nuṣūṣ*] *ʿan murād* [*al-shāriʿ*]) (Ibn al-Qayyim, *Aʿlām al-Muwaqqiʿīn*, vol. 1, p. 222). In other words, he distinguishes between what he calls *al-ẓawāhir wa-l-alfāẓ* and the objectives and (deeper? hidden?) meanings of texts (*al-maqāṣid wa-l-maʿānī*) (*ibid.*, vol. 3, p. 115). In this understanding, those who focus on the former miss the latter.

 | DOI 10.1163/9789004279650_007

previous chapter dealt with the first issue. This chapter continues this interrogation of Ẓāhirism by tackling the issue of literalism. It begins with comparing Ẓāhirism as elaborated by Ibn Ḥazm al-Andalusī with the version of textualism expounded by a contemporary American jurist, Justice Antonin Scalia. The second part of the chapter deals with literalism from a linguistic point of view.

1 Textualism

Justice Antonin Scalia—who has been Associate Justice of the United States Supreme Court since 1986—is known to be the most outspoken advocate of textualism in the United States in recent decades. Here, I investigate the extent to which his version of textualism corresponds to Ẓāhirism with respect to its premises, goals, and methodology.[2]

2 This section deals with constitutional interpretation in the United States. I find American textualism, as articulated by Justice Antonin Scalia in particular, a useful interpretative theory to compare with (and to) Ẓāhirism. There has been a previous attempt by Asifa Quraishi to draw some analogies between textualism and Ẓāhirism ("Interpreting the Qur'ān and the Constitution: Similarities in the Use of Text, Tradition, and Reason in Islamic and American Jurisprudence," pp. 76–80). Quraishi's almost complete reliance on secondary sources for Islamic law, however, has limited her ability to comprehend some of its aspects. For example, she believes that Mālik can be compared to American originalists who focus on the practice at the time when the US Constitution was written to identify the intent of its authors. She then compares Mālik with al-Shāfiʿī, who, for his part, focused on the verbal traditions that were transmitted from the Prophet. This comparison is problematic, for Mālik did not use the practice of the Medinese (*ʿamal ahl al-Madīnah*) to determine the meaning of verbal traditions, nor did al-Shāfiʿī neglect the historical context in determining the meaning of the Prophet's utterances. We have seen earlier that al-Shāfiʿī stressed that the Qur'ān was revealed in the language of its direct audience (the Arabs), and that full mastery of this language as it was used by the Arabs during the time of the Prophet was absolutely required to understand legal/religious texts. Furthermore, unlike American originalists who use history to determine the intended meaning of texts by examining how the "Americans" who lived in the late 18th century would have understood the Constitution (i.e., they use history to determine meaning rather than practice), Mālik usually used history to determine the law, *not* the interpretation thereof. Mālik simply rejected any textual evidence that contradicted Medinan *ʿamal*. Arguably, Shāfiʿī would have given weight to Medinan *ʿamal* that would support one understanding of a certain reading of a textual evidence rather than the other. In addition, Quraishi compares reliance on Prophetic traditions to using other textual evidence from the period when the US Constitution was written to determine the intent of its authors. This, however, does not take into account that the Prophetic Sunnah did not just explain general or ambiguous Qur'ānic statements. However it was also considered an independent source of the law. Moreover, if we use Prophetic traditions to determine the intent of God in the Qur'ān, by

1.1 *Textualism and Ẓāhirism*

A theory of language (by which I mean a set of assumptions about the nature and workings of language) is central to all interpretative methodologies.[3] In describing textualism, Scalia contends that textualists are neither literalists nor nihilists. "Words," he explains, "... have a limited range of meanings, and no interpretation that goes beyond that range is permissible."[4] This indicates two significant aspects of Scalia's perception of language; first, he believes that although we may need to exert some effort in order to determine the intended meaning of a given term, we are dealing primarily with a *finite* number of possibilities, which we can learn from many sources, as explained below. The second and probably the more important aspect is that it is assumed here that we *can* understand the language (of the law) in a correct way. For his part, Ibn Ḥazm argues that the first language that man used was not man-made, but was rather taught to man by God himself. According to him, Q. 2:31, "And He taught Adam all the Names ...,"[5] clearly indicates that God taught Adam all the words that He had assigned to everything.[6] This first language must have been the most perfect of all languages in its clarity, straightforwardness, and freedom from ambiguity.[7] As for other languages, they may too have been taught to Adam by God, or may have been derived (but not developed separately) from the first language. Yet even in the latter case, Ibn Ḥazm's view on how language functions remains the same; he holds that when people invented new languages, they had already learned how language works.[8] In every language, therefore, there is a word that corresponds to a certain thing, and this is what makes communication among people who speak the same language possible. This is a conclusion that is dictated by both reason and Revelation, he argues,

---

which methodology can we verify that our understanding of the Prophet's intent is correct if he is using the same language that God uses? Or, if there is a means by which we can determine the Prophet's intent, can we not use the same methodology to directly determine God's? In brief, Quraishi's attempt was a step in the right direction, but more remains to be said about this subject, which is what this chapter seeks to contribute to.

3 Crapanzano, *Serving the Word: Literalism in America from the Pulpit to the Bench*, p. 10.

4 Antonin Scalia, *Matter of Interpretation*, p. 24.

5 Ibn Ḥazm also held that the first language could not have been developed by people, for developing a language requires a high degree of reason and knowledge, which can only be obtained through the use of language (Ibn Ḥazm, *Iḥkām*, vol. 1, p. 28).

6 Ibn Ḥazm, *Iḥkām*, vol. 1, pp. 28–29.

7 *Ibid.*, vol. 1, p. 30. Ibn Ḥazm argues that we do not know now what that language was, and against the "arbitrary" view of some scholars that it was Arabic (a view that he believes is highly unlikely) (*ibid.*, vol. 1, pp. 30–31).

8 *Ibid.*, vol. 1, pp. 30–31.

for language is meant to explain rather than confuse matters.[9] Consequently, Ibn Ḥazm insists that a Muslim jurist must be accomplished in the Arabic language, the language of Revelation. This requires full knowledge of the words that are assigned to things and the grammatical rules of Arabic.[10]

The important analogy we can draw between Ibn Ḥazm's and Scalia's understanding of language here is their conviction that each word refers to a specific thing (its referent) and that "correct understanding" is possible. Whereas Ibn Ḥazm does not—to the best of my knowledge—make an explicit statement with regard to having more than one word referring to one thing (i.e., synonymity), this does not seem to have been a problem that he worried much about. As for assigning one word to many things, he refers to this question in his discussion of *majāz*—the metaphoric use of language—which he defines as assigning to a word a meaning that is different from the meaning that was first assigned to it. In religion, only another text or consensus can establish that a word is used figuratively in a certain text. If this is done by God, however, the metaphorical meaning ceases to be metaphorical and becomes a true meaning of the word, for it is God who assigns meanings to words in the first place, Ibn Ḥazm states.[11]

Another assumption that Scalia has relates to the purpose of the law and its relation to the social environment in which it is applied. Criticizing the "Living Constitution" philosophy—according to which the American Constitution must always be reinterpreted to remain in tune with changing circumstances—Scalia argues that the Constitution's "whole purpose is to prevent change."[12] Scalia is *not* against legal change on principle, but he does believe that this should be done in a particular way as explained below. As long as a certain law stands, it should be followed as it is without attempting to render it compatible

---

9 Ibn Ḥazm, *Iḥkām*, vol. 1, p. 260.

10 *Ibid.*, vol. 2, p. 693.

11 *Ibid.*, vol. 1, p. 44. Apparently, Ibn Ḥazm did not notice that this view would lead to a conclusion that he would have wanted to avoid, for if God uses a certain word to refer to something other than the meaning that people know, how do we know the meaning that God intends when he uses the same word elsewhere? In this case, it could be argued, a willful jurist would be able to pick up the meaning that serves his preference to a certain legal ruling, something that is in sharp contradiction with Ibn Ḥazm's perception of the law as explained below. Furthermore, it stands to reason that God was the one who assigned words to things in the first language, which Ibn Ḥazm does not believe was the Arabic language. It is not clear, however, why Ibn Ḥazm says here that God's use of an Arabic word to refer to a thing other than its original referent would not be a case of figurative use of language as he defines it.

12 Scalia, *Matter of Interpretation*, p. 40.

with a particular social reality or the subjective views of the legal interpreter. For his part, Ibn Ḥazm maintained that God's law that was revealed to the Prophet Muḥammad was the grounds on which life should be organized. His main criticism of other *madhhab*s was their—in his view—allowing their whimsical and arbitrary understandings of the purpose and spirit of the law to change God's law according to the circumstances. For him, God's message to the Prophet Muḥammad was God's last communication to mankind, and its legal aspect was intended to remain valid and operative until the end of time.[13]

A third assumption that Scalia holds concerns the distinctive roles of legislators or lawmakers, on the one hand, and that of legal interpreters—be they jurists or judges, on the other. In his view, the legislative power is the "power to make laws, not the power to make legislators." "Congress can no[t] … authorize one committee to 'fill in the details' of a particular law in a binding fashion."[14] On the other hand, "judges have no authority to pursue th[e] broader purposes [of the law] or write … new laws."[15] Similarly, this uncompromising distinction between the lawgiver and the legal interpreter is at the core of Ibn Ḥazm's jurisprudence. He insists that there is only one lawmaker in Islam—God, and that this lawmaker has not authorized anyone to assume the function of legislation (including the Prophet Muḥammad, whose Sunnah is mandated by God himself). Thus, the role of the jurist is not to legislate by declaring things permissible or forbidden, but only to determine and report God's rule in cases presented to him.[16] To do this, both Scalia and Ibn Ḥazm believe that the right methodology must be used. The discussion on their methodology below, therefore, deals with the way jurists and judges interpret the law, and not with the actual making of the law. In other words, it deals with how textualists and Ẓāhirīs deal with language as interpreters.

∴

The rejection of the notion of legislative intent is generally seen as the main characteristic of textualism, for which reason it is always contrasted with "intentionalism." In fact, textualism is regarded as emanating from "originalism," which refers to the search for original *meaning* rather than original

13 Fort this, see Ibn Ḥazm, *al-Nubdhah al-Kāfiyah fī Uṣūl Aḥkām al-Dīn*, p. 17.

14 Scalia, *Matter of Interpretation*, p. 35.

15 *Ibid.*, p. 23.

16 Ibn Ḥazm, *Iḥkām*, vol. 2, p. 659.

intent.[17] This position is both a principle that textualism maintains, as well as (or perhaps as a result of) a pragmatic, epistemological assumption about what they believe legal interpreters can and cannot do (here, what they can and cannot *determine*). "Textualists," Caleb Nelson points out, "emphasize that the legislative process is set up to achieve agreement over words, not motives or purposes."[18] Unlike intentionalism, textualism "treat[s] the legislative process as a black box that spits out the law to be interpreted but whose internal workings in any particular case are not part of the context that should be ascribed to an 'appropriately informed reader'."[19] (What is meant by "appropriately informed reader" will be discussed shortly.) What textualists seek to find out when interpreting a certain law, therefore, is that which lawmakers intended to say rather than what they intended to achieve or bring about by making a given law. It is not surprising, then, to learn that in this view, "[u]nfairness is irrelevant when the rule applies as a matter of plain textual meaning," as William Eskridge comments on one of Scalia's legal arguments.[20] Scalia argued that "judges should allow *even stupid laws* to stand … I do not think … [that] the avoidance of unhappy consequences is adequate basis for interpreting a text."[21] Another scholar explains that "[a]lthough textualists find it appropriate in cases of ambiguity to consult a statute's apparent purpose or policy …, they resist altering a statute's clear semantic import in order to make the text more congruent with its apparent background purpose."[22] It is also argued that textualism "rests upon the notion that enforcing the clear semantic meaning of a statute represents the best, if not the only, way to preserve the *unknowable* legislative bargains that produced the final text."[23] Scalia, it is believed, does not lend credence to the notion of legislative intent because it is not, most of the time, ascertainable.[24] Scalia himself argues that determining the original intent is almost impossible for a number of reasons (most of which relate to issues of American legal history, which is beyond the scope of this study).[25] Textualism, therefore, "might be understood as a judgment

17 Ring, *Scalia Dissents: Writings of the Supreme Court's Wittiest, Most Outspoken Justice*, pp. 8 and 25.
18 Nelson, "What is Textualism," p. 370.
19 *Ibid.*, p. 358.
20 Eskridge, "Textualism, the Unknown Ideal?," p. 1510.
21 Quoted in Ring, *Scalia Dissents*, p. 25 (emphasis mine).
22 John F. Manning, "Textualism and Legislative Intent," pp. 339–340.
23 *Ibid.*, p. 447 (emphasis mine).
24 Ring, *Scalia Dissents*, p. 25.
25 Scalia, "Originalism: The Lesser Evil," p. 856.

about the most reliable (or perhaps the least unreliable) way of discerning legislative instructions."[26]

Textualism, however, does not entirely disregard legislative intent, for the intent that matters in their view is "the *rule* that legislators meant to adopt rather than the real-world *consequences* that legislators expected the rule to have."[27] Textualism seeks after what is called the "objectified intent," which is "a concept predicated on the notion that a judge should read a statutory text just as any reasonable person conversant with applicable social conventions would read it."[28] The intention of the lawmakers, in other words, is to "enact a law that will be decoded according to prevailing interpretative conventions."[29] In Scalia's own words, "[w]e [should] look for a sort of 'objectified' intent—the intent that a reasonable person would gather from the text of the law, placed alongside the remainder of the *corpus juris*… [for] it is incompatible with democratic government, or indeed, even with fair government, to have the meaning of a law determined by what the lawgiver meant, rather than by what the lawgiver promulgated."[30] Thinking of what lawmakers meant would lead one to think in terms of his understanding of how an *intelligent* person "*should* have meant" and thus what the law "*ought* to mean."[31]

Ibn Ḥazm's concern about the usurpation of God's absolute prerogative as the sole lawmaker cannot be articulated better than Scalia's argument here (with Congress replacing God, of course).[32] In both views, legal interpreters should not be allowed to assume the role of lawmaking. Textualists, therefore, address various issues that could potentially give room to legal interpreters to assume this role. Scalia is critical of "certain presumptions and rules of construction that load the dice for or against a particular result."[33] Criticizing their vagueness and uncertainty, he argues that these rules are not textual, and can facilitate the job of a willful judge and increase judicial unpredictability.[34]

---

26 Manning, "Textualism," p. 433.

27 Nelson, "What is Textualism," p. 356 (emphasis mine).

28 Manning, "Textualism," p. 433.

29 *Ibid.*, pp. 432–433.

30 Scalia, *Matter of Interpretation*, p. 17.

31 *Ibid.*, p. 18 (emphasis in original).

32 In Ibn Ḥazm's view, disagreement among people is natural given their different personal characteristics, ideas, and preferences. Since they usually do not agree on a view, following them is impossible. Therefore, only God and his Messenger should be followed, and the Muslim community has agreed on this principle despite their disagreement on how to carry it out (for this, see Ibn Ḥazm, *Iḥkām*, vol. 1, pp. 502–503).

33 Scalia, *Matter of Interpretation*, p. 27.

34 *Ibid.*, pp. 27–28.

Accordingly, textualists reject the notion of "imaginative reconstruction," a process by which legal interpreters imagine how lawmakers would have decided on a given case. Rather than doing this, textualists focus on "the implications of what the enacting legislature actually *did* decide."[35] In contrast, intentionalism focuses more on the *spirit* rather than the *letter* of the law, seeking to figure out the intentions—meaning the goals—of lawmakers by resorting to imaginative reconstruction as well as to other tools. For example, "[w]hen a sufficiently dramatic mismatch between means and ends occurs (or, more accurately, appears to occur), classical intentionalists ascribe that divergence to legislative inadvertence."[36] In other words, an intentionalist legal interpreter can go so far as to assume that the law as it stands cannot be the law that the lawgivers had intended to promulgate. In Scalia's view, this type of judge intentionally manipulates the law to impose what a judge regards as an appropriate judgment in a particular case.[37]

Intentionalists, thus, can be regarded as meddling with the law at times to reflect more faithfully what they believe to be the real goals of the lawmaker. In so doing, they can assume that lawmakers may not be cognizant of the full implication of everything they say. Textualists, on the contrary, do not proceed on a similar assumption. They begin from the assumption that lawmakers are deliberate in choosing the language of the law, which language, they hold, reflects the outcome of a lengthy process which the law had to go through in order to be agreed upon by the majority of lawmakers.[38] Therefore, they focus on what an "informed reader"—by which they mean a learned but unspecialized person—would understand when reading a legal text. Focusing on what is thought to be the intent of the legislator rather than what the law could reasonably be understood to be saying, they argue, puts people outside the legislature in a situation where they have to abide by laws of which they cannot be fully aware since they may be interpreted by judges in a way that they could not understand or predict.[39]

It was noted in a previous chapter that Ẓāhirism is notorious for rejecting the notion of *ʿillah*, which is primarily used to determine the immediate objective of the lawgiver so that analogy can be drawn between new and existing

35 Nelson, "What is Textualism," p. 411 (emphasis mine).

36 Manning, "Textualism," pp. 429 and 440.

37 Paul J. Weithman, "The Precise Word," p. 181.

38 Manning, "Textualism," pp. 424ff.

39 Nelson, "What is Textualism," p. 352.

cases.[40] Ibn Ḥazm distinguishes very carefully and categorically between the lawgiver's (i.e., God's) intent—which is basically that we obey his law, and his objective in creating a certain law. Just as Scalia argues that "the text is the law, and it is the text that must be observed,"[41] he argues that *ẓāhir* is what we recite, and we are not required to go beyond that.[42] We are required to follow only what we understand, and do not need to consider the rationale or anything else beyond what we understand from a given legal text.[43] At the outset of his *Iḥkām*, he points out that what believers would be better off doing in this life is to seek to determine that which God has ordered us to do and abide by it.[44] This *is*, so to speak, the meaning of submission to God. Ẓāhirīs, then, do not concern themselves with original intent. However, they look for the "original meaning." The way Ibn Ḥazm deals with legal texts evinces his conviction that God uses language in the clearest and most efficient way, for which reason the first language that He created must have been the most perfect, as it was the clearest, the most straightforward and the least ambiguous, as noted earlier.[45] This, for Ibn Ḥazm, is the use of language that befits God. As noted in CHAPTER ONE, it is for this reason that some Ẓāhirīs rejected the idea that the Qur'ān contained metaphoric expressions, for this was regarded as a degraded form of language that created ambiguity and uncertainty. On this ground, the possibility that the language of the law was insufficient or not clear enough was categorically ruled out in principle.[46]

God, then, speaks in the clearest way in the Ẓāhirī understanding, and this clarity is intentional. Muslim scholars have disagreed on whether the *bayān* (clarification) of a certain ruling can follow its being made incumbent upon people. In other words, can God impose a duty on people by means of an ambiguous statement and only clarify what he exactly means in a later statement? In Ibn Ḥazm view, the actual obligation of a command cannot in

40 As explained earlier, if intoxication is the *'illah* of prohibiting wine, any intoxicating beverage would be similarly prohibited on the basis of this *'illah*. Why intoxication should be avoided in the first place, however, is a question that Muslim jurists referred to as the *ḥikmah*, or the wisdom of the law.

41 Scalia, *A Matter of Interpretation*, p. 22.

42 Ibn Ḥazm, *Iḥkām*, vol. 1, p. 293.

43 *Ibid.*, vol. 2, p. 1137.

44 *Ibid.*, vol. 1, p. 8.

45 *Ibid.*, vol. 1, p. 30.

46 This is not to say that Ibn Ḥazm thought that everyone can understand legal texts. He argues that "*bayān*" has several degrees, some of which can only be comprehended by a few scholars who have mastered the language well enough to understand them (*ibid.*, vol. 1, p. 79).

principle precede its *bayān* because this would be tantamount to burdening us, the subjects of the law, with what we cannot tolerate (*taḥmīlunā mā lā yuṭāqu*). God would not do this, not because he cannot do it, and not because it does not befit him, but according to his own words in the Qur'ān.[47] Similar to textualists' belief that people should not be held accountable for a law that they do not fully understand, Ẓāhirīs argue that God's promise that he would not inflict on people a burden that is beyond their capacity to carry out certainly indicates that he would not speak to them in an unclear or ambiguous way.[48] In other words, God would not mislead people when they are sincere in attempting to submit to His will.

It is worth noting here that while originalists in general assume that lawmakers are aware of the full import of the language that they use,[49] textualists, according to Nelson, do not categorically rule out the possibility of what is called "scrivener error," which roughly refers to any error in drafting a law. However, "[b]efore they will reinterpret a statutory text on the ground that it reflects a drafting error, textualist judges insist on a very high degree of certainty that Congress as an institution did indeed make a mistake."[50] For instance, if an error is "obvious," textualists are willing to act on the basis of what they thought lawmakers really intended to say.[51] This notion of scrivener error is only comparable to Ḥadīth transmission in the context of Islamic law, when a transmitter inadvertently changes one or more words in a Prophetic tradition.[52] It may be for the purpose of avoiding this kind of error (which would undermine the certainty of the law) that Ibn Ḥazm insisted that a transmitter has to transmit traditions verbatim without making any changes in their wording or structure,[53] whereas others were generally tolerant of changes pro-

---

47 Ibn Ḥazm, *Iḥkām*, vol. 1, p. 75. For an example of Ibn Ḥazm's rejection of the view that God may impose on people a duty without explaining it, see *ibid.*, vol. 9, p. 56.

48 Ibn Ḥazm's argument here is not purely theological. It relies on textual evidence to proceed through reason to specific conclusions. The belief of American textualists that lawmakers choose their language carefully and their ruling out the possibility of scrivener's errors, however, seem to be assumptions based on their understanding of how laws are made.

49 Nelson, "Originalism," p. 557.

50 Nelson, "What is Textualism," p. 380.

51 *Ibid.*, p. 356.

52 This possibility was, of course, not entertained by most Muslim scholars with respect to the Qur'ān.

53 Ibn Ḥazm, *Iḥkām*, vol. 1, pp. 205–206. Many Ḥadīth scholars held that a transmitter can change the wording of a tradition if he knows that the words that he uses mean exactly

vided that the traditionist who makes them know that they do not change the meaning.

∴

According to some contemporary legal scholars, what really distinguishes textualists is not what they think about the content and intent of the rules that Congress promulgate, but rather how they set about determining these rules.[54] As noted, identifying the underlying purposes of the lawmaker is not an objective for either textualists or Ẓāhirīs. Identifying the *meaning* of the text of the law, however, is what they seek to accomplish. Therefore, the first thing that a judge or a jurist (the legal interpreters) needs to do when working on a certain case is to find a relevant textual basis upon which he can proceed. Scalia argues that "judges should focus on the text. If someone claims he or she is being denied the exercise of a right or if the government asserts it has authority to take a given action, courts must make certain there is specific textual support for each assertion."[55] Accordingly, if a judge is confronted by a case that the law does not directly address, what should be done is that "instead of simply assuming the authority to engage in … [a] reconstructive project, courts should find the statute inapplicable unless it 'plainly hands [them] the power to create and revise a form of common law' with respect to the issue."[56] That is, if the judge is *not* given the authority to decide on certain cases, he should abstain from making judgments that do not follow from specific legal texts. Likewise, Ibn Ḥazm argues that the authoritative legal texts (the Qur'ān and Ḥadīth) are our only bases for knowing God's ordinances.[57] Texts for Ibn Ḥazm are not more important than other sources of Islamic law; they are its *only* sources. In fact, a view that distinguished Ẓāhirīs and that demonstrates their insistence on the absolute supremacy of texts was their dismissal of the Prophetic "practical Sunnah" (*al-sunnah al-ʿamaliyyah*) as a valid source of law.[58] Ibn Ḥazm argues that only verbal Ḥadīth is a valid source of law. The

---

the same thing as the words they replace (for this, see al-Khaṭīb al-Baghdādī, *al-Kifāyah*, pp. 232ff.).

54 Nelson, "What is Textualism," p. 357.

55 Ring, *Scalia Dissents*, p. 1.

56 Nelson, "What is Textualism," p. 407.

57 Ibn Ḥazm, *Iḥkām*, vol. 1, p. 64.

58 By practical *sunnah* I mean the deeds of the Prophet Muḥammad, in contrast to his sayings, or Ḥadīth in its strict sense.

Prophet's practice, irrespective of how habitual it was, is only recommended for us to follow but is not legally/religiously binding.[59]

Having identified a relevant text or texts, textualists begin the crucial process of interpretation. The most distinguishing feature of textualism here is their "rule-like" approach, which is contrasted with the "standard-like" approach of intentionalists. The difference between these two approaches is that whereas a "rule" is a directive that "requires for its application nothing more than a determination of the happening or non-happening of physical or mental events," a standard-like directive is one that "can be applied only by making, in addition to a finding of what happened or is happening in the particular situation, a qualitative appraisal of those happenings in terms of their probable consequences, moral justification, or other aspect of general human experience."[60] In general, rules provide jurists with well-defined and fixed regulations on how they should go about interpreting the law. For example,

> a rule might tell implementing officials to ignore some factors that they otherwise would have thought relevant to the goal behind the rule and to focus exclusively on a narrower set of issues identified by the rule. Or it might permit implementing officials to consider all the circumstances they like, but still make some binding generalizations about how those circumstances usually play out or about the proper weight of various factors.[61]

The rule-like attitude, in other words, seeks to regulate the legal process by carefully informing the legal interpreter of what he can and cannot do. In contrast, the standard-like approach of intentionalism gives legal interpreters more flexibility in deciding each case by allowing a degree of value-judgment. Accordingly, insisting that the development and use of hermeneutical tools is central to textualism,[62] Nelson points out that "[a] formalist theory has got to have *rules about rules*."[63] The rule-like attitude of textualism, a formalist theory according to Scalia (see below), is even more evident in cases where textualists use some of the techniques of other legal trends without giving up their

59 Ibn Ḥazm, *Iḥkām*, vol. 1, pp. 138–139.
60 Quoted in Nelson, "What is Textualism," p. 374.
61 *Ibid.*, p. 375.
62 For some hermeneutical tools of American Originalism, see Nelson, "Originalism," pp. 561ff.
63 Eskridge, "Textualism," p. 1542.

convention that rules and only rules must rule.[64] For example, "textualists try to keep their attempts at imaginative reconstruction within the rule-based framework that they understand the enacting legislatures to have chosen, and they are more likely than intentionalists to presume that this framework applies notwithstanding changed circumstances."[65] In commenting upon how textualist interpreters deal with legal texts, Scalia argues that:

> textualists are willing to deviate in certain ways from the baseline that conventional meaning provides. Still, textualists prefer such deviations to be guided by relatively rule-like principles. While textualists are willing to invoke some regularized canons that bear on the intended meaning of statutory language even though they are not part of normal communication, textualists are more reluctant than other interpreters to make ad hoc judgments that the enacting legislature must have intended something other than what conventional understandings of its words would suggest.[66]

This insistence on the necessity of both having/developing rules as well as abiding by them is, in fact, consistent with textualists' understanding of the all-importance of consistency, determinacy, and predictability in the law—notions that they regard as both crucial and indispensable for any just legal system.[67] Realizing these, however, requires that the process of legal interpretation be governed by specific, pre-defined rules. Therefore, Scalia believes that "general rules are beneficial because they provide notice and certainty to the public that is expected to obey the law. They also ensure that Americans will receive equal and consistent treatment and not be subjected to the predilections of the current justices on the Court or to shifting popular opinion."[68] On the other hand, "by using unclear standards," he points out, "consistency suffers." Rules are thus required and applied "to all situations."[69]

---

64 According to Frederick Schauer ("Formalism," p. 510), "at the heart of the word 'formalism,' in many of its various uses, lies the concept of decisionmaking according to *rule*. Formalism is the way in which rules achieve their 'ruleness' precisely by doing what is supposed to be the failing of formalism: screening off from a decisionmaker factors that a sensitive decisionmaker would otherwise take into account" (italics in original).

65 Nelson, "What is Textualism," p. 413.

66 Quoted in *ibid.*, p. 376.

67 Eskridge, "Textualism," p. 1512.

68 Ring, *Scalia Dissents*, p. 2.

69 Paul Weizer, *The Opinions of Antonin Scalia: The Caustic Conservative*, p. 16.

Textualism, accordingly, makes use of numerous interpretative rules. One of its basic rules is that "it [is] imperative, given the complexities of the legislative process, to respect the level of *generality* at which Congress speaks; for them, legislative compromise is reflected in the detail of the text produced. So they subscribe to the general principle that texts should be taken at face value—*with no implied extensions of specific texts or exceptions to general ones*—even if the legislation will then have an awkward relationship to the apparent background intention or purpose that produced it."[70] When the Constitution speaks of "any person," Scalia takes this to mean *any person* regardless of anything, whereas the same article could be read by other, non-textualist interpreters in view of the circumstances of its promulgation in a certain context with the aim to ensure specific rights for specific groups of citizens (mostly minorities).[71] Furthermore, if a law could be read in two different ways, one of which would make another law, or part of the same law, superfluous, a textualist would prefer the other reading which allows the two laws to stand together and complement each other.[72] In other words, a textualist would assume that the lawmaker intended to say something new or different in the new law even if this was not clear enough. Remarkably, in a chapter on the contradictions among legal texts (*taʿāruḍ al-nuṣūṣ*), Ibn Ḥazm argues against scholars who held that in cases like these (when authentic pieces of textual evidence seem to contradict each other), all texts fall and we proceed as if no text was available as evidence in the case at hand. If two *authentic* texts contradict each other (a possibility that Ibn Ḥazm does not acknowledge but only mentions to make a certain point),[73] both of them are to be used, for there is no good reason to follow one of them rather than the other.[74] This view does not seem to have been influential in Ibn Ḥazm's jurisprudence, not only because he did not abstain from dismissing a large number of textual pieces of evidence on account of their (lack of) authenticity,[75] but also because he was always willing to question and dismiss the *relevance* of particular textual evidence to a particular case on the basis that we do not know enough about its circumstances.

70 Manning, "Textualism," pp. 424–425 (italics mine).

71 Ring, *Scalia Dissents*, pp. 12–13.

72 Nelson, "What is Textualism," p. 355.

73 On the different methods according to which two seemingly contradictory pieces of textual evidence can be reconciled, see Ibn Ḥazm, *Iḥkām*, vol. 1, pp. 152ff.

74 *Ibid.*, vol. 1, p. 151.

75 In his discussion of prohibited beverages, for instance, Ibn Ḥazm dismisses more than twenty traditions related to this issue alone (for this, see Ibn Ḥazm, *al-Muḥallā*, vol. 6, pp. 177–186).

What is noteworthy about the rule-like and standard-like approaches is the implied inverse relationship between rules and the degree of subjectivity involved in the process of legal interpretation. Textualists and Ẓāhirīs sought to minimize subjectivity in legal interpretation by introducing hermeneutical rules. Ibn Ḥazm judges earlier scholars by the extent to which they use rules in their jurisprudence. He admires al-Shāfiʿī because he was, in his view, an *imām* in language and religion who introduced many rules, the sound among which outnumber the faulty.[76] As we have noted earlier, the insistence of Ẓāhirīs on the use of interpretive rules makes their methodology closer to the *Ahl al-Raʾy*'s and far from that of the *Ahl al-Ḥadīth*, who, in fact, seems to have loathed having to abide by rules that would limit their ability to serve their moral agenda, as reports about Ibn Ḥanbal's hesitation and indecisiveness strongly suggest.

Another major issue concerning the way textualists seek to identify what they call the "objectified intent" of the law is their attitude towards the context of any given legal text. According to Nelson, "when a statement has multiple and equally valid interpretations, textualists use internal and external evidence to ascertain the meaning intended by the lawmakers."[77] These kinds of internal and external evidence that textualists consider in order to identify the meaning intended by the lawmaker include historical as well as linguistic and social contexts.[78] When dealing with the historical context, a distinction must be made between two points: the historical context of a certain legal text, and what is called "legislative history." The historical context refers to the place and time in which a legal document or rule was produced. Legislative history, on the other hand, refers to all the interpretations of that legal doctrine since it was produced. In the American legal system, for example, the late 18th-century (would-be) United States is the historical context of the US Constitution. Subsequent interpretations of and writing on the Constitution are known as its legislative history. This similarly applies to statutory laws. In the Islamic context, the late 6th- and early 7th-century Arabia represents the historical context of the Qurʾān, for instance. All subsequent scholarship on its legal aspects, however, belongs to the legislative history of its law.

It has been argued that "[d]octrinally, the new textualism's most distinctive feature is its insistence that judges should almost never consult, and never rely on, the legislative history of a statute."[79] Several reasons are provided for this position. The first is that Congress itself (i.e., the lawmaker) does not authorize

76 Ibn Ḥazm, *Iḥkām*, vol. 1, p. 233, and vol. 2, p. 893.

77 Nelson, "What is Textualism," p. 409.

78 *Ibid.*, p. 348.

79 Eskridge, "Textualism," 1512.

this kind of quest for intended meaning in the legislative history. What it authorizes, however, is only the use of the laws that are approved and which are submitted to the President.[80] Secondly, textualists assume that the lawmakers choose their language carefully because they are aware that their laws would be used by the courts.[81] Furthermore, textualists are generally skeptical of the judge's ability to distinguish between reliable and unreliable or misleading materials in the legislative history.[82] Finally, they assume that the final legal product was one emerging from many compromises, and thus relying on how the law is formulated is the best way to "identify the compromises that members of the enacting legislature collectively intended to strike."[83]

Nevertheless, textualists do use history. What is important is that they do not use it to determine the intent of the law, which is not a goal for textualist legal interpreters in the first place. They, however, use history "only as a guide to meaning."[84] In Scalia's view, it is not contrary to sound interpretation to "give the totality of context precedence over a single word."[85] He argues that "when confronting a statute, all mainstream interpreters start with the linguistic conventions (as to syntax, vocabulary, and other aspects of usage) that were prevalent at the time of enactment. Those conventions help determine the 'ring' that the statutory language would have had to 'a skilled user of words ... thinking about the ... problem [that the legislature was addressing]'."[86] For his part, Ibn Ḥazm is not less than textualists in considering the historical context for identifying the intended meaning, a point that will be discussed in more detail below. This attitude towards historical context is remarkably reminiscent of both al-Shāfiʿī's and al-Ṭabarī's attitudes towards the same question, and differs from the attitude of the Mālikī *madhhab*, for instance, for which history is a source of knowledge for the *practice* rather than the *meaning* of the law.

The issue of the historical or physical context is at the heart of the difference between literalism and textualism, for whereas the former focuses only on the "semantics" (words and grammatical structures and the meaning that they convey) of sentences, the latter approaches the texts in light of the textual and historical contexts. Having said this, it must be noted that some scholars have expressed some uncertainty about the real attitude of textualists towards the

80 Nelson, "What is Textualism," p. 365.
81 *Ibid.*, p. 391.
82 *Ibid.*, p. 377.
83 *Ibid.*, p. 371.
84 Weizer, *Opinions of Antonin Scalia*, p. 9.
85 Scalia, *Matter of Interpretation*, pp. 20–21.
86 Nelson, "What is Textualism," p. 376.

historical context. For example, it has been argued that Scalia's interests are only linguistic rather than historicist, for he "often devotes little or no effort to figuring out how contemporaries actually would have understood the terms used in statutes."[87] In other words, he only cares about how a legal statement would be understood by a reasonable speaker of the English language.[88] Others have argued that Scalia and his ilk seek to determine the meaning of words as they were understood when a legal document was produced. Manning, for example, argues that textualists "are not literalists; they do not look exclusively for the 'ordinary meaning' of words and phrases. Rather, they emphasize the relevant linguistic community's . . . shared understanding and practices."[89] We have seen a similar statement made by Scalia himself. Eskridge's understanding of Scalia's attitude towards the historical context, therefore, is inconsistent with how others view his legal theory.

It is noteworthy that a similar uncertainty about the role of the historical context can be detected in Ibn Ḥazm's Ẓāhirism. A staggering fact about Ibn Ḥazm's legal writings is his rare references to Arabic poetry and disagreements among scholars of the Arabic language.[90] Ibn Ḥazm regularly mentions linguistic rules without providing historical evidence for their authenticity and soundness. For example, at the very beginning of his *Iḥkām*, he mentions the function, role, and indication of many conjunctive particles (like *wāw, fa-, thumma*, etc.) without providing any examples from Arabic poetry to prove his views on their indication.[91] Ibn Ḥazm probably assumed that these rules were known to everyone, for which reason he may have felt that he did not need to prove them.[92] In fact, he does make numerous references to linguistic usages of the Arabs, even though he does not always produce evidence for that. For example, he asserts that when the Arabs spoke about a group of men and women, they used masculine pronouns. No evidence is given here except the argument that since the Prophet was sent to men and women alike, and the

87 Eskridge, "Textualism," p. 1520.

88 *Ibid.*, p. 1516.

89 Manning, "Textualism," p. 434.

90 I am aware of only one citation of Arabic poetry in *al-Iḥkām* to demonstrate a linguistic point (Ibn Ḥazm, *Iḥkām*, vol. 1, p. 392).

91 A modern Tunisian scholar, Aḥmad Bakīr Maḥmūd, mentions that Ẓāhirīs did not condone the use of Jāhilī Arabic, pre-Islamic poetry, or poetry of non-Muslims to make conclusions about the use of the Arabic language (Maḥmūd, *al-Madrasah al-Ẓāhiriyyah*, p. 27). Unfortunately, Maḥmūd does not mention his evidence for this contention.

92 Ibn Ḥazm, *Iḥkām*, vol. 1, pp. 46–47 and p. 319, where Ibn Ḥazm argues that even those with minimal knowledge of Arabic cannot be ignorant of his understanding of the function of "*aw*." No evidence is given here for this understanding.

Qur'ān uses the masculine pronouns more often than not, this *must* indicate that these pronouns referred to both men and women.[93] He also asserts, without demonstration, that there is no disagreement among the Arabs that the dual has a form that differs from the plural. Therefore, the plural only indicates three or more (in contrast to another view that he mentions, according to which it can also refer to two).[94] Ibn Ḥazm is probably talking here about what, in his view, *ought* to be, but he does not demonstrate that this rule was actually invariably followed by the Arabs.

History for Ibn Ḥazm was important not only as a means for determining the intended meaning by informing jurists of how the language was used when legal texts were produced, but also because the historical context provides a "circumstantial evidence" for the intended meaning. In one Prophetic tradition, a woman asks the Prophet about the permissibility of kissing while fasting, to which the Prophet replies by saying that he used to do that. She then said to the Prophet that since God had forgiven all his sins, he was not similar to other men in this regard, meaning that his behavior in this case could be one of his prerogatives as the Messenger of God. This answer actually upset the Prophet, a context on which Ibn Ḥazm relies to prove that the permissibility of kissing during fasting was not a prerogative of the Prophet, but was rather valid for all Muslims, even if the Prophet did not say this explicitly to the woman who asked him about it.[95] It is important to note that the fact that we do not find comparable use of the historical context in American textualism can simply be accounted for on the basis of the nature of the two legal systems. In the American legal system, laws must be promulgated in a "formal" way. Congress, for example, cannot outlaw a practice by the mere expression of displeasure with or disapproval of it.

Finally, textualists take into consideration the textual context of words. In textualism, the language of the statute as a whole is considered essential in the process of determining the meaning of terms.[96] Scalia argues that "... the Court should ensure the meaning makes sense within the context of the law or code of which it is part,"[97] which is part of the "totality of context" that he believes should be given precedence over individual words.[98] Because

93 Ibn Ḥazm, *Iḥkām*, vol. 1, p. 324.
94 *Ibid.*, vol. 1, p. 395.
95 *Ibid.*, vol. 1, p. 141.
96 Eskridge, "Textualism," p. 1512.
97 Ring, *Scalia Dissents*, p. 24.
98 See page 186.

of the centrality of this point, it will be discussed in more detail in a later context, after discussing two case studies that illustrate Scalia's juridical thought.

1.2 *Case Studies*

In American criminal law, the sentence of a person who "uses" a machine gun in drug trafficking is thirty years in jail. In what is known as the Smith case,[99] J. A. Smith and a friend of his took part in a drug trafficking operation, during which Smith sought to sell or barter his machine gun with a drug dealer. Through an undercover agent, the police was informed about the operation, whereupon Smith fled the hotel in which the operation took place and was arrested later after a car chase. The police found the machine gun with Smith when he was arrested. He was indicted and sentenced to 30 years for knowingly "using" the machine gun "during and in relation to a drug trafficking crime."[100] When the case reached the Supreme Court, the judge who was in charge of the case decided that what Smith did constituted "use" of his machine gun and the statute was thus relevant to the case. The judge referred to the meanings of "use" in some dictionaries to demonstrate that Smith did use his machine gun in the operation.[101]

Scalia dissented, arguing that the Court's logic that the dictionary definition of the word "use" is very broad is fallacious. In his view, "[i]t is a 'fundamental principle of statutory construction' (and indeed, of language itself) that the meaning of a word cannot be determined in isolation, but must be drawn from the context in which it is used."[102] "That is particularly true," he adds, "of a word as elastic as 'use,' whose meanings range all the way from 'to partake of' (as in 'he uses tobacco') to 'to be wont or accustomed' (as in 'he used to smoke tobacco')." Citing other cases of the Supreme Court, Scalia adds that "[i]n the search for statutory meaning, we give nontechnical words and phrases their ordinary meaning," on the basis of which we can conclude that "[t]o use an instrumentality ordinarily means to use it for its intended purpose."[103] On this ground, considering that what Smith did constituted use of the machine gun is similar to saying that he would have been indicted for scratching his head with

99 A PDF file for the syllabus and concurring and dissenting opinions in SMITH vs. UNITED STATES, 508 U.S. 223 (1993) is available on http://supreme.justia.com/cases/federal/us/508/223/ (last accessed 15/03/2014). References are made to the pagination in this file.

100 For a more detailed description of the events of this case, see Crapanzano, *Serving the Word*, pp. 262–263.

101 "SMITH vs. UNITED STATES," pp. 228–229.

102 *Ibid.*, p. 241.

103 *Ibid.*, pp. 241–242.

the machine gun during the crime. This is an extraordinary understanding of "use," which is a nontechnical word the meaning of which is "inordinately sensitive to the context,"[104] and the ordinary meaning of which in this kind of cases is the use of the machine gun "as a weapon," which Smith did not do. The statute relied on, therefore, intended to refer to the use of a machine gun as a weapon during drug trafficking, and not to using it as a medium for exchange or barter, and the Court has failed to distinguish between how a word *could* be used, and how it is ordinarily used. The petitioner, Scalia points out, was not "seeking to introduce an 'additional requirement' into the text..., but is simply construing the text according to its normal import."[105]

The judge of the Supreme Court—Sandra Day O'Connor—responded to Scalia's dissent by pointing out that even though Scalia's understanding of "use" is the ordinary meaning of the word, this does not warrant excluding other meanings of the word, according to some of which Smith *did* use his machine gun during the crime.[106] This was probably a response to Scalia's view that the addition of a direct object (firearms here) to the verb ("use," in this case) narrows the meaning of the verb.[107]

The dispute in the second case—Maryland vs. Craig (or the Craig case), is on the sense of another word, "confrontation," as used in the Sixth Amendment of the US Constitution.[108] A Maryland statute permits an abused child to testify through a one-way closed-circuit television if the court feels that the physical presence of the child in the court could cause him or her emotional suffering that would affect his ability to testify. In our case, a child testified via closed-circuit television against S. A. Craig, who was subsequently indicted by the court for child abuse. Craig, however, argued that the Constitution requires a face-to-face courtroom encounter between the two litigants, which was not done in her case. The case reached the Supreme Court, and it was ruled that

---

104 "SMITH vs. UNITED STATES," pp. 244–245.

105 *Ibid.*, pp. 242–244.

106 Crapanzano, *Serving the Word*, pp. 263–264.

107 "SMITH vs. UNITED STATES," p. 245. Scalia adds that "[t]he word 'use' in the 'crimes of violence' context has the unmistakable import of use as a weapon, and that import carries over... to the subsequently added phrase 'or drug trafficking crime.' Surely the word 'use' means the same thing as to both, and surely the 1986 addition of 'drug trafficking crime' would have been a peculiar way to *expand* its meaning (beyond 'use as a weapon') for crimes of violence" (*ibid.*, p. 246. Italics in original).

108 According to this, "In all criminal prosecutions, the accused shall enjoy the right... to be confronted with the witnesses against him..." (see Crapanzano, *Serving the Word*, p. 264). The case (497 U.S. 836, 1990) can be reviewed here: http://supreme.justia.com/cases/federal/us/497/836/case.html (last accessed 15/03/2014).

the Confrontation Clause of the Constitution does not disallow use of procedures that secure reliable evidence while preserving "the essence of effective communication."[109]

Scalia dismissed the validity of this argument as "antitextual,"[110] and insisted that "[t]he Sixth Amendment provides, with unmistakable clarity, that '[i]n all criminal prosecutions, the accused shall enjoy the right... to be confronted with the witnesses against him.'"[111] In his view, this Confrontation Clause "means, *always and everywhere*, at least what it explicitly says: the 'right to meet face to face all those who appear and give evidence at trial,'"[112] and this is what it means regardless of "whatever else it may mean in addition."[113] Scalia harshly criticized the Court's view that "a State's interest in the physical and psychological well-being of a child abuse victims may be sufficiently important to outweigh, at least in some cases, a defendant's right to face his or her accusers in court," regarding this as a "subordination of explicit constitutional text to currently favored public policy."[114] Adding that he did not think that things were significantly different when this constitutional amendment was adopted,[115] he stressed that "the Constitution is meant to protect us against, rather than conform to, current 'widespread belief,'"[116] the widespread belief here being not exposing children to particular kind of emotional suffering. Furthermore, Scalia criticized the court's agreement with some states' laws in this kind of cases for the purpose of "protect[ing] child witnesses from the trauma of giving testimony in child abuse cases,"[117] which could make him unable to "reasonably communicate."[118] He wonders why a prosecutor would want "to call a

---

109 For a more detailed description of the events of this case, see Crapanzano, *Serving the Word*, pp. 264–265.

110 Weizer, *The Opinions of Justice Antonin Scalia*, p. 212.

111 *Ibid.*, p. 211.

112 *Ibid.*, p. 212 (italics mine).

113 *Ibid.*, p. 214.

114 *Ibid.*, p. 211.

115 Scalia argues that "no extrinsic factors have changed since that provision was adopted in 1791." "Sexual abuse," he points out, "existed then, as it does now; little children were more easily upset than adults, then as now; a means of placing the defendant out of sight of the witness existed then as now" (quoted in Crapanzano, *Serving the Word*, p. 266).

116 Weizer, *The Opinions of Justice Antonin Scalia*, p. 212.

117 *Ibid.*, p. 211.

118 *Ibid.*, p. 216. Scalia adds here that if we do not apply the Confrontation Clause on the ground that the pressure on the allegedly abused child could cause the witness to testify, why not deprive the defendant of his right to counsel if this would save him? For Scalia, this logic only reflects what he believes to be the typical State's interest: to convict as many defendants as possible (*ibid.*, p. 216).

witness who cannot reasonably communicate [in the first place],"[119] arguing that that this Constitution clause intended to "induce *precisely* that pressure [which the Maryland statutes intended to spare the abused children] upon the witness which the little girl found it difficult to endure." It is difficult, he points out, "to accuse someone to his face, particularly when you are lying."[120] In addition to this, since children are generally unable to separate fantasy from reality, this is a stronger reason to insist on bringing them to the courtroom and confronting them with whom they accuse.[121] Finally, the Supreme Court *has no right* to decide that this requirement of direct confrontation is dispensable, for this reduces the Confrontation Clause to "only one of many 'elements of confrontation,'" and could also justify regarding trial before a jury indispensable. The "interest-balancing analysis" that Scalia believes motivated the Court's decision is simply not permitted by the Constitution.[122]

Scalia has many detractors, one of whom is Vincent Crapanzano, whose critique of Scalia can help us shed more light on his legal thought and reinforces some of our conclusions. Commenting on these two cases, Crapanzano speaks of "Scalia's epistemological naiveté," that is, "his unquestioned assumptions that words are spiritless . . ., that meaning can be divorced from intention, and that texts can have a context-independent meaning that is at least potentially immune from the interlocutory effects of reading and interpretation." Furthermore, these two cases reveal Scalia's inconsistency, for while he relies in the Smith case on the ordinary meaning of words, in Craig he opts for the

119 *Ibid.*, p. 216.

120 Quoted in Crapanzano, *Serving the Word*, p. 266 (italics in original). Scalia points out that the objective of the Confrontation Clause "is to place the witness under the sometimes hostile glare of the defendant," which could "confound or undo the false accuser," as one Court's decision that Scalia quotes says (Weizer, *The Opinions of Justice Antonin Scalia*, p. 216). Scalia's analysis of the court's decision is as follows: "The Confrontation Clause guarantees not only what it explicitly provides for—face-to-face confrontation—but also implied and collateral rights such as cross-examination, oath, and observation of demeanor (TRUE); the purpose of this entire cluster of rights is to ensure the reliability of evidence (TRUE); the Maryland procedure preserves the implied and collateral rights (TRUE), which adequately ensure the reliability of evidence (perhaps TRUE); therefore the Confrontation Clause is not violated by what it explicitly provides for—'face-to-face' confrontation (unquestionably FALSE)." In Scalia's view "[t]his reasoning abstracts from the right to its purposes, and then eliminate the right. It is wrong because the Confrontation Clause does not guarantee reliable evidence; it guarantees specific trial procedures that were thought to ensure reliable evidence, undeniably among which was 'face-to-face' confrontation" (*ibid.*, p. 212).

121 Weizer, *The Opinions of Justice Antonin Scalia*, p. 216.

122 *Ibid.*, p. 218.

"literal" meaning.[123] Arguably, this does not do justice to Scalia's argument that the word "use" is a general word that must be interpreted in light of the textual context, unlike the word "confrontation" which he seems to regard as a more technical word that has a specific meaning in law.

Noting Scalia's belief that he "can bypass the human, humane, and social dimension of the cases before him,"[124] Crapanzano argues that, contrary to his proclaimed faith in "literalist hermeneutics," he, like other judges, does not separate interpretation of the law from his personal values and interests.[125] His view about children's inability to separate fantasy from reality and how this makes necessary their physical presence in the court reveals his concern for the adults who may be wrongly accused, and lack of sympathy towards terrorized children in child abuse cases. In other words, in Crapanzano's view, Scalia, similar to the other judges, also made an "interest-balancing analysis." This, it must be noted, seems to be another unfair critique of Scalia, and one that does not take into account that his logic could be that when a case of alleged child abuse is being investigated, whether or not the child or children involved were actually abused is not certain. Therefore, he is not willing to jeopardize justice on the basis of uncertainty, especially considering that he actually referred to other cases in which adults were falsely accused on the basis of children's testimonies, as Crapanzano himself mentions.[126] Yet since there is a possibility that a child involved in a case like these was in fact abused, this indicates that Scalia is not willing to give up his belief that the proper procedures of the law should be followed regardless of the case and without exceptions, which he states quite explicitly.

For our purposes, these cases reveal much about Scalia's legal thought. In both cases, he appears to be completely certain that a correct meaning of the words used does exist and is identifiable. As the Smith case demonstrates, he considers the textual context central to sound interpretation, for it can restrict or narrow the sense of a word with a potentially broad meaning (like "use"). These cases also demonstrate Scalia's understanding of the role of the judge and what he can, or, rather, cannot do. A court cannot decide without textual evidence, nor can it decide on the basis of its understanding of the interests of the litigants because there is no textual evidence for this. This point is consistent with Scalia's formalism and also illustrates his understanding of the

123 The distinction that Crapanzano makes between the "ordinary" and "literal" meanings here is not clear to me.

124 Crapanzano, *Serving the Word*, p. 260.

125 *Ibid.*, p. 261.

126 *Ibid.*, p. 266.

overall purpose of the law, which is to ensure that our *changing* values do not influence the judicial process. This case also demonstrates that Scalia *does* believe that the "rationale" of the law (which, in the Craig case, is exposing the witness or plaintiff to the pressure of direct confrontation with the defendant) could be reasoned. However, whether he would make a judgment on its basis is a question that is beyond the scope of this study.[127]

As Crapanzano has rightly observed, in these two cases, Scalia "resists expanding meaning."[128] That is, in the Smith case, he argued against considering all the senses of "use" and insisted that only one of its meanings was relevant to this case, a view that Crapanzano believes was motivated by Scalia's "pleasure of textual play and argument." In the Craig case, Scalia rejected the expansion of the word "confrontation" to mean anything other than direct, face-to-face confrontation. Crapanzano seems to regard this attitude against expanding meaning as a feature of literalism, for he says that Scalia "takes... laws as *literally* as possible..., resisting any expansion of meaning, any metaphorization, and translation, and thereby freezes meaning—the meaning *he* claims, often on scant evidence, was the original (and therefore only valid) meaning."[129] To this observation, we can add another that is significant in demonstrating the resemblance of Scalia's textualism and Ibn Ḥazm's Ẓāhirism. In the Smith case, Scalia notes:

> Even if the reader does not consider the issue to be as clear as I do, he must at least acknowledge, I think, that it is eminently debatable—and that is enough, under the rule of lenity, to require finding for the petitioner here. At the very least, it may be said that the issue is subject to some doubt. Under these circumstances, we adhere to the familiar rule that, 'where there is ambiguity in a criminal statute, doubts are resolved in favor of the defendant.'[130]

This view obviously relies on the presumption of continuity. The innocence of any defendant must be presumed, and if there exists any doubt in the evidence

127 I am assuming here that a judge may seek to show how his understanding of the law is justifiable on the basis of what he considers the purpose or logic of the law. This, however, does not necessarily mean that this understanding plays a role in the actual process of interpreting the law. In other words, this could only be a process of post-facto ratiocination.

128 Crapanzano, *Serving the Word*, p. 262.

129 *Ibid.*, p. 264 (italics added).

130 "SMITH vs. UNITED STATES," p. 246.

provided to prove the opposite, his original, default innocence of which we are certain must continue to be presumed. We have discussed earlier the centrality of the principle of *istiṣḥāb al-ḥāl* in the Ẓāhirī jurisprudence and how it relates to the broader issue of certainty.

1.3 *Conclusion*

Before we make some concluding remarks about Scalia's textualism and Ibn Ḥazm's Ẓāhirism, some points regarding the validity of comparing these two legal/hermeneutical theories must be addressed. The first concerns authorship of the law. In Islam, the lawgiver (God) is one and is regarded by Muslims as divine. In the American legal system, the lawgiver is also one, but it is a secular institution (Congress) that is made up of hundreds of persons. So whereas in the latter system we can, if only in theory, debate whether "original meaning" meant the subjective view of the lawmakers or not and whether it is at all possible to determine it,[131] we cannot do the same in Islamic law, undermining thereby the validity of this comparison. Fortunately, Scalia's textualism has ruled out the possibility of identifying the intention of the lawmakers, simply because it cannot be assumed that there exists only one such intention in any given case to begin with.[132] This means that the two theories are similar in this respect even if for two different reasons. Whereas Ẓāhirī jurists proceed on the basis that we cannot "read God's mind" and can only know what he tells us, American textualists do not hold that Congress has a readable mind in the first place.

The second question concerns the nature of the law. Whereas the core of Islamic law is regarded by Muslim jurists as divine or God-made, Western law (including those documents that are considered sacred, such as the US Constitution for Americans) is at the end of the day man-made, and alienating "reason" from interpreting it is, by definition, self-contradictory. Unsurprisingly, even staunch American originalists would agree that there are some "sensible" principles that should be respected when interpreting a legal document. "Many canons of construction reflect the sensible principles that interpreters would not be too quick to read a law to do something strange; other things being equal, they should prefer readings that comport with prevailing attitudes or established practices," Nelson points out regarding textualists' view on this issue.[133] It is probably for this reason that some scholars have argued that "it appears that norms are not absent from Scalia's interpretation of statutes;

131 Crapanzano, *Serving the Word*, pp. 287–288.

132 Nelson, "Originalism," p. 553.

133 *Ibid.*, p. 520.

he is merely influenced by different norms."[134] In fact, Scalia himself speaks about a number of what he regards as "commonsensical rules" of interpretation that textualists employ; for example, *expression unius est exclusion alterius* (expression of the one is exclusion of the other),[135] and *noscitur a sociis* (it is known by its companions) which simply refers to the understanding of words in their textual context.[136]

Similar rules are used by Ibn Ḥazm, who begins his work on *uṣūl al-fiqh* by defending reason (*al-ʿaql*) as one of several means to the truth. According to him, God has provided us with ideas and concepts that do not even require reflection on our part (like the belief that the whole is larger than the part, that a person is not another person, or that a person cannot be standing up and sitting down at the same time). In these and similar things, he explains, no inference (*istidlāl*) is even required.[137] Commenting on Q. 49:6 ("O you who believe, if an evil-doer (*fāsiq*) comes to you with any news, verify it ..."), he argues that since the verse requires the verification of the testimony of an impious person in particular, we are not required to do so with pious people (according to the notion of *dalīl al-khiṭāb*, which is the same thing as *expression unius est exclusion alterius*).[138] Another example that is based on the same principle is Ibn Ḥazm's rejection of the tradition mentioned in an earlier context in which the Prophet is reported to have said: "Disagreement among my community is mercy." In refuting this tradition, he argues that if disagreement was mercy, agreement would be the opposite, which cannot be the view of a "true Muslim."[139]

---

134 Eskridge, "Textualism," p. 1553.

135 Scalia, *Matter of Interpretation*, p. 25.

136 *Ibid.*, pp. 25–26.

137 Ibn Ḥazm, *Iḥkām*, vol. 1, p. 17.

138 *Ibid.*, vol. 1, p. 100.

139 *Ibid.*, vol. 2, p. 642. Ironically, Ibn Ḥazm makes these points notwithstanding his unconditional rejection of *dalīl al-khiṭāb*, according to which, what is not stated in the textual sources has the opposite ruling of what is (for this, see, *ibid.*, vol. 2, pp. 887ff.). In this example, since it is stated that disagreement is mercy, then it follows that agreement is the opposite. In explaining his point concerning this tradition, Ibn Ḥazm argues that there is either agreement or disagreement, on the one hand, and mercy and anger, on the other hand. If disagreement is mercy, agreement must be a source of God's anger. On the issue of testimony, however, he seems to be suggesting that testimonies of all persons are acceptable except for those excluded by textual evidence, such as impious people according to the verse he quotes here. As such, he seems to be avoiding using *dalīl al-khiṭāb*. This logic of assuming a general rule and excluding exceptions that are based on textual evidence, to my mind, is difficult to apply to the example of legal disagreements among Muslims, and we probably have to take this as an inconsistency on the part of Ibn Ḥazm

Reason, as must be clear, is only a *means* to discover God's law in the Ẓāhirī *madhhab*, but it cannot itself be a *source* of law. Similar to American textualists who reject the use (or abuse) of reason by legal interpreters to reach legal conclusions that cannot be supported by legal texts, reason, in Ibn Ḥazm's view, has a specific function and role, and that is to understand God's ordinances without interference with their actual content.[140] And while Ibn Ḥazm held that reason and revelation *can* agree on the goodness (*ḥusn*) and evilness (*qubḥ*) of beliefs and practices, he insists that the former cannot play a role in making something licit or otherwise.[141]

A third issue concerns legal change. "To be a textualist in good standing," Scalia writes, "one need not be too dull to perceive the broader social purposes that a statute is designed, or could be designed, to serve; or too hidebound to realize that new times required new laws. One need only hold the belief that judges have no authority to pursue those broader purposes or write those new laws."[142] Criticizing elsewhere some other legal theories, he points out that amendments were added to the Constitution when earlier generations of Americans wanted to assert new rights. These Americans, however, did not try to read those rights into the Constitution.[143] Evidently, Scalia is not against the principle of legal and constitutional change *per se*, but he insists that it can only be done by lawmakers and not by legal interpreters. However, as far as Islamic law—or at least that part of it that is based on explicit textual ground in the Qur'ān which Muslim scholars have generally regarded as outside the

---

who is unequivocal about his belief that any proposition establishes a ruling only for that to which it refers and nothing about what is similar to or different from its referent (for which reason *qiyās*, which depends on similarity between two things, and *dalīl al-khiṭāb*, which depends on difference, are both invalid). It is also possible (but unlikely, given that he states it when he uses a certain view for the sake of argument) that he is using *dalīl al-khiṭāb* that his adversaries accept to demonstrate their inconsistency. Both Vishanoff (*The Formation*, pp. 95ff.) and Nūr al-Dīn al-Khādimī have observed that Ibn Ḥazm does make conclusions on the basis of textual evidence that does not explicitly state them. The most important examples in this respect are *mafūm al-mukhālafah* and *mafhūm al-muwāfaqah*. Unlike al-Khādimī, however, Vishanoff is obviously aware that what is dealt with here are essentially different forms of syllogism, where conclusions are contained in the premises. This applies to almost all kinds of "textual evidence" (*al-dalīl al-naṣṣī*) that he mentions (al-Khādimī, *al-Dalīl ʿInda al-Ẓāhiriyyah*, pp. 92ff.).

140 Ibn Ḥazm, *Iḥkām*, vol. 1, pp. 27–28.

141 *Ibid.*, vol. 1, p. 52.

142 Scalia, *Matter of Interpretation*, p. 23.

143 Ring, *Scalia Dissents*, p. 5. Legal activism has gained a derogatory connotation in legal studies because it suggests the manipulation of law by judges to produce rulings that do not solidly rely on the Constitution (*ibid.*, p. 15).

realm of *ijtihād*—is concerned, legal change as such is not an option, for the lawmaker in Islam—according to the dominant Muslim view—has stopped communicating new laws or amending existing ones. This is probably the major difference between Ẓāhirism and textualism, for whereas any sort of legal change, including significant change, can occur in the latter system if proper procedures are followed, a significant part of the former—that part that is based on "fixed" texts, such as the Qur'ān and a great deal of Ḥadīth—is beyond *any* addition, omission, or alteration of the kinds possible in American law.[144]

With the exception of this last point, comparing Ẓāhirism to textualism is thus essentially sound. We have already seen that they concur on their understanding of the nature of the law, as well as its objectives and methodology. To these, one more important point can be added. Both Ẓāhirīs and textualists justify their methodologies. Speaking of originalism, Scalia believes that any interpretative methodology must be based on textual or historical evidence.[145] Arguing for some of his views on interpretation, he states that "the Constitution tells us not to expect nit-picking details, and to give words and phrases an expansive rather than narrow interpretation—though not an interpretation that the language will not bear."[146] Scalia is here seeking to prove that the Constitution itself is the source of some of his hermeneutical assumptions. In other words, it is the same document on which disagreements occur that provide the right methodology in Scalia's view.

Ibn Ḥazm similarly felt the need to defend the legitimacy of his methodology, but he does this on a number of grounds,[147] the first of which is to argue for its

144 I am talking here about the texts themselves, not the interpretation thereof, which, of course, can and does change. Admittedly, there have been attempts to do away with either part of or the entire Ḥadīth corpus. The prospects of success of these attempts, however, do not seem to be high.

145 Scalia, "Originalism," p. 862.

146 Scalia, *Matter of Interpretation*, p. 37.

147 Ibn Ḥazm, *Iḥkām*, vol. 1, p. 20. He points that good scholars should be confident, indeed certain, of their tools before they are certain of their conclusions. It was imperative for Ẓāhirīs, had they wanted to be true to their methodology, to legitimize it, and that, arguably, could be done in two ways. The first was to refer to an authoritative text. This, however, would lead to a circular argument, for Ẓāhirīs would interpret that text by the same methodology the soundness of which they seek to prove. The other method was to refer to extra-textual factors (such as reason, for instance), or to a general theory of the nature of divine command and the human capacity to comprehend it. This, however, would be self-defeating for Ẓāhirīs who dismissed the methodologies of other schools precisely on

authenticity. It was the methodology inherited from the Prophet Muḥammad and followed by his Companions and their followers, and it was the methodology that all early Muslim scholars followed. In this juncture, he distinguishes between those whom he describes as the notable scholars of early generations, on the one hand, and their blind followers, on the other,[148] excluding thereby the former from his criticism of the latter.[149] Furthermore, he relies on textual and non-textual evidence to argue for the validity of particular aspects of his methodology. For example, to demonstrate that commands should be taken to indicate absolute obligation if no indication suggests otherwise, he refers to Q. 5:67 ("O Messenger! Make known that which has been revealed unto you from your Lord, for if you do it not, then you have not delivered His message"). Since the Prophet would be disobeying God if he does not carry out the command, then he was required to take the command to mean absolute obligation.[150] Furthermore, it is reported that when the Prophet said "God had made pilgrimage an obligation unto you," one of the attendees asked him: "Do we need to do this every year?" The Prophet did not reply and the man had to repeat the question two more times, when the Prophet said: "If I were to say yes, it would be obligatory on you every year." This, in Ibn Ḥazm's views, demonstrates that we should presume that any command should be taken to indicate absolute obligation, for the Prophet was asked about the required frequency of performing pilgrimage, *not* the obligatoriness thereof.[151] As for non-textual evidence, Ibn Ḥazm uses his overall understanding of Islamic law to argue for the validity of specific legal or linguistic views. For example, he believes that when a pronoun occurs in a sentence, we must take it to be referring to the nearest referent; otherwise, there would be sheer confusion.[152] This, arguably, is a view that is based on a certain assumption about the lawgiver, which is that God does not want to confuse us. This confusion could well be avoided by taking the pronoun to be referring to the farthest possible referent. Ibn Ḥazm would probably not disagree with this in principle. What is important, however, is that we have to have fixed rules about such cases.

---

the basis of their reliance on this kind of factors. Using such factors to legitimize the very methodology that dismisses them as arbitrary and illegitimate would, of course, be contradictory and self-destructive.

148 Ibn Ḥazm, *Iḥkām*, vol. 1, p. 233, and vol. 2, p. 1114.

149 *Ibid.*, vol. 1, p. 233, and vol. 2, p. 1114.

150 Ibn Ḥazm, *Iḥkām*, vol. 1, p. 275.

151 *Ibid.*, vol. 1, p. 272. For other cases, see pp. 273–274.

152 *Ibid.*, vol. 1, p. 412.

To sum up, for both Ẓāhirism and textualism as legal and hermeneutical theories, the only intention of lawgivers that concerns legal interpreters is following the actual laws that they communicate through language. Both theories assume that the "correct" understanding of language is possible through mastery of its conventions and rules, and by examining textual and historical contexts. What is behind the communicated law is not for legal interpreters to worry about, for it is not something that they can verify in the first place. Both are formalistic theories of law that emphasize the soundness of their methodologies and the necessity of following the rules and the procedures that the law specifies. Scalia openly describes his legal philosophy as formalist, arguing that formalism "is what makes a government a government of laws and not of men."[153] Similarity, Ẓāhirism for Ibn Ḥazm is what makes Islamic law the law of God rather than the law of men.[154] And it is this understanding that constitutes in his view the sound meaning of submission to God's will.

2 Literalism

Just like Ẓāhirism, textualism has been, similarly uncritically, regarded as a "literalist" legal theory without a proper interrogation of the meaning and the very possibility of a "literal" reading of any text. This section, therefore, presents some views on different aspects of literalism as used in religion (Christianity in particular), law, and the all-important field of linguistics, with the aim of investigating the extent to which Ẓāhirism—and textualism, for that matter—can be viewed as literalist.

2.1 *Literalism in Religion and Law*

Speaking of literalism, the American anthropologist Vincent Crapanzano writes:

153 Scalia, *Matter of Interpretation*, p. 25.

154 It is remarkable to note that both Ibn Ḥazm (and some other Ẓāhirī scholars as noted earlier) and Justice Scalia share a common feature for which they were notorious, that is, their sharp and uncompromising criticism of other scholars and legal methodologies. Just as many scholars believe that Ibn Ḥazm's aggressiveness towards earlier and contemporary scholars was responsible to a large degree for the failure of Ẓāhirism, Scalia's "sharp pen and biting comments" (Ring, *Scalia Dissents*, p. 18) and his "brutal public attacks on some of his colleagues" (Weizer, *The Opinions of Justice Antonin Scalia*, p. 21) are blamed for alienating many of his colleagues from him and for leaving only few people on his side.

> [L]iteralism does not result from dull wit, though it is often taken to, even by those of us who are sometimes, despite ourselves, caught in it. It demands discipline… [meaning] a strict commitment to what is taken to be 'literal' or 'true' meaning. It is associated with a set of assumptions about the nature of language, language's relationship to reality, its figurative potential, its textualization, and its interpretation and application. It is the object of considerable philosophical reflection among Fundamentalist Christians, for example, and certainly among those legal scholars who interpret the Constitution in terms of what they claim to be its 'plain meaning.' It encourages a closed, usually (though not necessarily) politically conservative view of the world: one with a stop-time notion of history and a we-and-they approach to people, in which *we* are possessed of truth, virtue, and goodness and *they* of falsehood, depravity, and evil. It looks askance at figurative language, which so long as its symbols and metaphors are vital, can open—promiscuously in the eyes of the strict literalist—the world and its imaginative possibility.[155]

Crapanzano believes that literalism is prevalent, nay dominant, in many aspects of American life, especially in Evangelical Christianity and legal originalism.[156] According to his words in this passage, literalism is, generally speaking, regarded (by non-literalists, of course) negatively, being associated often with "dull wit." Accordingly, literalists are regularly thought of as fundamentalists and conservatives (both terms evidently bear a negative connotation here) who proceed on the conviction that they, and they alone, hold the absolute truth.

Literalism, as Crapanzano notes, is essentially a theory about language, and similar to all theories, it has assumptions about various issues. Central to literalism is the belief in the possibility of sound interpretation.[157] Literalists do not, in and on principle, acknowledge the possibility of having multiple, equally valid interpretations of a single text. This conviction is based on their concern for meaning, that is, only when the possibility that one text could be

155 Crapanzano, *Serving the Word*, p. xvi.

156 *Ibid.*, p. xvii. Another scholar agrees with Crapanzano, arguing that "[a]lthough its days of glory are past, the philosophical onslaughts of the past thirty years have not entirely unseated the notion of literal meaning" (Ellen Spolsky, "The Limits of Literal Meaning," p. 419). Spolsky goes on to show how works that assume that "linguistic forms have literal meaning" or that depend on the "existence of literal meaning" are welcomed and celebrated (*ibid.*, p. 419).

157 Crapanzano, *Serving the Word*, p. 67.

read in different, and equally valid, ways is excluded can we maintain the notion that every text has one true meaning and sound interpretation.[158] This conviction also relies on the belief that words have "plain meaning," which is the same thing as the "original meaning" and the "original intent."[159] "Plain meaning" is defined as the single, unambiguous meaning of a word, or the one understood by users of the language when they read a text.[160] Determining this plain meaning requires solid knowledge of the "original" meanings of words in the language of the text,[161] which knowledge requires in turn reference to the specific time when a text was written with the aim to determine the "original meaning," viz. the "original intent" of the author of the text. Reference to this context, however, is not meant to provide a social and cultural *context* to understand the text. As Crapanzano points out, whereas Christian literalists *freeze* the meaning by not acknowledging later changes in the use of language,[162] they resist interpreting the Bible "historically" in the sense of regarding it as being a product of a specific time, with the aim to avoid the notion that the Bible was written in a specific cultural context. Other than challenging the relevance of the Bible to modern times, this could "undermine the literalist understanding of Scripture."[163] Finally, Christian literalists insist that the authority of the Bible is based on the Bible itself, and that it is the Bible that must be the source of authority and legitimacy of anything else. The Bible is not authoritative because people see it as such; however, it is the Bible that establishes its own legitimacy and legitimizes or delegitimizes the views of those who write or talk about it.[164] For this reason, Christian literalists are suspicious of many aspects of medieval Christian scholarship, which suspicion similar to that of legal precedents by legal literalists.[165]

Crapanzano notes that literalism seeks to promote social order and continuity by "stabilizing" the law, which is achieved by controlling meaning.[166] To do this, it seeks to "bracket off human and social considerations" by rendering

---

158 Crapanzano, *Serving the Word*, p. 24.

159 *Ibid.*, p. xviii.

160 *Ibid.*, p. xx.

161 *Ibid.*, p. 66.

162 Monaghan, "Doing Originalism," p. 34, and Crapanzano, *Serving the Word*, p. 267. Crapanzano contrasts this with the liberals or pragmatists who regard a text as a living document and "try, within limits, to incorporate charge into their understanding of it" (*ibid.*, p. 209).

163 *Ibid.*, pp. 69–70.

164 *Ibid.*, pp. 75ff.

165 For this, see *ibid.*, pp. 75ff. and 258.

166 *Ibid.*, p. 16.

extra-textual factors irrelevant and treating law as a closed "autonomous system."[167] Literalists oppose attributing to a text unstated principles or underlying goals.[168] Here Crapanzano draws a comparison between what some scholars call legal "conservatives," "formalists," "originalists," "interpretivists," "strict-constructionists," "intentionalists," and "textualists." Whereas formalists and textualists are literalists, intentionalists are pragmatists. Legal formalists maintain that the role of the judiciary is to enforce "norms that are stated or clearly implicit in the Constitution as it was understood by those who ratified it," and insists that judges "must rely on value judgments 'within' the Constitution." On the other hand, non-originalists or intentionalists hold that "judges should, or at least can, look 'outside' the Constitution and the decisions based on it." These pragmatists speak in terms of the Constitution's "spirit, its aspiration, its unwritten presuppositions, the thrust of the whole, its need to be in tune with the times."[169]

Literalism, furthermore, rejects analogy and insists on a textual basis for any ruling.[170] It also rejects metaphorical and allegorical interpretations of religious and legal texts, stressing that "[an interpreter] should assume a literal interpretation unless there is some indication in the text to do otherwise."[171] It separates the exegesis of a text and its application. A text is usually independently interpreted and then applied to a particular situation, rather than being interpreted in light of the particular circumstances of that specific situation. Furthermore, literalism valorizes the written word and prefers it over oral communication. This preference, according to Crapanzano, is due to the perception of the written word as stable and autonomous, unlike the oral word, which is always flexible, context-dependent, and ephemeral.[172] Literalists, he adds, usually identify as foundational specific passages of authoritative texts and make frequent references to them. Not only do they refer to these authoritative texts at all times, literalist can even go so far as to physically carry them at all times.[173]

It should not be surprising now to envisage why Ẓāhirism could be regarded as a literalist legal theory. Ẓāhirism and literalism share some fundamental assumptions, foremost among which is the belief in the attainability of

167 Crapanzano, *Serving the Word*, pp. 210 and 252–253.
168 *Ibid.*, p. 209.
169 *Ibid.*, pp. 209–210.
170 *Ibid.*, p. 210.
171 *Ibid.*, p. 65.
172 *Ibid.*, pp. 2–4.
173 *Ibid.*, p. 62.

"correct" meaning and the necessity of belief in the possibility of achieving sound interpretation as well as the ability to distinguish it from wrong interpretations. Both believe that one and only one interpretation of any given text is sound, a view that Ibn Ḥazm holds, not only with regard to interpretation, but also with regard to all aspects of the law, where there exists only one correct ruling.[174] Both Ẓāhirism and literalism believe in the ability of sound hermeneutics to determine the original and true meaning without allowing personal biases to interfere in and corrupt the interpretative process. Both reject allegorical interpretation and analogy, which either change or add new elements to what a text explicitly says. Both share the same concern for social stability, and seek to have the society governed by the law (be it religious or positive), rather than subjecting the law to the norms of the society. Both value the written word, and both rely on specific passages on which to build their entire methodology and understanding of the law. Ibn Ḥazm, for example, argues that Q. 4:59, "O you who believe! Obey God, and obey the Messenger and those of you who are in authority. And if you differ on anything, refer it to God and the Messenger if you [truly] believe in God and the Last Day," encapsulates the core of Islamic law, such that he does not consider his voluminous *Iḥkām* save an explanation of what this verse says in terms of what we need to do and how we should deal with the legal tradition.[175] Other similarly key verses include Q. 2:29, "He it is Who created for you all that is in the earth," and Q. 6:119, "He [God] has explained to you in detail that which is forbidden unto you)," which demonstrate in his view that if something is not prohibited, it is (religiously/legally) permitted according to the text of the Qur'ān, a belief that is central to Ẓāhirī jurisprudence, as has been discussed.[176] Even when discussing specific cases, Ibn Ḥazm would determine specific verses as the most pertinent to the case at hand.

What this discussion of literalism leaves unanswered, however, is the very meaning of literalism and the possibility of identifying literal meaning. Literal

---

174 Ibn Ḥazm, *Iḥkām*, vol. 1, p. 15.

175 *Ibid.*, pp. 10–11. According to Crapanzano (*Serving the Word*, p. xix), "Christian literalism," as a hermeneutic methodology, assumes the inerrancy of the texts that it interprets literally—such as the Bible—and argues for the exactness of their wording (Crapanzano, *Serving the Word*, p. 67). In other words, reading these texts literally is related to the belief in their unquestionable truthfulness (*ibid.*, pp. 56ff). Arguably, this perception of the nature of the Bible and their keenness to prove its authenticity, inerrancy, and the exactness of its wording must have influenced the way they thought the Bible should be read. In Islam, however, a similar belief in the inerrancy of the Qur'ān did not necessarily lead Muslim scholars to read the Qur'ān literally; only a minority of them approached the Qur'ān as such.

176 Ibn Ḥazm, *Iḥkām*, vol. 12, p. 407.

meaning is defined here as the plain, single, and unambiguous meaning. This evidently refers to meanings of words only, and the cases that Crapanzano has chosen to discuss Scalia's legal philosophy shows that his discussion primarily deals with words, although Scalia himself evidently appeals to the textual context. When we deal with legal texts, however, we do not deal with words *per se*; rather, we deal with words as part of larger statements or sentences. Even if all the words of a given sentence have plain, single, and unambiguous meaning, this does not necessarily mean that the sentence as a whole yields a plain, single and unambiguous meaning. What is important, then, is to see how literalism deals with sentences and how this corresponds to the way Ẓāhirism does the same thing. As for the possibility of identifying literal meaning, we have seen that literalism seeks to "bracket off" all sorts of extra-textual considerations. In other words, interpreting a text is, so to speak, a mechanical process, the result of which should be the same regardless of who performs it. What we need to investigate, then, is whether Ibn Ḥazm's interpretation is truly free from extra-textual considerations. The following discussing seeks to examine to which extent similarities between literalism and Ẓāhirism can justify regarding them as essentially similar.

2.2 *Literalism in Linguistics*[177]

There are two main theories in the study of natural languages, which languages evolve through actual usage. The first is formal semantics, which assumes that language can be studied independently of any context of speech and irrespective of the intention of the speaker. This theory focuses on the "lexical" meanings of words and rules of syntax and grammar when interpreting a text. In formal semantics, the French linguist François Recanati explains, "[t]he meaning of a sentence ... is determined by the meanings of its parts and the way they are put together." Therefore, knowing a language for a formal semanticist is "like knowing a 'theory' by means of which one can deductively establish the truth-conditions of any sentence of that language."[178]

The other theory is pragmatics, which insists that language makes sense only when in use. Pragmatics does not deal with sentences; it deals with

---

177 According to Hipkiss, "[s]emantics is derived from the Greek *semaino*, meaning, to signify or mean. Semantics is part of the larger study of signs, semiotics. It is the part that deals with words as signs (symbols) and language as a system of signs (words as symbols)" (Hipkiss, *Semantics: Defining the Discipline*, p. ix).

178 François Recanati, *Literal Meaning*, p. 2 (emphasis omitted).

"speech acts,"[179] or "utterances," the meanings of which depend primarily on the context of use.[180] For a pragmatist like Keith Allan, "the source of linguistic data is the speech act: where a speaker S makes an utterance U in language L to hearer H in context C." This context C consists of the "physical setting" of the utterance (i.e., the time and place in which S utters and H hears or reads U), the "textual environment" in which a certain utterance appears, as well as what Allan calls "the world spoken of," which provides an infinite number of assumptions about the larger context or background information needed for an utterance to make sense.[181] For example, an utterance like "Almond Eyes ate her Kornies and listened to the radio" invokes a world in which a female (we know that Almond Eyes is a female from the pronoun "her") ate something and listened to the radio, which must have been broadcasting something. While this could have taken place in any moment in the past, we know that it must have taken place after the invention of the radio. If we do not have evidence to the contrary, we assume that an utterance like this is meant to be understood according to these specific assumptions which the sentence itself invokes when thought of carefully.[182]

Because of the centrality of context in pragmatic theory, it is regarded as a "contextualist" theory, one that takes the context of speech to be "an essential feature of natural languages,"[183] and maintains that "speech acts are the primary bearers of content."[184] On the other hand, semantic theory corresponds to a notion that some scholars call "literalism." Literalism, however, is a very elusive concept, and scholars of natural languages have put forward various

179 A speech act is any utterance that we make. According to Keith Allan (*Linguistic Meaning*, vol. 2, p. 164), John Austin was first to point out that "in every utterance, [the speaker] performs an act such as stating a fact or opinion, confirming or denying something, making a prediction or a request, asking a question, issuing an order, giving advice or permission, making an offer or a promise, greeting, thanking, condoling, effecting a baptism, or declaring an umpire's decision—and so forth." "[T]he list of speech acts is enormously long, and possibly boundless," he adds (*ibid.*, vol. 2, p. 164).

180 *Stanford Encyclopedia of Philosophy*, *c.v.* "Pragmatics." According to Hurford *et al.*, sentence meaning is "what a sentence means, regardless of the context and situation in which it may be used." In contrast, utterance meaning is "what a speaker means when he makes an utterance in a particular situation" (Hurford *et. al., Semantics*, p. 304).

181 Allan, *Linguistic Meaning*, vol. 2, pp. 36–37.

182 *Ibid.*, vol. 2, p. 41. Mohamed Yunis Ali points out that whereas Arab grammarians focused on semantics, legal theorists were pragmatists who focused on the language in use (Ali, *Medieval Islamic Pragmatics*, pp. 6–7). Legal theorists were definitely, and expectedly, pragmatists, but their strong interest in semantics is also evident.

183 Recanati, *Literal Meaning*, p. 96.

184 *Ibid.*, p. 3 (emphasis omitted).

definitions of it. Recanati, for instance, defines literalism as "ascrib[ing] truth-conditional content to natural language *sentences*, quite independently of what the speaker who utters this sentence means."[185] A "literal" meaning of a linguistic expression here is "its conventional meaning: the meaning it has in virtue of the conventions of the language endow with a particular meaning." Donald Davidson rejects identifying literal meaning with conventional meaning, arguing that literal meaning is what he calls the "first meaning," which meaning "comes first in the order of interpretation."[186] Delving into the details of this controversy over literalism is beyond the scope of this section, but we can note here that various theories on literal meaning define it in terms of its relationship to the context of speech. Unlike contextualism, literalism seeks to minimize or disregard context sensitivity by focusing on the semantic interpretation of words and sentences and insists that we appeal to the "speaker's meaning" only when the sentence requires it.[187]

This notion of literal meaning, however, has been questioned by many scholars, who insist that any understanding relies, to varying degrees, on the

---

185 Recanati, *Literal Meaning*, p. 3 (emphasis in original). "Truth conditional content" is what makes a sentence propositional, which is central to semantics. A proposition can generally be defined as "that part of the meaning of the utterance of a declarative sentence which describes some state of affairs" (Hurford *et al., Semantics*, p. 20). According to Hipkiss, "[f]ormal Semantics, also called 'set theoretic semantics' ... is a logic expressed as symbolic propositions that include and exclude each other entirely or in part. Propositions are, by definition, true statements, so truth and falsity are a major concern in this form of semantics" (Hipkiss, *Semantics*, p. xiii). Hipkiss explains this by referring to the founding fathers of modern linguistic philosophy—such as Bertrand Russell (d. 1970), Ludwig Wittgenstein (d. 1951) and Rudolf Carnap (d. 1970)—who regarded metaphysical propositions as false and unworthy of investigation, and focused not on words *per se*, but on how they are parts of a larger proposition. "The propositions themselves were restricted to matters of fact; attitudes, desires, motivations, and value judgments were all excluded. Feelings and beliefs could not be scientifically versified, so they were dismissed as not true" (*ibid.*, pp. xi–xii). In this view, accordingly, "truth and meaning [are] the same" (*ibid.*, p. 26).

186 Davidson, "A Nice Derangement of Epitaghs," p. 435. Davidson is critical of the term literal meaning, regarding it as "too incrusted with philosophical and other extras to do much work." He therefore suggests "first meaning" as a good alternative that can "appl[y] to words and sentences as uttered by a particular speaker on a particular occasion." "[I]f the occasion, the speaker, and the audience are 'normal' or standard," he points out, "then the first meaning of an utterance will be what should be found by consulting a dictionary based on actual usage" (*ibid.*, pp. 343–345).

187 Recanati, *Literal Meaning*, p. 85.

context of speech. This requires pragmatically rather than linguistically mandated processes (discussed below). For example, John Searle challenges

> the view that for every sentence the literal meaning of the sentence can be constructed as the meaning it has independently of any context whatever. I shall argue that in general the notion of the literal meaning of a sentence only has application relative to a set of contextual or background assumptions and finally I shall examine some of the implications of their alternative view. The view I shall be attacking is sometimes expressed by saying that the literal meaning of a sentence is the meaning that it has in the 'zero context' or the 'null context.' I shall argue that for a large class of sentences there is no such thing as the zero or null context for the interpretations of sentences, and that as far as our semantic competence is concerned we understand the meaning of such sentences only against a set of background assumptions about the contexts in which the sentence could be appropriately uttered.[188]

Searle gives numerous examples of sentences traditionally thought to yield meaning solely on the strength of their semantic value and without consideration of the context in which they are uttered. He then demonstrates that the interpretation of these sentences relies, in reality, on presumed contextual settings and background assumptions. In the same vein, Recanati gives other examples, arguing that under scrutiny, even such primary processes which literalists take to be "linguistically required" in order for a sentence to be propositional also appeal to the speaker's meaning according to the context of speech.[189]

Recanati has studied the issue of literalism in more depth in recent years. He points out that while "in ideal cases of linguistic communication, the speaker means exactly what she says . . ., in real life, . . . what the speaker means typically goes beyond, or otherwise diverges from, what the uttered sentence literally says. In such cases the hearer must rely on background knowledge to determine what the speaker means."[190] In this view, what is said (the sentence) does not necessarily correspond to what is meant or communicated (the utterance). One sentence can be used in various contexts (where each use of the sentence is a distinct utterance) to communicate different things, even if the words and syntax of the sentence are the same. For instance, "Muḥammad is a

188 Searle, "Literal Meaning," p. 207.

189 Recanati, *Literal Meaning*, p. 65.

190 *Ibid.*, p. 3.

prophet" is a sentence, but not a propositional one.[191] Before we know who Muḥammad is (we know that he is a human being and not a thing from the word "prophet") it only means that somebody named Muḥammad is a prophet.[192] However, when a person like Abū Bakr, the Prophet Muḥammad's Companion, goes to one of his Qurashī tribesmen and says to him "Muḥammad is a prophet" (assuming that the person knows the Muḥammad whom Abū Bakr has in mind), the sentence becomes propositional, and here it communicates a specific information about a specific person. But if a person goes to Abū Bakr and asks him: "Does Muḥammad communicate with God?," to which Abū Bakr replies, "Muḥammad is a Prophet," the sentence (still propositional) communicates something other than what it meant in the previous utterance. Here it says, "Yes, Muḥammad does communicate with God because he is a Prophet" (assuming, again, that there is an agreement that prophets, *qua* prophets, are believed to have some kind of communication with God).[193] In this example, what is communicated or "implicated" (implied) is different from that which would be understood from this sentence if it is uttered independently of this particular context.[194] This distinction between what is said and what is meant or implicated assumes that we can distinguish between the linguistic meaning of a sentence and what it intends to convey in different contexts where it is uttered. In Recanati's view, however, "there is... no such thing as 'what the sentence says' in the literalist sense, that is, no such thing as a complete proposition autonomously determined by the rules of the language." "In order to reach a complete proposition," he argues, "we *must* appeal to the speaker's meaning."[195] In this view, literalism is illusory, and "the notion of what the sentence says is incoherent," for "what is said... is nothing but an aspect of speaker's meaning."

Debates over the issue of literal meaning have apparently softened the views of scholars belonging to the two camps of formal semantics and pragmatics. Now a relationship between the semantic value of a sentence and the context in which it is uttered is more or less acknowledged by all scholars, even if they still disagree on the emphasis that they place on each. This has essentially

---

191 This example is of course only modelled on Recanati's examples.

192 For a similar example, see Hipkiss, *Semantics*, p. 28, where Hipkiss mentions that a sentence like "John is late" means "very little to a person who does not know who John is."

193 This, of course, assumes that it is understood in a world in which prophets communicate with God.

194 In semantics, an "implicature" is "a form of reasonable inference... [that] exists by reason of general social conventions" (Hurford *et al.*, *Semantics*, p. 20).

195 Recanati, *Literal Meaning*, p. 59 (emphasis in original). For a good example on this, see *ibid.*, p. 73.

reduced the difference between semantics and pragmatics to the kinds of contextual clues that are admissible in the process of interpretation rather than to whether contextual clues are ever admissible to begin with. On this basis, Recanati identifies two camps of modern linguists: minimalists and non-minimalists. Minimalism—the dominant literalist position, according to him[196]—holds that what is said must relate to the "conventional" meaning of the words used in a given sentence, and that departing from this conventional meaning is acknowledged as a possibility "only when this is necessary to 'complete' the meaning of the sentence and make it propositional." In other words, for minimalists what is said must correspond to the potentials of the semantics of the sentence.[197] They also admit only of linguistically mandated constituents that are necessary to make a sentence propositional, rejecting any "pragmatically determined element in utterance content that is not triggered by grammar."[198] For non-minimalists, on the other side, what is said is just as pragmatically determined as what is implied.[199] In other words, they maintain that it is often the case that pragmatically rather than linguistically required constituents are needed for a sentence to be propositional.[200]

A process is linguistically required when the sentence is not propositional without it. In other words, if a sentence cannot be a proposition (i.e., a statement that conveys meaning and can be described as being true or false) as it is, the process that we have to perform to make it propositional (viz. meaningful) is linguistically mandated. For example, the only contextual process that minimalists acknowledge, according to Recanati, is called "saturation," which refers to the process by which "slots" in sentences are filled out by a linguistically required constituent.[201] "He is tall" can only be a proposition when we know to whom the pronoun "he" refers, and this can differ from one context to another. Before we know the referent of "he" from the context, "he is tall" is almost meaningless in any obvious way. This requirement to assign a referent (which is not stated in the sentence) to the pronoun "he" only follows a rule of use in

196 Recanati, *Literal Meaning*, p. 160.

197 *Ibid.*, pp. 6–7.

198 *Stanford Encyclopedia of Philosophy, c.v.* "Pragmatics."

199 Recanati, *Literal Meaning*, p. 6.

200 When we discussed al-Shāfiʿī's and al-Ṭabarī's use of the term *ẓāhir*, we have seen that some of what they say suggest that they thought that there could be more than one *ẓāhir* meaning, and al-Ṭabarī's use of the superlative form of *ẓāhir* (*al-aẓhar*) also suggests that two readings could be *ẓāhir*, yet one of them is more *ẓāhir* than the other. This can be related to Recanati's discussion of a continuum between minimalism and non-minimalism. Pursuing this point, however, is beyond the scope of this chapter.

201 *Ibid.*, pp. 7 and 10.

the language which does not assign this demonstrative (and other demonstratives, for that matter) to a specific referent. This process of assigning referents to pronouns is thus linguistically mandated. The interpretation of these demonstratives and similar indexical expressions,[202] Recanati points out, takes us "beyond what the conventions of the language give us, but that step beyond is still governed by the conventions of the language." In other words, this interpretation of the utterance is predetermined by the very use of the demonstrative or similar expressions. Extra meanings that are not necessary to make a sentence propositional, therefore, are considered "external to what is said." Minimalists, thus, hold that with the exception of saturation, all pragmatic processes are secondary and presuppose the existence of a literal interpretation of what is said.[203]

Scholars who reject the validity of the notion of literalism do not do so only by ruling out the possibility of identifying a literal meaning of a sentence without considering the context of speech. However, they maintain that literal meaning "has no compositional privilege over derived meanings [that pragmatic processes other than 'saturation' mandate]." In Recanati's view, "literal" (to the extent that this is possible) and "non-literal" meanings compete, and it is possible for some derived meaning to be retained while the literal interpretation is suppressed.[204] It happens regularly that one moves immediately, through pragmatic processes, to what an utterance communicates (i.e., what the speaker intends to convey) without even considering what the sentence explicitly says (which is considered the "literal" meaning). In order to do this, Recanati distinguishes between two kinds of pragmatic processes, one primary and the other secondary. Primary pragmatic processes—which concern us here—are neither conscious nor inferential.[205] They take place unconsciously at the same time the literal meaning of a sentence is construed and do not even require reflection on the part of the interpreter. "Only when the unreflective normal process of interpretation yields weird results," Recanati argues, "does a genuine inference process take place whereby we use

---

202 Recanati, *Literal Meaning*, p. 69. Indexicality refers to "the pervasive context-dependency of natural language utterances, including such varied phenomena as regional accent (indexing speaker's identity), indicators of verbal etiquette (marking deference and demeanor), the referential use of pronouns (I, you, we, he, etc.), demonstratives (this, that), deictic adverbs (here, there, now, then), and tense. In all of these cases, the interpretation of the indexical form depends strictly on the context in which it is uttered" (William Hanks, "Indexicality," p. 124).

203 Recanati, *Literal Meaning*, p. 27.

204 *Ibid.*, pp. 28–29.

205 *Ibid.*, p. 38.

evidence concerning the speaker's beliefs and intentions to work out what he means."[206] In other words, some pragmatic processes that are not linguistically required to make a sentence propositional and thus meaningful have to be made and are in fact regularly made mostly unconsciously.

3 Ẓāhirism between Literalism and (Con)Textualism

Although the notion of literalism is controversial, it is generally assumed that literalist interpretation depends solely on the lexical meaning of words and the grammar of the language. A true literalist does not consider the context of speech and only allows linguistically required processes to play a role in interpretation. However, modern research is now paying greater attention to cases where what people intend to communicate or express by their utterances does not correspond to the semantic value of the sentences that they use, or where interpreters move directly to a pragmatically determined meaning without even entertaining the literal meaning of a given statement. To be sure, Recanati's views on the inherently pragmatic nature of natural languages (which other scholars, notably Relevance theorists, maintain too)[207] have been severely criticized by scholars who regard them as a return to "the pessimistic conclusions of the past," when it was thought that "the context-dependence and vagueness of natural language undermined the possibility of providing a systematic account of the meaning of natural language sentences."[208] As noted, engaging in this controversy is beyond the scope of this chapter, but it is essential to see how views like Recanati's can help us better understand the way Ẓāhirīs (and textualists) perceived and dealt with religious/legal texts.

It is important, however, to distinguish between how a *speaker* uses the language and how an interpreter (a reader or hearer of an utterance) processes what is said and understands it accordingly. As noted earlier, Ẓāhirīs, including Ibn Ḥazm, held that the Qur'ān does not contain any *majāz*. Whatever God says should not be taken to be metaphorical. This ensues from the notion that metaphorical language is a degraded, deceitful, and harmful form of speech. But do Ẓāhirīs also assume that God's speech does not require distinction between what is said or expressed and what is implicated or intended to be said? In other words, are we to regard the Qur'ānic text as made up of sentences, or utterances the understanding of which requires reliance on the con-

206 Recanati, *Literal Meaning*, p. 23.
207 For this, see *Stanford Encyclopedia of Philosophy*, *s.v.* "Pragmatics."
208 Stanley, "Literal Meaning."

text? Furthermore, when interpreting the Qur'ān, do we need to focus only on its semantic content, or do we have to use pragmatic processes to grasp its meaning? In what follows, some of Ibn Ḥazm's interpretation of Qur'ānic verses will be discussed in order to demonstrate that he did acknowledge the possibility that what the Qur'ān "says" is not necessarily what it "means" (vis. intends to communicate), and that the language of some Qur'ānic verses admits more than one reading. Ibn Ḥazm did not focus only on the semantic content and structure of sentences. Rather, he engaged in pragmatic processes and appealed to contextual, historical, and even doctrinal evidence to determine the meaning that the Qur'ān seeks and intends to convey. Unlike literalists, he did not deal with Qur'ānic statements as sentences that could provide meaning without context, but dealt with them as utterances and speech acts that required examination of the context of use to achieve sound interpretation. Where Ibn Ḥazm stands on the continuum of minimalism/non-minimalism, however, is a subject that will hopefully be examined in a separate study.[209]

An example that Recanati gives to illustrate his view of the indispensability of pragmatic processes in any process of interpretation is when one says "the city is asleep." He argues that when we hear this, we immediately and intuitively infer that either the word "city" is used non-literally to refer to the "inhabitants of the city," or that "asleep" is used metaphorically to denote that "the city is quiet."[210] The "literal" meaning of this sentence (i.e., that much of it, if any, that could be understood independently of any context) is not considered here. Taking "asleep" in this example to mean "quiet" is a pragmatic process called "loosening," whereby "a condition of application packed in to [a] concept literally expressed by a predicate is contextually dropped so that the application of the predicate is widened."[211] This is the case when we say, for example, "the ATM machine has swallowed my credit card." We make sense of an utterance like this by widening the scope of application of the word "swallow" so that we can imagine the ATM as something that can swallow and the credit card as something that can be swallowed. However, if we take "city" to refer to its inhabitants, we do this on the basis of a pragmatic process called "semantic transfer," by which what we understand only has a systematic

209 This chapter seeks to demonstrate that Ibn Ḥazm was *not* a literalist. However, it is both instructive and interesting to see where Ẓāhirism stands on the continuum of minimalism/non-minimalism and how this differs from the position of other *madhhabs*. If this shows that Ibn Ḥazm was not even a minimalist (which should not be surprising in light of our discussion here), considering Ẓāhirism literalist should be laid to rest once and for all.

210 Recanati, *Literal Meaning*, p. 34.

211 *Ibid.*, p. 26.

relation to what is being literally expressed. Thus, although the "city" and the "city dwellers" are two different concepts, they are obviously related to each other. Similarly, in "the ham sandwich has left without paying," the "ham sandwich" would be processed by the interpreter immediately as the "ham-sandwich-orderer," without the "absurd" literal meaning "being ever computed," Recanati states.[212]

A third primary pragmatic process is "free enrichment," which is the "paradigm case" of such pragmatic processes, according to Recanati. Free enrichment is simply the opposite of loosening, for it "consists in making the interpretation of some expression in the sentence contextually more specific." For this reason, this process is described by some linguists as "specifization" (remember *takhṣīṣ*). For example, we take "he eats rabbits" to mean rabbit meat (a specific part of the rabbit), while "she wears rabbit" to mean rabbit fur (another part of the rabbit).[213] Recanati argues that what distinguishes these three pragmatic processes from what he regards as secondary pragmatic processes is that whereas the latter are "post-propositional"—i.e., can only take place when a proposition is assumed to have been expressed, primary pragmatic processes are "pre-propositional," viz. they do not require a proposition to serve as input to the process of interpretation. Therefore, this kind of processes is not conscious: "[n]ormal interpreters need not be aware of the context-independent means of the expressions used." "Saturation," which is a linguistically mandated process, is an example of these primary pragmatic processes, but the three other processes that we have just mentioned are "optional and context-driven," Recanati argues.[214]

To what extent does Ibn Ḥazm's interpretation of the Qur'ān conform to Recanati's views? In Q. 12, the Hebrew patriarch Jacob (a prophet in Islam) asks his sons about their brother Benjamin and they tell him that he was arrested for stealing the cup of the king when they were in Egypt. Because Jacob was suspicious of them, they said: "Ask the town where we were (*is'al al-qaryah*) and the caravan (*al-ʿīr*) in which we have returned" (Q. 12:82). In dealing with this verse, Ibn Ḥazm mentions two interpretations, according to the first of which, what is meant here are the "people of the village" and the "travelers in the caravan,"[215] an obvious case of semantic transfer. The second interpretation is that given that Jacob was a prophet, had he asked the village and the

212 Recanati, *Literal Meaning*, pp. 29 and 33. For further discussion of this and more examples, see *ibid.*, pp. 61–64.

213 *Ibid.*, p. 24.

214 *Ibid.*, p. 23.

215 Ibn Ḥazm, *Iḥkām*, vol. 1, p. 369.

caravan themselves, they would have answered him. These two interpretations, Ibn Ḥazm argues, are *both* valid and possible. It is evident, however, that he is more inclined to the first interpretation, which he mentions first and then attributes the other one to some unnamed scholars.[216] What is worth noting here is that Ibn Ḥazm does not argue that the "village" and the "caravan" are things that can be asked. Jacob is only miraculously capable of doing so on the strength of him being a prophet.[217] The first interpretation demonstrates that Ibn Ḥazm admits that some constituents or components are missing in the verse, and these are the "people" of the village and the "travelers" in the caravans. The same applies to Q. 2:93, "And the calf was made to sink into their hearts (*wa-ushribū fī qulūbihim al-ʿijl bi-kufrihim*)." Ibn Ḥazm explains that the verse does not mean the calf itself, but rather the "love" of the calf which God made to sink into the hearts of the disobedient Jews to whom the verse refers.[218] In these two cases, there exists a relation between what is "literally" expressed and what is implicated and understood, although these remain two different things.

"He went to the cliff and jumped" is an example of free enrichment. Everyone, Recanati argues, would understand from this sentence that the referent of the pronoun "he" went to the cliff and jumped *off* it, rather than jumped in his place. Similarly, when a child cuts his finger and his mother says to him: "You are not going to die," we understand immediately that she means that he would not die *from that cut*, rather than not dying at all. In both cases, the proposition is made more specific: the referent of "he" in the first example jumped in a specific manner, while "death" in the second example was connected to a specific condition. This is particularly what Justice Scalia did in the Smith Case: he appealed to the context to restrict the meaning of "use" to a specific kind of use.

Two Qurʾānic verses are useful for comparison here: Q. 2:60, "We said [to Moses]: Strike the rock with your staff, and there gushed out from it twelve springs,"[219] and Q. 26:63, "Then We revealed to Moses: Strike the sea with your staff. So it divided…"[220] In commenting on these verses, Ibn Ḥazm argues

216 Ibn Ḥazm, *Iḥkām*, vol. 1, p. 415.

217 In other words, this sentence can only be read "literally" if we assume a different world in which it is uttered. Ibn Ḥazm's preference for the other interpretation, however, demonstrates that he was in favor of interpreting the Qurʾānic text according to the rules of our world.

218 *Ibid.*, vol. 1, p. 416.

219 The verse reads in Arabic: *fa-qulnā iḍrib bi-ʿaṣāk al-ḥajar fa-infajarat min-hu ithnata ʿashrata ʿayn.*

220 In Arabic: *wa-awḥaynā ilā Mūsā an iḍrib bi-ʿaṣāk al-ḥajar fa-infalaqa.*

that every *reasonable* person (*dhū ʿaql*) understands that there is something missing in them and that what they mean to say is that *upon* God's command, Moses struck the rock with his staff before the water gushed, and that he struck the sea with his staff before it divided.[221] What Ibn Ḥazm does here is rendering the propositions in these verses more specific by filling in gaps in them with the aim of specifying how and when the springs gushed and the sea divided.

"Everybody went to Paris" is another example of free enrichment. Here, "everybody" is construed to mean everyone from *specifically* such and such group (rather than everyone on earth) went to Paris. In commenting on Q. 46:25, "Destroying [i.e., the wind] everything (*kull shayʾ*) by the command of its Lord," Ibn Ḥazm argues that we conclude from the historical "fact" that the wind did not destroy everything on earth (otherwise not human beings would have survived) that this verse only means everything of the things that the wind passed over, or everything of the things that God had ordered it to destroy.[222] Just as the "literal meaning" of "everybody went to Paris" is not even entertained because we know that in no certain point in time all living people went to Paris, so is the meaning of *kull shayʾ* in this verse. In both cases, however, we do not need to engage in this pragmatic process for the sentence to be propositional; in theory, both could mean just what they "say." However, we, unconsciously in Recanati's view, intuitively sense absurdity in what these sentences say and appeal to external (that is, extra-textual) knowledge to identify the implicated or intended meaning.

Ibn Ḥazm's interpretation of Q. 18:77, "They [Moses and a righteous man whom he met] found there [in a village that they visited] a wall that *yurīdu an yanqaḍḍa ...*," represents another example of pragmatic processes. In "zero context," *yurīdu an yanqaḍḍa* means "wants to fall." Ibn Ḥazm argues that we know by reason and through the customary use of language that the wall does *not* have a will, which only living things possess. Therefore, *yurīdu* here *cannot* mean that the wall wanted to fall, and we can be certain that God uses this word to refer to something other than to that which it is usually used to refer.[223] In his view, it here means that the wall was physically inclined (*māʾil*). "Were it not for this necessity [of reason]," Ibn Ḥazm asserts, "we would not have allowed ourselves to take a word to mean something other than that which it normally means." In fact, he argues *against* the view that *yurīdu* could mean that the wall wanted to collapse in reality since God is able to create a will in it.

---

221 Ibn Ḥazm, *Iḥkām*, vol. 1, p. 181.

222 *Ibid.*, vol. 1, pp. 340 and 342.

223 As noted earlier, Ẓāhirīs do not believe that the Qurʾān uses *majāz*. Ibn Ḥazm is evidently conscious here to avoid saying that the Qurʾān uses *yurīdu* here figuratively.

In his view, we must have a textual basis for regarding this as having been a miracle.[224] Without this textual evidence, we have to interpret the verse in terms of its lexical meaning, and the lexical meaning of this verse indicates that one of its words is not used to refer to what it conventionally refers to. While this example is very close to Recanati's example of the ATM machine, Ibn Ḥazm, arguably, does not use "loosening" to interpret the verse (i.e., he does not relax the conditions of *yurīdu* to expand its application). Instead, he treats it as a case of "semantic transfer," although the relation between what is expressed (*yurīdu*) and what he takes to be implicated here (that the wall was inclined) is not clear. This, in Recanati's understanding, is regularly done without even considering the absurd literal meaning, which Ibn Ḥazm is aware of but explicitly and categorically dismisses.

Ibn Ḥazm, thus, engaged in some of what Recanati calls "primary pragmatic processes" when interpreting the Qur'ān. But as the last example demonstrates, this was not performed unconsciously as Recanati says, probably because of Ibn Ḥazm's career as jurist and his careful attention to the text with the aim to identify the "correct" meaning thereof. Ibn Ḥazm was definitely aware of what he was doing when interpreting these Qur'ānic verses that we have seen, and he seems to have felt the need to justify his "pragmatic" reading of them. Ibn Ḥazm's hermeneutical methodology, furthermore, relies on non-textual materials in light of which texts are interpreted. In other words, Ibn Ḥazm does *not* read, and does *not* pretend to be reading, religious texts solely on the basis of their semantic meaning. He obviously believed that these texts were to be read pragmatically within the broader context of, not only reason, but also history and theology.

In addition to engaging in these pragmatic processes that are not linguistically mandated, Ibn Ḥazm's treatment of some other verses also reveals that he viewed them as "speech acts" or utterances the understanding of which requires appeal to the context, rather than viewing them as mere sentences, the understanding of which only requires knowledge of the lexical meaning of the words and how they are put together in the verses. For example, to demonstrate that a woman's hands (*kaffān*) are not part of her private parts (*ʿawrah*) and do not therefore have to be covered in public, he refers to an incident where the Prophet asked women to donate to the poor when they began to throw their rings on a garment. Ibn Ḥazm argues that these women would not

---

224 Ibn Ḥazm, *Iḥkām*, vol. 1, pp. 415–416. Again, this demonstrates that Ibn Ḥazm was not in favor of interpreting the Qur'ān with reference to a world other than ours. For him, the "world spoken of" is always assumed to be ours, unless a valid indicator suggests otherwise (e.g., when we are told that something is a miracle).

be able to take off their rings unless their hands were not covered.[225] Obviously, he appeals here to the context of speech to make conclusions on the meaning (and legal rulings that can be inferred on the basis thereof) of this report, although there is nothing in the text itself that says that these women were not covering their hands.[226]

In another context, Ibn Ḥazm points out that a command can take the form of a declarative sentence (*jumlah khabariyyah*) and does not have to be in the imperative mood. For example, Q. 2:183, *kutiba ʿalay-kum al-ṣiyām* means that fasting is made obligatory upon Muslims, even if the sentence does not use the imperative form. Similarly, Q. 4:23, *ḥurrimat ʿalay-kum ummahātukum* means that mothers are forbidden. This issue, however, can be very problematic, for how are we to determine the intended meaning of some other declarative sentences? For instance, in Q. 3:97, *wa-man dakhalahu kāna āmin*?, the pronoun in *dakhala*-hu refers to the Sacred Mosque in Mecca. If interpreted as a declarative statement, this verse would be informing us that whoever enters the Sacred Mosque in Mecca *is* safe. However, if it is read as an imperative statement (similar to the two examples above), it would mean that securing whoever enters the sacred mosque is obligatory on Muslims. Ibn Ḥazm argues that since God does not tell but the truth, the fact that people have not always been safe in the Sacred Mosque evinces that this verse is *not* declarative. It must therefore be a command to Muslims that they must secure people who enter the Sacred Mosque.[227] The appeal here is obviously to history with the aim of determining the intended meaning, which is only one of many possible meanings of the verse. However, in Q. 4:92, *wa-man qatala muʾmin khaṭaʾan fa-taḥrīru raqabah muʾminah* and Q. 4:93, *wa-man yaqtul muʾmin mutaʿammidan fa-jazāʾuhu jahannam*, Ibn Ḥazm appeals to reason. These two verses use

---

225 Ibn Ḥazm, *Iḥkām*, vol. 9, p. 162.

226 Remarkably, Ibn Ḥazm does not entertain the possibilities that these women were not wearing their rings in the first place, or were wearing them but took them off after taking off their gloves, for instance. Compare this example with "Mary took out her key and opened the door." Recanati mentions this as an example of optional pragmatic processes. He explains that "[i]n virtue of a 'bridging inference', we naturally understand the second conjunct as meaning that Mary opened the door with the key mentioned in the first conjunct; yet this is not explicitly articulated in the sentence." This is an example of what some scholars describes as "specifization," which "consists in making the interpretation of some expression in the sentence contextually more specific" (Recanati, *Literal Meaning*, pp. 23–24).

227 Ibn Ḥazm, *Iḥkām*, vol. 1, p. 286. This command to protect people who enter the Sacred Mosque would therefore be inclusive of all people, Muslims as well as non-Muslims, since "people" is not restricted by another textual evidence.

almost the same words and are structurally similar, but do they convey the same thing? Ibn Ḥazm acknowledges the difficulty of this, but decides that whereas the first verse is prescriptive in that it establishes an obligation to set free a Muslim slave in case a Muslim kills another Muslim by mistake, the second verse is declarative, i.e., it only mentions that a Muslim who kills another Muslim intentionally would reside in Hellfire forever. We know this, he explains, because while we can obey the command in the first verse (by freeing a slave), we cannot carry out the punishment of the murderer in the second.[228] It stands to reason, then, that whereas the first verse is prescriptive, the second has to be only informative.

Ibn Ḥazm uses other kinds of evidence that are related to the broader context of Islam, including theology and law. For instance, commenting on Q. 4:59, "O you who believe, obey God, and obey the Messenger and those who are in authority among you, and if you have a dispute concerning any matter, refer it to God and his Messenger," he argues that *ijmāʿ* has established that God does not mean only the direct addressees of the Qurʾān (i.e., the Prophet's Companions) by this, but rather all subsequent Muslim generations too.[229] In another context, he mentions a report where the Prophet prohibits the killing of women. Ibn Ḥazm points out that the *ẓāhir* meaning of this tradition (viz. its general, unrestricted meaning) means that no woman shall be killed under any circumstance. A consensus exists among Muslims, however, that the *ẓāhir* of this tradition is qualified (i.e., restricted), and that women can be killed in certain circumstances. It has also been proven (*ṣaḥḥa*) that this tradition meant the killing of female prisoners of war in particular.[230] In both these cases, *ijmāʿ* is used, not only to determine the intended meaning, but also to qualify the *ẓāhir* meaning.

Elsewhere, Ibn Ḥazm acknowledges an apparent contradiction between Q. 2:47, "O Children of Israel! Remember my favor wherewith I favored you and how I preferred you to all creatures (*ʿalā ʾl-ʿālamīn*)", and Q. 3:110, "You [i.e., the Muslim community] are the best community that has been raised up for mankind." In commenting on these two verses, he says that either the first verse means that the Children of Israel were preferred by God to all creatures except Muḥammad's *ummah*, or that the second means that the Muslim *ummah* (which can here refer either to the generation of the Prophet Muḥammad

228 Ibn Ḥazm, *Iḥkām*, vol. 1, pp. 285–286.

229 *Ibid.*, vol. 1, pp. 87–88.

230 *Ibid.*, vol. 1, p. 175. Ibn Ḥazm probably had to resort to this interpretation to reconcile this tradition with another, according to which the Prophet ordered the killing of anyone who changed his religion (*man baddala dīnahu fa-uqtulūhu*).

exclusively or to all generations of Muslims at all times) was morally superior to all other communities except the Children of Israel. We know, Ibn Ḥazm argues, that the first verse is qualified, for it is established that the angles are better than the Jews (a theological view). At the same time, we do not have any textual or non-textual evidence that suggests that the second verse is similarly qualified. Therefore, we can conclude that the second verse is more general in its scope than the first, meaning that the Muslim *ummah* is superior to all other communities *including* the Children of Israel.[231] In other words, to solve the problem, Ibn Ḥazm relies on a theological view (which he takes to be granted) to argue for the restrictedness of the first verse, and against the unrestrictedness of the second. Similar to the case of killing women, he is clearly struggling here between two apparently general statements, and what he tries to do is to justify why one of them is, in fact, restricted. In other words, one of them cannot be taken at face value (*ʿalā ʾl-ẓāhir*), viz. its scope of application has to be restricted.

This and earlier examples also clearly demonstrate the relationship between Ẓāhirism and the *ʿumūm/khuṣūṣ* dichotomy. Ibn Ḥazm's dealing with these verses is consistent with the argument made earlier that the issue of the *ẓāhir* meaning was primarily associated with the scope of application and range of referents of terms and statements. In some of the cases discussed above, Ibn Ḥazm evidently struggles to justify his qualification of the default generality of some Qurʾānic verses by limiting its scope and rejecting its full potential range of reference. In other cases, he is even more explicit about the subject of *ʿumūm* and severely criticizes what he considers arbitrary restriction of terms. For example, he argues against those who held that Q. 2:34, "And when we said to the angles: Prostrate yourselves to Adam ...," did not mean all the angles, but rather only those who were present. He goes so far as to call this "madness" (*junūn*) that cannot be supported on the basis of the quoted text.[232] Similarly, relying on a Prophetic tradition that says that "the blood of Muslims is equal" (*al-muslimūn tatakāfaʾu dimāʾuhum*), he argues that any Muslim who murders another is to be killed, regardless of the gender and freedom of either the killer or the victim.[233] This is the *ẓāhir* meaning, which meaning is inclusive of all possible referents and maintains the absoluteness of words and statements unless another piece of textual evidence suggests otherwise.

Remarkably, Ibn Ḥazm mentions clearly the relationship between *ẓāhir* and the issue of the imperative, another subject that we have discussed earlier, and

231 Ibn Ḥazm, *Iḥkām*, vol. 1, p. 158.
232 *Ibid.*, vol. 2, p. 918.
233 *Ibid.*, vol. 2, p. 928.

his discussion of this subject also indicates how it is related to the issue of the scope of application of terms.[234] Since every term should be interpreted to be *ʿalā ʾl-ẓāhir* (i.e., not restricted),[235] the *ẓāhir* meaning of Q. 5:38, "As for the thief, both male and female, cut off their hands," is that *all* thieves should be punished by cutting off their hands *irrespective* of the value of what they have stolen. Here, the obligation to cut off the hand of a thief is absolute and unconditional, and it has to be carried out immediately. The *ẓāhir* meaning of commands, Ibn Ḥazm mentions explicitly, is that they should be taken to indicate absolute obligation (*wujūb*) and the requirement of the immediate performance of what is commanded (*ʿalā ʾl-fawr*).[236]

∴

The purpose of this chapter has not been to demonstrate that Ẓāhirism is not literalism because Ẓāhirī scholars themselves regarded it as such. Ẓāhirism has been considered—mistakenly, as should be obvious now—literalist only by modern and possibly some medieval scholars. The previous discussion is an argument against this understanding of Ẓāhirism which has been presumed but never in fact demonstrated. Similarly, textualism, which is almost identical with Ẓāhirism as both legal and hermeneutical theory, has also been conceived of as literalist by some Western scholars. This conception of both Ẓāhirism and textualism ignores an important fact: literalism is, and will probably continue to be, a controversial subject among linguists. Recanati's discussion shows that even minimalists, who believe that a "literal meaning" of a sentence can be determined with only a minimal appeal to the context of speech, can easily be shown to be wrong when they assume that certain concepts, for instance, are inherent in the meanings of certain words or verbs. This indicates that any meaning identified as literal by some scholar could be demonstrated to be a mixture of literal and derived, or stated and implicit, meaning. Furthermore, conceiving of Ẓāhirism as literalism ascribes views to the former that it does not in fact expound.

According to the definition of literal meaning that most linguists seem to agree on—the lexical meaning of the words of a sentence read in light of the rules of language without consideration of the context of speech, it can easily be demonstrated that Ibn Ḥazm, the only Ẓāhirī scholar whose views we can

234 Ibn Ḥazm, *Iḥkām*, vol. 1, pp. 85–86 and 362.

235 *Ibid.*, vol. 1, p. 40.

236 *Ibid.*, vol. 1, p. 259. Ibn Ḥazm accepts a Prophetic report that determines a minimum value for this punishment to be applicable.

discuss with sufficient depth, was anything but a literalist in this sense. He did not regard the Qur'ānic text as one that only required the minimal appeal to the context to be understood. Not only did he engage in pragmatic processes (which, to be sure, are not linguistically required) when interpreting the Qur'ān, but he also interpreted it against the backdrop of particular assumptions about God, religion, and language, as well as its textual and historical contexts. This does not mean that Ibn Ḥazm thought that he was deviating from what the text said in his view. What this says is that if we regard his methodology as literalist, we deprive ourselves of the opportunity to comprehend what he actually does and says. This is probably the mistake that Crapanzano made when he speaks about Scalia's "literalist hermeneutics." His perception of Scalia as a literalist prevented him from understanding that Scalia's appeal to the context to understand what a word like "use" meant was not due to his alleged inconsistency, but rather to his not being a literalist who disregards the context. Scalia himself does not regard his hermeneutics as being literalist, and those scholars who regard his methodology as literalist attribute to him what he does not acknowledge and judge him accordingly. In other words, they deal with fiction that they have created themselves. Accordingly, we must disagree with the statement that the Ẓāhirī approach was "based primarily on the non-pragmatic givens of the language and stresses the predetermined conventions of the language which are encoded in the linguistic structure of the texts as the essential, and perhaps the only requirements for communication," and that "[e]xtra-linguistic contexts are generally ignored and the inferential capacity of the hearer has almost no role to play in interpretation."[237]

In a revealing debate that Abū Isḥāq al-Shīrāzī mentions in his discussion of one form of textual implication, a disagreement took place over Q. 17:23, "And Say not fie (*uff*) to them [i.e., your parents],"[238] and Q. 4:40 "Surely Allah does not do injustice to the weight of an atom."[239] Is it possible to conclude from the first verse, scholars wondered, that beating one's parents is prohibited, and from the second verse that God does not do injustice to a weight that is more than that of an atom? Al-Shīrāzī argues that we can make these conclusions on the basis of the meaning (*maʿnā*) of the two verses, which indicates that these conclusions can only be validly derived from the meaning of the two verses in a "pragmatic" way. We take this to be a pragmatic reading of the two verses because according to the other view that al-Shīrāzī mentions, these two conclusions can be reached on "linguistic grounds" (*min nāḥiyat al-lughah*), i.e.,

237 Ali, *Medieval Islamic Pragmatics*, p. 9.
238 *Wa-lā taqul la-humā uff wa-lā tanharhumā.*
239 *Inna Allāh lā yaẓlimu mithqāl dharrah.*

they can be linguistically mandated. Al-Shīrāzī attributes to a certain scholar the view that what is more than an atom is two or more individual atoms, each of which is covered by the text of the second verse. Therefore, the language itself allows us to conclude from this verse that God does not do injustice to the weight of more than one atom, even though the verse speaks about one atom only. As for the first verse, al-Shīrāzī does not explain the view that we can conclude from the prohibition to say fie to one's parent that one cannot beat them, and it is difficult to imagine the logic of this argument since beating does not consist of several instances of saying fie. Al-Shīrāzī himself refutes this view (of the possibility to make these two conclusions about the verse on the strength of their wording) by arguing that the Arabic word *uff* is not used to refer to beating, just as the word atom is not used to refer to more than an atom. Therefore, scholars and lay people alike make these two conclusions on the basis of the meaning, rather than the wording, of the two verses.[240]

What is remarkable here is that the view that the wording of Q. 4:40 is the basis of our conclusion that God does not do injustice to more than the weight of an atom is attributed to Muḥammad ibn Dāwūd. Al-Shīrāzī adds that Ibn Surayj refuted this view by referring to half an atom, which is not made of single atoms as is the case with two or more atoms. Therefore, if we are to understand from this verse that God does not do injustice to the weight of half an atom, we can only do this on the basis of the meaning, rather than the wording, of the verse.[241] While al-Shīrāzī does not mention how Ibn Dāwūd responded to this point, it is not difficult to imagine that he could have simply retorted by saying that this point does not deal with the question in the first place. It is not against reason to say that while we can conclude on the basis of the wording of the verse that God does not do injustice more than the weight of an atom, we can make a similar conclusion about half an atom only pragmatically on the basis of the meaning of the verse. Be this as it may, this account seems to suggest that Ibn Dāwūd in this example was a "literalist" in the technical sense of the term. He was of the view that one can only resort to pragmatic processes if, and only if, there is no possibility to appeal to the language itself, or make conclusions that are derived from the very wording of a text. This view is also attributed by al-Shīrāzī to some Shāfiʿī scholars, the majority of theologians (*ʿāmmat al-mutakallimīn*), and some Ẓāhirīs (*baʿḍ ahl al-ẓāhir*). In other words, not all Ẓāhirīs held Muḥammad ibn Dāwūd's view.

240 Al-Shīrāzī, *al-Tabṣira*, pp. 227–228.

241 *Ibid.*, p. 228.

Ibn Ḥazm was not a literalist, but we can, with due caution, regard his legal philosophy to be almost identical to Justice Scalia's textualism.[242] Truly, there are obvious and at times significant similarities between Ẓāhirism, textualism, and literalism, the most important of which is their conviction that "[f]or any conversation, dialogue, or debate to move in a meaningful way, its participants must share, or at least have the illusion of sharing, a set of assumptions about language, communication, interpersonal relations, the nature of their world of reference, the way to make sense of it, and how to evaluate divergent understandings and adjudicate differences."[243] The three hermeneutical theories assume that the correct, intended meaning is determinable. This notwithstanding, Ẓāhirism—and textualism, for that matter—is not literalist for several reasons. Ẓāhirīs make use of pragmatic processes that are not linguistically required when interpreting texts. Rather than focusing on the semantic value of the text, they rely on the historical and textual contexts to determine the intended meaning of its author. Their consideration of the context allows them to depart from the semantic meaning of the sentence (or what the sentence "says") to what they believe the sentence intends to convey in a particular context (what it "communicates"). Finally, they interpret texts in light of various extra-textual considerations. Ẓāhirīs, however, are textualists because they insist on the supremacy of the text and take the context of speech into consideration in order to determine the intended meaning. This is the main difference between Ẓāhirism and textualism, on the one hand, and literalism, on the other hand. As legal theories, Ẓāhirism and textualism share many assumptions about the division of labor between lawgivers and legal interpreters, the objectives of the law, and the necessity to follow the methodology that is dictated and approved by the lawgiver irrespective of the result. Their differences only emanate from the nature of the two legal systems that they deal with, Ẓāhirīs with a religious law that is fixed in important aspects, and textualists with a positive law that can and does change.

---

242 To give one example of how literalism and textualism could be easily confused, Nabil Shehabi, giving an example of Ibn Ḥazm's literalism that adheres to "what is clearly stated in the established texts," mentions Ibn Ḥazm's rejection to attribute a body to God since "nowhere in the Qur'an is He so described" (Shehabi, "Illa and Qiyas," p. 32). Obviously, this view is not based on any reading of any text; rather, it is based on the absence of any relevant text. In other words, it is Ibn Ḥazm's textualism rather than his presumed literalism that led him to this and other views.

243 Crapanzano, *Serving the Word*, pp. 332–333.

CHAPTER 6

Case Studies

Several arguments have been made about Dāwūd al-Ẓāhirī and his juridical thought (i.e., Ẓāhirism) in the previous chapters. One of these is that what we know about him strongly suggests that he was closer in both personal profile and jurisprudence to the *Ahl al-Raʾy* than to the *Ahl al-Ḥadīth*, the two leading legal trends in his time. A strong connection between the general, unrestricted meaning of terms (*al-ʿumūm*) and the *ẓāhir* meaning has been argued in the previous two chapters. We have also discussed the relationship between the subject of *ʿumūm* and other key notions in Ẓāhirī jurisprudence, namely, the principles of *al-ibāḥah al-aṣliyyah* and *istiṣḥāb al-ḥāl*, as well as the rejection of *qiyās*. It has been argued that Ẓāhirīs, like the *Ahl al-Raʾy* and American textualists, give consistency and systematization a special emphasis in their jurisprudence. This concern for consistency requires that legal thinking be governed by specific assumptions and proceed on the basis of well-defined rules that regulate the process of determining the right meaning of legal texts and systematize the use of textual evidence. On the other hand, the *Ahl al-Ḥadīth*, particularly Aḥmad ibn Ḥanbal, were less interested in consistency and more concerned about "morality," meaning that ethical considerations were given priority in his jurisprudence. In this, he resembles intentionalist jurists who maintain that the law has a "spirit" and general objectives that it seeks to secure or protect more than the strict adherence to the text of the law or even the immediate benefits for the society and individuals. Another feature of Ibn Ḥanbal's jurisprudence, which feature is strongly related to his moral approach to legal issues, is his keenness to reconcile and synthesize all available evidence on a given issue. This concern for morality and for not abandoning any part of the evidence in a given question was the source of the main tension in his jurisprudence, which tension his reported hesitation about many issues makes evident.

The following case studies, including those that belong strictly to the ritualistic part of Islamic law, have a clear social dimension. This makes possible drawing conclusions about the concerns that may have underlined various views thereon, as well as putting to the test some of our conclusions about Dāwūd and his Ẓāhirism and how it compares with the juridical thought of both the *Ahl al-Raʾy* and the *Ahl al-Ḥadīth*. In the first two case studies, which are discussed at length, the evidence that could have been available to jurists starting from the second half of the 2nd century AH is presented and

 | DOI 10.1163/9789004279650_008

discussed. This includes Qurʾānic verses as well as Prophetic traditions and non-Prophetic reports. Qurʾān commentaries that were written in the first three centuries AH are used to examine how the relevant verses were interpreted. Ḥadīth compilations are used to identify relevant traditions and reports, paying particular attention to works compiled in the second half of the 2nd century AH in order to investigate whether the evidence that was available to Ibn Ḥanbal and Dāwūd in the 3rd/9th century was also available to Abū Ḥanīfah a hundred years earlier.

Works on legal disagreements (*ikhtilāf*) provide an idea about the evidence that may have been used by early jurists on each question under discussion, although they can at times be reticent about why a certain jurist held a certain opinion and on the basis of what evidence. To remedy this, some legal works of the *madhhab*s of Abū Ḥanīfah, Ibn Ḥanbal, and Dāwūd are consulted. These works have the advantage of offering lengthier presentations and detailed argumentation. Their downside, however, is that they tend to confuse what the purported founders of their *madhhab*s held and what its later scholars thought. It is not always clear whether an argument made in a given case goes back to the founder of the *madhhab*, to later scholars who belonged to that *madhhab*, or even to the author of the work itself. Furthermore, while some of these works—many of which are also works on legal *ikhtilāf* (such as Ibn Ḥazm's *Muḥallā*, the Ḥanbalī scholar Ibn Qudāmah's *Mughnī*, and the Shāfiʿī scholar al-Nawawī's *Majmūʿ*)—seem generally "objective" in presenting various points of view on each question, it is natural that they would provide a more extensive and better-argued presentation of the views of their *madhhab*s. Because of the succinct nature of the first set of works (the *ikhtilāf* works) and the indeterminate and possibly biased nature of the second, it is crucial to note that the analysis put forward here of how and why each jurist may have come to a certain conclusion is admittedly presumptive rather than demonstrative.

It must also be noted that while the exact history of these works and their authenticity are beyond the scope of this study, it is here assumed that when taken together, all these sources can provide us with a reliable sense as to what was in circulation in the 2nd/8th and 3rd/9th centuries and how that may have been used in jurisprudence.

1 Long Case Studies

1.1 *"Touching" Women and Men's Ritual Purity*

This case deals with the question of whether touching a member of the other sex invalidates the ritual purity of either one or both of the two parties involved, assumed to be in a state of ritual purity (*ṭahārah*). The loss of ritual purity requires the performance of ablution (*wuḍūʾ*) before praying. Following the tradition of our primary sources, it is here presumed that the question has to do with whether a man loses his ritual purity if he touches a woman.

On this question, Abū Ḥanīfah held that touching any woman (including women forbidden to men, such as their mothers, daughters and sisters) does not influence the ritual purity of a Muslim man.[1] On the contrary, Dāwūd is reported to have held the opposite, insisting that a man who touches a woman loses his ritual purity and has to perform ablution before praying.[2] Without reference to Ibn Ḥanbal's view on this issue, this is how the opinions of these two scholars would have been reported to us. With reference to Ibn Ḥanbal's view, however, Abū Ḥanīfah's view would be that touching a woman does not invalidate the ritual purity of either the woman who is being touched, or the man who touches her, irrespective of whether *the touching is with or without (sexual) desire* (*shahwah*). Dāwūd's view would be that touching any woman invalidates the ritual purity of the man (but not the woman) who touches her, *be this with or without desire*. The reason why the two positions would be characterized differently if we bring Ibn Ḥanbal into the picture is that he made the argument that if touching a woman involved sexual desire on the part of the man who touches her, it invalidates his ritual purity; whereas if it does not involve any desire, it does not affect his ritual purity.[3]

Works on *ikhtilāf* mentions one Qurʾānic verse that was used as a source of legal evidence on this issue. This verse does not directly address the question

---

1 For the attribution of this opinion to Abū Ḥanīfah, see, for instance, Abū Yūsuf, *Kitāb al-Āthār*, pp. 34–35, and Abū Jaʿfar al-Ṭaḥāwī, *Ikhtilāf al-ʿUlamāʾ* (abridged by Abū Bakr al-Jaṣṣāṣ), vol. 1, p. 162. In his *Kitāb al-Aṣl*, Muḥammad ibn al-Ḥasan al-Shaybānī attributes to Abū Ḥanīfah the view that touching, even one that involves sexual desire, or even touching the genitals of the wife, does not invalidate a man's ritual purity. The only exception is when a naked couple lay together skin to skin and the husband's penis becomes erect (*idhā bāsharahā laysa bayna-humā thawb wa-intashara la-hā*) (vol. 1, pp. 47–48).

2 This is attributed to Dāwūd in, for example, al-Qaffāl al-Shāshī, *Ḥilyat al-ʿUlamāʾ*, vol. 1, p. 186, and Sharaf al-Dīn al-Nawawī, *al-Majmūʿ*, vol. 2, p. 32. In *al-Muḥallā* (vol. 1, p. 227), Ibn Ḥazm mentions that this is the opinion of the *Aṣḥāb al-Ẓāhir*.

3 Aḥmad ibn Ḥanbal did not in fact invent this argument, but it was thanks to him that it became an established opinion on this issue. Had it not been for him, this opinion would probably have been of minor significance in any discussion of this issue, just as was the case with other views attributed to earlier authorities on this and other issues. For Ibn Ḥanbal's opinion on this question, see *Masāʾil al-Imām Aḥmad ibn Ḥanbal*, by his sons ʿAbd Allāh, pp. 19–20 and Ṣāliḥ, p. 160, by Isḥāq ibn Manṣūr al-Kawsaj, *Masāʾil al-Imām Aḥmad ibn Ḥanbal wa-Isḥāq ibn Rāhawayh*, p. 77, and by Isḥāq ibn Hāniʾ al-Naysābūrī, p. 10.

of the things that invalidate a Muslim's ritual purity, but it speaks about the situation when a Muslim needs to perform minor or major ablution (*wuḍūʾ* and *ghusl*) but does not find water. In this case, "dry" ritual wash (*tayammum*) is licensed *in lieu* of the regular ritual ablution with water. Before giving this permission, however, the Qurʾān mentions some things that invalidate a Muslim's ritual purity, one of which is *lāmastum al-nisāʾ*.

> O you who believe! Draw not near prayers when you are drunken, untill you know that which you utter, nor when you are ritually impure (*junuban*), unless you are travelling, untill you have bathed. And if you be ill, or on a journey, or one of you comes from the closet, or you have touched/made love to women (*aw lāmastum al-nisāʾ*), and you do not find water, then go to high clean soil (*fa-tayammamū ṣaʿīd ṭayyib*) and rub your faces and your hands (therewith). Lo! Allāh is Pardoning, Forgiving (Q. 4:43).

In one of the earliest available Qurʾān commentaries, Mujāhid ibn Jabr reports, seemingly approvingly, only one tradition that goes back to al-Ḥasan al-Baṣrī (d. 110/728), according to which "*al-mulāmasah*" in this verse refers to sexual intercourse (*al-jimāʿ*).[4] Both Zayd ibn ʿAlī (d. 122/740) and Muqātil ibn Sulaymān held the same view.[5]

In the late 3rd century, there existed many reports from earlier scholars on the meaning of *lāmastum* in this verse. Al-Ṭabarī gives a list of the early jurists who held various opinions on it meaning. Ibn ʿAbbās is mentioned as the Companion who held that *lams, mass* and *mubāsharah* all refer to sexual intercourse (*al-jimāʿ*) and that God only alludes to it out of decency (*wa-lākinna Allāh yaʿiffu wa-yaknī*). This report was transmitted by the famous jurist Saʿīd ibn Jubayr (d. 95/714) and a son of Ibn ʿAbbās's. Saʿīd ibn Jubayr also reports a number of anecdotes, with various names, according to which some jurists disagreed on this question on ethnic lines: while the Arabs argued that *lams* in the verse was used figuratively to refer to sexual intercourse, non-Arab clients (*mawālī*) stuck to the *ẓāhir* meaning of the verb and argued that it referred to any skin to skin contact. When they asked Ibn ʿAbbās about it, he said that the Arabs won and the *mawālī* lost, meaning that the Arabs understood it correctly. Ibn ʿAbbās was followed on this by al-Ḥasan al-Baṣrī, Mujāhid ibn Jabr, and Qatādah ibn Diʿāmah (d. 117/735). ʿAbd Allāh ibn Masʿūd and ʿAbd

4 Mujāhid ibn Jabr, *Tafsīr Mujāhid ibn Jabr*, vol. 1, p. 159.

5 For this, see Zayd ibn ʿAlī, *Tafsīr Zayd ibn ʿAlī*, p. 119, and Muqātil ibn Sulaymān, *Tafsīr Muqātil ibn Sulaymān*, vol. 1, p. 375.

Allāh ibn ʿUmar are mentioned as the Companions who maintained that any touching of any woman invalidates men's ritual purity.[6] Among the Successors, al-Ḥakam ibn ʿUtaybah (d. 115/733) and Ḥammād ibn Abī Sulaymān held this opinion, whereas Ibrāhīm al-Nakhaʿī is reported to have believed that touching invalidates ritual purity only when it involves desire.[7]

Al-Ṭabarī's own position on this subject is ambivalent. He begins his discussion by stating that *lāmastum* means "you touched women with your hands" (*bāshartum al-nisāʾ bi-aydīkum*).[8] Later, he mentions a number of anecdotes according to which the Prophet kissed one of his wives and went to the prayers without performing ritual ablution. With the exception of only one tradition that was attributed to Umm Salamah (Hind bint Abī Umayyah, d. 59/678), a wife of the Prophet (who mentioned that the Prophet once kissed her while he was fasting and did not break his fast or repeat his ablution), all these traditions were narrated by ʿĀʾishah bint Abī Bakr (d. *c.* 58/678)—apparently the wife whom the Prophet kissed—and transmitted by a certain ʿUrwah, a certain Ibrāhīm al-Taymī, and a certain Zaynab al-Sahmiyyah. Commenting on these traditions and concluding his discussion of this subject, al-Ṭabarī argues that they offer "clear evidence" that *lams* in this context means sexual intercourse.[9]

In addition to the evidence from the Qurʾān, works on *ikhtilāf* and some Ḥadīth compilations that have chapters on this issue mention a number of Prophetic traditions in the context of this subject. There are generally two major sets of traditions (with various versions) and a few other traditions that were brought to the discussion by some isolated scholars.

The recurrent theme in the first set of traditions is that the Prophet kissed one of his wives and prayed without performing ritual ablution. With the exception of one version by Umm Salamah, which is mentioned by al-Ṭabarī and very few other scholars, and the isolated version of Ḥafsah bint ʿUmar ibn al-Khaṭṭāb (d. 41/661), which was transmitted by Abū Ḥanīfah himself,[10] most versions of this tradition feature ʿĀʾishah as transmitter. From very early it became one of the most popular traditions in discussions of this subject, and in later works of jurisprudence it became the standard source of Prophetic Sunnah on the matter. As early as the late 2nd century AH, it was mentioned as evidence for

6 Muḥammad ibn Jarīr al-Ṭabarī, *Jāmiʿ al-Bayān*, vol. 5, pp. 102–104.

7 *Ibid.*, vol. 5, pp. 104–105.

8 *Ibid.*, vol. 5, p. 101.

9 *Ibid.*, vol. 5, p. 106. For these traditions, see *ibid.*, vol. 5, pp. 105–106.

10 *Musnad Abī Ḥanīfah*, collected by Abū Nuʿaym al-Iṣbahānī. Abū Ḥanīfah transmitted this tradition from the Kufan Abū Rawq ʿAṭiyyah ibn al-Ḥārith. I have not found this tradition anywhere else.

Abū Ḥanīfah's view in al-Shaybānī's *al-Ḥujjah ʿalā Ahl al-Madīnah*,[11] and later used by ʿAbd al-Razzāq al-Ṣanʿānī and Ibn Abī Shaybah in their *Muṣannaf*s in the context of discussing factors that invalidated ritual purity.[12] This tradition was transmitted by three persons from ʿĀʾishah. The most famous version was transmitted by ʿUrwah, whom most scholars take to be ʿĀʾishah's nephew and son of al-Zubayr ibn al-ʿAwwām (d. *c.* 94/712). ʿUrwah's version of this tradition is reported by Ibn Mājah, Abū Dāwūd, al-Tirmidhī, and al-Nasāʾī in their *Sunan* compilations.[13] Al-Ṭabarī's version from Ibrāhīm al-Taymī is reported by Abū Dāwūd[14] and al-Nasāʾī,[15] and his version from Zaynab al-Sahmiyyah is reported by Ibn Mājah in his *Sunan*.[16]

ʿĀʾishah also figures in another set of traditions that involves touching the Prophet, mostly while he was prostrating. According to one of these, the Prophet used to pray while ʿĀʾishah slept in front of him and her legs were in the direction of the *qiblah*. ʿĀʾishah mentions that when the Prophet wanted to prostrate himself, he would squeeze her so that she would fold her leg and then stretch it again when the Prophet stood up. This tradition is reported by al-Nasāʾī, who reports a similar tradition according to which the Prophet would touch ʿĀʾishah with his leg when he was praying. In a third tradition (also reported by al-Nasāʾī), ʿĀʾishah did not find the Prophet sleeping next to her one night when she started searching for him with her hand until she touched his feet while he was prostrating. She then mentions the prayer (*duʿāʾ*) that the Prophet was saying while he was in that position,[17] from which it was assumed that the Prophet did not interrupt his prayers because he did not consider his ablution void when she touched him.

A last Prophetic tradition that was used in this context was one that has the Prophet carry his grand-daughter Umāmah bint al-Ḥārith while he was praying. The relevance of this tradition was refuted by Ibn Ḥazm in *al-Muḥallā*,[18] which suggests that it was used by some earlier scholars as evidence for one opinion or another.

---

11 Muḥammad ibn al-Ḥasan al-Shaybānī, *Kitāb al-Ḥujjah ʿalā Ahl al-Madīnah*, pp. 65–66.

12 ʿAbd al-Razzāq al-Ṣanʿānī, *al-Muṣannaf*, vol. 1, p. 103; Ibn Abī Shaybah, *al-Muṣannaf*, vol. 1, p. 83.

13 Ibn Mājah, *Sunan*, vol. 1, p. 406; Abū Dāwūd, *Sunan*, p. 34; al-Tirmidhī, *Sunan*, vol. 1, p. 57; al-Nasāʾī, *Sunan*, vol. 1, p. 74.

14 Abū Dāwūd, *Sunan*, p. 34.

15 Al-Nasāʾī, *Sunan*, vol. 1, p. 75.

16 Ibn Mājah, *Sunan*, vol. 1, p. 406.

17 Al-Nasāʾī, *Sunan*, vol. 1, pp. 73–74.

18 Ibn Ḥazm, *al-Muḥallā*, vol. 1, p. 229.

In his *Muwaṭṭa'*, Mālik ibn Anas mentions the views of two Companions on our question. 'Abd Allāh ibn 'Umar is reported to have said that when a man kisses and touches his wife with his hand, this constitutes *mulāmasah* that requires performance of ritual ablution before praying. The same view is attributed to 'Abd Allāh ibn Mas'ūd.[19] As noted earlier, al-Ṭabarī attributes the same opinions to these two Companions, and during that time, reference to their opinions was made in almost all discussions of this subject. While most of the reports of Ibn 'Umar mention kissing in particular, others speak of all kinds of touching. In some of these reports, Ibn 'Umar defines kissing in terms of touching (arguing that "kissing is [a kind of] touching"),[20] which may indicate that for him it invalidated ritual purity for being just that. The same opinion is attributed to Ibn Mas'ūd, but in some versions, he adds to it lying with one's wife skin to skin (*al-mubāsharah*) and touching by hand. In his view, *lāmasa* in Q. 4:43 means pressing or squeezing with the hand (*al-ghamz*).[21]

Ibn 'Abbās, as we have seen, figures from early on as the Companion who held that touching women had no effect on the ritual purity of the man who touches or kisses her.[22] The story that Sa'īd ibn Jubayr reported on the dispute between the Arabs and non-Arabs on the meaning of *lāmastum* in the Qur'ānic verse is also reported in some early Ḥadīth compilations.[23] Other reports have Ibn 'Abbās argue that kissing does not require performance of ritual ablution.[24] In an isolated report, 'Abd al-Razzāq al-Ṣan'ānī mentions that 'Umar ibn al-Khaṭṭāb once kissed his wife and went to the prayers without performing ablution.[25] No direct statement, to my knowledge, is attributed to 'Umar himself.[26]

In the generation of the Successors (*tābi'ūn*), there are more statements that directly address our issue. In the Ḥijāz, Sa'īd ibn al-Musayyab (who mentions kissing in particular),[27] and Muḥammad ibn Shihāb al-Zuhrī (d. 124/742)

---

19 Mālik ibn Anas, *al-Muwaṭṭa'*, vol. 1, p. 87.

20 *Al-qublah min al-lams*. For this, see al-Ṣan'ānī, *al-Muṣannaf*, vol. 1, pp. 101–102, and Ibn Abī Shaybah, *al-Muṣannaf*, vol. 1, p. 84.

21 Al-Ṣan'ānī, *al-Muṣannaf*, vol. 1, p. 101.

22 See, for instance, *Masā'il Aḥmad ibn Ḥanbal* (by his son 'Abd Allāh), p. 20.

23 See, for instance, al-Ṣan'ānī, *al-Muṣannaf*, vol. 1, p. 102.

24 See, for instance, Ibn Abī Shaybah, *al-Muṣannaf*, vol. 1, p. 83.

25 Al-Ṣan'ānī, *al-Muṣannaf*, vol. 1, p. 103.

26 In *al-Majmū'* (vol. 2, p. 31), however, al-Nawawī mentions 'Umar among those who held that any kind of direct touching (*mubāsharah*), regardless of whether or not it involves intention or desire, invalidates ritual purity.

27 Al-Ṣan'ānī, *al-Muṣannaf*, vol. 1, p. 103.

(following Ibn ʿUmar in considering kissing a kind of touching)[28] were reported to have held that touching invalidated ritual purity. In Iraq, al-Shaʿbī is reported to have said that if a man kisses [his wife], he has to perform ablution.[29] The same opinion is also attributed to Qatādah ibn Diʿāmah,[30] Sulaymān ibn Mihrān al-Aʿmash (d. 148/765), al-Ḥakam ibn ʿUtaybah, and Ḥammād ibn Abī Sulaymān.[31] Contrary to this, Masrūq ibn al-Ajdaʿ (d. *c.* 63/682), al-Ḥasan al-Baṣrī, and ʿAṭāʾ ibn Abī Rabāḥ (d. 114/732) are mentioned as having held that kissing did not invalidate a man's ritual purity.[32] Sufyān al-Thawrī is also reported as having argued that if a man kisses his wife he does not have to perform ablution before praying.[33]

Ibrāhīm al-Nakhaʿī, who transmitted the traditions of Ibn Masʿūd and Ibn ʿUmar on this subject,[34] ruled that "if a man kisses or touches [his wife], he has to perform ablution."[35] In other reports, however, he is said to have argued that only when kissing and touching involve sexual desire does it invalidate ritual purity.[36] A similar opinion is attributed to ʿAbd al-Raḥmān ibn Abī Laylā (d. *c.* 83/702), who held that "if a man touches his wife with lust, he [has to] perform ablution unless he ejaculates."[37] Ḥammād ibn Abī Sulaymān agrees with this view, but adds another element to the discussion. Reported as having held that any touching invalidated ritual purity,[38] he thought that if a man kisses his wife when she does not want it, he has to perform ablution but she does not have to, unless she feels sexual desire. By the same token, if a wife kisses her husband while he does not want that, she needs to perform ablution, but he does not have to unless he feels sexual desire.[39] To those scholars who made similar arguments, al-Nawawī adds al-Ḥakam, Mālik ibn Anas, al-Layth

28 Ibn Abī Shaybah, *al-Muṣannaf*, vol. 1, p. 84.

29 Al-Ṣanʿānī, *al-Muṣannaf*, vol. 1, p. 102.

30 *Ibid.*, vol. 1, p. 102.

31 Ibn Abī Shaybah, *al-Muṣannaf*, vol. 1, pp. 84–85.

32 *Ibid.*, vol. 1. pp. 83–84.

33 Al-Marwazī, *Ikhtilāf al-Fuqahāʾ*, p. 183.

34 For al-Nakhaʿī's transmission of Ibn Masʿūd's tradition, see Al-Ṣanʿānī, *al-Muṣannaf*, vol. 1, pp. 101–02, and for his transmission of Ibn ʿUmar's, see Ibn Abī Shaybah, *al-Muṣannaf*, vol. 1, p. 84.

35 Ibn Abī Shaybah, *al-Muṣannaf*, vol. 1, p. 84.

36 Al-Ṣanʿānī, *al-Muṣannaf*, vol. 1, p. 102. See also Ibn Abī Shaybah, *al-Muṣannaf*, vol. 1, p. 84.

37 *Ibid.*, vol. 1, p. 87. This, of course, means that he has to perform *ghusl* (washing the entire body) if he ejaculates.

38 Ibn Abī Shaybah, *al-Muṣannaf*, vol. 1, p. 86.

39 *Ibid.*, vol. 1, p. 85.

ibn Saʿd, Isḥāq ibn Rāhawayh, al-Shaʿbī and Rabīʿah ibn Abī ʿAbd al-Raḥmān (Rabīʿat al-Raʾy) in one opinion attributed to each of them.[40]

∴

The Qurʾānic evidence on this issue obviously triggered the controversy over it. The verb that Q. 4:34 uses for touching is not used in the first form (*lamasa*), but rather in the third form (*lāmasa*), which led jurists to interpret the verse variously. In general, some of them took *lāmasa* to refer to sexual intercourse, while others held that it only meant the mere touching of a woman, an understanding that the first form would probably have indicated straightforwardly.[41] What complicated the matter is that some Companions did read the verb in this verse in the first form, which reading is attributed to ʿAbd Allāh ibn Masʿūd[42] and maintained in the readings of the two Kufan scholars Ḥamzah ibn Ḥabīb al-Zayyāt (d. 156/772) and ʿAlī ibn Ḥamzah al-Kisāʾī (d. 189/805).[43]

In the earliest available Qurʾān commentaries, *lāmastum* was understood to mean *jāmaʿtum*, viz. having sexual intercourse. The first Qurʾān commentary in which a controversy about this verb is reported is al-Ṭabarī's, which suggests that in the two centuries between Mujāhid and al-Ṭabarī something heated up the debate about this issue in Iraq, an observation discussed in a later context. Needless to say, the various ways this verb was construed by early scholars must have had a correlation with what they thought about this issue. Those who believed that *lāmasa* meant sexual intercourse, like Ibn ʿAbbās, would be able to exclude this verse from the debate over the issue of touching a woman and its effect on the validity or otherwise of men's ritual purity when they

40 Al-Nawawī, *al-Majmūʿ*, vol. 1, p. 31.

41 Some scholars held that *lamasa* (the first form of the verb) is a homonym, which means that even if this form had been used, the controversy over the meaning of the verb would still have taken place. This view was not mentioned by most of the *ikhtilāf* works consulted here, although it was used by some others (see, for instance, Ibn Rushd, *Bidāyat al-Mujtahid*, vol. 1, pp. 77–78). Most other scholars, however, seem to have discussed the use of the third form in this verse in terms of the *ḥaqīqah* vs. *majāz* dichotomy, probably following Ibn ʿAbbās's anecdote where the Arabs, with their genuine sense of the language, won over the *mawālī* who failed to differentiate between God meaning what he says or only alluding to something else.

42 See Ibn Qudāmah, *al-Mughnī*, vol. 1, p. 258.

43 For this, see Abū ʿAmr al-Dānī, *Mukhtaṣar fī Madhāhib al-Qurrāʾ al-Sabʿah*, p. 113. The verb was read in the third form by all other readers (*ibid.*, p. 113). In *al-Muqniʿ*, al-Dānī mentions this as a case in which *alif* was removed for the sake (or by way) of brevity (*mā ḥudhifa min-hu ʾl-alif ikhtiṣāran*), p. 11.

touch women. On the other hand, for those to whom the verb meant the mere touching of a woman, such as Ibn ʿUmar, the verse could have provided the basis of the ruling on the question that all other relevant pieces of evidence would then be assessed against its backdrop. These pieces of evidence include reports about and from the Prophet Muḥammad.

Remarkably, none of the reports that involve the Prophet that were used by early scholars were immune from criticism by medieval scholars with regards to both their relevance and authenticity.[44] It has been noted that the tradition of ʿĀʾishah (in which the Prophet would kiss one of his wives and then go to the prayers without performing ablution, the assumption being, again, that he was already in a state of ritual purity when he kissed) became almost standard in most medieval discussions of this subject (although its relevance to the issue was not accepted by all early scholars, as discussed below). This tradition, however, was the target of much criticism regarding its authenticity. It is conspicuously absent from some early works where we would expect to find it. Zayd ibn ʿAlī, for instance, does not mention any tradition—including those reports from wives of the Prophet other than ʿAʾishah—in his *Majmūʿ* when he mentions that kissing does not invalidate ablution.[45] Mālik, too, does not mention this tradition, but not necessarily because it would contradict his opinion.[46] Nor does al-Ṭayālisī (d. 204/819) mention any version of this tradition in his *Musnad*.[47] In the 3rd/9th century, each of the three versions of this tradition was rejected by one or more traditionists. Its ʿUrwah version,

44 It is worth noting that although it may be expected to find traditions with clear-cut rulings on the issue of touching, which is most likely to happen on a regular basis for both men and women, early Muslim jurists did not invent Prophetic traditions to back their respective legal opinions. Finding no Prophetic traditions with unequivocal bearing on the subject, what they did was to try to find traditions that could be helpful, even if indirectly, in supporting their views. Arguably, the fact that no Prophetic traditions address this issue directly indicates that disagreements among early Muslims did not necessarily lead to fabrication of traditions. It also indicates that traditions used in this debate on the issue of touching are probably authentic, if they do not serve as conclusive evidence in another context.

45 Zayd ibn ʿAlī, *Al-Majmūʿ*, p. 65. As noted earlier, there existed other versions of the tradition that were transmitted by other wives of the Prophet which Zayd could have used, had he been aware of them.

46 Mālik did not have a problem with mentioning a tradition and contradicting it, as noted in chapter four. It is indeed striking that not a single tradition of those used in later discussions of the subject is found in his *Muwaṭṭaʾ*, which suggests that he either was not aware that they existed, did not think they were authentic, or did not think that they were relevant to the issue.

47 Sulaymān ibn Dāwūd al-Ṭayālisī, *Musnad al-Ṭayālisī*.

which was the most popular, was rejected by al-Bukhārī (and probably Muslim who does not mention it in his *Ṣaḥīḥ*) on the basis that Ḥabīb ibn Abī Thābit (d. 117/735) (who is supposed to have transmitted the tradition from 'Urwah) never in fact heard from 'Urwah.[48] Notably, it is even reported that Ibn Ḥanbal himself had some doubts about it.[49] Abū Dāwūd, however, quoted the 'Urwah version approvingly, but had to defend his selection of this version. He mentions that Yaḥyā ibn Sa'īd al-Qaṭṭān, the famous Ḥadīth critic, rejected it (al-Qaṭṭān is quoted as having said that this tradition was "nothing"). Abū Dāwūd also mentions that al-A'mash identified the 'Urwah in the tradition as 'Urwah al-Muzanī, from whom, according to al-Thawrī, Ḥabīb ibn Thābit used to transmit. Abū Dāwūd disagreed with this view, insisting that Ḥabīb did transmit sound traditions from 'Urwah ibn al-Zubayr himself.[50] Al-Tirmidhī mentions that "our fellow traditionists have abandoned the 'Ā'ishah tradition because they do not consider it sound on account of the condition of its chain of transmitters."[51] A few centuries later, al-Nawawī mentions that this tradition is weak according to the consensus of the traditionists, as it was declared weak by Sufyān al-Thawrī, Yaḥyā ibn Sa'īd al-Qaṭṭān, Aḥmad ibn Ḥanbal, Abū Dāwūd, Abū al-Ḥasan al-Dāraquṭnī (385/995), Abū Bakr al-Bayhaqī (458/1066), and others.[52] Ibn Rushd, however, mentions that while the Ḥijāzīs considered this version weak, the Kufans "found it sound" (*ṣaḥḥaḥahu 'l-kūfiyyūn*).[53]

The version of Ibrāhīm ibn Yazīd al-Taymī (d. 92/710) was similarly rejected by some scholars. Abū Dāwūd considered it weak because he believed that Ibrāhīm never heard from 'Ā'ishah.[54] Despite his view that there was "nothing better than [this tradition] in this chapter," al-Nasā'ī considered this version *mursal*, a tradition from the chain of transmission of which a transmitter is missing.[55] Ibn Mājah mentions this and the other two versions of the tradition

---

48 This is reported by al-Tirmidhī in his *Sunan* (vol. 1, p. 57) in the context of his discussion of the views on this tradition.

49 Ibn Qudāmah, *al-Mughnī*, vol. 1, p. 257.

50 Abū Dāwūd, *Sunan*, pp. 34–35.

51 Al-Tirmidhī, *Sunan*, vol. 1, p. 58.

52 Al-Nawawī, *al-Majmū'*, vol. 2, p. 34.

53 Ibn Rushd, *Bidāyat al-Mujtahid*, vol. 1, p. 78. Most likely, *ṣaḥḥaḥahu 'l-Kūfiyyūn* here means they were able to authenticate it, either by finding a better *isnād* (viz. one that is both connected and consists of reliable transmitters), or by supporting it with other traditions or simply demonstrating its consistency with any other source of the law.

54 Abū Dāwūd, *Sunan*, p. 34. Abū Dāwūd mentions that this tradition is *mursal* for the above-mentioned reason.

55 Al-Nasā'ī, *Sunan*, vol. 1, p. 74. In *mursal* traditions, the missing transmitter is usually the Companion, but in this case it was either the Companion or the Successor who

without commenting on their authenticity.[56] As for the version of Zaynab al-Sahmiyyah [bint Muḥammad ibn ʿAmr ibn al-ʿĀṣ]—which was mentioned by Ibn Ḥanbal in his *Musnad*,[57] Ibn Mājah in his *Sunan*, and al-Ṭabarī in his *Tafsīr* but was nonetheless the least popular version of this tradition—al-Dāraquṭnī is reported to have considered her an unknown person (*majhūl*). Later, al-Nawawī does not mention it even to say that it was yet weaker than the other versions of the tradition, which he also rejected.[58] The similar tradition of Umm Salamah, to my knowledge, does not exist in any source other than al-Ṭabarī, which holds true for the tradition of Ḥafṣah that Abū Ḥanīfah transmitted.[59]

In addition to the problem of authenticity, this set of traditions had another problem regarding their relevance to our case. Strictly speaking, this set of traditions deals with kissing, which is probably why Ibn Masʿūd and Ibn ʿUmar had to explain that kissing is a kind of touching. Although this set of traditions was brought to the discussions of this subject very early, a medieval Ḥanbalī scholar still felt the need to prove that kissing was a form of touching.[60] But if the relevance of this to the issue was dubious, this is even more so for the other important set of traditions, where the Prophet touches ʿĀʾishah while prostrating. For example, al-Bukhārī and Muslim, who have no chapters on *lams al-marʾah* ("touching women," which is usually mentioned in the *kitāb al-ṭahārah* among the things that affect ritual purity and make ablution necessary), report the various ʿĀʾishah traditions in chapters that have nothing to do with our subject. For example, al-Bukhārī mentions it in a chapter in *Kitāb al-Ṣalāh* (chapter on the prayers) on the issue of "Can a man squeeze his wife to prostrate himself?"[61] and by Muslim in the context of the prayers (*duʿāʾ*)

---

transmitted the tradition from ʿĀʾishah and from whom Ibrāhīm al-Taymī, supposedly, heard the tradition.

56 Ibn Mājah, *Sunan*, vol. 1, p. 406.

57 Ibn Ḥanbal, *Musnad*, vol. 6, p. 73.

58 Al-Nawawī, *al-Majmūʿ*, vol. 2, p. 34.

59 The person from whom Abū Ḥanīfah reportedly got the tradition was Abū Rawq, who, according to al-Nawawī (who mentions him as a transmitter in one version of the ʿĀʾishah tradition as well), was deemed unreliable by Yaḥyā ibn Maʿīn (*ibid.*, vol. 2, p. 34).

60 For an interesting discussion of the various kinds of touching, see Abū Jaʿfar al-Hāshimī, *Ruʾūs al-Masāʾil fī al-Khilāf*, vol. 1, p. 62, where the author argues that the "reality of touching" is when two "skins" meet, but it then differs according to the skin involved. If the touching is by mouth, it is called kissing (*qublah*), if by the sexual organ (*farj*), it is called sexual intercourse (*waṭʾ*), and if by hand, it is called touching (*lams*).

61 *Hal yaghmizu ʾl-rajul imraʾatahu ʿinda ʾl-sujūd li-kay yasjuda* (al-Bukhārī, *Ṣaḥīḥ*, vol. 1, p. 339).

that can be recited while bowing and prostrating, also in the *Kitāb al-Ṣalāh*.[62] The other similar tradition by ʿĀʾishah, where she mentions that her leg would be in the direction of the *qiblah* in front of the Prophet while he was praying, is mentioned by al-Bukhārī in a chapter on *al-taṭawwuʿ khalfa ʾl-marʾah* (saying supererogatory prayers behind a woman).[63] For his part, Ibn Ḥazm openly dismisses this set of traditions, not on the basis of their authenticity, but on the basis of the fact that we do not know much about their context. He argues that we do not even know that the Prophet was praying in the first place. Furthermore, the tradition as it is does not rule out the possibility that the Prophet did interrupt his prayers, if he was indeed praying, to perform his ablution anew. But the main ground on which Ibn Ḥazm dismisses the relevance of this tradition is his argument (which meshes well with his opinion on the matter) that in all circumstances the Prophet was the one who was touched, not the one who did the touching. It was the absence of *intention* (*qaṣd*) here that allowed the Prophet to maintain his ritual purity and go on with his prayers.[64] Ibn Ḥazm dealt similarly with the tradition that has the Prophet carrying his grand-daughter Umāmah, which al-Bukhārī reports in a chapter on "carrying a young girl while praying."[65] He argues that the tradition does not indicate whether the Prophet's skin touched Umāmah's, or whether he did not interrupt his prayers, performed ablution, and then prayed again. Be this as it may, Ibn Ḥazm points out, this set of traditions and even the first one were abrogated by the Qurʾānic *aw lāmastum al-nisāʾ*.[66]

Finally, acknowledging many of the weaknesses of this tradition, al-Nawawī similarly dismissed them as evidence for the argument that touching and kissing do not affect men's ritual purity.[67] The logical conclusion of all this for al-Tirmidhī was, "nothing from the Prophet on this subject [of touching women and how this affects ritual purity] is sound" (*wa-laysa yaṣiḥḥu ʿan al-nabī fī hādha ʾl-bāb shayʾ*).[68]

It is noteworthy that non-Prophetic reports associated with this subject reveal that it was purely Iraqi. Although there was some controversy on this

62 Muslim, *Ṣaḥīḥ*, vol. 1, p. 295.

63 Al-Bukhārī, *Ṣaḥīḥ*, vol. 1, p. 336.

64 Ibn Ḥazm, *al-Muḥallā*, vol. 1, pp. 228–229.

65 Al-Bukhārī, *Ṣaḥīḥ*, vol. 1, p. 338.

66 Ibn Ḥazm, *al-Muḥallā*, vol. 1, pp. 227–229.

67 Al-Nawawī, *al-Majmūʿ*, vol. 2, p. 34.

68 Al-Tirmidhī, *Sunan*, vol. 1, p. 58.

issue in the Ḥijāz,[69] Ḥijāzīs seem to have made up their minds very early that all kissing, as well as any touching that involved sexual desire, invalidated ritual purity. This opinion was probably established by Saʿīd ibn al-Musayyab and al-Zuhrī, following the example of Ibn Masʿūd and Ibn ʿUmar. In Iraq, however, the differences in opinion between ʿAbd Allāh ibn Masʿūd and ʿAbd Allāh ibn ʿAbbās seem to have instigated a disagreement that was never resolved either by their followers, or by the students of their followers. The majority of Iraqi Successors apparently accepted Ibn Masʿūd's opinion, according to which touching invalidated the ritual purity of the one who touches. While some accepted this categorically (like Shuʿbah, al-Ḥakam, and al-Shaʿbī), others sought to qualify it by introducing further elements into the discussion. Ibrāhīm al-Nakhaʿī and Ibn Abī Laylā, in an opinion attributed to each of them, introduced the element of sexual desire. Al-Nakhaʿī's student Ḥammād introduced the element of intention. Some other Iraqi scholars, such as ʿAṭā', al-Ḥasan, Masrūq, and Sufyān al-Thawrī, however, sided with Ibn ʿAbbās, not only on his opinion that touching does not invalidate ritual purity, but also regarding his view that *lāmasa* in Q. 4:43 refers to sexual intercourse.

The aim of this lengthy discussion of what was taken as textual evidence in this issue and of the opinions that were attributed to the earlier authorities is not to assess the evidence or the opinions. Rather, it is to find out what sort of evidence was used, even by later scholars, and how much of it could have been available to the three scholars whom we are dealing with here. What we have seen is much disagreement and contradictory opinions that the generation of Abū Ḥanīfah and later generations of jurists inherited and had to deal with. This is exactly what we need to be looking at to investigate how Abū Ḥanīfah, Ibn Ḥanbal and Dāwūd may have dealt with the legal legacy on this issue.

∴

On the question of what evidence was available to the three scholars on this issue, it seems fair to say that the evidence they confronted was similar. Abū Ḥanīfah was aware of the various views of the Companions and the Successors on the matter (i.e., their views of the meaning of *lāmastum* and on the issue of touching more broadly)[70] and a tradition very similar to the first tradition of ʿĀ'ishah (which he actually may have been aware of and have considered

69 For the views of Ḥijāzī Successors and early scholars on this issue, see al-Nawawī, *al-Majmūʿ*, vol. 2, pp. 31–32.

70 Abū Yūsuf, *Kitāb al-Āthār*, p. 5.

relevant to the subject).[71] By the time of Ibn Ḥanbal and Dāwūd, all the traditions used in this controversy were used and considered relevant by at least some scholars. It can be safely assumed, then, that the three scholars had similar raw material to work with.

Abū Ḥanīfah, Ibn Ḥanbal, and Dāwūd, nevertheless, came to three different conclusions on this question. When facing the various views on *lāmastum*, Abū Ḥanīfah chose the view that it referred to sexual intercourse, most likely on the basis of either one or both of the following two reasons. The first is the use of the third form of the verb, which was the most popular reading even if Ibn Masʿūd's reading, which had the verb in the first form, was popular in Iraq. This form must have suggested to him, just as it did to many other jurists, that it was *not* the basic meaning of the root *l-m-s* that was meant. If this is how he thought of the verse, then the case was almost done for him since there was no other evidence that he would consider on the issue of touching. However, it is also possible that Abū Ḥanīfah had rendered the Qur'ānic verse irrelevant to the discussion in a different way. The fact that even the Prophet's Companions were uncertain about the meaning of *lāmastum* may have undermined it as evidence in his view. If the Qur'ānic evidence is uncertain, there was no reason for him to ignore the evidence from the Sunnah, which is at least not less certain than the Qur'ānic evidence. In this case, only one text should be accepted and the other one assessed accordingly. Abū Ḥanīfah chose the Prophetic traditions (for reasons that are discussed below) and assessed all other pieces of evidence accordingly. In both cases, having neutralized the Qur'ān (by rendering the Qur'ānic verse irrelevant, or reducing its epistemological value as evidence), he was ready to turn to Sunnah, where most reports about the Prophet did not seem to indicate that touching women invalidates men's ritual purity.

But even if Abū Ḥanīfah had some Prophetic traditions from which it could be understood that touching women voided men's ritual purity, he would probably not have accepted them. This case falls under the category of what Ḥanafīs call *ʿumūm al-balwā*, meaning that it is a matter that happens frequently, no matter how unfavorable it may be. Touching a member of the other sex is very likely to happen frequently and on a daily basis. Accordingly, Ḥanafīs would maintain that if this was an issue that affected people's ritual purity (which means that they would not be able to pray unless they perform ablution), the Prophet would have made this clear, and the Muslim community would have transmitted it by way of (either verbal or practical) *tawātur*, just as is the case with other things that affect ritual purity. It was on this very ground that Ḥanafīs did not accept the isolated traditions according to which touching the

71 This is probably so because al-Shaybānī mentioned it in his *Kitāb al-Ḥujjah*, pp. 65–66.

male sexual organ voided ritual purity, as noted earlier. Since this was something that was liable to happen frequently, there should not be any uncertainty about it among the Companions and the succeeding generations.[72] In fact, it may have been for this reason that Abū Ḥanīfah did not consider Ibn Masʿūd's reading of the verb in the first form, for this would have had catastrophic consequences on one of the basic assumptions of his jurisprudence. He did not think that it was plausible for an issue like this to be handed down from the Prophet to the latter generations with all that confusion. He must have thought that this could not happen, and he was most likely unwilling to challenge his assumption of how such issues ought to be transmitted on account of an isolated reading of a Qur'ānic verse.

Abū Ḥanīfah, therefore, probably had no other choice but to proceed under the presumption of continuity, according to which, in this case, nothing voids ritual purity unless we know for certain that either God or his Prophet had so specified. Since this was not done regarding our issue, it followed that *no* touching of *any* woman had any effect on the ritual purity of men. The isolated reports of the Prophet's conduct must have added further confirmation for him. This does not necessarily means that this issue falls within the second category of knowledge that Jaṣṣāṣ would discuss (the category of uncertain evidence and of *ijtihād* which only yields probable results). Rather, it falls within the first category of knowledge, one in which we *know* for certain what the law has to say and how it should say it. But since the law is silent on this issue (for it cannot be explicit and ambiguous at the same time), then we have to adhere to the general rule, viz. nothing voids ritual purity other than that which is explicitly mentioned by God or His Prophet.

There are two points that are worth noting about Abū Ḥanīfah's view on this issue. He ruled against what seems to have been the general attitude in his region. Not only did he reject Ibn Masʿūd's reading, but he also rejected the views that were attributed to him and to Ibn ʿUmar concerning kissing and touching. More significantly, he rejected the views of his more immediate teachers: Ibrāhīm al-Nakhaʿī and Ḥammād. Other than pointing to Abū Ḥanīfah's independence as a jurist (as well as the diversity within the camp of the *Ahl al-Raʾy*), his rejection of both his teachers' views as well as the elements that they introduced into the discussion (sexual desire by al-Nakhaʿī and intention by Ḥammād) is significant. While it is not clear why he did not consider the element of intention (although we can speculate that the reason may be that Ḥammād did not provide evidence for his view), his rejection of

72 For the Ḥanafī notion of *ʿumūm al-balwā*, see al-Jaṣṣāṣ, *al-Fuṣūl*, vol. 2, pp. 6–7, and al-Sarakhsī, *al-ʿUddah*, vol. 2, p. 276.

the more popular, but fuzzy element of sexual desire seems to be in perfect line with what has been discussed earlier about his jurisprudence and his predilection for systematization. The reason is that the element of sexual desire suffers from two important weaknesses, subjectivity and uncertainty. Each of these elements suffices to disqualify it in a legal system like Abū Ḥanīfah's, where only an exact and objective criterion would be admitted. The only element that Abū Ḥanīfah is reported to have considered on this issue is that only when a man lies naked with his wife and erection occurs does he need to perform ablution. While it could be argued that erection here serves as the "objective" criterion for which he was looking, some later scholars—probably seeking to demonstrate that Abū Ḥanīfah was not as whimsical by considering this factor as other scholars (since there is no textual evidence for erection as a criterion)—argued that what he probably had in mind is the fact that more often than not, when a man reaches this stage of intimacy with his wife, he would discharge some pre-ejaculatory fluid that voids ritual purity,[73] as all *madhhab*s maintain.

Unlike Abū Ḥanīfah, considering the Qur'ān and Prophetic Sunnah two epistemologically and authoritatively equal textual sources, Dāwūd was considering the evidence from the Qur'ān and Sunnah simultaneously. He believed that the verb in the verse meant the mere and, apparently, the unconditional touching of women. He probably did not see why it should be understood otherwise. It is certain that the root *l-m-s* means touching, and even if it is assumed that the use of the third form of the verb *could* be suggesting something else, this does not furnish a valid reason for abandoning that of which we are certain for a possibility that could be right or wrong. Dāwūd's Ẓāhirism is quite obvious here: he takes the word to its fullest possible extension and potential range of referents, including any and all kinds of touching. Therefore, on the basis of the Qur'ānic evidence, *any* touching of *any* woman (be she the mother, sister, wife, or daughter of the man who does the touching) invalidates men's ritual purity.

But what about those Prophetic traditions that could be taken to suggest otherwise? The only element that Dāwūd was willing to accept and consider in this discussion was the element of intention, an element that is both objective and exact in the sense that the person who does the act can be certain of it (i.e., that he intended to touch).[74] This, Ibn Ḥazm argues, is an element that

73 Pre-ejaculatory fluid is called *madhy*. For this, see, for instance, Ibn Qudāmah, *al-Mughnī*, vol. 1, p. 230 and pp. 232–233. In Jaʿfarī Shīʿī law, however, *madhy* does not invalidate ritual purity (for this, see al-Sharīf al-Murtaḍā, *al-Intiṣār*, p. 30).

74 For this, see, for instance, al-Qaffāl al-Shāshī, *Ḥilyat al-ʿUlamāʾ*, vol. 1, p. 187.

is *inherent* in the very third form of *l-m-s* that the verse uses. While Ibn Ḥazm does not explain how this is so, it seems that for him the use of the third form rather than the first one indicates that the one who touches does so intentionally, which means that if a man unwittingly touches a woman, his ritual purity remains in effect, but if he touches her deliberately, regardless of any other factor, his ritual purity is void and he has to perform ablution again before praying.[75]

This understanding resolved any contradiction between the verse and the second set of traditions (where the Prophet was touched while, apparently, he was praying). As for the first set (where the Prophet kissed and then went to the prayers), Dāwūd must have concluded that these traditions referred to a time when the verse had not yet been revealed. The verse, in other words, abrogated the original rule and established touching as one of the causes of the loss of ritual purity (which Ibn Ḥazm argued), for in the case of contradiction in the available pieces of textual evidence, only one of them can be the valid source of the law in light of which all other pieces of evidence are to be assessed, either through reconciliation, if possible, or by the outright exclusion of one or more pieces of evidence on the basis of relevance, authenticity, or abrogation, which methods were all used by Ibn Ḥazm in his discussion of this subject.

For his part, Aḥmad ibn Ḥanbal had more pieces of evidence to consider on this issue. He had to deal with various views inherited from earlier generations on the meaning of the verse and the practice of the Prophet, and he had to do this in a way that would incorporate all or most pieces of the available evidence. He probably had two options which would both reveal the tension that was inherent in his jurisprudence. The first was to accept Abū Ḥanīfah's view, which was also the most popular view among the Companions and Successors (and this would have saved him from any embarrassment). But not only would this have put him at odds with the views of some great Companions like Ibn Mas'ūd and Ibn 'Umar, but he must have also felt uneasy about not considering the possibility that touching, especially when it involves a member of the other sex (who might not be related to the touching man) may have an effect on ritual purity, if only as a precautionary measure. Ibn Ḥanbal's scrupulousness was probably why he could not accept this view as it was. The second option was to accept the logic of the Ẓāhirīs, which was in all likelihood expressed by someone at that time, if not by Dāwūd himself. This, however, would have put him in sharp contradiction with the Prophetic traditions, the abandonment of which was not an option for him. His desire to consider all evidence was probably why he could not accept this option either.

75 Ibn Ḥazm, *al-Muḥallā*, vol. 1, p. 227.

If the following is a convincing approximation of how Ibn Ḥanbal resolved the problem, it clearly demonstrates the synthesizing nature of his jurisprudence and his moral approach at the same time. He adopted the element that Ibrāhīm al-Nakhaʿī had introduced into the discussion (and which Mālikīs partially used)[76] by making the entire argument revolve around the existence or absence of a particular factor, that is, (sexual) desire. If a man touches a woman with desire, or if he touches her and (unintentionally) feels desire, he loses his ritual purity. However, when he neither seeks nor feels sexual desire, his ablution remains in effect. This way, Ibn Ḥanbal combined all the seemingly contradictory evidence that reached him. If the Qurʾānic verse refers to sexual intercourse, this would make it irrelevant to this subject because intercourse has its own rules. However, if it means touching, then the evidence of the traditions *qualifies* this touching by *restricting* it to a particular kind of touching, viz. one that involves sexual desire. This would exclude women who are forbidden to men to marry (such as mothers, sisters, and daughters etc.), and would also neutralize "innocent" touching that could take place between a man and his wife. When it comes to women who are not related to a man, however, it is conceivable that Ibn Ḥanbal's scruples would have had him perform his ablution anew, and advise others to do so, every time they touch such women, for one may not always be able to exclude the possibility that sexual desire was accidentally involved.

This possible simulation of how Ibn Ḥanbal may have dealt with the seemingly conflicting evidence on this issue was in fact entertained by the Ḥanbalī scholar Ibn Qudāmah. He argues that Ibn Ḥanbal probably thought that touching invalidated ritual purity on account of the generality of Q. 4:43 (*li-ʿumūm al-āyah*), and thought that it did not because of the traditions of ʿĀʾishah in which she touched the Prophet while he was praying in addition to the kissing traditions. He then decided that touching invalidated ritual purity only if it was accompanied by sexual desire, combining thereby the verse and the reports (*jamʿan bayna ʾl-āyah wa-l-akhbār*).[77] What is remarkable in this view is that the element of desire has no basis in the Qurʾān or Sunnah whatsoever. Discussing the various views on the subject, the famous Mālikī scholar Ibn Rushd concluded that each of the early scholars (who had views on the

76 Mālikīs held that kissing, regardless of whether or not it involves desire, invalidates ritual purity. "Regular" touching, however, only does so if it involves sexual desire. For this, see Saḥnūn, *al-Mudawwanah al-Kubrā*, vol. 1, p. 131. Mālik also mentions the opinion of ʿUmar according to which both kissing and touching (*jass*) invalidate ritual purity and require new ablution.

77 Ibn Qudāmah al-Maqdisī, *al-Kāfī fī Fiqh al-Imām Aḥmad*, vol. 1, p. 90.

matter) had predecessors among the Companions, with the exception of those who made sexual desire (*ladhdhah*) a conditioning factor. "I am aware of no Companion," he points out, "who made it a condition."[78] But Ibn Ḥanbal had to deal with the tension that always existed in his juridical thought between, on the one hand, his moral commitments, which would have him wish to hold that the mere touching would invalidate ritual purity, and, on the other hand, his keenness to incorporate all available evidence. This tension is evident in the fact that two other views were attributed to him, according to one of which touching does not invalidate ritual purity irrespective of anything, and according to the other one it does, also irrespective of any factor.[79] This proves that Ibn Ḥanbal was hesitant about this issue,[80] but he (or his followers, following his example) later managed to find a way to reconcile and synthesize all the relevant evidence around a moral principle, where sexual desire serves as the basis of judgment.[81]

1.2 *Breastfeeding and Foster Relationships*

The second case deals with the number of incidents of breastfeeding (*raḍʿāt*) that makes an infant a son or daughter of the woman suckling him (who could be a relative or a wet nurse), with all the serious consequences that this entails in Islamic law.[82] On this question, we also get three different answers from the three scholars who concern us here. Abū Ḥanīfah held that even a single incident of breastfeeding establishes a foster relationship between the infant and the woman who suckles him or her.[83] Dāwūd held that at least three such

78 Ibn Rushd, *Bidāyat al-Mujtahid*, vol. 1, p. 79.

79 For this, see, for instance, Yaḥyā ibn Muḥammad ibn Hubayrah, *Ikhtilāf al-A'immah al-ʿUlamā'*, vol. 1, p. 53, and Ibn Qudāmah, *al-Mughnī*, vol. 1, p. 257.

80 Having various opinions attributed to Ibn Ḥanbal on one issue is not uncommon. For possible reasons for this, see Abū Zahrah, *Aḥmad ibn Ḥanbal*, pp. 189–199.

81 Remarkably, from the 5th/11th century the discussion of this subject would involve many other considerations, such as the presence of sexual desire or intention, the presence or absence of a barrier between the two people who touch, the age of the woman who is being touched, whether or not the woman is lawful for the man to marry, and the organs that are being used in touching (for this, see Ibn Qudāmah, *al-Mughnī*, vol. 1, pp. 256–262, and al-Nawawī, *al-Majmūʿ*, vol. 2, pp. 24–35).

82 All schools of law have accepted the tradition in which the Prophet is reported to have said that "Whatever is forbidden through lineage is also forbidden through breastfeeding" (*yaḥrumu min al-riḍāʿ mā yaḥrumu min al-nasab*). This tradition exists in almost all works of Ḥadīth and jurisprudence.

83 I did not find any reference to this in the works of Abū Ḥanīfah's immediate students (who do not mention the issue in the first place), but many medieval sources attribute this

incidents are required to establish such a relationship.[84] Aḥmad ibn Ḥanbal held that at least five separate sessions of breastfeeding are required.[85]

Q. 4:23 gives a list of various categories of women who are "prohibited" to men, i.e., women whom men cannot marry, either temporarily (such as a sister-in-law) or perpetually (such as the mother, sister, daughter, etc.). One of these categories of women is "your mothers who have suckled you" (*ummahātukum allāti arḍaʿnakum*). For legal and other purposes, suckling women become the baby's (foster) mothers whom (and whose mothers, daughters, and sisters, etc.) he cannot marry. Unlike the Qur'ānic verse in the previous case, there is no special difficulty in this verse, which is probably why Mujāhid ibn Jabr, Zayd ibn ʿAlī, Muqātil ibn Sulaymān, and al-Ṭabarī had nothing especially significant to say on this part of it. Furthermore, and also unlike the previous case, there are many direct and indirect reports from the Prophet on this question, which are arranged here in different sets on the basis of their content.

In the first set of traditions, the Prophet is reported to have said that a single incident of sucking (*muṣṣah*), or even two such incidents, do not establish prohibitive foster relationship (*lā tuḥarrimu 'l-muṣṣah wa-l-muṣṣatān*). The first tradition in this set was transmitted from ʿĀ'ishah by ʿAbd Allāh ibn al-Zubayr, and was mentioned by many traditionists in their Ḥadīth compilations.[86] In an almost identical tradition (whose only difference from this one is the addition of *min al-raḍāʿah* after *lā tuḥarrimu*), Ibn al-Zubayr relates directly from the Prophet himself a version that was used by, among others, al-Shāfiʿī, al-Ṣanʿānī, and Ibn Abī Shaybah.[87] A third tradition is related from Umm al-Faḍl bint al-Ḥārith (died during ʿUthmān's caliphate), a wife of the Prophet's uncle al-ʿAbbās (d. 32/653), from the Prophet, according to which the Prophet said that one or two incidents of breastfeeding (*imlājah*) do not establish foster relationship (*lā tuḥarrimu 'l-imlājah wa-l-imlājatān*).[88] This tradition

opinion to him and to all the *Ahl al-Ra'y* (see, for instance, al-Marwazī, *Ikhtilāf al-Fuqahā'*, p. 294, and al-Qaffāl al-Shāshī, *Ḥilyat al-ʿUlamā'*, vol. 7, p. 369).

84 For this, see, for instance, al-Hāshimī, *Ru'ūs al-Masā'il*, vol. 2, p. 196, al-Qaffāl al-Shāshī, *Ḥilyat al-ʿUlamā'*, vol. 7, p. 369, and Ibn Qudāmah, *al-Mughnī*, vol. 11, p. 311.

85 For this, see, for instance, al-Kawsaj, *Masā'il*, vol. 1, p. 386, and Ibn Qudāmah, *al-Kāfī*, vol. 2, p. 218.

86 See, for instance, al-Ṣanʿānī, *al-Muṣannaf*, vol. 7, p. 377, Muslim, *Ṣaḥīḥ*, vol. 2, p. 870, and Abū Dāwūd, *Sunan*, vol. 1, p. 517.

87 Al-Shāfiʿī, *al-Umm*, vol. 5, p. 44, al-Ṣanʿānī, *al-Muṣannaf*, vol. 7, p. 377, and Ibn Abī Shaybah, *al-Muṣannaf*, vol. 6, p. 206.

88 *Muṣṣah* refers to the act of sucking by the infant, while *imlāj* refers to the suckling of the nursing woman (for *m-l-j* and its derivatives, see Ibn Manẓūr, *Lisān al-ʿArab*, vol. 13, p. 167).

is reported by Muslim in his *Ṣaḥīḥ*,[89] and in his *Muṣannaf*, Ibn Abī Shaybah mentions the same tradition with *al-raḍʿah wa-l-raḍʿatān or al-muṣṣah wa-l-muṣṣatān*, instead of *al-imlājah wa-l-imlājatān*.[90]

In the second, and equally popular, set of traditions on this subject, ʿĀʾishah is said to have reported that a verse of the Qurʾān that was revealed to the Prophet and dealt with the issue of *riḍāʿ* specified that ten incidents of breast-feeding were needed to establish prohibition. This, she adds, was then abrogated by another verse which mentioned only five such incidents, which verse she says was still recited when the Prophet died. This tradition is reported in almost all Ḥadīth compilations and some early legal works.[91] In one report in this set, included by Ibn Mājah in his *Sunan*, ʿĀʾishah mentions that she had under her bed a sheet on which this verse was written, but it was eaten by a domestic animal while they were busy preparing the Prophet's body for burial.[92]

Some other Prophetic traditions are reported in the context of this subject and used by some later scholars for one reason or another. In one of these, the Companion ʿUqbah ibn al-Ḥārith went to the Prophet and told him that he had married a woman when a black slave girl told them later that she had suckled both of them. When ʿUqbah first mentioned this to the Prophet, the Prophet turned away from him. But when he mentioned it to him again, the Prophet said: "How [can you remain her husband] when she [the slave woman] has claimed that she had suckled you?" (*kayfa wa-qad zaʿamat anna-hā arḍaʿatkumā*?).[93] This tradition was reported by al-Bukhārī, al-Dārimī, and al-Tirmidhī in their compilations.[94]

In a different set of traditions, the Prophet is reported to have advised Sahlah bint Suhayl, a wife of the Companion Abū Ḥudhayfah ibn ʿUtbah, to "breast-feed" Sālim—who used to be Abū Ḥudhayfah's adopted son and then his *mawlā* when the Qurʾān prohibited adoption—so that he becomes prohibited to her. This tradition is reported without any number of suckling sessions in many Ḥadīth compilations.[95] In another version of it, however, the Prophet

89 Muslim, *Ṣaḥīḥ*, vol. 2, p. 870.

90 Ibn Abī Shaybah, *al-Muṣannaf*, vol. 6, p. 209.

91 See, for instance, Mālik, *al-Muwaṭṭaʾ*, p. 411, al-Shāfiʿī, *al-Umm*, vol. 5, p. 44, al-Ṣanʿānī, *al-Muṣannaf*, vol. 7, p. 373, and Abū Dāwūd, *Sunan*, vol. 1, p. 516.

92 Ibn Mājah, *Sunan*, vol. 2, 462.

93 A transmitter of this tradition seems to have inserted *fa-nahāhu ʿan-hā* to emphasize that the Prophet made ʿUqbah's wife forbidden to him.

94 Al-Bukhārī, *Ṣaḥīḥ*, vol. 3, p. 12, and al-Dārimī, *Sunan*, vol. 2, pp. 209–210.

95 See, for instance, al-Ṣanʿānī, *al-Muṣannaf*, vol. 12, pp. 366–367, and Muslim, *Ṣaḥīḥ*, vol. 2, pp. 872–873.

is said to have told Sahlah to suckle Sālim five times (*arḍiʿīhi khamsa raḍaʿāt fa-yaḥrumu bi-labanihā*),[96] or, in yet other versions, ten times.[97]

Related to this is a set of reports in which ʿĀʾishah would send the same Sālim, and other men whom she wanted to allow to be able to interact with her, to her sister Umm Kulthūm, asking her to breast-feed them. This tradition too appears without mention of the number of breastfeeding sessions,[98] but also with the ten such sessions that were required by ʿĀʾishah.[99] However, after mentioning the ʿĀʾishah abrogation tradition (where she says that ten was abrogated by five in the Qurʾān), al-Shāfiʿī says that none would enter ʿĀʾishah's house without completing five sessions of breastfeeding. He then mentions the tradition of Sālim where the latter says that he was only breast-fed three times by Umm Kulthūm, and was thus unable to see ʿĀʾishah because he did not complete the required ten.[100] A similar tradition has Ḥafṣah bint ʿUmar doing the same thing with her sister Fāṭimah, sometimes without mentioning a specific number of breastfeeding sessions,[101] and in other versions specifying ten such sessions.[102] Ibn Abī Shaybah mentions another report in which it was ʿĀʾishah who sent a certain ʿĀṣim ibn Saʿd to Fāṭimah bint ʿUmar to be breast-fed ten times, after which he was allowed to enter her place and meet her.[103]

In another set of traditions, the relevance of which to our subject will become apparent later, the Prophet is reported to have said that the breastfeeding that is effective in establishing prohibition (i.e., establishes foster relationships) is one which moves the stomach and takes place before weaning (*lā yuḥarrimu min al-raḍāʿah illā mā fataqa ʾl-amʿāʾ wa-kāna qabla ʾl-fiṭām*).[104] In ʿĀʾishah's version of this tradition, the Prophet once went home and found a man talking to her. The Prophet's face, ʿĀʾishah reports, changed (meaning that it became clear that he was angry). When she told him that the man was her brother's foster-son, the Prophet said: "Mind whom you take as your brothers; [effective] breastfeeding is one that results from hunger [in infancy] (*unẓurna man ikhwānukunna; inna-mā ʾl-raḍāʿah min al-majāʿah*)."[105]

---

96 See, for instance, Mālik, *al-Muwaṭṭaʾ*, pp. 408–409, al-Shāfiʿī, *al-Umm*, vol. 5, pp. 44–45, and Abū Dāwūd, *Sunan*, vol. 1, p. 516.

97 See, for instance, Ibn Qudāmah, *al-Mughnī*, vol. 2, p. 311.

98 See, for instance, Muslim, *Ṣaḥīḥ*, vol. 2, pp. 872–873, and al-Nasāʾī, *Sunan*, vol. 11, pp. 77–78.

99 Mālik, *al-Muwaṭṭaʾ*, p. 407.

100 Al-Shāfiʿī, *al-Umm*, vol. 5, pp. 44–45.

101 See, for instance, al-Ṣanʿānī, *al-Muṣannaf*, vol. 7, p. 376.

102 See, for instance, Mālik, *al-Muwaṭṭaʾ*, p. 408.

103 Ibn Abī Shaybah, *al-Muṣannaf*, vol. 6, p. 211.

104 Al-Tirmidhī, *Sunan*, vol. 2, p. 102.

105 Al-Bukhārī, *Ṣaḥīḥ*, pp. 1011–1012; al-Dārimī, *Sunan*, vol. 2, p. 210.

Views that are attributed to the Companions and their followers are not less numerous. Ibn Abī Shaybah attributes to ʿAlī ibn Abī Ṭālib (through Ibrāhīm al-Nakhaʿī), ʿAbd Allāh ibn Masʿūd (through al-Nakhaʿī and Mujāhid ibn Jabr), ʿAbd Allāh ibn ʿUmar, and ʿAbd Allāh ibn ʿAbbās (through Ṭāwūs ibn Kaysān) the view that any number of breastfeeding sessions suffices to establish foster relationships.[106] To ʿAbd Allāh ibn Masʿūd is also attributed the opinion that "[effective] breastfeeding is only one that leads to the growth of the flesh and strengthening of the bones (*lā riḍāʿ illā mā shadda ʾl-ʿaẓm wa-anbata ʾl-laḥm*)."[107] Abū Mūsā al-Ashʿarī is reported to have held a similar view, in which he speaks about the flesh and the blood.[108]

Zayd ibn Thābit, however, maintained that prohibitive breastfeeding requires three occasions of suckling,[109] while ʿAbd Allāh ibn al-Zubayr, who transmitted the Prophetic report according to which one or two incidents of breastfeeding do not make it prohibitive, is reported to have said that one, two, or three such incidents are not sufficient to make breastfeeding effective in establishing prohibition.[110] A few centuries later, Ibn Qudāmah attributes the view of his school (five breastfeeding sessions) to ʿĀʾishah, Ibn Masʿūd, and Ibn al-Zubayr, and the requirement of ten such sessions to Ḥafsah bint ʿUmar.[111]

Saʿīd ibn al-Musayyab, al-Ḥasan al-Baṣrī, ʿAmr ibn Dīnār, Makḥūl, Ibn Shihāb al-Zuhrī, Qatādah ibn Diʿāmah, al-Ḥakam ibn ʿUtaybah, Ḥammād ibn Abī Sulaymān, ʿAbd al-Raḥmān al-Awzāʿī, Sufyān al-Thawrī, al-Layth ibn Saʿd, Mālik ibn Anas, and the *Aṣḥāb al-Raʾy* are reported to have held that *any* breastfeeding is sufficient to establish prohibition.[112] To Abū Thawr and Dāwūd is attributed the opinion that three breastfeeding sessions are required to establish prohibition.[113] In his *Darārī al-Muḍiyyah*, al-Shawkānī attributes to, among others, ʿAṭāʾ ibn Abī Rabāḥ, Ṭāwūs ibn Kaysān, Saʿīd ibn al-Jubayr, ʿUrwah ibn al-Zubayr, al-Layth ibn Saʿd, al-Shāfiʿī, and Ibn Ḥanbal the view that effective breastfeeding requires five incidents.[114] Ṭāwūs is said elsewhere to have held that only ten incidents of breastfeeding can be effective.[115]

∴

106 Ibn Abī Shaybah, *al-Muṣannaf*, vol. 6, p. 211.
107 Abū Dāwūd, *Sunan*, vol. 1, p. 517.
108 Ibn Abī Shaybah, *al-Muṣannaf*, vol. 6, p. 210.
109 Al-Muṭīʿī, *al-Takmilah al-Thāniyah—al-Majmūʿ*, vol. 20, p. 91.
110 Ibn Abī Shaybah, *al-Muṣannaf*, vol. 6, p. 210.
111 Ibn Qudāmah, *al-Mughnī*, vol. 11, pp. 310–311.
112 Ibn Abī Shaybah, *al-Muṣannaf*, vol. 6, p. 211.
113 Ibn Qudāmah, *al-Mughnī*, vol. 11, p. 311.
114 Al-Shawkānī, *al-Darārī al-Muḍiyyah Sharḥ al-Durar al-Bahiyyah*, p. 346.
115 Ibn Abī Shaybah, *al-Muṣannaf*, vol. 6, p. 211.

If it was the Qur'ān that instigated the controversy in the previous case, it was, arguably, brought into the controversy over this issue quite unjustly. As it stands, the Qur'ān mentions the term *arḍaʿnakum* without qualifying it, which could be and was indeed taken to indicate that any breastfeeding is effective. This is in all likelihood why Mujāhid ibn Jabr, Zayd ibn ʿAlī, Muqātil ibn Sulaymān and al-Ṭabarī did not comment on it.[116]

The only issue that is relevant to the Qur'ān does not come from the Qur'ān that we have today, but has to do with evidence that stands, "literally," outside the Qur'ān itself, namely, ʿĀ'ishah's tradition of the abrogation of the Qur'ān, where she said that one Qur'ānic verse, which was part of the Qur'ān until the Prophet died, specified the exact number of incidents necessary to make breastfeeding prohibitive. It does not take an expert to realize how problematic this could be, for it simply suggests that part of the Qur'ān that was recited during the Prophet's life did not find its way to the Qur'ānic vulgate later on. This is an issue whose significance goes far beyond Islamic law and is beyond the scope of this study. For our purposes, however, this is a case of what may be called "compound abrogation." Not only was the verse that mentioned ten incidents of breastfeeding abrogated by another that mentioned only five (a typical case of abrogation), but the whole revelation on this issue was also dropped from the text of the Qur'ān, an incident that is referred to as the "abrogation of recitation" (*naskh al-tilāwah*) Those who used this tradition in the debate on this issue said that this was a case of *naskh al-tilāwah dūna 'l-ḥukm*, i.e., the abrogation of only the recitation of the verse but not the legal ruling that it establishes, a notion that is not without its problems in both Islamic law and theology.[117]

This tradition does not seem to have enjoyed much popularity in the first two centuries of Islam. Ḥijāzīs, for instance, seem to have rejected it completely. In his *Muwaṭṭa'*, Mālik commented on the tradition by saying that that was not the practice in Medina.[118] Since the *Ahl al-Ra'y* in Iraq apparently did not accept it, it seems that it was not popular there either. Pointing out how problematic this report was, the Ḥanafī al-Jaṣṣāṣ argued that, to be consistent, anyone who accepted this tradition had to either hold that the Qur'ān could be abrogated after the Prophet's death or that it could not. If yes, he would be making a truly blasphemous statement that puts him in the category of the

116 Mujāhid transmitted Ibn ʿAbbās's view (considering any breastfeeding as effective), a view that was also shared by Zayd ibn ʿAlī (see Zayd ibn ʿAlī, *al-Majmūʿ*, p. 217). The fact that neither Muqātil nor al-Ṭabarī comment on this part of the verse indicates that they held the same view.

117 On this, see al-Jaṣṣāṣ, *al-Fuṣūl*, vol. 1, pp. 389ff.

118 Mālik, *al-Muwaṭṭa'*, p. 411.

enemies of the Qur'ān. If he does not believe that it is possible, however, that the Qur'ān be abrogated in any way after the Prophet's death, then he cannot use this tradition as evidence in this case. This report, therefore, is baseless either on the basis of the (lack of) integrity (*ʿadālah*) of its transmitters, or on the basis of their (in)accuracy (*ḍabṭ*). In other words, the tradition, as it is, was either deliberately fabricated, or was transmitted by careless traditionists who inadvertently made changes to its content.[119] This is not to say that the report was abandoned. In fact, it was this report in particular that al-Shāfiʿī and later Ibn Ḥazm (against his school) relied on as a basis for the requirement of five incidents of breastfeeding.

In this case, it was the various traditions that were attributed to the Prophet that clouded the picture, especially since every set of traditions that different scholars used had some problems. The first set of traditions (where the Prophet says that one or two incidents of breastfeeding do not suffice to make it effective) seems to have been accepted, in one of its versions or another, by many early and medieval scholars, although the fact that neither the majority of the *Ahl al-Raʾy* in Iraq nor the Ḥijāzīs accepted it (witness their view on this issue) suggests that there were some uncertainties surrounding it. Again, because of the limitations of the sources, speculation is inevitable here. It is possible that early scholars noticed that in the ʿUrwah version of the tradition (which was by far the most famous one from ʿĀ'ishah), he transmitted the tradition from ʿĀ'ishah at times, and directly from the Prophet (whom he never actually saw) at other times. He was also reported to have transmitted other reports from ʿĀ'ishah in which she mentioned five, seven, and ten incidents of breastfeeding that were required to make it effective in establishing foster relationships.[120] All this must have cast doubt not only on the attribution of the traditions to the Prophet, but also on the strength of the evidence that it could furnish as to the number of incidents that make breastfeeding effective.[121] Furthermore, this and the similar traditions were problematic for both groups of scholars, those who held that any breastfeeding was effective, and those who argued that fewer than five incidents of it were not effective, although the latter group must have been in a better position to reconcile the two sets of traditions (by arguing, for instance, that the Prophet said that one or two incidents were not effective, which we know for certain, but did not say that three or four were, which could be taken to admit other possibilities).

---

119 Al-Jaṣṣāṣ, *al-Fuṣūl*, vol. 1, pp. 399–400.

120 For this, see, for instance, Ibn Ḥazm, *al-Muḥallā*, vol. 10, pp. 189–191.

121 See, for instance, *ibid.*, vol. 10, p. 201, where Ibn Ḥazm mentions this opinion to refute it.

Furthermore, the ʿUqbah tradition could have been easily neutralized. Those who used the tradition must have made the argument that the Prophet did not ask about the number of breastfeeding sessions (which the slave women spoke about) because, they would say, it was not relevant. We have seen in the first case that those traditions the context of which was not clearly identified could be easily dismissed. Just as we do not know whether the Prophet's skin touched his grand-daughter's, as Ibn Ḥazm argued in the previous case study, we also do not know whether or not he knew that ʿUqbah was not aware of what constituted effective breastfeeding. In all circumstances, this tradition, probably for this or similar reasons, did not seem to have been very popular on this subject. Al-Bukhārī, for instance, mentions it only in a chapter on the testimonies of nursing women, and not in the chapter on the number of breastfeeding sessions required to establish foster relationships, which suggests that he did not consider it relevant to our subject.

The remaining set of traditions, that of Sahlah bint Suhayl and Sālim, and the other traditions of ʿĀʾishah and Ḥafṣah (where they are reported to have had their nieces or sisters breast-feed men), were used as evidence on two different issues. When no number of breastfeeding incidents was mentioned, they were primarily used in the chapter on the notion of "adult breastfeeding" (*riḍāʿ al-kabīr*). They were brought to the context of our question only when they mentioned the number that was required by the Prophet and his wives to establish the "desired" prohibitive relationship. In both cases, where the numbers are mentioned and where they are not, adult breastfeeding is an integral part of these traditions, which means that if a scholar rejects this notion, he cannot use these traditions, even when they give numbers, to substantiate his view on our subject. This notion of adult breastfeeding, however, has caused heated controversies in Islamic law and has been rejected by many scholars on the basis of its content.[122]

But this set of traditions could have been, and was indeed countered by, the other Prophetic traditions, some of which were also narrated by ʿĀʾishah,

122 These traditions still stir controversies today. In 2007, the Head of the Ḥadīth Unit in al-Azhar University in Egypt was fired from his position because he argued that these traditions could provide a solution for the prohibited *khalwah*—viz. a situation where a man and an unrelated woman are alone such that they can have a intimate relationship without being seen, which situation many Egyptian men and women find themselves in for many reasons, especially in the work place. An emergency meeting was called for and the Shaykh al-Azhar, the President of al-Azhar University, and other top officials in al-Azhar University agreed that what the Head of the Unit said disqualified him as a scholar.

in which the Prophet apparently says that effective breastfeeding is one that takes place before weaning and contributes to the growth of the body (which usually happens to infants but not to adults). Therefore, breastfeeding an adult is not valid and consequently does not establish any prohibitive relationship. This, it must be noted, is the context in which these traditions were mentioned very early. In his *Kitāb al-Āthār*, al-Shaybānī mentions that a husband went to Abū Mūsā al-Ashʿarī and told him that after his wife gave birth, their child died and her breast was full of milk. To get rid of the milk, she asked him to suck and spit it out. The husband unintentionally swallowed some of the milk. Abū Mūsā told him that this made his wife forbidden to him. When he went to Ibn Masʿūd, however, Ibn Masʿūd told him that he was attending to her medical needs (*inna-mā kunta mudāwiyan*), and that "there is no breastfeeding after weaning; [effective] breastfeeding is that which contributes to the growth of flesh and bones."[123]

The notion of adult breastfeeding, therefore, was reportedly rejected by the majority of the Companions, such as ʿUmar ibn al-Khaṭṭāb, Ibn Masʿūd, ʿAlī ibn Abī Ṭālib, Abū Hurayrah, Abū Mūsā, Ibn ʿAbbās, and Umm Salamah, and by the Successors Saʿīd ibn al-Musayyab, Sulaymān ibn Yasār, ʿAmr ibn Dīnār, ʿAṭāʾ, and al-Shaʿbī.[124] It is even reported that all the Prophet's wives told ʿĀʾishah that the Sālim tradition provided a special ruling for that particular case, and rejected allowing any men to enter to them through this method.[125] Many reports mention that ʿUmar ibn al-Khaṭṭāb used to punish those women who would breast-feed other women to make them forbidden to their husbands.[126] Just as the majority of Iraqi and Ḥijāzī scholars rejected the ʿĀʾishah abrogation reports, so also they rejected her opinion on this matter. Al-Zuhrī reportedly said that ʿĀʾishah continued to hold that breastfeeding after weaning was effective until she died, and it is not clear whether he wanted to say that she was the only one who held that view, or that she did not give up her unpopular view. In what could be taken as innuendo regarding the reports of her asking her niece to breast-feed men, al-Zuhrī also says that she mentioned five incidents of breastfeeding, in "what was reported to us, and God knows better" (*fī-mā balaghanā, wa-Allāh aʿlam*).[127]

123 Abū Yūsuf, *al-Āthār*, p. 134.

124 For this, see, for instance, al-Ṣanʿānī, *al-Muṣannaf*, vol. 7, pp. 368–373, and Ibn Abī Shaybah, *al-Muṣannaf*, vol. 6, pp. 215–217.

125 See, for instance, al-Ṣanʿānī, *al-Muṣannaf*, vol. 7, p. 366, and Muslim, *Ṣaḥīḥ*, vol. 2, p. 873.

126 Al-Ṣanʿānī, *al-Muṣannaf*, vol. 7, pp. 369–370.

127 *Ibid.*, vol. 7, pp. 367–368. For a full discussion of how these traditions were and could have been used as evidence here, see al-Muṭīʿī, *al-Takmilah al-Thāniyah*, vol. 20, pp. 83ff.

There is nothing significant about the views attributed to the Companions and the following generations except that they were sharply divided between those who held that any breastfeeding was effective for the purposes of our question here, and those who held that there must be a specific number of incidents of it (the minority). This last group was divided between those who held that there must be two or more such incidents (the minority), and those who held that there must be at least five such incidents to make breastfeeding effective in establishing foster relationships. Only a few scholars held the view that ten sessions of breastfeeding were required. The first view, of the unqualified breastfeeding, was dominant in the Ḥijāz and the most popular in Iraq. The other views were held by some scholars here and there in different regions.

∴

The way Abū Ḥanīfah, Ibn Ḥanbal, and Dāwūd dealt with the conflicting evidence and diverse opinions of earlier authorities on this issue seems to corroborate the arguments made about their jurisprudence in previous chapters. It is safe to assume that even if we cannot be completely certain that they were dealing with exactly the same raw material, the three of them were probably dealing with evidence that could have suggested to them any of the possible conclusions on this issue, which makes this case too suitable for comparing them.

Possibly starting with the Qur'ān and thinking on the basis of his assumption that any term must be understood in an all-inclusive, unrestricted manner unless its scope of application is restricted by a valid piece of evidence, Abū Ḥanīfah must have thought that the Qur'ān did not qualify (i.e., restrict) *riḍāʿ* (from *arḍaʿnakum*) which can possibly refer to suckling one drop of milk. It follows from this that any number of incidents of breastfeeding makes it effective in establishing foster relationships. Qualifying this term requires evidence that has the same epistemological value as the Qur'ān. But there were two main problems with the traditions that reached Abū Ḥanīfah from the Prophet. All these traditions were *āḥād* traditions, i.e., they rested on shaky ground in his understanding. Furthermore, and probably more importantly, they were contradictory and problematic. Similar to the first case, this issue, which took place regularly at that time, also falls within the category of *ʿumūm al-balwā*, where Abū Ḥanīfah would expect a clear ruling from the Prophet that is transmitted by *tawātur*. But this was not the case, for even if many Companions held that one or two incidents of breastfeeding did not make it effective, others held that *any* breastfeeding was effective, not to mention the other views that required more than three incidents of breastfeeding to establish prohibition.

This must have rendered all these traditions uncertain and therefore useless for Abū Ḥanīfah's purposes. This in fact is how the medieval Mālikī scholar Ibn Rushd accounts for Abū Ḥanīfah's (and al-Thawrī's and al-Awzāʿī's) view.[128] Abū Ḥanīfah, therefore, must have held that the evidence of the Qur'ān was the only relevant evidence, and without seeking to incorporate all reported views or consider extra-textual values of any sort, he simply argued that the Qur'ān mentioned *riḍāʿ* without qualifying it, so *any* breastfeeding was effective.

Dāwūd would have come to the same conclusion had he held the same view of the epistemological value of the *akhbār al-āḥād*. But since he thought that this category of traditions had the same epistemological value of the Qur'ān, he was willing to qualify the relevant Qur'ānic verse on the basis of one tradition or another. The real problem that must have faced him was that he had to deal with contradictory reports from the Prophet. Since he proceeded on the assumption that only one of the relevant traditions could be the source of the law on this issue, he was left with only two options: to show that all the traditions were sound but only one of them was the source of the law because the others were abrogated, or to argue that only one tradition was the source of the law because it was the only authentic tradition relevant to the question at hand. Our sources are not useful in indicating which route Dāwūd took, and what complicates the issue further is that Ibn Ḥazm himself differed with him and with all other Ẓāhirīs on this issue. He accepted the traditions, including ʿĀ'ishah's abrogation report that required five incidents of breastfeeding to make it prohibitive.[129] He refuted the use of all other traditions either on the basis of the unreliability of the transmitters or on the basis of their relevance, and defended the ʿĀ'ishah abrogation tradition against all the views that rejected it.[130] Rather than undermining our theory on how Dāwūd dealt with the evidence, Ibn Ḥazm's disagreement with him demonstrates that Ḥanafīs and Ẓāhirīs dealt similarly with the evidence. They considered only one textual source to be the source of the law and neutralized others, either by reconciliation, when possible, or by rejecting them as inauthentic or irrelevant. In either case, no factor, other than the certainty and authenticity of the evidence, is used to resolve the contradiction between the traditions.

---

128 Ibn Rushd argued that the reason why the three scholars came to this opinion was the contradiction between the *ʿumūm* of the Qur'ānic verse and the traditions, and among the traditions themselves (Ibn Rushd, *Bidāyat al-Mujtahid*, vol. 3, p. 315).

129 Ibn Ḥazm, *al-Muḥallā*, vol. 10, pp. 197–198.

130 For this, see *ibid.*, vol. 10, pp. 189–201, where Ibn Ḥazm also deals with other reports that other scholars relied on to substantiate their views on this subject.

Ibn Ḥanbal was almost in Dāwūd's position, but unlike Dāwūd, he was unwilling to give up any piece of evidence and was also seeking to define a criterion or factor, mostly of a moral nature, that would be the basis of reconciling, in his view, the various traditions on this issue. As in the first case, three opinions were attributed to him, in the first of which he said that only one incident of breastfeeding was enough to establish foster relationship, whereas in the second he said three, and in the third five.[131] Remarkably, the first source that mentions his opinion shows that he was hesitant about it. Al-Kawsaj mentions that when he asked him about the number of incidents of breastfeeding that establishes prohibition, Ibn Ḥanbal replied that one or two such incidents were not sufficient for that, which indecisive reply evinces his desire to avoid giving a definite answer. When al-Kawsaj repeated the question, Ibn Ḥanbal said: "If somebody says five I would not blame him, but I have some hesitation, although I see it [this opinion] as more solid."[132]

Ibn Ḥanbal, who had no problem with the issue of the Qur'ān being qualified by a Prophetic tradition, seems to have liked to consider any number of incidents of breastfeeding sufficient to establish prohibitive relationship as a precautionary measure that is inspired by his scrupulous character. It is indeed possible that this was the opinion that Ibn Ḥanbal held for some time in his life, and probably for this reason. Apparently, however, he eventually had to choose the many reports of ʿĀ'ishah about the five sessions of breastfeeding, without, at the same time, challenging the authenticity of the other reports from which it could be understood that any number of breastfeeding sessions that exceed two was sufficient for the purpose of establishing prohibition. But it seems that he did not make this choice to accept one piece of evidence and abandon another arbitrarily. The fact that most later Ḥanbalī scholars insisted that the "growth of the flesh and strengthening of the bones" was the conditioning factor that distinguished between effective and ineffective breastfeeding suggests that this was probably the basis that he considered. In a sense, he used another Prophetic tradition, which relates to an entirely different context (the context of adult breastfeeding) to judge the contradictory evidence that he had on our issue. Remarkably, while he used this part of the *riḍāʿ al-kabīr* tradition, Ibn Ḥanbal, and probably on the same moral ground, rejected the notion of *riḍāʿ al-kabīr* itself.[133] He must have used this same criterion to rule

131 For this, see Ibn Hubayrah, *al-Ifṣāḥ*, vol. 2, p. 148, and Taqī al-Dīn al-Subkī, *Takmilat al-Majmūʿ*, vol. 11, p. 310.

132 *In dhahaba dhāhib ilā khamsah lam aʿibhu, wa-ajbunu ʿan-hu baʿḍ al-jubn illā annī arāhu aqwā* (al-Kawsaj, *Masā'il*, vol. 1, p. 386).

133 For this, see Ibn Hāni' al-Naysābūrī, *Masā'il al-Imām Aḥmad*, vol. 1, p. 202.

on the questions of drinking the milk of the nursing woman indirectly, such as from a cup—either through the throat (called *wajūr*), or through the nose (called *saʿūṭ*)[134]—or eating the milk as cheese rather than drinking it,[135] opinions that only this factor (of contributing to the growth of flesh and strengthening of the bones) can account for, and that also point to the moral aspect in his thought (as it could be argued that he probably held these views as a precautionary measure).

Be this as it may, the similarity between this criterion that Ibn Ḥanbal relied on in this case and the element of lust which he relied on in the first case study above is unmistakable. Both are flexible enough to be used to reconcile various pieces of evidence. Furthermore, the fact that he did not try to hide his hesitation about this issue indicates that certainty was not an element that he worried seriously about. Abū Ḥanīfah and Dāwūd (and Ibn Ḥazm), however, were absolutely certain of the soundness and basis of their views, even if they disagreed, and did not seek to rest or qualify these views on the basis of any factor similar to the one that Ibn Ḥanbal selected and used. The only factor that they considered was what they accepted as evidence, and they followed that without seeking to relate it to any other factor.

2 Short Case Studies

2.1 *The Status of* Imraʾat al-Mafqūd

On the question of the marital status of a woman whose husband has disappeared, Abū Ḥanīfah and Dāwūd are reported to have held that she remains his wife until he re-appears or his death is confirmed.[136] Ibn Ḥazm cites various views of Companions on this issue, among which is ʿUmar ibn al-Khaṭṭāb's view, also held by many other Companions and Successors, that the woman has to wait for four years and then start a waiting period of four months and ten days (according to Q. 2:34, which specifies this waiting period for a wid-

---

134 For this, see Ibn Qudāmah, *al-Kāfī*, vol. 3, p. 221.

135 For the attribution of this opinion to Ibn Ḥanbal, see Ibn Qudāmah, *al-Mughnī*, vol. 11, p. 314. For the view that this is the basis of the prohibition, see *ibid.*, vol. 11, p. 315. Earlier than Ibn Qudāmah, the Ḥanbalī scholar Abū Jaʿfar al-Hāshimī had argued that, contrary to Abū Ḥanīfah, cheese made of a woman's milk is a valid way of breastfeeding, for what is effective as a liquid (*māʾiʿ*) is also effective as a hard substance (*jāmid*). Obviously, there is an attempt here to say that adult breastfeeding does not necessarily have to involve direct suckling. A woman can squeeze her milk into a cup from which the man would drink.

136 Ibn Ḥazm, *al-Muḥallā*, vol. 9, p. 323.

owed woman).[137] After the waiting period, she is free to get married.[138] ʿUmar's view was held by Ibn Ḥanbal, but he distinguished between a husband who disappears in war or at sea, and one who does not return home and nothing is known about his whereabouts. ʿUmar's view applies to the former case. In the latter case, the woman remains her husband's wife until his whereabouts are known.[139] Ibn Ḥazm criticizes all views on this issue, arguing that they rely only on Companions' opinions without any basis in the Qur'ān or the Sunnah. In his view, a wife whose husband disappears remains his wife and no one has the authority to declare her otherwise. Additionally, there is no waiting period for a woman whose husband has not died, and in the case under consideration, we do not know that her husband has actually died or not.[140]

Abū Ḥanīfah and Dāwūd probably came to their conclusion on the basis of Ibn Ḥazm's logic, for both accepted the notion of *istiṣḥāb al-ḥāl*.[141] Since it is certain that that the woman was her husband's wife, there must exist a valid reason to consider a change of her status.[142] Both rejected ʿUmar's view because it has no textual basis. Ibn Ḥanbal, however, accepted his view, but as expected, he does not apply it across the board. He had to deal with various views from the earlier generations of Muslims and find a solution that served the moral character of the community at the same time. When a husband disappears in war or at sea, while there is a considerable chance that he may have perished for reasons that are outside his control, there is also a chance of his return. In both cases, it is worth having his wife wait for him. Here he probably thinks of the husband and of what the community may expect of a wife whose husband disappears while fighting or working to provide for his family (if he is a fisherman, for instance). After four years and the expiration of the waiting period, however, his concern shifts to the fact that the woman has remained effectively unmarried for a long period. Ibn Ḥanbal is reported to have held

137 The verse reads: "And as for those of you who die and leave wives behind, they shall keep themselves in waiting (*fa-ʿiddatuhunna*) for four months and ten days."

138 Ibn Qudāmah, *al-Mughnī*, vol. 11, p. 248, and Ibn Ḥazm, *al-Muḥallā*, vol. 9, pp. 316–321.

139 Ibn Ḥazm, *al-Muḥallā*, vol. 9, p. 323.

140 *Ibid.*, vol. 9, pp. 326–327.

141 Ibn Qudāmah mentions that those who held the view that the wife has to wait until she gets news about her husband relied on a Prophet tradition in which the Prophet says that the wife of a lost person remains his wife until she learns news about him (*imra'at al-mafqūd imra'atuhu ḥattā ya'tiyahā 'l-khabar*) (Ibn Qudāmah, *al-Mughnī*, vol. 11, p. 249). The authenticity of this tradition, he says, was not confirmed and it was not mentioned by (earlier) traditionists (*ibid.*, vol. 11, p. 251).

142 This is the logic of some scholars who held this view, Ibn Qudāmah points out (*ibid.*, vol. 11, p. 250).

that marriage was obligatory (*wājib*) and that celibacy was not part of Islam.[143] But if a husband disappears mysteriously, his wife has to wait for him because there is always a chance of his return. Ibn Ḥanbal's concern for the marriage bond here and for not letting a woman marry a man while she is still another's wife overcomes his concern for her being unmarried. It is even reported that he expressed some hesitation about his view on the first case, when a husband disappears in war or at sea, preferring instead to keep his wife waiting until she dies or her husband appears or is confirmed dead. This is a more precautionary approach to the question, he is reported to have said, especially given that earlier authorities disagreed on it.[144] In both cases, Ibn Ḥanbal relies on Companions' views, yet he cannot provide any evidence from the Qurʾān or Ḥadīth for either view.

2.2 Ṭalāq al-Sakrān

On the question of the marital status of a woman whose husband divorces her while he is drunken, Abū Ḥanīfah is reported to have held that the divorce is valid,[145] whereas Dāwūd held that it was invalid and the woman remained his wife.[146] Three responses, expectedly, are attributed to Ibn Ḥanbal: she remains his wife, she is divorced, and a third response where he abstains from answering this question because the Companions disagreed on it.[147] Ibn Qudāmah mentions that those authorities who held that the divorce was valid relied on a Prophetic tradition according to which any divorce is valid except that of a madman (*maʿtūh*).[148] Some of the Companions and Successors who held that the divorce was invalid relied on this tradition, arguing that by analogy, actions of any person who is not in his right mind are invalid. Ibn Ḥazm, who did not accept the authenticity of the tradition,[149] accepted this view but not on the basis of this analogy. He referred to Q. 4:43[150] to demonstrate that a drunken person does not know what he says, for which reason uttering the divorce formula has no effect on his marriage.[151]

---

143 *Laysat al-ʿudhrah fī amr al-islām fī shayʾ*. For this, see Ibn Qudāmah, *al-Mughnī*, vol. 9, pp. 340–341.

144 *Ibid.*, vol. 11, p. 249.

145 *Ibid.*, vol. 10, p. 346.

146 Ibn Ḥazm, *al-Muḥallā*, vol. 9, p. 474.

147 Ibn Qudāmah, *al-Mughnī*, vol. 10, p. 346.

148 *Kullu ṭalāq jāʾiz illā ṭalāq al-maʿtūh* (*ibid.*, vol. 10, p. 346).

149 Ibn Ḥazm, *al-Muḥallā*, vol. 9, p. 475.

150 *Wa-lā taqrabū ʾl-ṣalāh wa-antum sukārā ḥattā taʿlamū mā taqūlūna* ([O you who believe] Do not approach prayer while you are drunken until you know [well] that which you say).

151 Ibn Ḥazm, *al-Muḥallā*, vol. 9, pp. 471–472.

Ibn Ḥanbal's—whose students adopted one or the other of the views attributed to him on this question—hesitation is not unusual. He could have chosen to follow any of the Companions' views on this issue or to rely on the *ṭalāq al-maʿtūh* tradition to come to a conclusion similar to Abū Ḥanīfah's. Apparently, he was hesitating between what he saw as two equally bad outcomes: the annulment of a marriage, and letting a couple live together when they may no longer be married. He does not seem to have thought of a possible formula that would allow him to say that it really depends on the situation and the parties involved. Be this as it may, his hesitation to decide on this question reflects the tension between his desire to reconcile and synthesize all available pieces of evidence (including views of the Companions) and his commitment to his moral worldview.

Abū Ḥanīfah relied on a text which mentions one condition that renders a divorce invalid. To remains faithful to his belief in *ʿumūm*, he considers this the only exception to the general rule that if a husband utters the divorce formula to his wife, their marriage is dissolved. It is remarkable that Abū Ḥanīfah did not use analogy in this case. He could have relied on what other scholars regarded as the "spirit" of the law on this question by considering not being in one's right mind, regardless of the cause, as sufficient reason to invalidate one's utterances. Dāwūd may have relied on Q. 4:43 to prove that a drunken person is unaware of what he says, for which reason he cannot actually divorce his wife in this state even if he utters the divorce formula.

2.3 Al-Luqaṭah

The final case concerns a find, known as *luqaṭah* in Islamic law. There are numerous questions about finds: what counts as a find, how should it be dealt with, if it should be publicized so that its owner can reclaim it, who would publicize it, how and where should it be publicized, what happens after it has been announced for one year (as discussed below), what happens if its owner appears after a year and his item has perished or been consumed, what happens if two people claim ownership of a find, etc.[152] Here we focus on the question of whether a person who finds something should take or leave it.

The Qur'ān does not speak about this issue, but there are seemingly contradictory Prophetic traditions on it. According to one tradition, when a person finds something, he has to declare it in public for one year, after which he is free to use it, but if its owner appears later, he has to return it to him.[153] According

152 For a complete discussion of this issue, see Ibn Qudāmah, *al-Mughnī*, vol. 8, pp. 290ff.

153 *ʿArrifahā sanatan, fa-in lam tuʿraf fa-istanfiqhā, wa-l-takun wadīʿah ʿinda-ka, fa-in jāʾa ṭālibuhā yawman min al-dahr fa-idfaʿhā ilay-hi* (*ibid.*, vol. 8, p. 290).

to another tradition, the Prophet told a person who asked him about a lost camel that he had no business with it, telling him to leave it until its owner finds it.[154] In a third tradition, the Prophet answers a question about a lost sheep by instructing the questioner to take it, for if he does not, another person or a wolf will.[155]

Abū Ḥanīfah is reported to have held that if a person finds something, he should take it,[156] or, in another view attributed to him, that he can take or leave it although taking it is preferable.[157] Relying on Prophetic traditions that indicate so, Ibn Ḥazm argues that it is obligatory to take a find and declare it for one year.[158] Ibn Qudāmah attributes to Ibn Ḥanbal the view that if one finds something, it is better to void taking it (*al-afḍal tark al-iltiqāṭ*), a view that is attributed to Ibn ʿAbbās and Ibn ʿUmar.[159] In Ibn Qudāmah's view, Ibn Ḥanbal held this view because of the risks involved in taking finds, which risks are evidently moral in nature. When a person takes a find, he risks consuming ("eating," in Ibn Ḥanbal's words, meaning taking into possession, sinfully here) something that is not his and is therefore forbidden to him (*ḥarām*). He may also be unable to publicize it in the proper fashion. It is more precautionary (*aslam*), therefore, to leave it altogether.[160]

Dāwūd apparently came to his legal conclusion on the basis of some traditions that indicated to him that one should take finds. It is likely that Abū Ḥanīfah did not consider any evidence on this issue valid, for which reason he held that it was up to the person, although he would prefer that he take it. Dāwūd may have thought about this issue in the same way. For both scholars, if there is no textual evidence on an issue, or if the evidence is too contradictory to be reconciled, the original rule of permissibility applies. Since there is no evidence that indicates otherwise, appropriating a find is lawful. As for

---

154 *Mā la-ka wa-la-hā? fa-inna maʿa-hā ḥidhāʾahā wa-siqāʾahā, taridu ʾl-māʾ wa-taʾkulu ʾl-shajar ḥattā yajidahā rabbuhā* (*ibid.*, vol. 8, p. 290).

155 *Khudhhā fa-innamā hiya la-ka aw li-akhīk aw li-l-dhiʾb* (Ibn Qudāmah, *al-Mughnī*, vol. 8, p. 290).

156 Al-Muṭīʿī, *al-Takmilah al-Thāniyah*, vol. 14, p. 503.

157 Ibn Ḥazm, *al-Muḥallā*, vol. 7, p. 115.

158 *Ibid.*, vol. 7, pp. 110–113. Ibn Ḥazm does not mention that this was Dāwūd's view, but the fact that he does not mention any disagreement among Ẓāhirīs on this issue suggests that this was the dominant view in his *madhhab*. The view that one should take a find is attributed to Dāwūd by Muḥammad al-Shaṭṭī without reference to any source (Muḥammad al-Shaṭṭī, *Majmūʿ*, pp. 23–24).

159 Ibn Qudāmah, *al-Mughnī*, vol. 8, p. 290.

160 *Ibid.*, vol. 8, p. 291.

Ibn Ḥanbal, what is remarkable is how he expressed his view on this issue. To avoid contradicting some Prophetic traditions and Companions' views (which indicate that one can take a find), he said that it is *more precautionary* that one does not take it. He does not say that taking it is sinful, and he did express views on what happens when a person does take it. Ibn Qudāmah's explanation of Ibn Ḥanbal's primary view on this question, however, is consistent with the contention made here that Ibn Ḥanbal was always grappling with the evidence, which, more often than not, is contradictory, and that his concern was focused on the morality rather than the legality of acts.

3 Conclusion

The purpose of these case studies has been to try to construct the arguments made by Abū Ḥanīfah, Ibn Ḥanbal, and Dāwūd al-Ẓāhirī on the five questions discussed on the basis of the textual evidence that was available to them and in light of what we have concluded about their respective juridical thought in the previous chapters. Admittedly, there is some circularity here, for we use what we have said about them to construct their arguments, and use this argument to support that which we have said. However, I hope that it has been clear that that was not done arbitrarily. No evidence has been deliberately twisted to be consistent with any pre-determined conclusion. The previous constructions were made smoothly and our previous discussions led them to specific directions in a rather natural way. However, as has been made clear at the outset, these constructions, despite all the evidence presented, remain presumptive to some extent.

The case studies discussed above reveal similarities between Ḥanafī and Ẓāhirī jurisprudence in terms of their assumptions and methodology. When dealing with a legal question, Ḥanafism and Dāwūdism typically accept one legal text (a Qurʾānic verse or a Prophetic tradition) as the primary source of evidence on the question and deal similarly with other problematic texts (which they usually reject as inauthentic or irrelevant). The presumption of *ʿumūm* helps them identify the *ẓāhir* meaning of the text they accept as primary. When formulating a certain ruling on the basis of this evidence, they consider it valid for all similar questions, regardless of the parties involved or any other personal or social considerations. Therefore, more often than not, they are able to say that something is either religiously/legally permitted (*ḥalāl*) or forbidden (*ḥarām*), but not that it depends on the situation. This is consistent with their concern for consistency and systematization of the law, as well as for a high degree of certainty.

In contrast, Aḥmad ibn Ḥanbal in all likelihood regarded morality as part of the religious law. For him, one thing can be *ḥalāl* in one situation but *ḥarām* in another. He therefore cannot answer a question like whether touching a woman invalidates a man's ritual purity in definitive terms. In his view, this depends on a *qualitative* aspect of the touching involved, just as the number of effective breastfeeding sessions is related less to their actual number and more to how much the milk that a baby suckles contributes to his growth. Yet Ibn Ḥanbal's other main concern was to synthesize all relevant legal evidence in each case, a job that was even harder for him than for other scholars given his consideration of evidence that others rejected (such as views of the Companions). The main tension in his jurisprudence, therefore, was his keenness to take all relevant evidence into account in a way that served his moral agenda. Striking a balance between these two concerns, or even prioritizing one over the other when reconciliation is difficult, requires flexibility in dealing with the available evidence. This need for flexibility may explain Ibn Ḥanbal's apparent lack of interest in, or perhaps dislike of, holding to rigid rules, as well as his hesitance in accepting some of them.

Conclusions

This study has begun with several questions about the Ẓāhirī *madhhab* and made three main contributions to our knowledge and understanding of its history and doctrines. These questions included whether we can study Ẓāhirism without exclusive reliance on Ibn Ḥazm's writings, what the term *ẓāhir* meant in the 3rd/9th century, and why Ẓāhirism failed to survive. It raised the question of what we can actually learn about the founder of the *madhhab*—Dāwūd ibn ʿAlī ibn Khalaf al-Iṣbahānī al-Ẓāhirī—and how this may confirm or call into question what is generally held apropos his scholarly profile and juridical thought. CHAPTER ONE has thus surveyed what medieval sources report about Dāwūd's life and doctrines. Biographical evidence on him has suggested that his overall profile was closer to that of the *Ahl al-Raʾy* scholars of his time, an issue taken up in more depth in CHAPTER THREE and CHAPTER FOUR. The meaning of the term *ẓāhir* and how it may have been used in the 3rd/9th century was discussed in CHAPTER FOUR. CHAPTER FIVE has questioned the received wisdom on the nature of Ẓāhirism, according to which it is a "literalist" legal and hermeneutical theory. Finally, CHAPTER SIX has discussed five case studies that sought to illustrate conclusions drawn in earlier chapters about Dāwūd and Ẓāhirism. The following conclusions summarize and expand on the findings of all these chapters.

The Ẓāhirī *madhhab* has regularly been regarded as a failed school of law. This belief, however, is based on a mischaracterization of it. If by a legal school is meant a set of doctrines attributed to a particular scholar, a hierarchical structure of scholars and legal works, and institutionalized transmission of knowledge, then our survey of the history of the Ẓāhirī *madhhab* demonstrates that at no point did it develop into anything similar to the *madhhab*s that have crystallized into the existing schools of law. In fact, there is no evidence that Dāwūd's students thought of themselves as belonging to a school of law, or that they sought to establish one.[1]

There is evidence that Dāwūd was not an insignificant scholar. However, statements about his scholarly status cannot always be substantiated on the basis of the information given in the same sources that make them. While this may be a purely historiographical issue that has to do with what the authors

1 See now, Vishanoff, *The Formation*, p. 87, where he says that "[t]he Ẓāhirī movement never quite became an institutionalized school of law, with a regular curriculum of instruction, after the manner of the other Sunnī schools, in part because of its opposition to the very idea of a humanly constructed set of rules."

© KONINKLIJKE BRILL NV, LEIDEN, 2014 | DOI 10.1163/9789004279650_009

of these sources—particularly biographical dictionaries—selected to report about him, it is here assumed that they would have mentioned what they actually knew about him had there been anything particularly special about his personal character or views as a legal scholar. Indeed, there are lengthy accounts in these sources about Dāwūd's asceticism and piety. Whereas this may or may not serve a particular or a significant purpose in a biography of a legal scholar, it suggests that if these authors had had other information about his life, they would have reported it. Be this as it may, whether they knew things about Dāwūd that for some reason they did not mention, or did not know more than what they actually reported about him, is, in the final analysis, an idle question for us. Accordingly, for Dāwūd's legal knowledge and scholarly interests, we have to rely on titles of works and views on *uṣūl* and *furūʿ al-fiqh* that are attributed to him in medieval sources in order to determine the subjects to which he may have contributed. While these do not constitute conclusive evidence for his legal doctrines, the fact that medieval sources do not attribute more than one view to him is significant. These sources attribute at times more than one view to Ẓāhirīs, but they are always consistent on views that they attribute to him. Views on the theory of law (*uṣūl*) that are attributed to Dāwūd are generally consistent with view that al-Qāḍī al-Nuʿmān, in his *Ikhtilāf Uṣūl al-Madhāhib*, attributes to Dāwūd's son Muḥammad. Arguably, this level of consistency among medieval scholars in attributing certain views to Dāwūd renders skepticism about these rather unwarranted.

Besides what Dāwūd himself left behind, his immediate students and followers are reported to have had differing views on many issues, such that the prominent 4th/10th-century Ẓāhirī scholar ʿAbd Allāh ibn al-Mughallis compiled a work designed to refute the views of another Ẓāhirī. Consequently, regardless of how coherent Dāwūd's views were, it is clear that he did not leave behind a unified group of students who shared similar views. In fact, he had a small number of students, and only two or three of them transmitted his legal knowledge. The most significant of these students was his own son Muḥammad, who was fairly young when his father died. Only through Muḥammad can we construct any meaningful chain of Ẓāhirī scholars. Muḥammad, however, had the same weakness as did his father in that he did not distinguish himself as a Ḥadīth scholar. It is probably for this reason, and also because he died relatively young, that Muḥammad had little success in spreading Dāwūd's *madhhab*. The fact that Ibn al-Mughallis, who was one of Muḥammad students, is credited with spreading the *madhhab* in Baghdād itself in the first half of the 4th/10th century indicates that neither Dāwūd nor his son had much success in propagating their views in their lifetimes.

Just as Dāwūd's students seem to have followed in the footsteps of their teacher in having little interest in Ḥadīth, their students seem to have had just as little. Scholars of the second generation of Ẓāhirīs—who traveled to various corners of the Muslim world—were not active in Ḥadīth transmission and criticism. Despite their many and significant disagreements, these scholars seem to have begun to develop a sense of belonging (many of them shared the eponym "Dāwūdī") and of connection with common past teachers. Chains of scholars who studied with and transmitted from each other can be constructed as of the 4th/10th century. However, the small number of these students was not sufficient to ensure continuity of the *madhhab* in the region that witnessed its emergence. In the 6th/12th century, Iraq ceased being a center of Ẓāhirism.

It probably was not just the number of scholars that adversely affected Dāwūd's *madhhab* very early and continued to undermine it, but also the "schizophrenic" nature of the careers of Ẓāhirī scholars. Of the 4th/10th-century Ẓāhirī scholars whose profession is reported, the majority were judges. Since judges were almost always appointed on the basis of their legal affiliation, the Ẓāhirism of these scholars must have been kept as a personal matter. These scholars were likely trained according to a certain *madhhab* (Ḥanafism in Iraq and Mālikism in Andalus, for example) and adjudicated according to its rules, but practiced religious rituals and perhaps gave private *fatwā*s according to the Ẓāhirī *madhhab*.[2] Those of them who did not hide their true affiliation—such as Ẓāhirīs who compiled legal works according to their *madhhab*—seem to have enraged other scholars by engaging in polemics against their *imām*s and ridiculing their views and methodologies. This must have alienated Ẓāhirīs from mainstream scholars and made affiliation with them risky and unrewarding. Over time, the number of Ẓāhirī scholars decreased until they completely disappeared in the early 10th/16th century.

The advent of Ibn Ḥazm was an extremely significant event in the history of the Ẓāhirī *madhhab*, but this is not only because of his accomplishments. Truly, Ibn Ḥazm provided Ẓāhirism with an extensive, well-articulated and coherent literature on *uṣūl* and *furūʿ al-fiqh* that was probably unprecedented in the history of the *madhhab*, and which subsequent Ẓāhirīs evidently took great interest in preserving and transmitting. It was probably Ibn Ḥazm who shifted the *primary* (but not necessarily exclusive) focus of Ẓāhirism from the Qurʾān (which the few titles of Ẓāhirī works before him suggest) to Ḥadīth (in conjunction with the Qurʾān), as indicated by the obvious interest of almost

2 In her study of Ẓāhirī scholars under Almohad rule, Adang found out that the majority of their teachers were Mālikīs (Adang, "Ẓāhirīs," p. 469).

all subsequent Ẓāhirīs in Ḥadīth transmission. In fact, he believed that knowledge of Ḥadīth and the ability to distinguish authentic reports from fabricated ones (such as those used by the *Ahl al-Raʾy*, in his view) were fundamental to any jurist's work.[3] As such, Ibn Ḥazm may have been, quite ironically, the founder of the misconception that Ẓāhirīs belonged to the *Ahl al-Ḥadīth* and were opposed to the *Ahl al-Raʾy*.

Furthermore, Ibn Ḥazm played a role (perhaps the most important one) in developing Dāwūd's image as the founder of Ẓāhirism. His evident keenness to connect himself to Dāwūd, his references to Dāwūd's views to support his own even against fellow Ẓāhirīs, and his agreement with him on almost all theoretical legal issues can be regarded as consciously securing Dāwūd's position as the founder of the *madhhab*. This was done in a very distinctive way, however. It has been noted that before Ibn Ḥazm, Dāwūd's *madhhab* was generally known as *al-madhhab al-Dāwūdī* or *al-Dāwūdiyyah* (Dāwūdism), and that a scholar who followed him was often referred to as "al-Dāwūdī." After him, however, Dāwūd's *madhhab* came to be known exclusively as *al-madhhab al-Ẓāhirī*, and his followers as the *Ahl al-Ẓāhir*, the *Ẓāhirīs*. What is remarkable here is that while Dāwūd's authority as the founder of the *madhhab* was being constructed, there was a simultaneous focus on his methodology rather than his personal authority. In other words, rather than focusing on the person, Ibn Ḥazm, who apparently had some of Dāwūd's legal works, focused on his methodology to demonstrate that Dāwūd was the founder of Ẓāhirism because he was the Ẓāhirī *par excellence*. In this respect, there was no process of authority construction similar to the one described by Wael Hallaq with regard to the surviving schools of law, where such process led to the replacement of regional with personal *madhhab*s the foundation of which a single scholar was credited, almost single-handedly, with having laid.[4]

Despite Ibn Ḥazm's accomplishments and contributions, the number of Ẓāhirī scholars in subsequent generations remained quite limited in comparison with the number of scholars belonging to other *madhhab*s, which *madhhab*s had become powerful enough—in terms of the number of their scholars and followers and their association with caliphal and regional governments—

3 In his *Risālah al-Bāhirah* (p. 21), Ibn Ḥazm argues that real jurists are the *Aṣḥāb al-Ḥadīth* who are knowledgeable about authentic traditions and can distinguish them from weak ones that are used by the *Ahl al-Raʾy*.

4 In Hallaq's view, the process of "authority construction,"—viz. constructing the authority of the four eponymous founders of the surviving Sunnī schools of law—involved two simultaneous processes: demonstrating their originality vis-à-vis earlier scholars, and attributing later views to them. For this, see Hallaq, *Authority*, pp. 24ff.

to prevent new schools from emerging or weaker ones from growing. After Ibn Ḥazm, Ẓāhirī scholars were generally on the defensive. Many of them had to conceal their affiliation with Ẓāhirism, and others seem only to have admired the Ẓāhirī *madhhab* such that Ibn Ḥajar was uncertain about their true affiliation. For these scholars, and for those Ẓāhirīs who worked as judges, Ẓāhirism remained a personal matter, and only one Ẓāhirī scholar (in the post-Ibn Ḥazm period)—Muḥammad ibn Saʿdūn ibn Murajjā al-ʿAbdarī—is reported to have given *fatwā*s in public according to the Ẓāhirī *madhhab*.

Admittedly, some Ẓāhirīs are reported to have engaged in defending Ẓāhirism. However, it was probably these same scholars who were also confronting the rulers of their times. We know that in one of these cases—that of Ibn al-Burhān—confrontation arose from Ẓāhirī doctrines, which must have made affiliation with Ẓāhirism a risky matter. Even under the Almohads rule, which is commonly believed to have favored Ẓāhirism, Ẓāhirī scholars do not appear to have fared much better than elsewhere. Despite the fact that al-Manṣūr [r. 580/1184–594/1198] actively sought to promote Ẓāhirism,[5] it has been argued that there was no "significant increase in the absolute number of Ẓāhirīs in the Iberian peninsula and North Africa during the Almohad period, nor in the number of Ẓāhirīs employed in the judiciary." Almohad Caliphs "continued to rely mainly on Mālikī, or at least non-Ẓāhirī, personnel, first of all because the pool of Ẓāhirīs from which judges, preachers, *imāms etc.* could be recruited, was apparently rather limited, and secondly because contrary to what has generally been assumed, the Almohad caliphs, with the exception of al-Manṣūr, did not adopt a policy of giving preferential treatment to Ẓāhirīs."[6] Be this as it may, neither the Almohads nor any other government would give preferential treatment to a *madhhab* that had only a few followers and a limited number of scholars who could fill judicial posts.

All this must have made it difficult for Ibn Ḥazm's students and later Ẓāhirī generations to establish a real school of law. Although they now had a founder—be he Dāwūd or Ibn Ḥazm himself for some of them—and a substantial literature on *uṣūl* and *furūʿ*, there is no trace of any coordinated effort on their part to defend the *madhhab* and secure its survival. We do not hear of any specific venue in which Ẓāhirī scholars taught their *madhhab*, and the transmission of Ẓāhirī knowledge from teachers to students seems to have been done in private and only for interested students. We do not even find any commentaries or abridgements of Ibn Ḥazm's works, which are often polemical in nature, that are intended to make them more suitable for educating new students.

5 Adang, "Ẓāhirīs," pp. 468–469.

6 *Ibid.*, p. 472.

A situation like this cannot continue indefinitely. Unsurprisingly, references to Ẓāhirīs in medieval sources steadily diminished. A survey of Ẓāhirī scholars until the 10th/16th century has shown that there was a sharp decrease in the number of Ẓāhirīs after the 8th/14th century, with only a few in the 9th/15th and one in the 10th/16th centuries. In biographical dictionaries of the 11th/17th, 12th/18th, and 13/19th centuries, there does not seem to be any Ẓāhirīs,[7] even in Egypt and Syria, where they existed in the 7th/13th and 8th/14th centuries.[8]

---

7 I could not find a single Ẓāhirī scholar in al-Sakhāwī's *Ḍaw' al-Lāmiʿ li-Ahl al-Qarn al-Tāsiʿ*, Najm al-Dīn al-Ghazzī's *Kawākib al-Sā'irah fī Aʿyān al-Mi'ah al-ʿĀshirah*, ʿAbd al-Qādir al-ʿAydarūs' *Nūr al-Sāfir ʿan Akhbār al-Qarn al-ʿĀshir* (which covers scholars from India in the east to Morocco in the west) and its *dhayl*, al-Shillī's *Sanā' al-Bāhir bi-Takmīl al-Nūr al-Sāfir*, which focuses primarily on scholars in the Muslim east, including Yemen, where al-Shillī comes from), Muḥammad Amīn al-Muḥibbī's *Khulāṣat al-Athar fī Aʿyān al-Qarn al-Ḥādī ʿAshar*, and Abū al-Faḍl al-Murādī's *Silk al-Durar fī Aʿyān al-Qarn al-Thānī ʿAshar*. These works, to my knowledge, are not yet on searchable CD-ROMs and they may contain Ẓāhirī names that I failed to notice.

8 In a late 19th-century work by a certain Egyptian Sufi named Ibrāhīm al-Manṣūrī and known as al-Samannūdī, the author speaks of a group of scholars who called themselves al-Sunniyyah, al-Aḥmadiyyah, and al-Muḥammadiyyah and had followers in many Muslim regions including Morocco, Egypt, Sudan, the Ḥijāz, and India (Ibrāhīm al-Samannūdī, *Saʿādat al-Dārayn fī al-Radd ʿalā al-Firqatayn al-Wahhābiyyah wa-Muqallidat al-Ẓāhiriyyah*, vol. 2, p. 221). Al-Samannūdī considers them followers of "al-Ẓāhiriyyah" who followed Ibn Ḥazm, hence the title of his book. The real identity of these scholars is not clear. According to al-Samannūdī, they were active in various areas in Upper (the southern part of) Egypt and the Nile Delta. They did not have leaders, although he heard that there was one in Mudīriyyat al-Sharqiyyah (now al-Sharqiyyah governorate) in the southern-eastern part of the Delta. He mentions some of their legal views, most of which *do not* coincide with classical Ẓāhirī views; for example, they shortened the daily prayers during any journey regardless of the distance, did not fast while traveling even during the month of Ramaḍān, said funeral prayers without the ritual ablution, and held that women could lead men in the prayers (*ibid.*, vol. 2, 401). According to Ibn Ḥazm, the distance that is considered "travel" for the purposes of prayers is one "*mīl*", or 2000 cubits (*dhirāʿ*) (Ibn Ḥazm, *al-Muḥallā*, vol. 3, pp. 192, and 213–214). Ibn Ḥazm reports that the distance between Mecca and Jedda, which is about 70 kilometers, is 40 miles (*ibid.*, vol. 3, p. 196), which makes *mīl* the same distance as a mile), and the duration of travel is twenty days (*ibid.*, vol. 3, p. 216). Within these days, a traveler has to shorten his prayers and can only fast voluntarily but not the obligatory fast of Ramaḍān (in other words, if he fasts, his fast does not count as the obligatory fast and he has to make up for the missed days later when he is no longer traveling). Additionally, I could not find any reference that mentions that any Ẓāhirī scholar ever held that ritual ablution was not needed for funeral prayers (for Ibn Ḥazm's views on funeral prayers, see *ibid.*, vol. 3, pp. 333–410). Ibn Ḥazm, furthermore, rejects clearly and categorically the idea that a woman can lead men in the prayers (*ibid.*, vol. 3, pp. 135–137). Their most important view, however, and one that motivated the author to

Despite Ibn Ḥazm's accomplishments, it has been suggested that they may have contributed to the failure of Ẓāhirism. His unconditional conviction of the soundness of his methodology and rulings, and the massive literature that he produced and the reception of this literature by later Ẓāhirīs put Ẓāhirism on the road of turning into a legal school, where *ijtihād* is restricted and *taqlīd* becomes the norm. Although Ẓāhirism never actually turned into a legal school similar to other schools, it seems to have frozen after Ibn Ḥazm, whose followers seem to have either lacked or abandoned his ingenious *ijtihād* in interpreting textual sources and weighing various pieces of evidence in each case.

The failure of the Ẓāhirī *madhhab* may also be related to its own doctrine. It has been noted in the INTRODUCTION that although medieval Muslim jurists were tolerant of what they may have regarded as a "literal" reading of religious commands (which was how some of the Prophet's Companions understood the Prophet's command to not pray *ʿaṣr* except in the abode of the Banū Qurayẓah), this toleration was more of an admiration that did not materialize in their actual jurisprudence.[9] The tension, which probably exists in all legal systems, between consistency and coherence on the one hand, and convenience and practicality on the other hand has been settled in Islamic legal history in favor of the latter. Dāwūd believed that in cases that are under the purview of the law, there must exist one, and only one, relevant and decisive piece of evidence, which can determine the outcome with complete certainty,

---

refute them in this book, was their proclamation that they were *mujtahid*s exercising *ijtihād muṭlaq* similarly to the founders of the legal schools, and their rejection of *taqlīd* by following early *imām*s and existing *madhhab*s (al-Samannūdī, *Saʿādat al-Dārayn*, vol. 2, pp. 221 and 348). These people were evidently actively seeking to convince people of their views and of the invalidity of following existing *madhhab*s (*ibid.*, vol. 2, 348), at times claiming to be Mālikīs to deceive people (*ibid.*, vol. 2, p. 418). Al-Samannūdī, therefore, goes to great lengths to refute them on the issue of the authority of the four *madhhab*s by arguing for the scholarly authority and exceptional qualities of their founders and the necessity of following them (*ibid.*, vol. 2, 230–348). At the same time, he mentions that some of them went so far as to halt the daily prayers and fasting during Ramaḍān (*ibid.*, vol. 2, p. 222), and even claimed that they learned their legal views directly from God and met with the Prophet Muḥammad while awake and consulted him. They even claimed that their leader was superior to Abū Bakr, the Prophet's close Companion and successor (*ibid.*, vol. 2, p. 393). These last points indicate that we are probably dealing with a group of Sufis who also happened to perhaps build on some legal views that al-Samannūdī takes to be characteristic of Ẓāhirīs. In the 14th/20th century, a group of scholars, also existing in various parts of the Muslim world, have espoused the Ẓāhirī *madhhab*, calling themselves al-Ẓāhiriyyah. For this, see Tawfīq al-Ghalbazūrī, *al-Madrasah al-Ẓāhiriyyah*, pp. 909–961. More information about these scholars is available on their website: http://www.zahereyah.com/vb/ (last accessed 15/03/2014).

9 For this, see pp. 1–2 above.

and because of which the soundness and validity of our legal views are also certain. Regardless of whether or not Dāwūd drew on the distinction that al-Jaṣṣāṣ presents between cases in which there is only one piece of evidence and others in which conflicting pieces of evidence exist, it is not clear why he would seek to collect traditions that contradicted each other and contradicted the Qurʾān too. However, although he was willing to argue that when there was no evidence in a certain case we can assume that it is not covered by the law, he probably drew on the traditions collected by the traditionists of his time, for which reason he was mistakenly thought to be their associate. Adopting the view that in every case there must exist only one relevant and sound piece of evidence and accepting at the same time the wealth of traditions that traditionists gathered must have left a mark on Dāwūd's juridical thinking, for he constantly and simultaneously had to argue for the relevance and authenticity of some pieces of evidence and the irrelevance and inauthenticity of others. This tension is very clear in Ibn Ḥazm's writings, and it was noted that he did not abstain from rejecting many Prophetic traditions, at times on the basis of their authenticity, and at other times on the basis of their relevance.

A juridical system with this inherent tension can only survive if scholars always have the freedom to assess the available evidence and select the one they deem relevant and sound in cases offered to them. Dāwūd and Ibn Ḥazm, and perhaps some scholars between them, were able to do this. The problem arose when social and cultural circumstances changed, and Ẓāhirī scholars whose mindset was shaped by different cultural mores had to deal with either new or old issues. In normal circumstances, even if a scholar openly rejects them as irrelevant to jurisprudence and the judicial process (as do Ibn Ḥazm and Justice Antonin Scalia), cultural mores and social conventions play an inevitable role in every stage of any juridical process, beginning with the selection and assessment of the legal evidence itself.[10] Ẓāhirī scholars must always have found themselves in an insoluble dilemma. Rethinking any legal issue which Ibn Ḥazm had an opinion on was a direct assault not only on the legal heritage of the *madhhab*, but also and primarily on its pivotal contention that in every legal issue there is one and only one valid piece of evidence which is necessarily identifiable. At the same time, following the legal views of any scholar, including Ẓāhirī scholars, is also detrimental to their belief in the absolute invalidity of *taqlīd*. Ibn Ḥazm, and perhaps earlier Ẓāhirīs, do not appear to have faced this dilemma. They disagreed with each other, and Ibn Ḥazm was able to disagree with them. However, Ẓāhirīs after him were choosing between

10 Eskridge, for example, argues that "it appears that norms are not absent from Scalia's interpretation of statutes; he is merely influenced by different norms" (Eskridge, "Textualism," p. 1553).

being faithful to the beliefs and views of their school (which were basically Ibn Ḥazm's beliefs and views at this point), and being able to practice independent thinking that by necessity takes social convenience into consideration even if they were not consciously operating on this ground. This dilemma must have made it difficult for the Ẓāhirī *madhhab* to survive as a popular *madhhab* (if it was ever one) and consequently as even an elitist one.

The second contribution of this study concerns the relationship between Ẓāhirism and the two main legal trends of the 3rd/9th century. Against the predominant view that Dāwūd was affiliated with the *Ahl al-Ḥadīth*, it has been argued that the available biographical and doctrinal evidence about him strongly suggests that he was closer to the *Ahl al-Ra'y*. Born to a Ḥanafī father, Dāwūd himself began his career as a Shāfiʿī. Among his teachers, Abū Thawr al-Kalbī, and possibly Abū ʿAlī al-Karābīsī, were probably the two scholars with the longest and strongest influence on him. These two scholars were affiliated with the *Ahl al-Ra'y*, and al-Karābīsī was an open enemy of the *Ahl al-Ḥadīth*. Furthermore, neither Dāwūd nor his immediate students were interested in Ḥadīth transmission and criticism, which was the main activity of the *Ahl al-Ḥadīth*. Finally, there is evidence that Dāwūd was not on good terms with Aḥmad ibn Ḥanbal and possibly with Isḥāq ibn Rāhawayh, two scholars that the *Ahl al-Ḥadīth* held in high esteem. Accordingly, there is hardly any evidence that suggests that Dāwūd belonged to the *Ahl al-Ḥadīth* in terms of his profile, activities, or interests as a scholar. In addition to this, what we know about his legal doctrines seems to confirm not only that Dāwūd was not a member of the *Ahl al-Ḥadīth*, but also and more importantly that he may in fact have been a member of the other camp, the camp of the *Ahl al-Ra'y* and those who shared some important views with them, such as some theologians.

CHAPTER FOUR examines how the term *ẓāhir* is used in two 3rd/9th-century works deemed potentially useful for the purpose of determining why Dāwūd was labeled al-Ẓāhirī—al-Shāfiʿī's *Risālah* and part of al-Ṭabarī's *Jāmiʿ al-Bayān*. Despite some ambiguities and inconsistencies (which could indicate merely that *ẓāhir* was just beginning to be used as a technical term), al-Shāfiʿī's and al-Ṭabarī's uses of this term suggest that the term was used in a specific context: the scope of application of terms. Both scholars seem to be using *ẓāhir* to refer to *al-maʿnā al-ʿāmm*, meaning the fullest possible extension or the broadest range of referents that is inclusive of everything that can potentially fall under a term's gamut. When the Qur'ān speaks of *al-nās*, for instance, *al-maʿnā al-ẓāhir* refers to all people everywhere rather than a specific group of them. Limiting the reference of this word to include only the Muslims or the Arabs, for example, is a *takhṣīṣ*, restriction or particularization, that excludes some of its referents. This *takhṣīṣ*, in the view of Ẓāhirīs and other scholars who adhere to *al-maʿnā al-ʿāmm*, requires a valid indicator, such as a Prophetic tradition, for example, the authenticity and indication of which are beyond doubt. Ibn Ḥazm, who, to the best of my knowledge, does not explain what the term *ẓāhir* actually means,[11] mentions clearly the relationship between it and *ʿumūm*. Remarkably, when describing his legal methodology, Shams al-Dīn al-Dhahabī points out that Ibn Ḥazm relied on the *ẓāhir al-naṣṣ* and the *general* terms and statements (*ʿumūmāt*) of the Qurʾān and Ḥadīth,[12] which suggests that al-Dhahabī saw a connection between *ẓāhir al-naṣṣ* and the scope of application of terms as suggested here.

What was Ẓāhirī about Dāwūd al-Ẓāhirī, then, was his unconditional belief that in the absence of indicators to the contrary, all words and sentences must be understood in an all-inclusive manner. The assumption that the unrestricted meaning is the intended meaning unless proven otherwise is one of the most important hermeneutical tools of the *Ahl al-Raʾy* scholars. Medieval sources attribute this view to Abū Ḥanīfah, the leading figure of the *Ahl al-Raʾy*. Dāwūd shared other theoretical legal views with Abū Ḥanīfah, such as the assumption that any imperative (*amr*) in the Qurʾān or Ḥadīth indicates absolute obligation (*wujūb*) rather than the mere recommendation or permissibility of doing something, and the assumption that any interdiction (*nahy*) indicates absolute prohibition rather than the mere recommendation that a certain act or belief be avoided. The two issues of *ʿumūm* and *amr* and the sense of each of them are foremost among the basic linguistic issues that the discipline of *uṣūl al-fiqh* deals with. More often than not, Muslim jurists have disagreed on how to construe a *ʿāmm* statement or a command.

That the term *ẓāhir* appears in the context of commands and prohibitions indicates that it had more than one application depending on the context. However, our survey of al-Shāfiʿī *Risālah* and al-Ṭabarī's *Jāmiʿ al-Bayān* strongly indicates that its most common application was in the context of the scope of application of terms. These two contexts, however, seem to share an underlying common element, that is, the unconditionality and absoluteness of the indication of legal texts. That is, that which is presumed to be the linguistic indication of a given expression, be it a term or an imperative, is taken to be absolute. Just as any term is presumed to be referring to everything that could be included under it, any command establishes an unconditional religious obligation on *all* those who are addressed by religious law to do something in *all* circumstances. Similarly, any prohibition establishes the absolute obligation

11 Al-Ghalbazūrī believes that because *ẓāhir* was the core of Ibn Ḥazm's *madhhab* and was therefore clear in his mind, he did not need to define it in a precise way (al-Ghalbazūrī, *al-Madrasah al-Ẓāhiriyyah*, p. 549).

12 Al-Dhahabī, *Siyar*, vol. 18, p. 186.

to avoid doing something regardless of other factors. In both cases, challenging the unconditionality and unrestrictedness of expressions requires a valid indicator, which indicator in both Ḥanafī and Ẓāhirī view must be certain in terms of both authenticity and relevance.

Remarkably, although Dāwūd shares this view with the *Ahl al-Ra'y* and with other scholars as well, what was distinctive about him was how his understanding of the meaning of *ẓāhir* led to the rejection of other tools of the *Ahl al-Ra'y*. It has been argued that there is an intimate relationship between *ẓāhir* and *qiyās*, and that Dāwūd's understanding of the former led to his rejection of the latter. *Qiyās* essentially limits or restricts the scope of applicability of legal rules. In Dāwūd's view, prohibiting something because of its resemblance to another that is prohibited infringes on God's prerogative as the only legislator. This happens by widening the scope of prohibition and thus limiting the general rule that what is not prohibited by the law remains in the default state of legality and permissibility (*al-ibāḥah al-aṣliyyah*) according to the presumption of continuity (*istiṣḥāb al-ḥāl*). If religious law prohibits a certain beverage, for instance, declaring another beverage forbidden because it shares a certain quality with the one that the law explicitly prohibits (a quality that scholars of *qiyās* regard as the cause of prohibition, *'illah*) is an assault on the presumed permissibility of all drinks except those prohibited specifically and explicitly by the law. In the case of *khamr*, therefore, it was imperative for Ẓāhirīs to argue that *khamr* was a generic term that referred to all intoxicating beverages.[13] Had they accepted the view that *khamr* referred to one kind of drink (grape-wine, for instance) only, there would have been no justification for maintaining that other intoxicating beverages were forbidden, for this would further limit the rule of general and presumed permissibility. The issue of *'umūm* thus came to play a central role in Dāwūd's jurisprudence, and together with the belief in the principles of *al-ibāḥah al-aṣliyyah* and *istiṣḥāb al-ḥāl*, it represents the core of his doctrine.

Other than sharing these particular theoretical views with the *Ahl al-Ra'y*, Dāwūd also had their interest in producing consistent and coherent jurisprudence. This interest is evident in proceeding in legal issues on specific legal and linguistic assumptions and according to certain procedures of weighing the often contradictory evidence. On the other hand, the *Ahl al-Ḥadīth* do not appear to have been interested in proceeding according to fixed assumptions and rules. Instead, they had an obvious moral agenda, and the legality or illegality of a certain act was not their primary concern. Ibn Ḥanbal explains his rejection of a marriage between a man and a woman with whom the man's

13 For this view, see Ibn Ḥazm, *al-Muḥallā*, vol. 6, pp. 176ff.

father has had a sexual relationship without producing conclusive evidence for the illegality of this marriage from the Qur'ān and the Ḥadīth. In his view, this act was simply immoral, regardless of whether or not it was forbidden. It is probably because of this moral dimension that the *Ahl al-Ḥadīth* were not interested in adopting and employing rules, for serving their moral agenda required a great deal of flexibility and freedom from the restriction of rules. They wanted to be able to judge every case on its own merits to produce a ruling that served their vision of the moral character of the Muslim individual and society.

The case studies discussed in CHAPTER SIX sought to demonstrate that in addition to producing rulings that reflected their moral character and worldview, the *Ahl al-Ḥadīth* also sought to reconcile and synthesize all relevant legal evidence in a given case. In the case of whether touching women affects men's ritual purity, for instance, Ibn Ḥanbal argued that this depends on whether or not he feels sexual desire. He came to this conclusion on the basis of a number of Qur'ānic verses and reports about the Prophet's practice, none of which refers to the element of sexual desire. For him, there cannot be one answer to this question; it all depends on the circumstances of each particular case. But whereas touching one's mother or daughter may not involve sexual desire, touching a woman who is unrelated to a man may well involve it. On the other hand, the Ḥanafī insistence that no such touching ever affects the ritual purity of men regardless of any factors, and the Ẓāhirī view that all touching, regardless of anything, invalidates men's ritual purity indicate that for these two groups of scholars, there must be a straightforward answer to each question, and this answer, if it must, has to rely on verifiable factors, a basic requirement of consistency. Both groups assume that touching does not affect ritual purity without textual evidence. Ẓāhirīs accepted a Qur'ānic text (the *aw lāmastum al-nisā'* verse) that indicated in their view that touching women invalidated men's ritual purity. Ḥanafīs interpreted the Qur'anic evidence differently and did not recognize it as relevant to the question. Whether their views contradicted any notion of morality (such as when a man touches a woman with lust and then prays without performing ritual purity), or caused unreasonable inconvenience or hardship (such as when one has to perform ablution every time he happens to touch his mother, sister or daughter—let alone wife), was not a concern for either of them. What is important is to follow the evidence regardless of any considerations.

In the second case study, Ḥanbalīs accounted for their choice of five sessions of breastfeeding to make a nursing woman a foster mother for the suckled baby by arguing that these ensure that the milk consumed contributed to the growth of the baby's flesh and strengthened his bones. This explanation reveals their desire to identify and rely on notions that could serve their moral agenda. Accordingly, they are reported to have held that if cheese is made out of a woman's milk and a baby happens to eat it five or more times, he becomes the woman's foster son. However, they rejected the notion of adult-breastfeeding despite reported traditions on this issue and also despite the fact that it can contribute to the growth of flesh and strengthening of bones. This clearly points to the moral dimension of their juridical thinking and the tension they sustained between following every piece of evidence in a single issue and remaining true to what they took to be moral considerations. Since this factor is not verifiable, however, it was of no use for either Abū Ḥanīfah or Dāwūd. The former relied on the *ʿumūm* of the word *riḍāʿ* in a Qurʾānic verse to conclude that even one drop of milk is sufficient to establish prohibition of marriage between the nursing woman and the suckled baby.[14] Dāwūd would have held the same view had it not been for one tradition which he accepted and according to which three sessions of breastfeeding are required to establish prohibition. Unlike Ḥanbalīs, neither Ḥanafīs nor Ẓāhirīs felt the need to determine a rationale of what they take to be the correct view on this and other issues.

The centrality of the principles of *ʿumūm, al-ibāḥah al-aṣliyyah*, and *istiṣḥāb al-ḥāl* in Ẓāhirī and Ḥanafī jurisprudence are also confirmed by the short case studies. Abū Ḥanīfah and Dāwūd insisted that the wife of a person who disappears remains his wife because we know that she was his wife when he disappeared but are not confident that he perished. A drunken person cannot divorce his wife in Abū Ḥanīfah's view because he relied on one textual source according to which divorce in only one state—madness—is invalid. The *ʿumūm* of the validity of divorces and utterances, therefore, prevails in the case of drunkenness. Dāwūd held the same view either on the same basis, or on the basis of a Qur'anic verse that indicates that a drunken person is unaware of what he says and therefore cannot make a conscious decision, which divorce has to be. Finally, if someone finds something (presumably lost), there is no reason why he should not take it in Abū Ḥanīfah's view. Dāwūd relied on a textual source—a tradition in which the Prophet commands a person to take what he finds—to come to the conclusion that one has to take lost items that he finds and deal with them in the way described by the Prophet (i.e., publicize their discovery for a year).

---

14 To show the relationship between morality and rules as I understand it, I would consider the possibility that Abū Ḥanīfah construed the Qur'anic evidence in this way on a moral ground only if he did not have a rule on the scope of application of term. But since he did have one, we can only assume that he simply followed his rule rather than (or at most, in addition to) having had other considerations in mind.

On these three issues, Aḥmad ibn Ḥanbal was also hesitant, not only because he had to deal with more pieces of evidence, but also because he sought to find solutions that served his moral worldview. While he was concerned not to let a wife get married to another man if her husband disappears, he was equally concerned for keeping her unmarried for a long time. Therefore, he decided that if her husband disappears in a context that suggested his death—such as in war or at sea—she should wait for four years and then begin a waiting period of four months and ten days, after which she was free to remarry. Not only does this reconcile in his view various opinions of the Companions on this issue, but it also takes into consideration the moral consequences of each alternative. When a drunken person divorces his wife, Ibn Ḥanbal struggled between the prospect of letting him live with her while they may not be married anymore, or separating them while they may still be married. His hesitation to decide on this issue reflects his inability to reconcile and synthesize the available evidence in a way that solves this moral dilemma. Finally, notwithstanding the Prophetic traditions that indicate that one should take a lost item that he happens to find, Ibn Ḥanbal's scruples and fear that he may not deal with it in the prescribed manner led him to hold that it is better, or safer, to keep away from it.

The historiographical issue of the attribution of theoretical and substantive legal views to Abū Ḥanīfah, Aḥmad ibn Ḥanbal, and Dāwūd al-Ẓāhirī has been noted and briefly discussed. It must be stressed that there is no attempt here to advance any contention that the three scholars were consistent in all their legal views. Proving the consistency of the views of any legal scholar is obviously difficult. However, this does not necessarily mean that we cannot or should not make general observations about these scholars or about their juridical thought. In fact, the lack of a reasonable degree of consistency and coherence can suggest either false attribution or outright fabrication, and a reasonable degree of inconsistency may indicate authenticity. In all circumstances, we should be able to assume that there existed some general and perhaps rudimentary guidelines that governed the legal thought of the three scholars that we have dealt with here.[15] To say this is one thing, and to assume

15 Obviously, I do not share Vishanoff's view that *uṣūl al-fiqh* emerged out of the desire to justify and legitimize legal views that had already existed earlier (Vishanoff, *The Formation*, p. 8 and *passim*), or his related view that al-Shāfiʿī's use of textual ambiguity in the Qur'an was meant to serve this purpose of bestowing further legitimacy on earlier views (see, for instance, *ibid.*, pp. 1–2 and *passim*). Proving these theses, I believe, requires more research than has been done by Vishanoff himself and others. I here maintain that there were basic linguistic and legal assumptions that all scholars must have had. In fact,

full or nearly full consistency is quite another. Furthermore, in relating the substantive views of these three scholars to the theoretical views attributed to them, it has only been assumed that if these theoretical views can explain their actual rulings in some cases, these latters should also confirm the former. This should allow us to question some the attribution of some views to these scholars on account of their being in sharp contradiction to our understanding of their overall legal thought. Admittedly, this is a tricky endeavor that can easily slide us into circularity and contradiction when we take inconsistency to say something about the authenticity of some views and reject others as being inconsistent with the overall legal thought of a scholar. To my mind, there is no solid formula to solve this dilemma. Engaging in informed and reasoned guesses is inevitable in deciding what to accept and what to reject. I have therefore sought to analyze the legal views attributed to these three scholars on the basis of what is generally known about their juridical thought among their followers. How historically true this might be is an issue that I have not sought to take up in depth here, if indeed it is at all possible to do that.

The third contribution of this study is challenging the commonly-held view that Ẓāhirism was literalist. CHAPTER FIVE has discussed two fundamental problems with this characterization of Ẓāhirism; first, it does not take into account the fact that literalism is a controversial subject in the field of linguistics; secondly and most importantly, Ẓāhirism is not literalist according to the current understanding of literalism, but rather contextualist, and as such it has strong affinity with textualism, an American legal theory that shares with Ẓāhirism its most fundamental premises, methodology, and objectives.

Ẓāhirism and textualism insist on the absolute supremacy of legal texts and dismiss all non-textual evidence. Both share views on the division of labor between the lawgiver and the legal interpreter—the former (God for Ẓāhirīs and Congress for American textualists) makes the law and formulates it in a certain and deliberate way, whereas the job of the latter (be he a judge or a jurist) is to identify the relevant textual evidence for a given case and apply

---

elsewhere, Vishanoff argues that the root of some linguistic and hermeneutical issues that exist in *uṣūl al-fiqh* works lie in theological debates that took place in the 2nd/8th and 3rd/9th centuries. These hermeneutical issues included clarity and ambiguity, the basis of verbal meaning, the scope of general references, the interpretation of various modes of speech, and implicit meaning, especially as regards commands. For example, the relation between general and particular statements emerged out of a debate over the fate of grave sinners in the Hereafter. This was adopted and used later by scholars of *uṣūl al-fiqh* in their discussions (*ibid.*, pp. 25–26). In this regard, see also Vishanoff's argument against the view that opinions of Muslim theologians on the issue of the general and particular statements were shaped by Greek Logic (*ibid.*, pp. 29–30).

it faithfully regardless of the outcome. In both theories, the only intent of the lawmaker that matters is applying the law as it is, not serving what the interpreter believes to be the objectives of the law or the interests that it seeks to protect. Obviously, both theories seek to rid the interpretation and application of the law of the subjective views and prejudices of interpreters. For this reason, proceeding in the legal process on the basis of specific assumptions and according to specific rules is essential, for abiding by rules is the guarantee that a willful judge would not be able to interpret the law according to his own liking.

However, while both textualism and Ẓāhirism share with literalism assumptions about the language and the ability of people to engage in meaningful communication, they differ from it in one crucial aspect that is generally regarded by philosophers of language to be the defining feature of literalism. Unlike literalism, which assumes that any text can be interpreted in "zero-context," or independently of any context, Ẓāhirism and textualism rely on the historical and textual contexts when interpreting a text. When interpreting a constitutional article, for example, a textualist appeals to the historical context in which that constitution was written and to other articles in the constitution itself to determine the intended meaning of the article at hand. A literalist, on the other hand, would focus only on what this particular article "says," disregarding the social and historical contexts in which it was written, or where it falls within the framework of the constitution at large. The two case studies of Antonin Scalia and Ibn Ḥazm's interpretation of some Qur'ānic verses that have been discussed in CHAPTER FIVE demonstrate that neither jurist interprets legal texts according to the precepts of the theory of formal semantics. Their reliance on the historical and textual contexts to identify the meaning intended by the lawgiver, and their drawing conclusions on the basis of linguistic assumptions that a strict literalist would not condone, indicate that their hermeneutics can only be understood with the help of pragmatics, a contextualist theory that is antithetical to literalist theory of formal semantics.

It has been noted earlier that the inherent tension in Ẓāhirī doctrine between the necessity for constant assessment of the evidence and the requirements of membership in a legal *madhhab* after Ibn Ḥazm may have contributed to the failure of the Ẓāhirī *madhhab*. It is this particular aspect of the Ẓāhirī doctrine that may have contributed to its demise, and not its purported rigidity, hostility to human reason, and failure to incorporate rationalism or meet it half-way as has been suggested. A relevant aspect of pragmatic interpretation, according to Recanati, is its inconclusiveness, or "defeasibility." According to this, "[t]he best explanation we can offer for an action given the availability of evidence may be revised in the light of new evidence... It follows that any piece of evidence may turn out to be relevant for the interpretation of an action. In other words, there is no limit to the amount of contextual information that can affect pragmatic interpretation." It would perhaps be assumed that Ibn Ḥazm would not be happy with this aspect of pragmatism. However, we have already seen how he appeals to contextual information or the lack thereof to argue for or against the relevance of some textual evidence. He also acknowledges the possibility of changing some of his conclusions, even if he claims to be limiting this to cases that have contradictory verses or traditions, or to cases where there exist traditions the authenticity of which is not certain but may become so.[16] In such cases, we hold only that our conclusions are sound to the best of our knowledge, but we cannot pretend to say that we know them for certain.[17] He is even willing to give the benefit of the doubt to scholars who abandon the *ẓāhir* of a text through an interpretation that they believe is sound.[18] Although he may have regarded this as a theoretical possibility that is unlikely to materialize, Ibn Ḥazm's acknowledgment of the possibility of new textual evidence coming to the light—which can easily put the very methodology or any Ẓāhirī view on *uṣūl* and *furūʿ* at risk—is significant in that it demonstrates that Ẓāhirism, as Ibn Ḥazm practiced it, had the potential of considering new and reassessing old evidence, not only in view of new, emerging evidence, but also in light of contextual information about existing evidence. If the context is allowed a role in the process of interpretation, possibilities for new interpretation remain open. Taking the context into consideration was one practice that allowed Ibn Ḥazm to disagree with earlier scholars and assert his own independence.

This also points to Ibn Ḥazm's possible damaging effect on the Ẓāhirī *madhhab*. If Ẓāhirism had the potential to renew itself, this was only possible when Ẓāhirī scholars made use of that potential. After Ibn Ḥazm, this does not seem to have been the case. Whether this was due to his absolute belief in the soundness of his understanding of the evidence and of his legal views, or was because subsequent Ẓāhirīs deferred to his authority and failed to follow his example by disagreeing with earlier Ẓāhirīs, does not change the fact that Ẓāhirism after Ibn Ḥazm became rigid and stagnant. However, this rigidity is *not* inherent in the doctrine itself. Ibn Ḥazm's Ẓāhirism was anything but rigid in its reading of the religious texts or assessment of the evidence. The rigidity resulted from forsaking the methodology and freezing the *madhhab after* Ibn Ḥazm. The Ẓāhirism that is rigid, therefore, is that of the Ẓāhirīs after Ibn Ḥazm. Prior

16 Ibn Ḥazm, *Iḥkām*, vol. 1, p. 21.

17 *Ibid.*, vol. 1, p. 67, and vol. 2, p. 657.

18 *Ibid.*, vol. 2, p. 829.

to Ibn Ḥazm, Ẓāhirīs disagreed, and he was able to disagree with them, opening up new possibilities for the *madhhab* by challenging some pieces of textual evidence on the basis of their authenticity or relevance (which his contextualist theory made possible) and introducing new ones.

Finally, the following observations on Ẓāhirism and textualism are in order. By emphasizing the historical context to determine the meaning of words, these two legal theories make an unwarranted assumption: they assume that all people who lived in a certain historical period—like the 7th-century Arabs for Ẓāhirīs and the late 18th-century "Americans" for American textualists—used language in exactly the same way. While this assumption is hard to prove in either case, it is harder to prove in the case of Ẓāhirīs due to the lack of dictionaries that registered the senses of words as the Arabs used them in the 7th century.[19] Using the evidence of pre-Islamic poetry is problematic. For one thing, using such evidence to determine the meaning of words requires considering every single instance in which a given word was used and its linguistic context in order to determine its meaning. To my knowledge, Ẓāhirīs, and textualists, for that matter, do not pretend to engage in this kind of exercise. This does not necessarily doom their methodology, but it calls into question their claim to stand on a solid ground of certainty (stated by Ibn Ḥazm and strongly evident in Scalia's arguments), for there always remains a chance that their understanding of a certain word is different from the intended meaning. Secondly, knowledge of the indication and denotation of single words does not suffice in the process of interpretation. Knowledge of how the Arabs would understand a complete sentence on the basis of its syntax and structure is not less, if not more, important. Ibn Ḥazm evidently assumes that the Arabs used rules of grammar and syntax consistently, an assumption that is impossible to prove historically. This also makes room for uncertainty in the Ẓāhirī scheme. Finally, Ẓāhirī and textualist scholars assume that the way they read the historical evidence that they use to determine the meaning of words is sound. This practically leads to circularity, for if there were a way to determine the correct meaning of pre-Islamic poetry, for instance, the direct identification of the correct meaning of religious texts themselves should not be problematic. On this point, Ẓāhirism and textualism have the disadvantage of not being literalist.

If textualism seeks after the right application of the rule of law, Ẓāhirism sought after the right way of submission to God, which is what Islam is all

---

19 American originalists use dictionaries that show how words were used when a certain text they examine was written (Nelson, "Originalism," p. 519). For the kinds of evidence that American originalists and textualists use, see Eskridge, "Textualism," p. 1532.

about, not just for Ẓāhirīs, but for all jurists for whom Islamic law constituted the core of Islam. A good Ẓāhirī jurist is one who accepts only texts (the Qur'ān and Ḥadīth) as valid sources of the law and rejects all non-textual sources such as *qiyās* (and its opposite, the *argumentum e contrario*), *istiḥsān*, and *maṣlaḥah*, etc. The process of dealing with these textual sources is strictly formalist, meaning that it abides by specific rules throughout. It begins by searching for pieces of evidence in each case and investigating how they may contribute to reaching one ruling. To do this, they rely on certain assumptions, foremost among which is that only interdiction (*nahy*) requires textual evidence, whereas permission (*ibāḥah*) does not require such evidence according to the principle of *al-ibāḥah al-aṣliyyah*, which principle has textual evidence in the Qur'ān. In interpreting textual sources, it is assumed that absent any valid evidence (i.e., another textual source the authenticity of which is accepted) to otherwise, all terms must be interpreted according to their broadest scope of application without any sort of qualification or restriction (i.e., *takhṣīṣ* is exceptional), such that it includes the full range of its potential referents. Similarly, any textual command, unless a valid indicator suggests otherwise, must be interpreted to establish absolute obligation to carry out the demanded action without delay and as frequently as is required. Together with these rules, all textual and non-textual pieces of evidence should be considered in order to ascertain the intended meaning of each text. Finally, the uncritical acceptance of views of earlier jurists (i.e., *taqlīd*, which is a, or *the*, basic feature of the *madhhab* system) is strictly forbidden, and each jurist is personally required to deal with textual sources directly (i.e., *ijtihād* within the bounds of textual sources is obligatory). If this methodology is followed correctly, believers should be able to determine God's ruling in each case with complete confidence. The next step would be for them to follow it. This *is* what submission to God means and requires.

Finally, and admittedly, missing in this monograph on the history of the Ẓāhirī *madhhab* is a discussion of the broader cultural significance of what seems to be its incompatability with the medieval Islamic cultures, of its recent (slow) resurgence, and of its potential prospects in "modern" cultures as a vigorous legal and hermeneutical theory. It was my intention to dissuss these all-important questions in a separate chapter on the contemporary rehabilitation of the *madhhab* either by individual jurists or institutions (such as the Islamic Research Assembly of al-Azhar University, where the Ẓāhirī *madhhab* is one of eight *madhhab*s that it accepts).[20] Unfortunately, however, it has not

20 In addition to the four existing Sunnī *madhhab*s, the Assembly accepts the Jaʿfarī, Zaydī, Ibāḍī, and Ẓāhirī *madhhab*s.

been possible to interview any of the contemporary Ẓāhirī scholars—the most important of whom is Shaykh ʿAbd al-Raḥmān ibn ʿAqīl in, significantly, Saudi Arabia—and the events in Egypt has made conducting research there since 2011 almost impossible. Hopefully, these questions will be duly discussed in a separate article.

Bibliography

Primary Sources

ʿAbd Allāh ibn Aḥmad ibn Ḥanbal. *Masāʾil al-Imām Aḥmad ibn Ḥanbal*. Beirut: al-Maktab al-Islāmī, 1981.

Abū Dāwūd, Sulaymān ibn al-Ashʿath. *Sunan Abī Dāwūd*. Beirut: Dār Ibn Ḥazm, 1998.

Abū Ḥanīfah, al-Nuʿmān ibn Thābit. *Musnad Abī Ḥanīfah* (by Abū Nuʿaym al-Iṣbahānī). Riyad: Maktabat al-Kawthar, 1994.

Abū al-Wafāʾ al-Qurashī, ʿAbd al-Qādir ibn Muḥammad. *Al-Jawāhir al-Muḍiyyah fī Ṭabaqāt al-Ḥanafiyyah*. Cairo: Hajr li-l-Ṭibāʿah wa-l-Nashr, 1993.

Abū Yūsuf, Yaʿqūb ibn Ibrāhīm. *Kitāb al-Āthār*. Cairo: Maṭbaʿat al-Istiqāmah, 1936.

Āl Taymiyyah (Majd al-Dīn, Shihāb al-Dīn, and Taqī al-Dīn ibn Taymiyyah). *Al-Musawwadah*. Cairo: Maṭbaʿat al-Madanī, 1964.

Āmidī, al-, ʿAlī ibn Muḥammad. *Al-Iḥkām fī Uṣūl al-Aḥkām*. Riyad: Dār al-Ṣumayʿī, 2003.

Awzāʿī, al-, ʿAbd al-Raḥmān. *Sunan al-Awzāʿī*. Beirut: Dār al-Nafāʾis, 1993.

ʿAydarūs, al-, ʿAbd al-Qādir ibn Shaykh. *Al-Nūr al-Sāfir ʿan Akhbār al-Qarn al-ʿĀshir*. Beirut: Dār Ṣādir, 2001.

Baghdādī, al-, Ismāʿīl. *Hadiyyat al-ʿĀrifīn: Asmāʾ al-Muʾallifīn wa-Āthār al-Muṣannifīn*. Istanbul: Wakālat al-Maʿārif, 1955.

Balawī, al-, al-Wādī Āshī, Aḥmad ibn ʿAlī. *Thabat al-Balawī*. Beirut: Dār al-Gharb al-Islāmī, 1983.

Baṣrī, al-, Abū al-Ḥusayn. *Al-Muʿtamad fī Uṣūl al-Fiqh*. Beirut: Dār al-Kutub al-ʿIlmiyyah, 1983.

Baṭaylawsī, al-, ʿAbd Allāh ibn Muḥammad. *Al-Tanbīh*. Cairo: Dār al-Iʿtiṣām, 1978.

Bazzār, al-, Abū Bakr. *Al-Baḥr al-Zakhkhār* (or *Musnad al-Bazzār*). Medina: Maktabat al-ʿUlūm wa-l-Ḥikam, 1988.

Bukhārī, al-, Muḥammad ibn Ismāʿīl. *Al-Jāmiʿ al-Ṣaḥīḥ*. Al-Majlis al-Aʿlā li-l-Shuʾūn al-Islāmiyyah, 1966.

Ḍabbī, al-, Aḥmad ibn Yaḥyā. *Bughyat al-Multamis fī Tārīkh Rijāl Ahl al-Andalus*. Beirut: Dār al-Kutub al-ʿIlmiyyah, 1997.

Dabūsī, al-, Abū Zayd. *Taqwīm al-Adillah fī Uṣūl al-Fiqh*. Beirut: Dār al-Kutub al-ʿIlmiyyah, 2001.

Dānī, al-, Abū ʿAmr. *Mukhtaṣar fī Madhāhib al-Qurrāʾ al-Sabʿah bi-l-Amṣār*. Beirut: Dār al-Kutub, 2000.

———. *Al-Muqniʿ*. Damascus: Maṭbaʿat al-Taraqqī, 1940.

Dārimī, al-, ʿAbd Allāh. *Sunan al-Dārimī*. Beirut: Dār al-Kutub al-ʿIlmiyyah, 1987.

Dhahabī, al-, Shams al-Dīn. *Al-ʿIbar fī Khabar man Ghabar*. Kuwait: Dāʾirat al-Maṭbuʿāt wa-l-Nashr, 1960–6.

———. *Siyar Aʿlām al-Nubalāʾ*. Beirut: Muʾassasat al-Risālah, 1981.

———. *Tadhkirat al-Ḥuffāẓ*. Beirut: Dār al-Kutub al-ʿIlmiyyah, 1998.

———. *Tārīkh al-Islām wa-Wafayāt al-Mashāhir wa-l-Aʿlām*. Beirut: Dār al-Kitāb al-ʿArabī, 1992.

Dimashqī, al-, Muḥammad ibn ʿAbd Allāh. *Tawḍīḥ al-Mushtabih*. Beirut: Muʾassasat al-Risālah, 1993.

Farrāʾ, al-, Ibn Abī Yaʿlā. *Al-ʿUddah fī Uṣūl al-Fiqh*. Riyad: n.p., 1973.

Ghazzālī, al-, Abū Ḥāmid. *Al-Mustaṣfā min ʿIlm al-Uṣūl*. Beirut: Dār al-Arqam ibn Abī al-Arqam, 1994.

Ḥalabī, al-, Burhān al-Dīn. *Al-Kashf al-Ḥathīth ʿam-man Rumiya bi-Waḍʿ al-Ḥadīth*. Baghdad: Maṭbaʿat al-ʿĀnī, 1984.

Ḥasanī, al-, ʿAbd al-Ḥayy ibn Fakhr. *Nuzhat al-Khawāṭir wa-Bahjat al-Masāmiʿ wa-l-Nawāẓir*. Haydarabad: Maṭbaʿat Dāʾirat al-Maʿārif al-ʿUthmāniyyah, 1946.

Hāshimī, al-, (Abū Jaʿfar) ʿAbd al-Khāliq ibn ʿĪsā. *Ruʾūs al-Masāʾil fī al-Khilāf ʿalā Madhhab al-Imām Aḥmad ibn Ḥanbal*. Beirut: Dār Khiḍr, 2000.

Ḥumaydī, al-, Muḥammad ibn Abī Naṣr. *Jadhwat al-Muqtabis fī Tārīkh ʿUlamāʾ al-Andalus*. Cairo: Dār al-Kitāb al-Miṣrī, and Beirut: Dār al-Kitāb al-Lubnānī, 1983.

Ibn ʿAbd al-Barr, (Abū ʿUmar) Yūsuf. *Al-Istidhkār li-Madhāhib Fuqahāʾ al-Amṣār wa-ʿUlamāʾ al-Aqṭār fī-mā Taḍammanahu al-Muwaṭṭaʾ min Maʿānī al-Raʾy wa-l-Āthār*. Cairo: al-Majlis al-Aʿlā li-l-Shuʾūn al-Islāmiyyah, 1971.

———. *Jāmiʿ Bayān al-ʿIlm wa-Faḍlihi*. Dammam, Dār Ibn al-Jawzī, 1994.

Ibn al-Abbār, Muḥammad ibn ʿAbd Allāh. *Al-Takmilah li-Kitāb al-Ṣilah*. Majrīṭ: Maṭbaʿat Rūkhas, 1887–1919.

Ibn ʿAlī, (al-Qāḍī) ʿAbd al-Wahhāb. *Al-Ishrāf ʿalā Nukat Masāʾil al-Khilāf*. Beirut: Dār Ibn Ḥazm, 1999.

Ibn ʿAqīl, ʿAlī ibn Muḥammad. *Al-Wāḍiḥ fī Uṣūl al-Fiqh*. Beirut: Muʾassasat al-Risālah, 1999.

Ibn ʿAsākir, ʿAlī ibn al-Ḥasan. *Tārīkh Madīnat Dimashq*. Beirut: Dār al-Fikr, 1997.

Ibn al-Athīr, ʿIzz al-Dīn. *Al-Lubāb fī Tahdhīb al-Ansāb*. Beirut: Dār Ṣādir, 1972.

Ibn ʿAṭiyyah al-Andalusī, ʿAbd al-Ḥaqq. *Fihris Ibn ʿAṭiyyah*. Beirut: Dār al-Gharb al-Islāmī, 1980.

Ibn Bashkuwāl, Khalaf ibn ʿAbd Allāh. *Al-Ṣilah*. Cairo: al-Dār al-Miṣriyyah li-l-Taʾlīf wa-l-Tarjamah, 1966.

Ibn al-Dahhān, ʿAlī ibn Shuʿayb. *Taqwīm al-Nazar*. Beirut: Dār al-Kutub al-ʿIlmiyyah, 2001.

Ibn al-Faraḍī, ʿAbd Allāh ibn Aḥmad. *Tārīkh ʿUlamāʾ al-Andalus*. Tunis: Dār al-Gharb al-Islāmī, 2008.

Ibn Farḥūn, Ibrāhīm ibn Nūr al-Dīn. *Al-Dībāj al-Mudhhab fī Maʿrifat Aʿyān ʿUlamāʾ al-Madhhab*. Beirut: Dār al-Kutub, 1996.

Ibn Ḥajar al-ʿAsqalānī, Aḥmad ibn ʿAlī. *Al-Durar al-Kāminah fī Aʿyān al-Miʾah al-Thāminah*. Cairo: Dār al-Kutub al-Ḥadīthah, 1966.

———. *Inbāʾ al-Ghumr bi-Anbāʾ al-ʿUmr*. Cairo: al-Majlis al-Aʿlā li-l-Shuʾūn al-Islāmiyyah, 1972.

———. *Lisān al-Mīzān*. Beirut: Dār al-Kutub al-ʿIlmiyyah, 1996.

———. *Tahdhīb al-Tahdhīb*. Beirut: Dār al-Kutub al-ʿIlmiyyah, 1994.

Ibn Hāniʾ al-Naysābūrī, Isḥāq. *Masāʾil al-Imām Aḥmad*. Beirut: Al-Maktab al-Islāmī, 1979.

Ibn Ḥanbal, Aḥmad. *Kitāb al-Ashribah*. Baghdad: Wazārat al-Awqāf, 1976.

———. *Musnad Aḥmad ibn Ḥanbal*. Beirut: Dār al-Kutub al-Islāmiyyah, 1993.

Ibn Ḥayyān al-Qurṭubī, Abū Marwān. *Al-Muqtabas min Anbāʾ Ahl al-Andalus*. Beirut: Dār al-Kitāb al-ʿArabī, 1973.

Ibn Ḥazm, ʿAlī ibn Aḥmad. *Al-Iḥkām fī Uṣūl al-Aḥkām*. Cairo: Maṭbaʿat al-Imām, n.d.

———. *Al-Iʿrāb ʿan al-Ḥayrah wa-l-Iltibās al-Mawjūdayn fī Madhāhib Ahl al-Raʾy wa-l-Qiyās*. Riyad: Dār Aḍwāʾ al-Salaf, 2005.

———. *Marātib al-Ijmāʿ fī al-ʿIbādāt wa-l-Muʿāmalāt wa-l-Iʿtiqādāt*. Cairo: Dār Zāhid al-Qudsī, 1983.

———. *Al-Muḥallā bi-l-Āthār*. Beirut: Dār al-Kutub al-ʿIlmiyyah, 1988.

———. *Al-Nubdhah al-Kāfiyah fī Uṣūl Aḥkām al-Dīn*. Beirut: Dār al-Kutub al-ʿIlmiyyah, 1985.

———. *Rasāʾil ibn Ḥazm al-Andalusī*. Beirut: al-Muʾassasah al-ʿArabiyyah li-l-Dirāsāt wa-l-Nashr, 1987.

———. *Al-Risālah al-Bāhirah*. Damascus: Majmaʿ al-Lughah al-ʿArabiyyah, 1989.

Ibn Hubayrah (al-Shaybānī), Yaḥyā ibn Muḥammad. *Al-Ifṣāḥ ʿan Maʿānī al-Ṣiḥāḥ*. Beirut: Dār al-Kutub al-ʿIlmiyyah, 1996.

———. *Ikhtilāf al-Aʾimmah al-ʿUlamāʾ*. Beirut: Dār al-Kutub al-ʿIlmiyyah, 2002.

Ibn al-Jawzī, ʿAbd al-Raḥmān ibn ʿAlī. *Al-Muntaẓam fī Tārīkh al-Mulūk wa-l-Umam*. Beirut: Dār al-Kutub al-ʿIlmiyyah, 1992.

Ibn al-Zubayr al-Thaqafī, Aḥmad ibn Ibrāhīm. *Ṣilat al-Ṣilah*. Morocco: Wazārat al-Awqāf wa-l-Shuʾūn al-Islāmiyyah, 1993–95.

Ibn Kathīr, Ismāʿīl ibn ʿUmar. *Al-Bidāyah wa-l-Nihāyah*. Beirut: Dār al-Kutub al-ʿIlmiyyah, 1994.

———. *Tafsīr al-Qurʾān al-ʿAẓīm*. Giza: Muʾassasat Qurṭubah, 2000.

Ibn Khaldūn, ʿAbd al-Raḥmān. *Al-Muqaddimah*. Beirut: al-Maktabah al-ʿAṣriyyah, 1995.

Ibn Khallikān, Aḥmad ibn Muḥammad. *Wafayāt al-Aʿyān wa-Anbāʾ Abnāʾ al-Zamān*. Beirut: Dār al-Thaqāfah, 1968.

Ibn al-Khaṭīb, Lisān al-Dīn. *Al-Iḥāṭah fī Akhbār Gharnāṭah*. Cairo: Maktabat al-Khānjī, 1973.

Ibn Khayr al-Ishbīlī, Abū Bakr Muḥammad. *Fahrasat ibn Khayr al-Ishbīlī*. Beirut: Dār al-Kutub al-ʿIlmiyyah, 1998.

Ibn Mājah, Abū ʿAbd Allāh Muḥammad. *Sunan ibn Mājah*. Beirut: Dār al-Jīl, 1998.

Ibn Mākūlā, ʿAlī ibn Hibat-Allāh. *Al-Ikmāl*. Haydarabad: Dāʾirat al-Maʿārif al-ʿUthmāniyyah, 1966.

Ibn Manẓūr, Jamāl al-Dīn. *Lisān al-ʿArab*. Beirut: Dār Iḥyāʾ al-Turāth al-ʿArabī, 1988.

Ibn al-Mulaqqin, Sirāj al-Dīn. *Al-ʿIqd al-Mudhhab fī Ṭabaqāt Ḥamalat al-Madhhab*. Beirut: Dār al-Kutub al-ʿIlmiyyah, 1996.

Ibn al-Mundhir (al-Naysābūrī), Muḥammad ibn Ibrāhīm. *Al-Ishrāf ʿalā Madhāhib Ahl al-ʿIlm*. Beirut: Dār al-Fikr, 1993.

Ibn al-Nadīm, Muḥammad ibn Isḥāq. *Al-Fihrist*. Beirut: Maktabat Khayyāṭ, 1966.

Ibn Qayyim al-Jawziyyah, Muḥammad ibn Abī Bakr. *Aʿlām al-Muwaqqiʿīn ʿan Rabb al-ʿĀlamīn*. Beirut: Dār al-Jīl, 1973.

Ibn Qudāmah al-Maqdisī, (Muwaffaq al-Dīn) Muḥammad ibn Aḥmad. *Al-Mughnī*. Cairo: Hajr li-l-Ṭibāʿah wa-l-Nashr wa-l-Iʿlān, 1986–1990.

———. *Al-Kāfī fī Fiqh al-Imām Aḥmad*. Beirut: Dār al-Kutub al-ʿIlmiyyah, 1994.

Ibn Qutaybah al-Dīnawarī, ʿAbd Allāh ibn Muslim. *Kitāb al-Ashribah wa-Dhikr Ikhtilāf al-Nās Fī-hā*. Cairo: Maktabat Zahrāʾ al-Sharq, 1998.

———. *Kitāb al-Masāʾil wa-l-Ajwibah*. Damascus: Dār Ibn Kathīr, 1990.

———. *Taʾwīl Mukhtalif al-Ḥadīth*. Amman: Dār al-Bashīr, 2004.

Ibn Rushd, Muḥammad ibn Aḥmad. *Bidāyat al-Mujtahid wa-Nihāyat al-Muqtaṣid*. Beirut: Dār Ibn Ḥazm, 1995.

Ibn Shaddād, Bahāʾ al-Dīn. *Dalāʾil al-Aḥkām*. Beirut: Dār al-Kutub al-ʿIlmiyyah, 1991.

Ibn Abī Shaybah, ʿAbd Allāh ibn Muḥammad. *Al-Muṣannaf*. Riyad: Maktabat al-Rushd, 2004.

Ibn Sīrīn, Muḥammad. *Tafsīr al-Aḥlām*. Beirut: Dār al-Ḥarf al-ʿArabī, 2000.

Ibn Taymiyyah, Aḥmad ibn ʿAbd al-Ḥalīm. *Ṣiḥḥat Uṣūl Madhhab Ahl al-Madīnah*. Beirut: Dār al-Nadwah al-Jadīdah, 1980.

Ismāʿīl al-Baghdādī. *Hadiyyat al-ʿĀrifīn: Asmāʾ al-Muʾallifīn wa-Āthār al-Muṣannifīn*. Istanbul: Wakālat al-Maʿārif, 1951.

Jaṣṣāṣ, al-, Abū Bakr. *Al-Fuṣūl fī al-Uṣūl*. Beirut: Dār al-Kutub al-ʿIlmiyyah, 2000.

Jazarī, al-, Muḥammad ibn Muḥammad. *Ghāyat al-Nihāyah fī Ṭabaqāt al-Qurrāʾ*. Cairo: Maktabat al-Khānjī, 1932.

Kawsaj, al-, Isḥāq ibn Manṣūr. *Masāʾil al-Imām Aḥmad ibn Ḥanbal wa-Isḥāq ibn Rāhawayh*. Riyad: Dār al-Hijrah, 2004.

Khalīl, al-, ibn Aḥmad al-Farāhīdī. *Kitāb al-ʿAyn*. Qum: Muʾassasat al-Nashr al-Islāmī, 1993.

Khaṭīb, al-, al-Baghdādī, Aḥmad ibn ʿAlī. *Al-Kifāyah fī ʿIlm al-Riwāyah*. Beirut: Dār al-Kitāb al-ʿArabī, 1985.

———. *Tārīkh Baghdād*. Beirut: Dār al-Kitāb al-ʿArabī, 1966.

Lablī, al-, Aḥmad ibn Yūsuf. *Fihrist al-Lablī*. Beirut: Dār al-Gharb al-Islāmī, 1988.

Laknawī, al-, Muḥammad ʿAbd al-Ḥayy. *Al-Fawāʾid al-Bahiyyah fī Tarājim al-Ḥanafiyyah*. Beirut: Dār al-Arqam, 1998.

Maktabat Āl al-Bayt. DVD-ROM. Qum: al-Mojam al-Feqhi Center and al-Mostafa Islamic Researches Center, 2005.

Al-Maktabah al-Shāmilah. CD-ROM. N.p., n.d.

Mālik ibn Anas. *Al-Muwaṭṭa'* (transmitted by Suwayd ibn Sa'īd al-Ḥadthānī). Beirut: Dār al-Gharb al-Islāmī, 1996.

———. *Al-Muwaṭṭa'* (transmitted by Yaḥyā ibn Yaḥyā al-Laythī). Beirut: Dār al-Gharb al-Islāmī, 1996.

Maqqarī, al-, Aḥmad ibn Muḥammad. *Nafḥ al-Ṭīb min Ghuṣn al-Andalus al-Raṭīb*. Beirut: Dār Ṣādir, 1968.

Marrākushī, al-, Muḥammad ibn Muḥammad ibn 'Abd al-Malik. *Al-Dhayl wa-l-Takmilah li-Kitābayy al-Mawṣūl wa-l-Ṣilah*. Beirut: Dār al-Thaqāfah, 1969–1973 (vols. 1–6); Rabat: Maṭbū'āt Akadimiyyat al-Mamlakah al-Maghribiyyah, 1984 (vol. 8).

Marwazī, al-, Muḥammad ibn Nasr. *Ikhtilāf al-Fuqahā'*. Riyad: Aḍwā' al-Salaf, 2000.

Miskawayh, Aḥmad ibn Muḥammad. *Tajārib al-Umam*. Cairo: n.p., 1332.

Mizzī, al-, Jamāl al-Dīn. *Tahdhīb al-Kamāl fī Asmā' al-Rijāl*. Beirut: Mu'assasat al-Risālah, 1992.

Mubārakfūrī, Abū al-Ma'ālī Aṭhar. *Rijāl al-Sind wa-l-Hind ilā al-Qarn al-Sābi'*. Cairo: Dār al-Anṣār, 1977.

Muḥibbī, al-, Muḥammad Amīn. *Khulāṣat al-Athar fī A'yān al-Qarn al-Ḥādī 'Ashar*. Beirut: Maktabat Khayyāṭ, n.d.

Mujāhid ibn Jabr. *Tafsīr Mujāhid*. Beirut: Al-Manshūrāt al-'Ilmiyyah, 1977.

Muqaddasī, al-, Muḥammad ibn Aḥmad. *Aḥsan al-Taqāsīm fī Ma'rifat al-Aqālīm*. Beirut: Dār Iḥyā' al-Turāth al-'Arabī, 1987.

Muqātil ibn Sulaymān. *Tafsīr Muqātil*. Cairo: Al-Hay'ah al-'Āmmah li-l-Kitāb, 1979.

Murādī, al-, Muḥammad Khalīl. *Silk al-Durar fī A'yān al-Qarn al-Thānī 'Ashar*. Beirut: Dār al-Kutub al-'Ilmiyyah, 1997.

Murtaḍā, al-, Aḥmad ibn Yaḥyā. *Al-Baḥr al-Zakhkhār al-Jāmi' li-Madhāhib 'Ulamā' al-Amṣār*. Beirut: Mu'assasat al-Risālah, 1975.

Muslim ibn al-Ḥajjāj. *Al-Jāmi' al-Ṣaḥīḥ*. Beirut: Dār ibn Ḥazm, 1975.

Muṭī'ī, al-, Muḥammad Najīb. *Al-Takmilah al-Thāniyah, al-Majmū', Sharḥ al-Muhadhdhab*. Cairo: Maṭba'at al-Imām, 1966.

Najm al-Dīn al-Ghazzī. *Al-Kawākib al-Sā'irah bi-A'yān al-Mi'ah al-'Āshirah*. Beirut: Dār al-Āfāq al-Jadīdah, 1979.

Nasā'ī, al-, 'Abd al-Raḥmān. *Sunan al-Nasā'ī*. Dār al-Kutub al-'Ilmiyyah, 1995.

Nawawī, al-, Muḥyī al-Dīn ibn Sharaf. *Al-Majmū', Sharḥ al-Muhadhdhab*. Cairo: Maṭba'at al-Imām, 1966.

———. *Tahdhīb al-Asmā' wa-l-Lughāt*. Damascus: Dār al-Fayḥā', 2006.

Pickthall, Marmaduke (trans.). *The Glorious Qur'an*. Albany: State University of New York Press, 1976.

Qāḍī, al-, 'Iyāḍ ibn Mūsā. *Fihrist Shuyūkh al-Qāḍī 'Iyāḍ* (or *al-Ghunyah*). Cairo: Maktabat al-Thaqāfah al-Dīniyyah, 2002.

Qāḍī, al-, al-Nuʿmān ibn Muḥammad. *Ikhtilāf Uṣūl al-Madhāhib*. Simla: Indian Institute of Advanced Study, 1972.

Qaffāl, al-, al-Shāshī, Muḥammad ibn Aḥmad. *Ḥilyat al-ʿUlamāʾ fī Maʿrifat Madhāhib al-Fuqahāʾ*. Mecca: Dār al-Bāz, 1988.

Qurṭubī, al-, Muḥammad ibn Aḥmad. *Al-Jāmiʿ li-Aḥkām al-Qurʾān*. Cairo: Dār al-Kitāb al-ʿArabī, 1967.

Rāzī, al-, Ibn Abī Ḥātim. *Al-Jarḥ wa-l-Taʿdīl*. Haydarabad: Maṭbaʿat Jāmʿiyyat Dāʾirat al-Maʿārif al-ʿUthmāniyyah, 1942.

Rāzī, al-, Fakhr al-Dīn. *Al-Tafsīr al-Kabīr*. Cairo: ʿAbd al-Raḥmān Muḥammad, n.d.

Ruʿaynī, ʿAlī ibn Muḥammad. *Barnāmaj Shuyūkh al-Ruʿaynī*. Damascus: Wazārat al-Thaqāfah wa-l-Irshād al-Qawmī, 1962.

Ṣafadī, al-, Khalīl ibn Aybak. *Aʿyān al-ʿAṣr wa-Aʿwān al-Naṣr*. Beirut: Dār al-Fikr al-Muʿāṣir, 1998.

———. *Al-Wāfī bi-l-Wafayāt*. Beirut: Dār Ṣādir, 1996–1997.

Sahmī, al-, Ḥamzah ibn Yūsuf. *Tārīkh Jurjān*. Beirut: Dār al-Kutub al-ʿIlmiyyah, 2004.

Saḥnūn ibn Saʿīd al-Tanūkhī. *Al-Mudawwanah al-Kubrā*. Beirut: Al-Maktabah al-ʿAṣriyyah, 1999.

Sakhāwī, al-, Shams al-Dīn Muḥammad. *Al-Ḍawʾ al-Lāmiʿ li-Ahl al-Qarn al-Tāsiʿ*. Cairo: Maktabat al-Qudsī, 1353–5 AH.

Ṣāliḥ ibn Aḥmad ibn Ḥanbal. *Masāʾil al-Imām Aḥmad*. Riyad: Dār al-Waṭan, 1999.

Samʿānī, al-, Abū Saʿd. *Al-Ansāb*. Beirut: Dār al-Janān, 1988.

Samannūdī, al-, Ibrāhīm ibn ʿUthmān al-Manṣūrī. *Saʿādat al-Dārayn fī al-Radd ʿalā al-Firqatayn al-Wahhābiyyah wa-Muqallidat al-Ẓāhiriyyah*. Nouakchott: Maktabat al-Imām Mālik, 2005.

Samarqandī, al-, Abū al-Layth. *Mukhtalif al-Riwāyah*. Riyad: Maktabat al-Rushd, 2005.

Samarqandī, al-, ʿAlāʾ al-Dīn. *Tuḥfat al-Fuqahāʾ*. Damascus: Maktabat Jāmiʿat Dimashq, 1958.

Ṣanʿānī, al-, ʿAbd al-Razzāq. *Al-Muṣannaf*. Beirut: Dār al-Kutub al-ʿIlmiyyah, 2000.

Sarakhsī, al-, Shams al-Dīn. *Kitāb al-Mabsūṭ*. Beirut: Dār al-Fikr, 2000.

———. *Al-Muḥarrar fī Uṣūl al-Fiqh*. Beirut: Dār al-Kutub al-ʿIlmiyyah, 1996.

Shāfiʿī, al-, Muḥammad ibn Idrīs. *Al-Risālah*. Cairo: Muṣṭafā al-Bābī al-Ḥalabī, 1938.

———. *Kitāb al-Umm*. Beirut: Dār al-Kutub al-ʿIlmiyyah, 1993.

Shahrastānī, al-, Muḥammad ibn ʿAbd al-Karīm. *Al-Milal wa-l-Niḥal*. Beirut: Dār al-Maʿrifah, 1990.

Shakir, M. H. (trans.). *The Holy Qurʾan*. Elmhurst: Takrike Tarsile Qurʾan, 1983.

Sharīf, al-, al-Murtaḍā, ʿAlī ibn al-Ḥusayn. *Al-Intiṣār*. Najaf: Al-Maṭbaʿah al-Ḥaydariyyah, 1971.

Shawkānī, al-, Muḥammad ibn ʿAlī. *Al-Darārī al-Muḍiyyah Sharḥ al-Durar al-Bahiyyah*. Sanaa: Dār al-Āthār, 2007.

Shaybānī, al-, Muḥammad ibn al-Ḥasan. *Kitāb al-Aṣl* (or *al-Mabsūṭ*). Karachi: Idārat al-Qur'an wa-l-'Ulūm al-Islāmiyyah, n.d.

———. *Kitāb al-Āthār*. Karachi: Al-Majlis al-'Ilmī, 1965.

———. *Al-Ḥujjah 'alā Ahl al-Madīnah*. Hyderabad: Maṭba'at al-Ma'ārif al-Sharqiyyah, 1965.

Shillī, al-, Muḥammad. *Al-Sanā' al-Bāhir bi-Takmīl al-Nūr al-Sāfir 'an Akhbār al-Qarn al-'Āshir*. Sanaa: Maktabat al-Irshād, 2004.

Shīrāzī, al-, Abū Isḥāq. *Al-Muhadhdhab* (*fī Fiqh al-Imām al-Shāfi'ī*). Damascus: Dār al-Qalam, 1992.

———. *Ṭabaqāt al-Fuqahā'*. Beirut: Dār al-Rā'id al-'Arabī, 1970.

———. *Al-Tabṣirah* (*fī Uṣūl al-Fiqh*). Damascus: Dār al-Fikr, 1980.

Sibṭ ibn al-Jawzī. *Īthār al-Inṣāf fī Āthār al-Khilāf*. Riyad: n.p., 1999.

———. *Wasā'il al-Aslāf ilā Masā'il al-Khilāf*. Beirut: Dār al-Kutub al-'Ilmiyyah, 1998.

Subkī, al-, Tāj al-Dīn 'Abd al-Wahhāb. *Ṭabaqāt al-Shāfi'iyyah al-Kubrā*. Cairo: Maṭba'at 'Īsā al-Bābī al-Ḥalabī, 1964–76.

Subkī, al-, Taqī al-Dīn 'Alī. *Al-Takmilah Sharḥ al-Majmū'*. Cairo: Maṭba'at al-Imām, 1966.

Suyūṭī, al-, Jalāl al-Dīn. *Bughyat al-Wu'āh fī Ṭabaqāt al-Lughawiyyīn wa-l-Nuḥāh*. Cairo: Maṭba'at 'Īsā al-Bābī al-Ḥalabī, 1965.

———. *Ṭabaqāt al-Ḥuffāẓ*. Cairo: Maktabat al-Thaqāfah al-Dīniyyah, 1996.

———. *Ṭabaqāt al-Mufassirīn*. Cairo: Maktabat Wahbah, 1976.

Ṭabarī, al-, Muḥammad ibn Jarīr. *Ikhtilāf al-Fuqahā'*. Beirut: Muḥammad Amīn Damaj, 1970.

———. *Jāmi' al-Bayān fī Ta'wīl Āy al-Qur'ān*. Cairo: Maktabat Muṣṭafā al-Bābī al-Ḥalabī, 1954.

Ṭaḥāwī, al-, Abū Ja'far. *Ikhtilāf al-Fuqahā'* (abridged by Abū Bakr al-Jaṣṣāṣ). Beirut: Dār al-Bashā'ir al-Islāmiyyah, 1995.

Tanūkhī, al-, 'Alī ibn al-Muḥsin. *Nishwār al-Muḥāḍarah wa-Akhbār al-Mudhākarah*. n.p., 1971–1973.

Ṭayālisī, al-, Sulaymān ibn Dāwūd. *Musnad al-Ṭayālisī*. Beirut: Dār al-Kutub al-'Ilmiyyah, 2004.

Tirmidhī, al-, Muḥammad ibn 'Īsā. *Sunan al-Tirmidhī*. Cairo: Maṭba'at al-Madanī, 1965.

Ṭūsī, al-, Muḥammad ibn al-Ḥasan. *Fihrist Kutub al-Shī'ah wa-Uṣūlihim wa-Asmā' al-Muṣannifīn wa-Aṣḥāb al-Uṣūl*. Qumm: Maktabat al-Muḥaqqiq al-Ṭabāṭabā'ī, 1999.

Ṭūsī, al-, al-Ḥasan ibn 'Alī. *Mukhtaṣar al-Aḥkām*. Medina: Maktabat al-Ghurabā' al-Athariyyah, 1994.

Yāqūt al-Ḥamawī, Shihāb al-Dīn. *Mu'jam al-Buldān*. Beirut: Dār al-Kutub al-'Ilmiyyah, 1990.

Yusuf Ali, Abd Allah (trans.). *The Holy Qur'an: Text, Translation, and Commentary*. Brentwood: Amana Corporation, 1989.

Zabīdī, al-, Muḥammad Murtaḍā al-Ḥusaynī. *Tāj al-ʿArūs*. Beirut: Dār al-Fikr, 1994.
Zayd ibn ʿAlī. *Al-Majmūʿ*. Amman: Muʾassasat al-Imām Zayd al-Thaqāfiyyah, 2002.
———. *Tafsīr Zayd ibn ʿAlī*. Beirut: Dār al-Kutub al-ʿIlmiyyah, 1992.
Zarkashī, al-, Badr al-Dīn Muḥammad. *Al-Baḥr al-Muḥīṭ*. Kuwait: Wazārat al-Awqāf wa-l-Shuʾūn al-Islāmiyyah, 1992.

Secondary Sources

ʿAbd al-Bāqī, Muḥammad Fuʾād. *Al-Muʿjam al-Mufahras li-Alfāẓ al-Qurʾān al-Karīm*. Cairo: Manshūrāt Dhawī al-Qurbā, 1988.
Abd al-Hādī, Abd al-Bāqī al-Sayyid. "Al-Madhhab al-Ẓāhirī wa-Nashʾatuhu wa-Taṭawwuruhu bi-l-Maghrib wa-l-Andalus ḥattā Nihāyat al-Muwaḥḥidīn." *Ḥawliyyat Siminār al-Tārīkh al-Islāmī wa-l-Wasīṭ* (Egypt), no. 2 (2012).
ʿAbd al-Majīd, ʿAbd al-Majīd Maḥmūd. *Al-Ittijāhāt al-Fiqhiyyah li-Ahl al-Ḥadīth fī al-Qarn al-Thālith al-Hijrī*. Cairo: Maktabat al-Khānjī, 1978.
———. *Al-Madrasah al-Fiqhiyyah li-l-Muḥaddithīn*. Cairo: Dār al-Shihāb, 1972.
ʿAbd al-Raḥmān, Ibrāhīm Muḥammad. *Al-Fikr al-Fiqhī li-Ibn Ḥazm al-Ẓāhirī*. Unpublished PhD dissertation. Cairo: Cairo University, 1981.
Abū ʿĪd, ʿĀrif Khalīl Muḥammad. *Al-Imām Dāwūd al-Ẓāhirī wa-Atharuhu fī al-Fiqh al-Islāmī*. Kuwait: Dār al-Arqam, 1984.
Abū Zahrah, Muḥammad. *Aḥmad ibn Ḥanbal: Ḥayātuhu wa-ʿAṣruhu, Ārāʾuhu wa-Fiqhuhu*. Cairo: Dār al-Fikr al-ʿArabī, n.d.
———. *Abū Ḥanīfah: Ḥayātuhu wa-ʿAṣruhu, Ārāʾuhu wa-Fiqhuhu*. Cairo: Dār al-Fikr al-ʿArabī, n.d.
———. *Ibn Ḥazm: Ḥayātuhu wa-ʿAṣruhu, Ārāʾuhu wa-Fiqhuhu*. Cairo: Dār al-Fikr al-ʿArabī, n.d.
———. *Tārīkh al-Madhāhib al-Islāmiyyah*. Cairo: Dār al-Fikr al-ʿArabī, n.d.
———. *Uṣūl al-Fiqh*. Cairo: Dār al-Fikr al-ʿArabī, n.d.
Adang, Camilla. "The Beginning of the Zahiri Madhhab in al-Andalus," in Peri Bearman et al. (eds.), *The Islamic School of Law: Evolution, Devolution, and Progress*. Cambridge, MA: Islamic Legal Studies Program, Harvard Law School, 2005.
——— *et al. Ibn Ḥazm of Cordoba: The Life and Works of a Controversial Thinker*. (*Handbook of Oriental Studies*, vol. 103). Leiden and Boston: Brill, 2013.
———. "Ibn Ḥazm on Homosexuality. A case-study of Ẓāhirī legal Methodology." *Al-Qanṭara*, vol. 24, no. 1 (2003).
———. "Ẓāhirīs of Almohad times," in Ávila, María Luisa and Maribel Fierro (eds.). *Biografías Almohades II* (vol. 10 of *Estudios Onomásticos-Biograficos de al- Andalus*). Madrid-Granada: Consejo Superior de Investigaciones Científicas, 2000.
Addī Shīr, al-Sayyid. *Kitāb al-Alfāẓ al-Fārisiyyah al-Muʿarrabah*. Cairo: Dār al-ʿArab, 1987–1988.

Afghānī, al-, Saʿīd. *Ibn Ḥazm al-Andalusī wa-Risālah fī al-Mufāḍalah bayna al-Ṣaḥābah*. Damascus: Dār al-Fikr, 1969.

Ahmed, Rumee. *Narratives of Islamic Legal Theory*. Oxford: Oxford University Press, 2012.

Ali, Mohamed Mohamed Yunis. *Medieval Islamic Pragmatics: Sunni Legal Theorists' Models of Textual Communication*. Surrey, UK: Curzon Press, 2000.

Allan, Keith. *Linguistic Meaning*. London: Routledge and Kegan Paul, 1986.

Amīn, Aḥmad. *Fajr al-Islām*. Cairo: Lajnat al-Ta'līf wa-l-Tarjamah wa-l-Nashr, 1961.

ʿAmmār, Rabīḥ. "Ibn Maḍā' al-Qurṭubī: Thawrah fī al-Fiqh, Thawrah fī al-Naḥw." *Majallat Kulliyat al-Ādāb wa-l-ʿUlūm al-Insāniyyah wa-l-Ijtimāʿiyyah* (Baskara, Algeria: Muhammad Khayḍar University), no. 5 (2009).

Arnaldez, Roger. *Grammaire et théologie chez Ibn Ḥazm de Cordoue: essai sur la structure et les conditions de la pensée musulmane*. Paris: Librairie Philosophique J. Vrin, 1956.

Ibn ʿAqīl, Abū ʿAbd al-Raḥmān. *Ibn Ḥazm khilāl Alf ʿĀm*. Beirut: Dār al-Gharb al-Islāmī, 1982.

De Bellefonds, Y. Linant. "Ibn Hazm et le Zahirism Juridique." *Revue Algérienne, Tunisienne, et Marocaine de Législation et de Jurisprudence*, No. 76 (1960).

Bernards, Monique, and John Nawas. "The Geographical Distribution of Muslim Jurists during the First Four Centuries AH." *Islamic Law and Society*, vol. 10, no. 2 (2003).

Biblioteca de al-Andalus: De Ibn al-Dabbāg a Ibn Kurz. Almería: Fundación Ibn Tufayl de Estudios Árabes, 2004.

Buḥṣalī, al-, Māzin ibn ʿAbd al-Raḥmān. *Ṭabaqāt Ahl al-Ẓāhir*. Beirut: Mu'assasat al-Rayyān, 2009.

Coulson, N. J. *A History of Islamic Law*. Edinburgh: Edinburgh University Press, 1964.

Crapanzano, Vincent. *Serving the Word: Literalism in America from the Pulpit to the Bench*. New York: The New Press, 2000.

Davidson, Donald. "A Nice Derangement of Epitaphs," in Ernest LePore. *Truth and Interpretation: Perspectives on the Philosophy of Donald Davidson*. Oxford: Basil Blackwell, 1986.

Dickinson, Eerik. *The Development of Early Sunnite Ḥadith Criticism: The Taqdima of Ibn Abī Ḥātim al-Rāzī*. Leiden: Brill, 2001.

Encyclopaedia of Islam (Second Edition). Leiden, E. J. Brill, 1960–2005.

Eskridge, William. "Textualism, the Unknown Ideal?" *Michigan Law Review*, vol. 96, no. 6 (1998).

Fadel, Mohammad. "Ibn Hajar's Hady al-Sari: A Medieval Interpretation of the Structure of al-Bukhari's al-Jami al-Sahih: Introduction and Translation." *Journal of Near Eastern Studies*, vol. 54, no. 3, 1995.

———. "Istiḥsān is nine-tenth of the Law: The Puzzling Relationship of Uṣūl to Furūʿ in the Mālikī Madhhab," in Bernard Weiss (ed.). *Studies in Islamic Legal Theory*. Leiden: Brill, 2002.

Fierro, Isabel. "The Introduction of ḥadīth to al-Andalus." *Der Islam*, no. 66 (1989).
Freeman-Grenville, G. S. P. *The Muslim and Christian Calendar*. London: Oxford University Press, 1963.
Ghalbazūrī, al-, Tawfīq. *Al-Madrasah al-Ẓāhiriyyah fī al-Maghrib wa-l-Andalus*. Riyad: Dār Ibn Ḥazm, 2006.
Gleave, Robert. *Islam and Literalism: Literal Meaning and Interpretation in Islamic Legal Theory*. Edinburgh: Edinburgh University Press, 2012.
Goldziher, Ignaz. *The Ẓāhirīs: Their Doctrine and their History* (trans. Wolfgang Behn). Leiden: E. J. Brill, 1971.
Gouraya, Muhammad Yousuf. *Origins of Islamic Jurisprudence* (*with Special Reference to Muwatta' Imam Malik*). Lahore: Shaikh Muhammad Ashraf, 1985.
Hallaq, Wael. *Authority, Continuity, and Change in Islamic Law*. Cambridge: Cambridge University Press, 2001.
———. *The Formation of Islamic Law*. Burlington (VT): Ashgate, 2004.
———. "From Regional to Personal Schools of Law? A Reevaluation." *Islamic Law and Society*, vol. 8, no. 1 (2001).
———. *The Origins and Evolution of Islamic Law*. Cambridge: Cambridge University Press, 2005.
———."Usul al-Fiqh: Beyond Tradition." *Journal of Islamic Studies*, no. 3 (1992).
Ḥālūb, Arkān Yūsuf. "Al-Ārā' al-Fiqhiyyah li-Abī Bakr Muḥammad ibn Dāwūd al-Ẓāhirī." *Majallat Diyālā*, no. 8 (2008).
Hanks, William. "Indexicality." *Journal of Linguistic Anthropology*, vol. 9, nos. 1–2 (1999).
Ḥasan, al-, Khalīfah Bābakr. *Al-Ijtihād bi-l-Ra'y fī Madrasat al-Ḥijāz al-Fiqhiyyah*. Cairo: Maktabat al-Zahrā', 1997.
Ḥijwī, al-, Muḥammad ibn al-Ḥasan. *Al-Fikr al-Sāmī fī Tārīkh al-Fiqh al-Islāmī*. Beirut: Dār al-Kutub al-ʿIlmiyyah, 1995.
Hipkiss, Robert. *Semantics: Defining the Discipline*. Mahwah (NJ): Lawrence Erlbaum Associates, 1995.
Hurvitz, Nimrod. *The Formation of Hanbalism: Piety into Power*. London: Routledge Curzon, 2002.
Hurford, James *et al*. *Semantics: A Coursebook*. Cambridge: Cambridge University Press, 2007.
Jackson, Sherman. "Fiction and Formalism: Towards a Functional Analysis of Uṣūl al-Fiqh," in Weiss, Bernard. *Studies in Islamic Legal Theory*. Leiden: E. J. Brill, 2002.
Juynboll, G. H. A. *Muslim Tradition: Studies in Chronology, Provenance and Authority of Early Hadith*. Cambridge: Cambridge University Press, 1983.
Khadduri, Majid. *Al-Risālah fī Uṣūl al-Fiqh* (of Muḥammad ibn Idrīs al-Shāfiʿī). Cambridge: The Islamic Texts Society, 1987.
Khādimī, al-, Nūr al-Dīn. *Al-Dalīl ʿinda al-Ẓāhiriyyah*. Beirut: Dār Ibn Ḥazm, 2000.

Khafīf, al-, ʿAlī. *Muḥaḍarāt fī Asbāb Ikhtilāf al-Fuqahā'*. Cairo: Maʿhad al-Dirāsāt al-ʿArabiyyah al-ʿĀliyah, 1956.

Lane, E. W. *Arabic-English Lexicon*. Beirut: Librarie du Liban, 1968.

Ljamai, Abdelilah. *Ibn Ḥazm et le polémique islamo-chretienne dans l'histoire de L'islam*. Leiden: E. J. Brill, 2003.

Lowry, Joseph. *Early Islamic Legal Theory: the Risālah of Muḥammad ibn Idrīs al-Shāfiʿī*. (Studies in Islamic Law and Society, vol. 30). Leiden and Boston: Brill, 2007.

———. "The Legal Hermeneutics of al-Shafiʿi and Ibn Qutaybah: A Reconsideration." *Islamic Law and Society*, vol. 11, no. 1 (2004).

Maḥmaṣānī, Ṣubḥī. *Falsafat al-Tashrīʿ fī al-Islām*. Beirut: Dār al-ʿIlm, 1975.

Maḥmūd, Aḥmad Bakīr. *Al-Madrasah al-Ẓāhiriyyah bi-l-Mashriq wa-l-Maghrib*. Beirut: Dār Qutaybah, 1990.

Makdisi, George. "Hanbalite Islam," in Swartz, Marlin (ed.). *Studies on Islam*. Oxford: Oxford University Press, 1981.

———. "The Significance of the Sunni Schools of Law in Islamic Religious History." *International Journal of Middle East Studies*, vol. 10, no. 1 (1979).

Makki, Mahmud Ali. *Ensayo sobre las Aportaciones Orientales en la España Musulaman y Su Influencia en al Formación de la Cultura Hispano-Árabe*. Madrid: Instituto de Estudios Islámicos, 1968.

Manning, John F. "Textualism and Legislative Intent." *Virginia Law Review*, vol. 91, no. 2 (1995).

Melchert, Christopher. *Ahmad ibn Hanbal*. Oxford: Oneworld, 2006.

———. *The Formation of the Sunni Schools of Law: 9th–10th Centuries* C.E. Leiden, E. J. Brill, 1997.

———. "The Formation of the Sunni Schools of Law," in Hallaq, Wael. *The Formation of Islamic Law*. Burlington (VT): Ashgate, 2004.

Monaghan, Henry P. "Doing Originalism." *Columbia Law Review*, vol. 104, no. 1 (2004).

Motzki, Harald. *The Origins of Islamic Jurisprudence: Meccan Fiqh before the Classical Schools*. Leiden: E. J. Brill, 2002.

———. "The Role of Non-Arab Converts in the Development of Early Islamic Law." *Islamic Law and Society*, vol. 6, no. 3 (1999).

Muʿjam Fiqh Ibn Ḥazm. Damascus: Damascus University, 1966.

Nelson, Caleb. "Originalism and Interpretative Conventions." *The University of Chicago Law Review*, vol. 70, no. 2 (2003).

———. "What is Textualism." *Virginia Law School*, vol. 91, no. 2 (2005).

Osman, Amr. "*ʿAdālat al-Ṣaḥāba*: The Construction of a Religious Doctrine." *Arabica*, vol. 60, nos. 3–4 (2013).

Qaddūrī, Samīr, "Al-Rudūd ʿalā Ibn Ḥazm bi-l-Andalus wa-l-Maghrib min khilāl Mu'allafāt ʿUlamā' al-Mālikiyyah." *Majallat al-Aḥmadiyyah*, no. 13 (1424/2003).

Qāḍī, al-, Muḥammad Mukhtār. *Al-Raʾy fī al-Fiqh al-Islāmī.* Cairo: Fu'ād the 1st University, 1949.

Quraishi, Azfa. "Interpreting the Qur'an and the Constitution: Similarities in the Use of Text, Tradition, and Reason in Islamic and American Jurisprudence." *Cordoba Law Review*, vol. 28, no. 1 (2006).

Raven, Wim. *Ibn Dâwûd al-Iṣbahânî and his Kitâb al-Zahra* (unpublished PhD dissertation, Leiden University, 1989).

Recanati, François. *Literal Meaning.* Cambridge: Cambridge University Press, 2004.

Ring, Kevin. *Scalia Dissents: Writings of the Supreme Court's Wittiest, Most Outspoken Justice.* Washington DC: Regnery Publishing, 2004.

Sabra, Adam. "Ibn Ḥazm's Literalism: A Critique of Islamic Legal Theory (I). *Al-Qanṭara*, vol. 28, no. 1 (2007).

———. Ibn Ḥazm's Literalism: A Critique of Islamic Legal Theory (II). *Al-Qanṭara*, vol. 28, no. 2 (2007).

Scalia, Antonin. *A Matter of Interpretation.* Princeton: Princeton University Press, 1997.

———. "Originalism: The Lesser Evil." *University of Cincinnati Law Review*, vol. 57, no. 3 (1989).

Schacht, Joseph. *An Introduction to Islamic law.* Oxford: Clarendon Press, 1964.

———. *The Origins of Muhammadan Jurisprudence.* Oxford: Clarendon Press, 1950.

Schauer, Frederick. "Formalism." *The Yale Law Journal*, vol. 97, no. 4 (1988).

Searle, John. "Literal Meaning." *Erkenntnis*, vol. 13, no. 1 (1978).

Shalabī, Muḥammad Muṣṭafā. *Taʿlīl al-Aḥkām: ʿArḍ wa-Taḥlīl li-Ṭarīqat al-Taʿlīl wa-Taṭawwurātihā fī ʿUṣūr al-Ijtihād wa-l-Taqlīd.* Cairo: Maṭba'at al-Azhar, 1949.

Shaṭṭī, al-, Muḥammad. *Majmūʿ yashtamil ʿalā Risālatayn.* Damascus: Maṭbaʿat Rawḍat al-Shām, 1912.

Shehabi, Nabil. "Illa and Qiyas in Early Islamic Legal Theory." *Journal of the American Oriental Society*, vol. 102, no. 1 (1982).

Shitā, al-Sayyid ʿAlī. *Al-Ẓāhiriyyah al-ʿArabiyyah.* Alexandria: al-Maktabah al-Miṣriyyah, 2001.

Spectorsky, Susan. *Chapters on Marriage and Divorce: Responses of Ibn Ḥanbal and Ibn Rāhwayh.* Austin: University of Texas Press, 1993.

———. "Ahmad ibn Hanbal's Fiqh." *Journal of the American Oriental Society*, vol. 102, no. 3 (1982).

Spolsky, Ellen. "The Limits of Literal Meaning." *New Literary Theory*, vol. 19, no. 2 (1988).

Stanley, Jason. Review of François Recanati's *Literal Meaning. Notre Dame Philosophical Reviews* (http://ndpr.nd.edu/review.cfm?id=3841).

Stewart, Devin. "Muḥammad b. Dāwūd al-Ẓāhirī's Manual of Jurisprudence: *Al-Wuṣūl ilā Maʿrifat al-Uṣūl*," in Bernard Weiss (ed.). *Studies in Islamic Legal Theory.* Leiden: E. J. Brill, 2002.

Ṭanṭāwī, Aḥmad Wadī', "Shawāhid al-Madhhab al-Ẓāhirī fī al-Dars al-Naḥwī 'inda Abī Ḥayyān." *Majallat Markaz al-Khidmah li-l-Istishārāt al-Baḥthiyyah* (Munūfiyyah, Egypt), no. 42 (2010).

Targhī, al-, 'Abd Allāh. *Fahāris 'Ulamā' al-Maghrib mundhu al-Nash'ah ilā Nihāyat al-Qarn al-Thānī 'Ashar li-l-Hijrah: Manhajiyatuhā, Taṭawwuruhā, Qīmatuhā al-'Ilmiyyah*. Titwan: Jāmi'at 'Abd al-Malik al-Sa'dī, 1999.

Thaqafī, al-, Sālim ibn 'Alī. *Asbāb Ikhtilāf al-Fuqahā'*. Cairo: Dār al-Bayān li-l-Ṭibā'ah wa-l-Nashr, 1996.

Turki, Abdel Magid. "Notes sur l'évolution du zâhirisme d'Ibn Ḥazm (456/1063) du *Taqrîb* à l'*Iḥkâm*," *Studia Islamica*, no. 59 (1984).

———. *Polémiques entre Ibn Ḥazm et Bāǧi sur les principes de la loi musulmane: Essai sur le littéralisme zahirite et la finalité malikite*. Alger: Etudes et Documents, n.d.

Versteegh, Kees. "Ibn Maḍā' as a Ẓāhirī Grammarian," in Camilla Adang *et al. Ibn Ḥazm of Cordoba* (Brill, 2013).

Vishanoff, David R. *The Formation of Islamic Hermeneutics: How Sunni Legal Theorists Imagined a Revealed Law*. American Oriental Series, New Haven (CT), 2011.

Weiss, Bernard (ed.). "Language and Law: The Linguistic Premises of Islamic Legal Science," in A. H. Green (ed.). *In Quest of an Islamic Humanism: Arabic and Islamic Studies*. Cairo: the American University in Cairo Press, 1984.

———. *Studies in Islamic Legal Theory*. Leiden: E. J. Brill, 2002.

Weithman, Paul J. "The Precise Word." *The Review of Politics*, vol. 60, no. 1 (1998).

Weizer, Paul. *The Opinions of Justice Antonin Scalia: The Caustic Conservative*. New York: Peter Lang, 2004.

Wiederhold, Lutz. "Legal Religious Elite, Temporal Authority, and the Caliphate in Mamluk Society: Conclusions drawn from the Examination of a 'Zahiri Revolt' in Damascus in 1386." *International Journal of Middle East Studies*, vol. 31, no. 2 (1999).

Zysow, Aaron. *The Economy of Certainty: An Introduction to the Typology of Islamic Legal Theory*. (Resources in Arabic and Islamic Studies). Atlanta (Georgia): Lockwood Press, 2013.

Index

www.ingramcontent.com/pod-product-compliance
Ingram Content Group UK Ltd.
Pitfield, Milton Keynes, MK11 3LW, UK
UKHW020846290926
15470UKWH00004B/1583

9 789004 276192